Jewi~
2245
P9-AFB-058
4¹⁵⁰

Antisemitism and the Constitution of Sociology

Antisemitism and the Constitution of Sociology

Edited and with an introduction by MARCEL STOETZLER

University of Nebraska Press | Lincoln and London

© 2014 by the Board of Regents of
the University of Nebraska. All
rights reserved. Manufactured
in the United States of America.

∞

Sections of the introduction and
of chapters 1, 2, 4, and 6 have
been previously published in the
journals *Patterns of Prejudice* and
Sociological Theory.

Library of Congress
Cataloging-in-Publication Data

Antisemitism and the constitution of
sociology / edited and with an introduction by Marcel Stoetzler.
pages   cm

Includes bibliographical references
and index.
ISBN 978-0-8032-4864-9 (hardback)
ISBN 978-0-8032-6671-1 (epub)
ISBN 978-0-8032-6672-8 (mobi)
1. Antisemitism—History.
2. Sociology—History. I. Stoetzler,
Marcel.
DS145.A639 2014
305.892'4—dc23
2014003786

Set in Lyon Text by Renni Johnson.

Contents

Acknowledgments

Most of the chapters collected in this volume have been developed from presentations at the conference Antisemitism and the Emergence of Sociological Theory that took place at the University of Manchester in November 2008. I am grateful to the Centre for Jewish Studies for hosting and partly financing this conference that was also supported by the University of Manchester's School of Arts, Histories and Cultures, the British Sociological Association Theory Study Group, and the Leo Baeck Institute, London. I am grateful to *Patterns of Prejudice* and *Sociological Theory* for granting permission to draw on materials previously published in these journals.

Antisemitism and the Constitution of Sociology

Introduction

The Theory of Society Talks Back to Its Travesty

MARCEL STOETZLER

> Without rancor or hatred, in the spirit of sociology and psychology,
> I seek to examine the debased condition into which France has
> fallen. . . . My mission as a sociologist is to show people as they are.
>
> EDOUARD DRUMONT, 1886, addressing reactions to his antisemitic
> tract, *La France Juive*

Thinking develops in the engagement with an object.[1] However, although thinking is always about an issue, the concepts that are developed in the process do not necessarily name that object or issue.

One of the principal issues that served as the catalysts around which European (or "Western") modern social and political thought evolved in the long nineteenth century was the question of Jewish emancipation, and after emancipation was achieved, the question of whether, how, or to what extent it ought to be revoked. These were the two incarnations of "the Jewish question" that centered in either form on discussing Jewish equality and difference. Modern social and political thought developed, consolidated, and translated itself from Enlightenment philosophy and critique into the modern, institutionalized discourses of disciplines such as sociology in the period when modern society itself materialized in the form of so many national societies; Enlightenment thought became thereby concerned—often explicitly, but always by implication—with the continuing creation and reproduction of societies *as nations*. The discourse of modern society was already there at the birth of that society and had to adapt itself to the requirements of the object whose fate it shared. The "discourse" was always a practice, and as such part of that wider societal practice that we call society. Emancipation (of national, ethnic, religious, and other "minorities," of the third and the fourth estate, of women, of the various groups of people with less than straight sexual preferences) was, and remains, crucial to that practice called "society," or at least it is safe to say that the promise and *hope* of emancipation always were and still remain crucial to its legitimacy—as this hope and promise are among the things that make its constituents continue to "do" society.

Marx's famous double essay "On the Jewish Question" exemplifies the way this "question" served as a field on which to develop modern thought: theoretical propositions of tremendous momentum and radicality were first formulated in a dispute on Jewish emancipation that had been triggered by some Prussian draft legislation that in the process was shelved and is since all but forgotten. Marx's text, though, was then already part of a tradition that earlier included, for example, Christian Wilhelm Dohm's "On the Civil Amelioration [*bürgerliche Verbesserung*] of the Jews" of 1781. This text too and the debate about it were about Jews, as announced by the title, but also about much more: they were about the emerging modern society and its historical dynamic, and "the Jewish question" was one of the fields on which these issues were discussed. It remained such a field for a long time, and perhaps still is today, to an extent.

Modern antisemitism and the discipline of sociology were two of the discourses that were part of the consolidation process of modern society in the nineteenth century, articulating, commenting on, and intervening in some of the problems that the constitution, or reconstitution, of modern society in the form of an ensemble of nation-states brought with itself. Beyond the obvious fact that they emerged in the same period, they also overlapped and complemented as much as struggled and competed with each other. This complicated relationship is the subject of the present volume: it explores and tests the hypothesis that the formation of sociology and that of antisemitism were related, partly cosubstantial, as much as competing, sometimes antagonistic phenomena.

This hypothesis is based on two observations: first, the discipline of sociology emerged out of the liberal response to crisis phenomena of modern society, aiming at that society's consolidation, regeneration, and its defense; second, modern antisemitism is likewise best understood as the "travesty of a social theory" responding to the same type of society, offering in its phantasmagorias of "the Jew" and "Jewification" an explanation of its deficiencies and crises. Both sociology and antisemitism also tended to be antagonistic to the social-democratic labor movement whose actual or anticipated successes both aimed to curb by proposing alternatives (and at times wooing sections of it).[2] The volume thus deals with two fundamental questions: What did sociologists (or those who helped constitute the discipline) have to say on antisemitism and "the Jewish question"? How did what sociologists had to say about subjects such as money, usury, modernity, work and labor, individualism, community, society, social reform, socialism, state and culture, religion, the spirit of capitalism, and capitalist development resemble or differ from what antisemites said on the same issues? The volume asks whether, how, and to what extent the makers of sociology were responding to the antisemites (among others) who were busy building their parallel discourse in the same vicinity, as it were, and whether, how, and to what extent they also shared or came to reflect some of their competitors' concerns. These questions have until now never been researched. The new perspective that this volume proposes and explores rests on the presupposition that antisemitism—in its various forms—was a more pervasive presence in the societies and in the period under discussion than is often acknowledged, including the milieus in which the liberals and socialists operated from whose ranks came the founders of sociology.[3] This volume thereby takes what conventionally would be considered a small subfield *within* the field of sociological theory and its history—the sociology and theory of antisemitism—as the central perspective from where general emergence and development of the discipline itself can be illuminated and understood afresh. It contributes to a general trend to historicizing and recentering theoretical discourses of modernity and modern society.

I came to this subject in a somewhat indirect fashion. Some ten years ago I completed a PhD that was initially meant to be about liberal and socialist conceptions of the nation and critiques of the textbook distinction between "civic" and "ethnic" nationalisms. While reading around for suitable source materials that would allow me to articulate my unease with this distinction, I came across the "Berlin antisemitism dispute," the *Treitschke-Streit* of 1879–81, which then became the sole topic of my thesis. I was fascinated by the ways Treitschke himself, but even more so his critics and also some of his radical antisemitic supporters, mobilized whole conceptions of society, state and individual, complete with accounts of culture, religion, and economy and how they threw all into the battle on "the Jewish question." A key figure in the Berlin antisemitism dispute on the side of the Jewish community was Moritz Lazarus, a social scientist of great importance (but known now mostly to specialists in this area of intellectual history), who was a teacher of Georg Simmel and of great influence on Franz Boas. Max Weber's father, Max Weber Sr., was involved in organizing a declaration of notables of German liberalism who found Treitschke's sympathies for antisemitism unhelpful. I decided to work on this material, a defining episode in the development of late nineteenth-century German liberalism, because it resonated strongly with concerns from contemporary social and sociological theory.[4] In the process, I began to see what would subsequently become (in Germany) the discipline of sociology emerge out of the context of (national) liberalism—which explains the resemblance. My hunch was that the dispute on antisemitism must have had an impact on the thinking of the founders of "classical sociology," many of whom (such as Weber and Simmel, but also visiting students like William Edward Burghardt Du Bois) sat in Treitschke's lectures. (The influence of the antisemitism dispute on the young Max Weber was pointed out by Gary Abraham in his 1992 monograph *Max Weber and the Jewish Question*.) Also Durkheim, at a crucial stage in his early career, had visited German universities and tapped into just this intellectual milieu. These initial observations led me to the question that is explored in the present volume.

In the introduction to the volume *Sociology Responds to Fascism*, Stephen P. Turner wrote in 1992 that "reformers of various political persuasions" felt ambivalent about fascism, as they saw it "as a potential catalyst for the changes they advocated." He wrote, "There are many very direct connections between fascist ideas and early sociology. . . . The romantic notion of reweaving a social order destroyed by impersonality, shared by Tönnies, Durkheim, and many others, such as Othmar Spann, contributed, however indirectly, to the climate of opinion in which fascism took hold. So did the elitism of Vilfredo Pareto and Gaetano Mosca."[5] The contributions to the present volume focus with sociology and antisemitism on a dimension of this topic that is both narrower and wider than the connection of sociology and fascism: narrower, as antisemitism is not the only and not even the most defining characteristic of fascism (arguably, with the exception of German National Socialism), and wider, because it occurs in all political traditions and functions universally as a bridgehead or gateway that allows, in specific historical situations, members, or whole sections of those traditions to support, join, or at least tolerate fascist movements and regimes. This marks the significance of the topic.[6]

The perspective taken by Turner was expressed earlier by the Danish sociologist Svend Ranulf in his 1939 article "Scholarly Forerunners of Fascism." Ranulf provides a highly critical reading of Auguste Comte's *Cours de philosophie positive* and Émile Durkheim's *De la division du travail social*, arguing that both authors' arguments rely on conceptions that are similar to what Ferdinand Tönnies in 1887 (i.e., six years before Durkheim's *On the Social Division of Labor*, fifty-seven years after the publication of the first volume of the *Cours*) conceptualized as the dichotomy of *Gemeinschaft* and *Gesellschaft* (community and society). While Tönnies's pair of concepts has been adopted by German political romantics and reactionaries of all stripes (not necessarily with his approval), Ranulf's main point is that if there is a shared ground between Tönnies's philosophical sociology and the "scientific" and positivistic sociology of Comte and especially Durkheim, and if indeed this was compatible with fascist social thought, then the discipline of sociology as a whole needs fundamental rethinking.[7] (To put it with Tönnies, this point could be expressed by saying that being complicit with fascism was against the *Kürwille*, the deliberate willing and wishing, but in line with the *Wesenswille*, the "essential will" or the intrinsic and not always conscious logic, of the sociological project, including Tönnies's own.) Ranulf concluded that "both these groups of sociologists have—for the most part unintentionally and unconsciously—served to prepare the soil for fascism by their propagation of the view that the society in which they were living was headed for disaster because of its individualism and liberalism and that a new social solidarity was badly needed."[8] Concerning Comte, Ranulf wrote, "If Comte could wake up and see the conditions now [i.e., 1939] prevailing in Germany, he would undoubtedly have to admit that the rule of positivism for which he was yearning has largely come true in the form of German naziism or, more generally, in the form of fascism."[9] Ranulf quotes the following aspects of Comte's thinking in support of his argument: Comte saw European society devastated by "intellectual anarchy," where individuals were called upon to decide on fundamental political issues "without any guide" or moral control.[10] This state of things was prolonged and exploited by "the class of publicists." (It is perhaps worth noting that polemics against "the press" have been one of the staples also of nineteenth-century antisemites and remain today a key concern of popular critiques of modern culture.) When every individual has the right to question the very foundations of society, the very possibility of social life is destroyed.[11] Government must therefore rein in unfettered intellectual freedom, the "demolition of public morals," the dissolution of the family, and the effacement of traditional class distinctions.[12] "Responsible for this misery" are, in Ranulf's paraphrase of Comte, "all kinds of rebels against the Catholic church, from the early Protestants onwards to the contemporary deists and atheists." (Jews are missing from this list, but when in the decades after Comte it became a common perception that Protestantism was inspired by Judaism it was but a small step to add them.)[13] According to Comte, "the Catholic system of the Middle Ages" that integrated politics and morality "is the most perfect political masterpiece that has been devised until now by the human mind." As Catholicism, though, has become a stranger to modern societies, its place needs to be taken by science, in particular "social physics" or else, indeed, "sociology" that will effect the scientific ("positive") reorganization of modern societies.[14] Ranulf argues that Durkheim too, like Comte, believed he lived in an age of moral dissolution and that sociology was called upon to remedy this evil.[15] He asks, "Is not the rise of fascism an event which, in due logic, Durkheim ought to have welcomed as that salvation from individualism for which he had been trying rather gropingly to prepare the way? In due logic, undoubtedly. But there are aspects of fascism which would probably have seemed unacceptable to Durkheim."[16] Ranulf seems on firmer ground with respect to Comte than to Durkheim, as Durkheim was ambivalent about individualism rather than hostile to it and explicitly departed from Comte in this as in other respects; after all, Durkheim diagnosed as a symptom of moral dissolution the Dreyfus affair, during which he *defended* individualism *against* antisemitic nationalists. Still, even in Durkheim the kind of ambivalence can be found that is explored throughout this volume; Ranulf could have added, for example, that Weber's notion that only charismatic leadership can break through the gray routine of bureaucratized modernity contributed to, as well as reflected, the rise of a societal atmosphere that facilitated the fascist takeover.[17]

It would seem that Ranulf's intervention of 1939 has not enjoyed any lasting influence. One reason for this might be that post–World War II (U.S.) sociology, especially due to the influence of Talcott Parsons, who successfully amalgamated its main traditions—including Weber and Durkheim—into liberal, progressivist modernization theory, stood on the side of Western democracy and against fascism.[18] Liberals and democrats cannot but be scandalized by the suggestion that Parsonian democratic, antifascist modernization theory could share, via Durkheimian and Comtean positivism, some of its roots with its hot and cold war enemies; after all, it was developed (along with the notion of Western "political," allegedly non-"ethnic" nationalism) first against Hitlerism and then further deployed as an alternative to Leninist-Stalinist modernization theory and praxis. If (as does critical theory) one counts structural-functionalism as a form of positivism, then it still needs to be acknowledged that it represents the human face of liberal-democratic positivism that is positioned against crude, totalitarian positivism that drives the social-engineering and -gardening projects of Stalinists, fascists, and all kinds of more ordinary dictators.[19]

If Ranulf's thesis is now taken as an inspiration to dig deeper into the matter, his account must necessarily be made more complicated, especially with respect to Durkheim. Furthermore it is notable that Ranulf's discussion seems to treat fascism and "naziism" as synonyms and does not mention antisemitism; as antisemitism has over the past decades been recognized as central at least to the German Nazi variety of fascism, the exploration of antisemitism seems a good vantage point to reopen the discussion. This is especially so as antisemitism tends to become relevant at the points where fascists construct their idea of *Gemeinschaft*. The perspective taken here is, however, different from Ranulf's also in another aspect: while Ranulf decided to align Comte and Durkheim, along with Tönnies, with fascism as its "forerunners," the present volume proposes instead to focus on their *ambiguities*, treating these as another instance of the internal dialectic of the enlightenment (to be precise, the dialectic of the enlightenment of the post-Enlightenment period, the nineteenth and twentieth centuries). The idea that liberals, democrats, and socialists who opposed fascism and antisemitism might themselves be implicated in what they oppose is unlikely ever to become a hugely popular proposition. When a few isolated theorists, including Horkheimer, Adorno, and Sartre, suggested it in the aftermath of World War II when the spirit of the anti-Hitler coalition still dominated the worldview of most people in "the West," their propositions, although celebrated in the world of "social theory," hardly managed to revolutionize the daily workings of scholarly or political discourse.[20] In the present period, though, after postmodernism popularized some of the claims critical theory had formulated earlier, the concern with the ways the liberal, democratic, and socialist manifestations of the "Enlightenment project" are implicated in what the latter was up against should seem less outlandish.[21]

The present volume aims to complicate and develop Ranulf's thesis. As for Durkheim, the principal ground on which Ranulf's claim has to be contested is the interpretation of Durkheim's direct and public engagement as a leading Dreyfusard. Crucial here is the paradox that positivist sociology was elementary to the intellectual conception that Durkheim threw into the battle against antisemitism in the Dreyfus affair, but it was also in partial agreement with the antisemitic worldview itself. It is perhaps not too far-fetched to say that the present volume is in its entirety an exploration of this ambiguity. (Another volume could be written to make the argument the other way around: that antisemites were fully aware and also part of the emerging new way of talking and thinking about the new society, as Edouard Drumont testifies in the statement that serves as the epigraph to this introduction.)

A case that could be quoted in support of Ranulf's argument on Comte is that of Charles Maurras, an important (though then still young) player in the Dreyfus affair and, in that context, the founder of the right-wing Action Française. Maurras was the theorist of what he termed "integral nationalism," which he understood to be "socialist," and as such an important if indirect influence on the early development of fascism. Although a declared agnostic, he supported and admired the Catholic Church and, perhaps more than anything else, was a follower of Comte.[22] Maurras wrote, for example, in 1904, "It is clear from the philosophy of Comte that the Jewish race is a race whose evolution has been stunted."[23] Likewise in a text from 1898 Maurras wrote that the Jews were a material force of societal degeneration, while there was also "a Protestant spirit . . .

[which] threatens not only the French spirit, but . . . every spirit, every nation, every State, and reason itself. . . . It dissolves societies; it constitutes, according to Auguste Comte's fine definition, a sedition of the individual against the [human] species."[24] Although in this quote Maurras seems to find Protestants even worse than Jews, it also points to the close relation between anti-Protestantism and antisemitism within Catholic reactionary discourse. (Inversely it also indicates that Weber's work on the "Protestant spirit" might have been written against anti-Protestant/ antisemitic critiques of modern society, including, within the sociological tradition, Comte's anti-Protestantism.)

Maurras, who was obsessively driven to combat individualism in what he saw as its two prevalent forms, (German) romanticism and the revolutionary tradition of 1789, had nurtured since the Dreyfus affair the idea of an alliance of positivists and Catholics (incidentally, with little practical success).[25] His hero was Comte, as explained in an essay bearing Comte's name as its title (1902): "Some amongst us were living examples of anarchy. To those of us who were, he restored order or, its equivalent, the hope of order; he revealed the beauty of Unity smiling out of a heaven that did not appear too far away." Maurras repeatedly quoted Comte's aphorism "Submission is the basis of perfection" and lauded his awareness of the vanity of rationalism and "revolutionary sophism."[26] Following Comte, Maurras saw the root of these evils in monotheism, as it led the believer to prioritize individual spiritual welfare and a personal relationship with deity over positive societal ties. This is expressed, for example, in an appendix to his book *Trois idées politiques* of 1898: "The idea of this invisible and distant master will quickly undermine the respect that the conscience owes to its visible and near masters. Such a conscience . . . will invoke the eternal and unwritten laws so as to extract itself from laws that have the most immediate pertinence, . . . on each and every pretext. . . . This mystical exchange [with God] leads to scepticism in the field of theory and to revolt in that of practice. . . . Every egoism is justified in the name of God."[27] Monotheism is what makes Protestantism antisocial. The monotheistic spirit of Christianity brought down Rome; subsequently it also destroyed Catholic civilization in the sixteenth century, and it did so again, in its Rousseauan incarnation, in 1789. This argument hinges on the idea that in Catholicism the element of monotheism (the Christian spirit) was rigorously circumscribed and attenuated by polytheistic elements as well as organic and hierarchical institutional structures, an argument that Maurras takes from Comte, supported with ample references to the *Cours* and the *Système*.[28] Maurras concludes that in Catholicism, "the stupid and the vile, bound by the chains of dogma, are not free to choose a master as they please and in their own image. . . . Catholicism proposes the only idea of God that is tolerable in a well organized State."[29] Likewise "morality in the Comtian State tends, in effect, towards a sort of moral socialism; but, with good logic, it excludes the leading articles of the Declaration of the Rights of Man and of liberal doctrine. By contrast, morality in the Kantian State leads to a form of mystical isolation, where everyone considers himself as a sort of god."[30] Only on the issue of nationalism does Maurras flag his divergence from Comte: while he applauds Comte's notion that the dignity of the individual results only from its "subordination to some compound existence," he does not follow Comte's notion that this "compound existence" is humanity. Maurras notes that "Humanity does not exist—at least not yet" and replaces the nation for it: "He who defends his Country, his nationality and his State is engaged in the defence of all that is real and all that is concrete in the idea of Humanity."[31] In this sense, the nation is the positive reality of humanity, which is a not inconsistent development of the positivist position in a historical period— the late nineteenth century—in which nation-states are indeed concrete, positive realities, while humanity (which Comte had expected would become a positive reality soon enough) is not (yet).[32]

It seems to have been in the context of the Dreyfus affair that Maurras came clear on what is the essence behind Protestant individualism, for he began to argue then that justice, pity, and compassion are Jewish ideas: "All individualist theory is of Jewish making."[33] In *Trois idées politiques* he declares, "The Protestant originates entirely from the Jew." It is from this point that Maurras was explicitly and radically antisemitic. As Michael Sutton notes, it is "ironic" that Maurras's antisemitism, or, to be precise, its "modern philosophical sub-structure," was derived from Comte, who was then widely regarded as the greatest French philosopher of the nineteenth century, including by Dreyfusards like Durkheim.[34]

When Maurras described his own nationalism as "socialist," he had in mind and often referred to Alphonse Toussenel, a Fourierist and the author of one of the key texts of mid nineteenth-century antisemitism in France, "The Jews, Kings of the Epoch."[35] It was first published in 1845 by a Fourierist publishing house with a three-page preface that alerted readers that this was not to be seen as an official statement of the school's doctrine.[36] The book was republished slightly extended and significantly more violent in its antisemitic language by another publisher in 1847 and went through several more editions. Significantly only these later editions contained the chapter "Saint-Simon et Juda," an antisemitic polemic that denounces the Saint-Simonians as being "Jewish."[37]

Crucial to the Fourierist critique of modern society is the notion of the "financial feudality," which implies a fundamental critique of the French Revolution: the Revolution has not actually abolished feudalism but merely changed its form and exchanged some of the actors. The new feudal lords are the *financial* aristocracy; the antifeudal revolution is still to come. Arguably this type of critique is more than an acknowledgment that the Revolution is incomplete or needs to be driven further, which would have been shared by any democrat or socialist; it seems to be implied that the entire Revolution was fake. While for Saint-Simon, for example, the Revolution certainly opened the door to the rule of the *industriels* (the productive Third Estate), whose domination and transformation of society now merely needed to be followed through, exactly this process is seen by Fourier as the continuation of feudalism in a different guise: it is the obstacle to the petit-bourgeois (i.e., based on small-scale commodity production) collectivist transformation he wishes to see.[38]

It is easy to see how Toussenel's position might dovetail with a proto-fascist's idea of "socialism" (as in Maurras's case), while his denunciation as "Jewish" of Saint-Simonianism's embrace of modernization, industrialization, and the modern banking required by the former fits a familiar antisemitic pattern.[39] However, things were more complicated. Rather bizarrely, another important antisemitic tract of exactly the same title was published one year after Toussenel's by an author of Saint-Simonian background, Pierre Leroux, who is nowadays usually referred to as a "Christian socialist."[40] In "The Jews, Kings of the Epoch," Leroux is critical of Saint-Simon because he understands that "industry" cannot unite bourgeoisie and proletariat into a "classe industrielle" that would be united and opposed to the class of the unproductive and the parasites, as Saint-Simon had expected.[41] Leroux also points out (correctly)

that Saint-Simon's notion of organization is elitist, hierarchical, and antidemocratic; Saint-Simon rejected general franchise, for example. It is
in this context that Leroux adopts the Fourierist notion that the allegedly new industrial society actually is a "féodalité industrielle."[42] Leroux's
text seems to result from the gradual merger of the Saint-Simonist and
the Fourierist movements in the 1830s and 1840s, which seems to have
overcome some theoretical dead-ends of Saint-Simonism but was also
part of the context of the development of radical modern antisemitism.

The milieus and intellectual traditions out of which in France in the
second third of the nineteenth century antisemitism and positivism, and
out of the latter, sociology, emerged, are closely related. When sociology
emerged out of "positive philosophy" and "positive politics," modern
radical antisemitism emerged out of what Marxists call "early" or "utopian" socialism. Henri de Saint-Simon was a crucial figure for both developments: Comte, the inventor of the word *sociology*, had been Saint-
Simon's disciple, collaborator, and secretary. After Saint-Simon's death
in 1825, Comte became an important member of the milieu of followers
of Saint-Simon out of which the "school" of Saint-Simonianism emerged.

Comte was Saint-Simon's secretary and collaborator from 1817 to 1824,
when he was fired in a bitter argument over the authorship of a seminal
essay.[43] Comte was excluded from the Saint-Simonian "school" in 1829 on
the basis of Saint-Simon's earlier denunciation of him as too indifferent to
the emotions and to religion. The Saint-Simonians represented Comte's
thinking as "the 'glacial' scientism" they rejected.[44] Out of this process
of distancing themselves from Saint-Simon's most famous disciple, the
group developed the 1829 manifesto of Saint-Simonianism, *The Doctrine
of Saint-Simon*, which was also a critique of (Comtean) positivism and a
crucial inspiration for subsequent socialist and communist traditions.[45]
The Saint-Simonian school was very influential around the time of the
Revolution of 1830 before it disintegrated in 1831, partly over the question of the emancipation and the role of women.[46] Mary Pickering argues
that Comte's *Cours de philosophie positive* (1830–42) constituted his ongoing "discourse with the Saint-Simonians, who remained unnamed,"[47]
emphasizing the necessary priority of science. From 1838, though, when
he started work on volume 4 of the *Cours* that first introduced "sociology," Comte increasingly included reflections on the emotions, the arts,
imagination and religion, that is, aspects of Saint-Simon's and his own

earliest work that he had suppressed in the preceding decade and a half. When the 1848 Revolution failed to usher in the kind of transformation he considered necessary, he concluded that positivism ought to enter the battle of doctrines in a more robust manner and henceforth presented it with the Saint-Simonian term "Religion of Humanity," detailed in the *Système de politique positive* (1851–4).[48] These details illustrate how close the emergence of Comtean positivism and sociology in France was interrelated with the development of "early socialism," which in turn provided the context for the emergence of some of the most momentous variants of modern antisemitism, and how much both traditions responded and reacted to one another.[49]

In the last decade of his life (he died in 1857) Comte developed an ethic centered on the idea that "the dictatorship of the proletariat would purify economic life of the commercial spirit by exercising a new moral hegemony," a conception he formed in his "Positivist Society" that stood in opposition to liberals as well as communists.[50] The proletariat would usher in the final, positive state of society, wherein parliamentary representation would be replaced by scientifically organized political forms. (The proletariat would of course first have to be converted to positivism, but would then, through its dictatorship, help install the new hierarchy led by the positivist "spiritual priesthood.") Although nothing suggests that Comte himself was antisemitic, the basic pattern of the positivist blueprint—under this name or another—dovetailed with the drive of (pro-modernization) antisemites for ethical, purified, noncommercial capitalism. In fact outside the very small world of "early industrialized," liberal societies (i.e., Britain and those who were in the position to copy her early on), positivism's commitment to "order and progress" carried much more weight and blended together with "state-socialist" and "economic-nationalist" doctrines like those that were formulated in nineteenth-century Germany into developmental regimes of varying brutality.[51] (The positivist-influenced founders of the republican Brazilian state, for example, inscribed Comte's motto "Order and Progress" onto their national flag of 1889: "Ordem e Progresso.") Such regimes are of course not in themselves antisemitic, but elements of antisemitism occur time and again—depending on historical, cultural, political, and economic circumstances—in the context of regimes that attempt to create "ethical economies" on the basis of robust assertion of national culture. The reason for this is arguably that the discourses that state and economy promote as "morality" can be more than abstract, normative claims only if they are backed up by positive (which usually means national) culture, fortified, more often than not, by a strong shot of religion.[52] It is hardly surprising, at least in the Christian-influenced world, that discourses that construct a conflict between money-economy and morality invite musings on "the Jews"; after all, the figure of that mild-mannered man who, in the name of love, drove the money changers out of the temple is central to the Christian religion. In modernity's formative period, Shakespeare gave this conflict a first monumental formulation: in *The Merchant of Venice* Shylock "the usurer" gives the brilliant antiracist speeches and points out that modern society and economy depend on contracts that are legally binding, while Antonio the "Christian merchant" and most others in the play wax lyrical about the power of mercy and cosmic harmony. Shakespeare himself—a thoroughly modern man who was both a successful entrepreneur and a political thinker who would have accepted the need for some kind of religion as the glue holding society together—does not seem to be taking sides. The cultural pattern that Shakespeare exploited for his play is still today so firmly in place that, every now and then, advocacies of the moral reform of the capitalist economy come adorned with mostly perfumed forms of antisemitism. (In the period since the late nineteenth century, such antisemitic undertones tend to stem from democratic populism's struggle for benign small-scale commodity production, uncorrupted by giant monsters of the Wall Street family of evils.)[53]

Orderly progress was also the concern of those right-wing liberals, "socialists of the chair," and state socialists in Imperial Germany within whose milieu the Verein für Sozialpolitik (Association for Social Policy) was founded in 1872 and out of which in turn, in Germany, the discipline of sociology slowly emancipated itself.[54] The Verein was committed to "bürgerliche Sozialreform," bourgeois social reform;[55] overt antisemitism was not the dominant tone in the Verein für Sozialpolitik, but neither was it entirely absent. The central, moderate figure, Gustav Schmoller, was only mildly antisemitic by the standards of time and context and apparently made explicitly antisemitic statements in public only late in his career,[56] but the equally central economist Adolph Wagner was at the same time a close ally of the populist-clerical antisemite, Adolf Stoecker. Wagner was a founding member and vice chairman of Stoecker's Christian Social Party and contributed crucial passages to its program.[57] Wagner was thus a key player in radical, political antisemitism, in the history of modern economics, and in the wider field from which the discipline of sociology emerged.[58]

The need to respond to, but also the inevitability of reflecting some of the concerns of contemporary antisemites have had their impact on the shape of "classical" just as on "early" sociology. The liberals who would become sociologists (such as Tönnies, Weber, and Sombart) and the liberals who would become antisemites (such as Heinrich von Treitschke, a teacher of Weber and the person whom Weber's father helped to challenge in the Berlin antisemitism dispute of 1879) worked on alternative conceptions of what kind of national culture, or societal religion, is necessary for modern society to continue to exist, and what kinds of degenerations and anomies this culture should be entrusted to avert.[59] Contemporary antisemites had already attacked Saint-Simonianism as a Jewish enterprise, partly because several of its leading members were indeed Jewish, partly because it embraced and celebrated modernization and central institutions linked with it such as money and banking.[60] (An equivalent phenomenon in the early nineteenth-century German context was that German antisemitic patriots accused Hegelianism and even Hegel himself of being Jewish, at least in spirit.)[61] These antisemitic slurs against bodies of thought that embraced crucial aspects of modernity set the pattern for later similar attacks on sociology itself and, much more violently so, on Marxism. (The Nazis, though, did not summarily dismiss sociology but instead developed "non-Jewish sociology," which amounted, in some aspects at least, to a kind of technocratic modernization of sociology).[62] Durkheim, Tönnies, Weber, and Sombart considered social reform crucial and looked for ways to draw the right wing of the labor movement, that is, the labor movement minus its Marxist, antinationalist elements, into projects of *bürgerliche Sozialreform*.[63] Also Simmel in his early career was associated with Gustav Schmoller's attempts at formulating an ethical, institutionalist version of political economy, reconnecting to Adam Smith the moral philosopher (as opposed to the Adam Smith imagined later by the economists), and was thus part of the same general tendency to formulate a social scientific basis for social reform. Simmel departed from this milieu by insisting in *Philosophy of Money* boldly and provocatively that money and all the bad—according to the antisemites, the Jewish—things it stood for were also very good things: emancipation and indeed individualism itself owed themselves largely to the abstraction and alienation that comes with what he called "the money economy."[64] Simmel, quite like Durkheim, rehabilitated therewith some of the "degenerations" of liberal society, contra its more wholesale rejection by antimodern antisemites.

The book is in three parts: part 1 contains chapters that survey how contemporary debates on antisemitism were reflected in works that contributed to the formation of classical sociological theory in France and Germany; part 2 contains chapters on sociological responses to antisemitism in different national contexts (Imperial Germany, the United States) and in the cases of several individual sociologists and social theorists who directly addressed antisemitism in their work, and/or whose work was significantly shaped by the experience of antisemitism (Marx, Boas, Simmel, Ruppin); part 3 contains chapters that look at how sociological treatments of antisemitism were rearticulated during and immediately after the challenge of fascist antisemitism and the Holocaust, that is, after sociology's "classical" period.

The first part begins with Chad Alan Goldberg's chapter "Durkheim's Sociology and French Antisemitism." He begins by delineating the two principal forms of nineteenth-century antisemitism: the reactionary form accused the Jews of having ushered in modernity, being responsible for the Revolution, and having destroyed the old regime's political and social order; conversely the "radical" form, in Goldberg's terminology, accused the Jews of conspiring against and corrupting the new order that the Revolution established. Goldberg discusses aspects of Durkheim's work that respond either explicitly or implicitly to either of these two forms of antisemitism: against "reactionary antisemitism" Durkheim argued that the French Jews were actually a rather traditionalistic and backward group, "far from constituting the advance guard of a dangerous and disruptive modernity." He also produced sociological arguments against racial antisemitism (and, by implication, race thinking in general). Central to Durkheim's stance against both forms of antisemitism (as well as to his sociology in general) was his specific interpretation of the French

Revolution itself: he embraced the Revolution as not an event destructive of social order but, to the contrary, as its indeed very productive reconstitution. Likewise he advocated a constructive brand of socialism, which, in Goldberg's view, set him apart from antisemitic socialists who tried to destroy in "the Jews" a neofeudal ruling elite. Rather than elimination of a (supposed or real) ruling elite, moral regeneration of society was the task at hand. Goldberg correlates Durkheim's embrace of the Revolution, including the realization that it did not destroy religion but, to the contrary, is the origin of the new "religion of the individual" central to the social imaginary of the new form of society, his invocations of Saint-Simon, and his opposition to antisemitism: it is this constellation rather than, for example, Durkheim's Jewishness that can explain his stance on antisemitism.

My chapter "Sociology's Case for a Well-tempered Modernity: Individualism, Capitalism, and the Antisemitic Challenge" offers a different perspective on the same question. My argument is chiefly built around analyses of Durkheim's intervention in the Dreyfus affair, "Individualism and the Intellectuals," and passages from Weber's *Protestant Ethic*. I argue that both sociologists developed a discourse that aimed at defending liberal society and modernization while at the same time attacking a caricature of "egotistical utilitarianism" on which they blamed the dismal sides of the emerging new form of society. By doing so they formulated an alternative to but also mimicked the discourse of the antisemites, even when—as in the case of Durkheim—explicitly opposing antisemitism. I argue that this is an intrinsic characteristic of classical sociology that weakened its ability to oppose antisemitism and fascism. In *Protestant Ethic* Weber develops the notion that once upon a time there was ethically driven, Calvinist capitalism when people (rather religiously, as it were) performed accumulation for its own sake and when concern with material goods was but a "light cloak." Along came utilitarianism and helped turn the light cloak into a "casing hard as steel." Jews are bracketed out of this account because they represent a backward, premodern form of capitalism, pariah-capitalism, that is of little relevance. In this respect Weber—quite like Durkheim in Goldberg's account— plays down the connection between Jews and modernity that is central to reactionary antisemitism. Weber's friend and colleague Werner Sombart, though, was able to take Weber's basic narrative of "good capitalism turning bad" but changed some of the value judgments: for Sombart good, early capitalism is robust, military, and heroic, while things went downhill (turned "utilitarian") when the Jews started commercializing everything and turned heroic into parasitic capitalism. He moved the "pariah" version of capitalism from the distant past, where Weber had exiled it, to the present. My argument is that the two narratives—both based on rumors about the Jews more than historical fact—are structurally related in spite of having been formulated as competing accounts. I conclude that as long as sociology remains committed—like its contemporary and competitor, antisemitism—to the notion that the creation of a reformed, benign form of capitalism combined with some form of communal, "re-binding" (religious) morality will halt the perceived dissolution of society by capitalism and individualism, images of "the Jews" (or, depending on context, some equivalent) as incongruent with this difficult and precarious effort are bound to retain their discursive power.

Irmela Gorges discusses in her chapter "Fairness as an Impetus for Objective, Scientific Social Research Methods: The Reports about Jewish Traders in the 1887 Usury *Enquête* of the Verein für Socialpolitik" a dispute that was of great importance for the development of empirical research in German sociology. This dispute of 1887–88 dealt with prejudices toward Jews and induced social researchers to take steps to develop objective methods of empirical social research; it may well have lingered in the back of the minds of members of the Verein, including Weber, when they subsequently returned repeatedly to the question of objectivity in social research.

Since the mid-1860s national liberal academics, especially those associated with the "historical school of national economics," addressed "the social question," the situation of the working class under the conditions of the Industrial Revolution. In 1872, the Verein für Socialpolitik (VfS) was founded from among these circles. One of the principal activities of the VfS was to conduct policy-relevant *enquêtes* (surveys). In the 1880s (the period of the Bismarckian antisocialist legislation), the VfS concentrated on research concerning "the rural question" rather than industrial problems. Usury was then generally considered a problem of crucial importance to the rural question, although the definition of usury was ambiguous. The enquête attracted enormous interest, as it highlighted a kind of usury that aroused particular resentment: usury not as a mere matter of "too high" interest rates but of cheating and outwitting poor peasants not well-versed in business matters. Furthermore the reports provoked outrage also because in most reports those accused of committing usury were said to be Jews; it seemed that for many authors *Jew* and *usurer* were nearly synonyms. One of the main critics was the statistician Gottlieb Schnapper-Arndt, who pointed to "a whole anthology of insulting comments on Jews." He criticized the survey for having been based on questionnaires that contained suggestive questions, such as questions about the consequences of a social fact before it was clear that the social fact was indeed existent. Schnapper-Arndt claimed that generalizations from single cases were made in an inadmissible manner and criticized the fact that reporters reproduced only "the Jewish jargon," although all reports were based on data collected among rural populations, all of whom obviously spoke a variety of dialects.

Michal Bodemann argues in his chapter "Coldly Admiring the Jews: Werner Sombart and Classical German Sociology on Nationalism and Race" that German sociology in its "classical" period by and large avoided dealing with "the Jewish question," let alone antisemitism, but discussed issues that can be understood as "displacements" of the former, whereas Sombart, in spite of formally rejecting racial categories, in fact put forward a racial, if not racist, account of "the Jews" based on the notion of a Jewish essence outside history and society.

Tellingly the first meeting of the German Sociological Society in 1910 featured a paper by the "racial biologist" Alfred Ploetz, indicating that the organizers of the meeting found positioning the emerging discipline of sociology in relation to "racial biology" a matter of urgency. Ploetz saw social problems as effects of racial impurities and perceived a dichotomy between society, altruistically committed to support and preserve the weak, and race, aiming to preserve itself by exterminating the weak. He implied that this conflict ought to be resolved in favor of race. Apart from the fact that Sombart leaned toward this perspective, one might be surprised by the terms in which the more progressive sociologists Tönnies and Weber criticized it: the former argued that preserving cripples, for example, might benefit the nation, as they might be "great minds" (he pointed to Moses Mendelssohn as an example), while Weber defended against Ploetz the concept of social policy as it might help people cope who have perfectly good genes but simply fell on hard times.

Weber dismissed the concept of racial instincts because scientific evidence was "so far" still wanting. Some issues, writes Bodemann, were studiously not discussed, such as the widely perceived (in these circles) decline of German national culture and the related issue of the "Jewish question." Bodemann argues that they were displaced by discussions on the decline of classical Greece and the "Negro question in America." It seems as if the sociologists felt they ought to bracket them out as their discussion might spin out of control and threaten the carefully guarded scientificity of the whole project of sociology.

Bodemann then compares three discourses on "the stranger" by Simmel, Sombart, and Tönnies. For Simmel, the stranger (of whom "the Jew" is only a prominent example) is the product of increasing division of labor. The "social type" of the stranger is socially constituted ("constructed," as "social constructionists" would say). Sombart described strangers in similar ways a few years later but "essentialized" them: the Jews remain Jews, products of the nomadic life in the desert that "they" once led. Sombart has no time for Simmel's sophisticated play with the idea that the stranger is both distant *and* close, indifferent *and* involved, which for Simmel makes the Jew/stranger but a slightly more extreme version of what any modern individual is anyway (a pattern of thought that bears comparison with Marx's argument from half a century earlier: that Christian society can emancipate the Jews because—even if the image of "the Jew" as drawn by the anti-emancipation discourse was accurate—they merely play back to it its own melody). Bodemann then draws our attention to an essay by Tönnies from whose analysis he concludes that both writers, coming from the same reform-oriented, national liberal milieu, had not hugely differing things to say about the Jews, although Tönnies soon was to join the Social Democrats (in 1930), while Sombart, at least temporarily, leaned toward the National Socialists.

Part 2 begins with Robert Fine's chapter "Rereading Marx on the 'Jewish Question': Marx as a Critic of Antisemitism?" With those who diagnose the existence of a Marxist form of antisemitism Fine agrees that among Marx's followers there were many who were—to say the least—ill-disposed toward either Jews or Judaism, but he finds no entirely convincing grounds for such a judgment in the case of Marx himself. More important, though, he argues that his texts on Bruno Bauer and "the Jewish question" should be appreciated as key texts in the (small enough) canon of texts that offer a basis for sophisticated interpretations and refutations of antisemitism.

Fine contextualizes Marx's position first within the Enlightenment tradition, which he describes as generally pro-emancipation, even though sometimes the abandonment of Judaism in assimilation was demanded, and second within the Hegelian tradition. Like the eighteenth-century enlighteners, Hegel (in spite of being likewise not incapable of unfriendly words about Judaism) strongly advocated Jewish emancipation against the propaganda of the nationalist populist antisemites of the time. So did Marx, who understood Bauer's opposition to Jewish emancipation as an aspect of his opposition to modern political life. Marx took up Bauer's argument that *political* emancipation (including freedom of religion) did not mean *human* emancipation (including freedom from religion), but he drew the opposite conclusion to that drawn by Bauer: given political emancipation was just that, there was no reason to demand of the Jews first to abandon their religion and then to be emancipated.

Fine demonstrates that the second essay against Bauer, which contains the notorious formulations about, for instance, money being the "jealous God of Israel," is difficult to interpret and admits that no final reading can be offered as we are not able to pick Marx's brain; the reading Fine suggests, though, sees Marx using a particular strategy of turning the anti-Jewish stereotypes on their head. Marx's strategy here was "not to challenge the veracity of antisemitic representations of Jews but to reveal their irrelevance." Different from other critics who had already pointed out that Bauer's characterization of the Jews had no basis in reality, Marx did not waste time on such blatantly obvious points and put forward instead the argument that all the things of which the Jews were accused were in fact general characteristics of modern society; the question whether these things *also* characterized the Jews—as they did everybody else—was therefore irrelevant. Fine concludes that in this reading, Marx's second essay on "the Jewish question" continued the first essay's argument for the detachment of the right of emancipation of Jews from all prior qualifications demanded by liberals and nationalists.

Amos Morris-Reich explores in "From Assimilationist Antiracism to Zionist Anti-antisemitism: Georg Simmel, Franz Boas, and Arthur Ruppin" how antisemitism shaped, in different ways, different layers in the arguments of these three social scientists (all of whom were born in what was then the German Empire). He attempts to distinguish but correlate their direct references to antisemitism and Jewish social issues and their more general theoretical frameworks. Morris-Reich emphasizes the "generational dimension": Simmel and Boas were both born in 1858 (incidentally, the same year as Durkheim), Boas, who never converted, to an assimilated Jewish family, Simmel, who was baptized a Protestant, to parents who had converted. Ruppin, by contrast, was born in 1876, which means that he grew up after the assimilationist ideal held by many Jews of the previous generation had been blown to pieces by the intensified antisemitism of the early 1880s. Morris-Reich identifies a delicate paradox: while the commitment to assimilation made many Jews hesitate to respond too directly to antisemitism but contributed, for example, in Boas's and Simmel's work, to the development of nonracial, (in today's terminology) anti-essentialist and culturally relativist conceptions, the breakdown of the assimilationist perspective resulted in Ruppin in a more robust reaction to antisemitism, but one that was itself colored by the racialism that characterized the intellectual environment in which Ruppin was educated.

Simmel never directly engaged in a critique of antisemitism, but the sociological categories he developed can be understood as an implicit critique, or deconstruction, of the category of race from within sociological theory. Morris-Reich argues that Simmel displaced any notion of "substance" by conceiving of "social form" and "social type"—his central categories—as constituted by individual "interaction." While "social form" is a more general term, "social types" are such forms constituted by "the specifiable reactions and expectations of others." Interestingly Simmel rules out that an actual individual could ever be grasped by the "types" that fellow members of society create: individuality is ultimately impossible to subsume under any categories, forms, or types (a position that points back to Kant and forward to Adorno). In this framework "racial difference" can be theorized only as a "social construct" (which does not mean, though, that, e.g., "Jewish difference" does not exist). Morris-Reich concludes that Simmel's radical epistemological and ontological individualism meant a "circumvention," a way of dealing with antisemitism while not dealing with it.

While resembling Simmel in some ways, Boas was less adverse to entering immediate battle with the enemy (he published at least two important texts against racism and antisemitism, in 1923 and 1934), but he also much less consistently excluded the category of race from his work, at least in his earlier period. Boas's strategy was to destabilize and transform the category of race, not to bury it. The real contrast, in Morris-Reich's chapter, is with Ruppin, who wrote extensively on antisemitism. Prompted perhaps by persistent experience and observation of antisemitism, Ruppin postulated an extrahistorical and irrational "group instinct" that made members of "groups" (or societies) force "aliens" to assimilate. Unlike Simmel and Boas, however, Ruppin, who was a leading functionary of the Zionist movement, opposed assimilation as being no less dangerous to Jewish existence than antisemitism, which he saw as a natural and inevitable reaction to actual Jewish difference. All three authors developed differing strategies to engage antisemitism.

Richard H. King looks at how sociology in the United States related to different aspects of "the Jewish question" in his chapter "The Rise of Sociology, Antisemitism, and the Jewish Question: The American Case." For the period preceding World War II, he observes a general avoidance of the subjects of Jews, Jewishness, and "the Jewish question" in favor of theorizations of (color-coded) "race." King argues that Thorstein Veblen's *The Theory of the Leisure Class* (1899) "could easily have picked out American Jews as symbols of the rampant materialism of the time" but did not do so. It seems that American sociology in that period tended to see Jews as carriers of a welcome modernization process that was in essence, though, coded as American rather than Jewish; by and large, they appeared at that point in time neither as too modern nor as obstacles to modernity, as was the case with antisemitism in Europe in its two main dimensions. King writes that "American sociology was historically more preoccupied with . . . alleged obstacles to modernity presented by African Americans than the dangers presented by the carriers of the modern spirit, the Jews of America." Arguably, in order to keep it that way, though, Jewish sociologists avoided working on "Jewish topics."

This situation changed after World War II. King writes that three factors—the Holocaust (and having escaped it), having gained unprecedented affluence as well as access to universities, and the foundation of the state of Israel—resulted in a newly configured, specifically American Jewish consciousness that was manifested in a more open concern with things Jewish also in academia. King discerns four areas in which "the Jewish question" was addressed, directly or indirectly, in that period: studies of the Holocaust (whereby comparisons with black slavery were formulated already in the late 1950s), studies of prejudice where antisemitism and color-coded racism were often treated in parallel, studies of contemporary Jewish life that included revisiting the old metaphor of the "melting pot," and the sociology of modernity and the self. King mentions in this context Benjamin Nelson's *The Idea of Usury* of 1949, which presented Jews as neither particularly traditional nor the sole inventors of capitalism; he argues that the distinction in Deuteronomy between those who might and those who might not be charged interest anticipated a modern but traditional duality of Gemeinschaft and Gesellschaft.

Roland Robertson's chapter "Civilization(s), Ethnoracism, Antisemitism, Sociology" bridges the second and the third parts. His principal proposition is that the most appropriate framework for discussions of race and antisemitism is what arguably is the widest framework one can think of: the concept of civilization. Touching upon a variety of differing uses of that concept, including by Norbert Elias and Shmuel Eisenstadt, he explores the relevance of the Jewishness of the proponents of these differing concepts of civilization and suggests that whether one understands civilization as process, as territorialized "entity" ("*a* society" as "*a* civilization"), or as project—the last especially in the context of catch-up development and postcolonial situations—cannot but affect the ways one also understands race, including the "Jewish question." He suggests that German theorists in particular, including those of the Frankfurt School, failed to examine the meeting and mixing of civilizations, implying that this has limited their interpreting of antisemitism. Especially in the context of globalization—again a topic Robertson implies is ill understood by theories framed in traditions prevalent in German sociology—when the meeting and mixing of civilizations becomes a dominant phenomenon, lack of a differentiated conception of civilization will limit the understanding of race and antisemitism too. Paralleling some of King's explorations, Robertson argues that the discourse on multiculturalism (or, better, multiculturality) has been a central concern for writers of Jewish background—in the United States, to be sure—because the civilizing process, as well as the project of civilization, and the problem of the meeting and mixing of distinct civilizations are central for those whose social identity is informed by the experience (or at least the "collective memory") of antisemitism.

The contributions in the third section discuss developments under the changed conditions of Nazi antisemitism and the Holocaust and their aftermath. Jonathan Judaken's chapter "Talcott Parsons's 'The Sociology of Modern Anti-Semitism': Anti-antisemitism, Ambivalent Liberalism, and the Sociological Imagination" discusses Parsons's wartime antifascist writings and the liberal ambiguities they reveal, connecting back not only to King's chapter on the earlier stages of American work on antisemitism but also to Morris-Reich's, mine, and others' accounts of the attempts of liberals to get to grips with antisemitism. The focus is on Parsons's essay "The Sociology of Modern Antisemitism" that was published in 1942 in the volume edited by Isacque Graeber and Steuart Henderson Britt, *Jews in a Gentile World*, one of the key publications in the history of the social sciences' engagement with antisemitism. Judaken argues that the wartime period brought about a shift in the discourse on antisemitism, from arguments about how Jews could change to avoid antisemitism—ranging from the rabbinic attempt to explain antisemitism with reference to what Jacob did to Esau, through the liberal and socialist attempts at the Jews' "amelioration" and the Zionist hope that antisemitism would disappear once the Jews will have become a "normal" nation—to explaining why antisemites hated Jews. Judaken argues that Parsons's essay was "caught in this shift," as if inhabiting both sides of it at the same time. Parsons's argument hinges on what he saw as the clash between the values and characteristics of Jewishness and modernity: antisemites project free-floating aggression resulting from the anomie typical of badly integrated modern society onto the Jews, who offer a particularly appropriate target due to their particular characteristics. Parsons's understanding of what this Jewish character is, is entirely derived from Max Weber's account in *Ancient Judaism* and *The Sociology of Religion*; short of actually using the word, Parsons describes the Jewish character as that of the self-ghettoizing "pariah-people" (a conception he later criticized in Weber). The friction between the Gentiles and the Jewish "pariah-people" is for the Parsons of 1942 "natural."

Eva-Maria Ziege discusses in her chapter "The Irrationality of the Rational: The Frankfurt School and Its Theory of Society in the 1940s" the Institute of Social Research's study *Antisemitism among American Labor* of

1944–45, which, although it remained unpublished, constituted a crucial step in the evolution of this particular sociological tradition. She frames her discussion of the Institute's work in the period of exile in the United States as an example of "scientific innovation through forced migration," whereby "marginal persons" (according to Paul Lazarsfeld) who are part of two different cultures become "institution men," the dynamic forces behind the formation of new institutions or, more generally speaking, of the institutionalization of an emerging practice, such as that of empirical social research informed by critical theory. She argues that the core members of the Institute were linked by "a discreet orthodoxy," namely adherence to Marx's critique of political economy and Freud's psychoanalysis, which they maintained throughout their careers as crucial to the "esoteric" side of their communication and production, while they de-emphasized the theoretical core of their work in their "exoteric" communications. Ziege writes that this split between what one says explicitly and what one only hints at had been important to critical thinkers since the Enlightenment, and, in the case of the Frankfurt theorists, it enabled them to cooperate with scholars who did not share their theoretical core conception to immensely productive and innovative effect.

Antisemitism among American Labor (the *Labor Study*) is the "missing link" between the *Dialectic of Enlightenment* and the most famous but least typical work of the School, *The Authoritarian Personality*. It is based on hundreds of semistructured interviews conducted by American workers (who got involved through the strategic involvement of the trade unions) with their peers and examines attitudes toward Jews in the context of World War II at a point when the Holocaust was a well-publicized fact in the United States. Ziege describes it as "not only the blue-collar but also the multicultural complement to *The Authoritarian Personality*": "the *Labor Study* conceptualized manifold 'fine distinctions,'" including those between men and women, blue and white collar, religious affiliations, ethnic and generational differences, ethnic and national belonging, and age cohort. It established as the "type" most susceptible to antisemitism "white male workers with neither vocational training nor education," and as the least susceptible, African American workers. For those inclined toward antisemitism, "the Jew" mainly represented "the bourgeois." Perhaps most shockingly it was found that not antisemitic agitation but rather the news about the Holocaust exacerbated antisemitic attitudes;

while the most atrocious aspects tended to be disbelieved, interviewees tended to assume, drawing on their own life experience, that one does not get "punished" without at least some guilt, an argumentative pattern that the theorists of the Institute termed the "guilty victim" pattern.

Daniel Lvovich's chapter "Gino Germani, Argentine Sociology, and the Study of Antisemitism" discusses the work of Germani, who immigrated—as an antifascist—to Argentina from fascist Italy in 1934, studied economics and philosophy in Buenos Aires, and became a key figure in the modernization of Argentine sociology, especially in the period from 1955, when he became director of both the School of Sociology and the Institute for Sociological Research at the University of Buenos Aires, to 1966, when he moved to Harvard. This process chiefly consisted of the transformation of a more old-fashioned, philosophically based sociology into a modern, institutionalized discipline driven by empirical research. As part of this process, Germani also pioneered sociological research on antisemitism in Argentina. The theoretical base of this work was broad; its influences included Parsons as well as the Frankfurt School. On a more practical level, the chief influence on Germani's sociology must have been his having lived under Mussolini as well as Perón.

Beginning in 1957 Germani headed a research project on "ethnocentrism and authoritarian attitudes" that included research on antisemitism in Argentina. The results of this research were published in 1963. Germani suggested distinguishing two levels of antisemitism: the antisemitism of the "general public," consisting of "certain adverse verbally expressed stereotypes," and political antisemitism, expressed through movements "'similar to the European totalitarian right-wing movements' known in Argentina as *nacionalistas*." These groups consisted of upper- and middle-class individuals with close connections to the Catholic Church and the armed forces. Following Germani's analysis, their societal power rested on their ability to exploit the nationalism of the Argentine working classes as well as "certain psychosocial elements liable to promote authoritarian political attitudes." (Concerning Peronism, though, Germani emphasized its important "democratic" aspects, as well as the relative absence of antisemitism.) The large empirical study on antisemitism Germani conducted in 1961, partly modeled on *The Authoritarian Personality*, showed that among the lower classes "traditional antisemitism" was more pertinent than "ideological antisemitism," and interestingly "traditional antisemitism" was not correlated with authoritarianism. Among the middle and upper classes the antisemitism tended to be "ideological antisemitism," which was correlated strongly with authoritarianism.

Werner Bonefeld's chapter "Antisemitism and the Power of Abstraction: From Political Economy to Critical Theory" completes the third part of the volume and points forward to Detlev Claussen's concluding comments. Presenting his argument in a style more reminiscent of political theory than of the intellectual history that is the predominant tone of the volume, Bonefeld weaves together theorems from Horkheimer and Adorno, Sartre, and Moishe Postone (as well as Hegel and Marx) and puts them to work in the context of the rise, or reemergence, of elements of antisemitism in contemporary "anti-imperialist" and (supposedly) "anticapitalist" movements. Bonefeld's chief suggestion is that antisemitism is not, as some on the Left seem to believe, essentially an expression of "resistance to capitalism" but is an expression of a form of resentment of selected aspects of capitalism (whose incarnation is deemed to be 'the Jews') that is in itself supportive of and indeed elementary to capitalism itself. Bonefeld challenges primarily the "anti-imperialist Left," especially those who recently have demanded solidarity with Islamists such as the Muslim Brotherhood while downplaying and rationalizing their antisemitism. It is significant that while in the past Leninists had argued for cooperation between communist parties and national liberation and anticolonial movements primarily (and quite overtly) for geopolitical and strategic reasons (especially the economic and power-political interests of the USSR), more recently anticapitalists have shifted to the argument that anticolonial movements as such *are* anticapitalist; in this context moral discourses against, for instance, "westoxication" (to use Khomeini's word)—liberalism, democracy, socialism, feminism, communism, all represented in "the Jew" and enjoying an imperialist bridgehead with Israel—are mistaken as progressive (or at least tolerated as harmless idiosyncrasies that need to be forgiven those who are most oppressed). Bonefeld sees as central to antisemitic anti-imperialism the underlying naturalization of the nation as an egalitarian community of honest, industrious, soil-bound *Volksgenossen* that is under siege by "society," representing evil and abstract forces of rootlessness, the "invisible hand" of the market, intellectualism, and finance capital. By destroying society, personified in the Jews, the community "liberates itself" and (seemingly) ends the exploitation of its members while in actuality being able relentlessly to develop capitalist production under the cover of the struggle against (Jewish) capitalism.

Detlev Claussen's "The Dialectic of Social Science and Worldview: On Antisemitism in Sociology" draws together some of the main lines of argument represented in this volume in light of his own perspective, which takes its cue from Max Horkheimer's comment that "the Jewish Question is the question of contemporary society." Central to Claussen's argument is that a sociology that tries to find rationalistic explanations of an irrational phenomenon cannot but fail; instead, by leaving unexamined the irrationalism that dwells at the heart of rationalism, sociology becomes complicit in the larger irrationality of which antisemitism is an extreme expression. Anything less than the self-critique of the Enlightenment will not suffice for the task of understanding antisemitism. This must involve a rational (in the sense of "guided by reason and reasoning") critique of rationalism itself in its irrational dimensions that stem from its inevitably being enmeshed in the structures of the modern society that produced it.

This volume is based on the following premise: If, first, antisemitism can be understood as a discourse that speaks to a set of actual or perceived conflicts, processes, and problems inherent in modern society—none of which of course have anything causally to do with Jews, except in the minds of the antisemites—and if, second, sociology is also a discourse that speaks to more or less the same conflicts, processes, and problems, then the two are inevitably competing discourses fighting over the same ground, trying to win over and mobilize the hearts and minds of the perplexed individual members of this society. If this is granted, it is unsurprising that the one will adopt characteristics of the other when their thought patterns (reasoning, ideology, imaginings, rhetoric) are seen to succeed: antisemites will become quasi-sociologists (see the quote from Drumont that opens this introduction), and sociologists—even if and when opposing antisemitism—will parallel, be ambivalent about, or partly resemble antisemites, or even join them to varying degrees. Their convergence will likely be stronger if the individuals in question originate from the same political, cultural, or social milieu, such as (in Germany) the late nineteenth-century national liberal milieu that produced most sociologists and some antisemites. But that is a minor point; the real issue is what one has to say (think, feel, imagine) on that tremendous and encompassing revolution: the emergence of modern capitalist, industrial, individualistic, national, liberal society.

Most of the chapters collected in this volume have been developed from presentations at a conference that took place at Manchester University in November 2008. I would like to thank the School of Arts, Histories and Cultures, the Centre for Jewish Studies, and the Department of Religions and Theologies at Manchester University and the British Sociological Association Theory Study Group for financing this conference, and those who, in addition to the contributors to this volume, made it such a pleasant and inspiring event: Bill Williams, Hae-Yung Song, David Seymour, Gary A. Abraham, Barbara Rosenbaum, Jean-Marc Dreyfus, Moishe Postone, Susie Jacobs, Christine Achinger, Kati Vörös, Rainer Niklaus Egloff, Philip Spencer, Lars Fischer, Ewa Morawska, Mathias Berek, Sebastien Mosbah-Natanson, and Malgorzata Mazurek. The present volume still reflects the spirit and the atmosphere of this conference that brought together scholars from critical theory, Weberian and Durkheimian backgrounds—with more than enough to disagree on—in a friendly but combative discussion of what is probably one of the most divisive and charged issues around. Most participants seemed to agree that it was one of those rare academic gatherings that are unmistakably "about something"; there are now probably not many conferences where a discussion of Talcott Parsons makes pulses race and produces silences of the kind wherein one could hear a pin drop. The more electric moments are of course neutralized when ink meets acid-free paper and controversies are exiled into endnotes, but the reader might still sense some of the excitement of finding quite differing perspectives on some famously thorny issues.[65]

Notes

Some sections of this introduction were previously published in "Antisemitism, Capitalism and the Formation of Sociological Theory," Patterns of Prejudice 44.2 (2010): 161–94.

1. Drumont is quoted in Birnbaum, *Jewish Destinies*, 106.
2. Rürup, *Emanzipation und Antisemitismus*, 115; Mommsen, *Max Weber*; Breuilly, "Eduard Bernstein and Max Weber"; Geary, "Max Weber"; Rehmann, *Modernisierung*.

3. This perspective also aims to displace the approach that has been taken by some in the past looking for intrinsic affinities between sociology and "Jewishness" (see, for example, Wiehn, *Juden in der Soziologie;* Käsler, *Judentum*). If sociology is about the search for a modern society healed from or reconciled with its contradictions, then it is less than surprising that many of those who suffer from antisemitism as one of the latter's foremost expressions would dedicate themselves to it.

4. This became Stoetzler, *The State, the Nation and the Jews.*

5. Turner, "Sociology and Fascism in the Interwar Period," 6, 7, 9.

6. On the response of sociology to the Holocaust, see Stoetzler, "Sociology."

7. Ranulf, "Scholarly Forerunners of Fascism," 33–34. Svend Ranulf (1894-1953) was primarily a sociologist of law; his main works are discussed in Barbalet, "Moral Indignation, Class Inequality and Justice." According to Barbalet, the failure of Ranulf's work to have had a significant impact on the sociological tradition may primarily be due to the lack of an institutional environment for sociology in Denmark before the 1980s.

8. See also Turner, "Sociology and Fascism in the Interwar Period." While Tönnies seems to have held (in private) antisemitic and antimodernist views in his early twenties, an impulse that lived on in his main work, *Gemeinschaft und Gesellschaft* (published in 1887 when he was just thirty-two), he was also vehemently opposed to the antisocialist laws, supported activities of the labor movement and, in 1930, actually joined the Social Democratic Party (Liebersohn, *Fate and Utopia in German Sociology*, 12). While "Tönnies integrated Hobbesian theory and utilitarianism into a postliberal dialectic" (21), the early formation of the concept of the Gemeinschaft was inspired by Nietzsche's concept of "Dionysian oneness," Hobbes's and Schopenhauer's emphasis on "the will," and the historical research by Lewis Morgan, Johann Bachofen, and Otto von Gierke. Liebersohn argues that Tönnies "spotted the subversive potential of their research" (they were conservatives) but also considers *Gemeinschaft und Gesellschaft* "implicitly" antisemitic (24, 26, 33, 34). Tönnies's actual politics were "restrained patriotism and support for social reform" (38).

9. Ranulf, "Scholarly Forerunners of Fascism," 26. Ranulf's intervention is particularly interesting because he was not a Marxist; his work on the concept of right was actually to a large extent Durkheimian. For a Marxist argument that links positivism to fascism, see Ball, "Marxian Science and Positivist Politics." In the 1930s Ranulf was not the only one who indicted Durkheim as a "forerunner of fascism"; Alexandre Koyré, for example, made the same point in a 1936 review article on French sociology in the Frankfurt School's *Zeitschrift für Sozialforschung* (Falasca-Zamponi, "A Left Sacred," 43). In his introduction to the German edition of Durkheim's *Sociology and Philosophy* (Adorno, "Einleitung zu Emile Durkheim") Adorno later challenged the authoritarian character of a theory that hypostatizes the "spirit" of a society as its essence because this obstructs the possibility of distinguishing between

right and wrong consciousness of that society itself, but he credits Durkheim
for acknowledging as a fact the thingness of society as it stands opposed
to the individuals. Philippe Burrin, *La dérive fasciste*, 41, however, points to
Durkheim's influence on Marcel Déat, one of those socialists who "drifted"
toward fascism. The conception of socialism that allowed this "drift" to take
place was Durkheim's, who continued in this respect "la pensée de Saint-
Simon et de Proudhon, celle de tout le vieux socialisme français." Burrin
sums up Durkheim's ambivalence succinctly: "Rationaliste et républic-
ain, mais préoccupé par la désagrégation social produite par le capitalisme
libéral, Durkheim avait vu dans les groupements professionels le moyen de
donner moralité et solidarité à une societé menacée d'anomie" (41).

10. Ranulf, "Scholarly Forerunners of Fascism," 19.
11. Ranulf, "Scholarly Forerunners of Fascism," 20.
12. Ranulf, "Scholarly Forerunners of Fascism," 21.
13. In one point also Weber the Protestant would have agreed with Comte the
    "secular Catholic": the particularly harsh critique of "the plainly immoral
    doctrine of Luther that a man can be saved by faith irrespective of what his
    works may be," in Ranulf's paraphrase of Comte ("Scholarly Forerunners of
    Fascism," 21).
14. Ranulf, "Scholarly Forerunners of Fascism," 22.
15. Ranulf, "Scholarly Forerunners of Fascism," 26.
16. Ranulf, "Scholarly Forerunners of Fascism," 31.
17. Some readers will object that Durkheim's corporations are not the cor-
    porations proposed by the fascists—that Durkheim *intended* a different
    meaning—and that Weber did not exactly dream of Hitler as his charismat-
    ic leader; it will be objected that the meaning of ideas depends on context,
    that is, that the same idea means something different in different contexts.
    Although this is undeniably true (I am tempted to say *banal*, certainly for a
    sociologist), I would hold against such objections that the *über*-historicizing
    type of intellectual historian is in danger of contextualizing the idea under
    consideration so much that nothing is left of the idea. The more completely
    historiography moves away from the social and political philosophy whose
    concern with the validity of ideas and arguments in and for the battles of the
    present drove us to the study of history in the first place, the less interest-
    ing it becomes. There is much more to the story than whatever Durkheim
    and Weber might have *intended* to say; part of what they *actually* said is also
    what others, at the time and later, *thought* they said. The mediating instance
    that makes the various intended and unintended meanings cohere is *soci-
    ety*, in critical theory conceived as "the totality" of social relations, in post-
    structuralism as discourse, episteme, and so on (which can be understood as
    amounting to the same thing): a structural dimension of society (the Durk-
    heimian "thing"; *It*) that expresses itself in the utterances of the speakers
    and gives them meaning and resonance beyond their *specific* contexts as

long as the *general* context (the "type" of society; the "mode of production"; "civilization" in the sense developed by Robertson in this volume) remains the same. Studying ideas in this perspective opens up the possibility for the thinker to reflect on what it is in society that "thinks" and "speaks" *through* him or her and to take at least some degree of responsibility for how he or she functions as a mouthpiece for *It*.

18. On Parsons, compare Gerhardt, *Talcott Parsons on National Socialism.*

19. The argument that, in spite of the obvious differences, there is a fundamental identity between Western democratic liberalism and Eastern "real socialism" was made by Immanuel Wallerstein, who in *After Liberalism* used the concept "lower case liberalism" as "the ideology of the modern world system" in this context. Wallerstein's concept of "lower case liberalism" bears some similarity to that of "positivism" as used here.

20. Adorno and Horkheimer, *Dialectic of Enlightenment*; Sartre, *Antisemite and Jew.*

21. See Bauman, *Modernity and the Holocaust*; on Bauman, see Stoetzler, "Sociology."

22. Hawthorn, *Enlightenment and Despair*, 85, called Comte a "Catholic atheist," which is also what Maurras was.

23. Quoted in Wilson, *Ideology and Experience*, 461. This was an opinion also shared by perfectly establishmentarian liberals such as Ernest Renan; the idea seems to have been common in all postrevolutionary traditions that inherited elements of the Enlightenment, including liberalism and socialism as well as positivism. On Renan's antisemitism, see Almog, "The Racial Motif in Renan's Attitude to Jews and Judaism."

24. Wilson, *Ideology and Experience*, 422. The same quote (from Maurras's article "La guerre religieuse"), in a slightly different translation, is in Sutton, *Nationalism, Positivism and Catholicism*, 18. I have not been able to verify this quote in Comte.

25. Sutton, *Nationalism, Positivism and Catholicism*, 1.

26. Sutton, *Nationalism, Positivism and Catholicism*, 13–14.

27. Quoted in Sutton, *Nationalism, Positivism and Catholicism*, 18–19. It would be perfectly possible, of course, to construct—in keeping with Luther and Kant, though probably less so with Rousseau—exactly the opposite argument, namely that monotheism *strengthens* "the respect that the conscience owes to its visible and near masters"; this would be the line of reasoning to be expected in a romantic-nationalist context, which Maurras rejected in theory, although in practice romantic and integral, classicist nationalism are not easily kept apart. Moreover this second line of argument would also be compatible with Durkheim's republican, anti-antisemitic nationalism, which indeed invokes both Comte and Kant: the French revolutionary and positivist, postrevolutionary traditions, and the German idealist tradition.

28. Wernick, *Auguste Comte and the Religion of Humanity*, 110–11, writes that Comte described monotheism, via the idea of "personal salvation," as the fount of egoism. Comte detected a contradiction in Catholicism between an

egoistic and abstract theology and love-engendering cultic practice and organizational structure. Positivism would replace the former and thereby salvage the latter.

29. Sutton, *Nationalism, Positivism and Catholicism*, 21. Maurras borrows from
Comte the concept of "subjective synthesis," denoting the idea that "thought
and action can be made properly coherent through their being ordered in the
service of a collective 'Great Being' in which the subject incorporates himself
through sentimental (or existential) choice" (241). This conception, a Comtean element that anticipates an aspect of "structural functionalism," vouches
for the modernity of Maurras's "integral nationalism."

30. Sutton, *Nationalism, Positivism and Catholicism*, 23.

31. Sutton, *Nationalism, Positivism and Catholicism*, 24, 26.

32. The fact of the positivity of the wrong state of things, or else the nonpositiv-
ity of the humane state of things that the Enlightenment still aims for, is of
course the main reason why critical theory (as defined by Horkheimer in 1937
in "Traditional and Critical Theory") defines itself in opposition to positivism, both the encompassing original Comtean conception and the "neoposi-
tivist" version whose focus is narrowed onto concerns of the philosophy of
science. Maurras accuses Comte of being slightly utopian also in other respects (his prophetic millenarian tendencies, dedication to progress, femi-
ninity, love and tenderness; Sutton, *Nationalism, Positivism and Catholicism*,
34). Against all this (i.e., against all that is interesting in Comte in spite of his
"system"), Maurras asserts that "from Aristotle and Xenophon to Dante as
well as to Thomas of Aquinas . . . there is a positive politics that the classical
spirit encourages and teaches faithfully over the centuries." In other words,
Maurras's classicist proto-fascism equals positivism minus its transcenden-
tal, as it were, feminine aspects. In a similar vein, for Maurras romantic love
is just narcissism and wreaks havoc on social and family life; pity is individualistic, hence barbaric (36).

33. Sutton, *Nationalism, Positivism and Catholicism*, 37.

34. Sutton, *Nationalism, Positivism and Catholicism*, 45. Marion Mitchell developed a similar argument in an article from 1931: she argued that Durkheim
"sought to reconcile the cosmopolitan ideal in a spiritualized patriotism";
while "retaining humanity as a god, he recognized the divinity of the nation,"
"the most exalted 'collective being' in actual existence." Aiming to achieve
"the closer integration of France by means of national professional groups,
meetings and symbols, and a national system of education," securing the
continued existence of "national personality," Durkheim "foreshadowed
what Charles Maurras has been pleased to call 'integral nationalism.' It is not
a far step from a conception of the nation as the supreme reality, and humanity as the highest ideal, to one in which the nation fulfils the requirements of
both. Where Durkheim clung to the vestiges of humanitarian pacifism and
abhorred violent upheaval, his successors openly discarded the Positivist re-

ligion and replaced it by the religion of nationalism" ("Emile Durkheim and the Philosophy of Nationalism," 106).

35. Toussenel, *Les Juifs, Rois de l'époque.*

36. "Le titre de l'ouvrage, qui consacre une signification fâcheuse donnée au nom de tout un grand peuple, suffirait à lui seul pour motiver une réserve de notre part" (Toussenel, *Les Juifs*, vii).

37. The 1847 edition was in two volumes, while the 1845 edition was in one. A German edition appeared already in 1851.

38. It should perhaps be added that there is a lot in Fourier—some of what he has to say on labor and on sex and gender—that is of great importance, in spite of his general political program and its antisemitism.

39. The antisemitic socialists' fixation on the Jews as an unproductive, exploitative, and corrosive "financial aristocracy" derived from a simple reversal of Saint-Simon's celebration of the struggle of the productive against the parasitical classes (whereby Saint-Simon and the Saint-Simonians themselves saw bankers and Jews in the camp of the productive).

40. Szajkowski, "The Jewish Saint-Simonians"; Silberner, "Pierre Leroux's Ideas on the Jewish People"; Kuhn, *Pierre Leroux.*

41. Kuhn, *Pierre Leroux*, 204.

42. Leroux's blending of Fourierism and Saint-Simonianism is thus based on the recognition of actual weaknesses in the Saint-Simonian doctrine—chiefly its authoritarian and antidemocratic character—and is therefore highly significant for the history of socialism: the more crucial it is to pay attention to the fact that exactly at this point of synthesis and radicalization, antisemitism also becomes virulent. A precise analysis of how and why antisemitism entered the equation at this crucial point still needs to be done. The Fourierist school seems to have been able to absorb a large number of dispersed former Saint-Simonians. There must have been a significant element of continuity between the two doctrines that allowed the antisemitism of the new doctrine to connect into the older doctrine; this connection seems to be the concept of productivity. Also the concept of exploitation as proposed by the Saint-Simonians is a weakness as it implies the idea of the "parasite"; the wage contract was considered "exploitative" because it "violated the principle of remuneration according to work": "owners were remunerated without working by not fully remunerating those who did" (Cunliffe and Reeve, "Exploitation," 71). The critique of capitalist exploitation properly speaking begins only with Marx's introduction of the concept of surplus-value and the distinction between the exchange-value of labor power and its use-value for the employer, which allows for the argument that the capitalist can appropriate surplus-value while paying a "fair wage," if "fair" means receiving the price equivalent to the labor power's exchange-value. This makes obsolete the ideas of the parasite and of remuneration being fraudulent. On the transformation of Fourierism after 1830, see Pamela Pilbeam, "Fourier and the Fourierists."

43. Pickering, "Auguste Comte and the Saint-Simonians," 213.

44. Pickering, "Auguste Comte and the Saint-Simonians," 220.

45. Pickering, "Auguste Comte and the Saint-Simonians," 222.

46. Pickering, "Auguste Comte and the Saint-Simonians," 228.

47. Pickering, "Auguste Comte and the Saint-Simonians," 228.

48. Pickering, "Auguste Comte and the Saint-Simonians," 233. "The irony was that just as he lost interest in the sciences and opened himself up to ridicule because of his outlandish religion, . . . former Saint-Simonians who had turned their back on their religion became important in the development of industrial capitalism in France" (236). See as well Manuel, *The Prophets of Paris*; Baker, "Closing the French Revolution."

49. I have discussed the dialectic between conservative and progressive antisemitisms in chapter 8 in *The State, the Nation, and the Jews*. See on this also the chapter by Goldberg in the present volume. For an examination of fascism in terms of the intellectual history of its active protagonists, nineteenth-century socialist antisemitism seems to me the most important element, whereas the "real," or political history of fascism's success depended more on the persistence of the "ordinary," widespread conservative antisemitism that continued to exist as a "cultural code" and undermined any resistance to the former.

50. Gane, *Auguste Comte*, 5.

51. The Second Reich was universally admired as the original catch-up economy; see Szporluk, *Communism and Nationalism*; Love, *Crafting the Third World*.

52. Even the Bolshevist state had to submit to this historical law and imposed itself as the new "religion of humanity." Likewise some of those associated with quasi-Leninist groupings (see Bonefeld in this volume for examples) are in cahoots with those who advocate, for example, some version of Khomeinist populism (and, before this came to look like a desirable option to metropolitan anti-imperialists, defended, for example, the corporatist-nationalist socialism of Saddam Hussein, who admired not only Stalin's moustache). On the Comtean roots of Stalinism, see Debray, *Critique of Political Reason*, 228–33; on Khomeinism, see Abrahamian, *Khomeinism*.

53. On populism, see Peal, "The Politics of Populism."

54. See, for example, Repp, *Reformers, Critics, and the Paths of German Modernity*; Loader, "Puritans and Jews"; Gorges, *Sozialforschung in Deutschland*; Bruch, Graf, and Hübinger, *Kultur und Kulturwissenschaften um 1900*; Lindenlaub, *Richtungskämpfe im Verein für Sozialpolitik*; Grimmer-Solem, *The Rise of Historical Economics and Social Reform*.

55. In the last third of the century, for the *Sozialreform* of German state socialists and the Verein für Sozialpolitik as well as for Durkheim, the point was not so much the need for state-driven development but rather the moral control of the economy that *resulted* from this development.

56. Grimmer-Solem, "'Every True Friend of the Fatherland.'"

57. Zumbini, *Die Wurzeln des Bösen*, 157–58. Wagner seems to have become more distanced from party political antisemitism in the course of the 1890s. For a comprehensive portrayal of Wagner, see Clark, "Adolf Wagner."

58. In his early but crucial survey of German debates, "La science positive de la morale en Allemagne," Durkheim reviewed Wagner's work rather favorably and without mentioning his antisemitism.

59. Abraham, *Max Weber and the Jewish Question*, 100.

60. While Silberner ("Pierre Leroux's Ideas," 375–76) states that Saint-Simon did not show any hostility to or contempt of the Jews in his writings, Szajkowski ("The Jewish Saint-Simonians," 34) writes that Saint-Simon had an "unfavourable opinion of the Jews," in spite of his doctrine's "philosem-itism" that was based on his positive view of the role of banking. Fourier-ists and, later, Proudhonists considered Saint-Simonianism "a Jewish ven-ture" (38); their antisemitism and their opposition to Saint-Simonianism seem to have reinforced each other. But also among the adherents of Saint-Simonianism "anti-Jewish feeling" and expressions of antisemitism can be found apparently from the mid-1840s onward (41). Many also embraced Ca-tholicism at the time, as Fourierists did, Toussenel being an example. "Under the July monarchy, the Fourierists had led French socialism into the antise-mitic camp. In the period of the Second Empire Proudhon and his friends played this role" (55).

61. Claussen, *Grenzen der Aufklärung*, 127.

62. Klingemann, *Rassenmythos und Sozialwissenschaften in Deutschland*.

63. On "bürgerliche Sozialreform," see Bruch, *Weder Kommunismus noch Kapi-talismus*.

64. Simmel, *The Philosophy of Money*; Simmel, "Money in Modern Culture." See Levine, "Simmel as Educator."

65. The conference itself, the research for my own contribution, and the first stages of the editing of this volume were made possible by a Simon Fellow-ship at the University of Manchester from 2006 to 2009. I also would like to thank the editors of *Patterns of Prejudice*, who invited me to edit a special is-sue on the subject (2010, containing earlier versions of the chapters by Bode-mann, Morris-Reich, and myself in the present volume, as well as an excel-lent paper on antisemitism and sociology in Hungary by Kati Vörös), and Vic Seidler, with whom I first discussed this project during my fellowship at Gold-smiths College in 2004–5.

References

Abraham, Gary. *Max Weber and the Jewish Question: A Study of the Social Outlook of His Sociology*. Urbana: University of Illinois Press, 1992.

Abrahamian, Ervand. *Khomeinism: Essays on the Islamic Republic*. Berkeley: University of California Press, 1993.

Adorno, Theodor W. "Einleitung zu Emile Durkheim, *Soziologie und Philosophie.*" In *Gesammelte Schriften Bd. 8, Soziologische Schriften*, 245-78. Frankfurt am Main: Suhrkamp, 1996.

Adorno, Theodor W., and Max Horkheimer. *Dialectic of Enlightenment: Philosophical Fragments*. Translated by Edmund Jephcott. Stanford CA: Stanford University Press, 2002.

Almog, Shmuel. "The Racial Motif in Renan's Attitude to Jews and Judaism." In *Antisemitism through the Ages*, edited by Shmuel Almog, 255-78. Oxford: Pergamon, 1988.

Baker, Keith Michael. "Closing the French Revolution: Saint-Simon and Comte." In *The French Revolution and the Creation of Modern Political Culture*. Vol. 3, *The Transformation of Political Culture 1789-1848*, edited by François Furet and Mona Ozouf, 323-39. Oxford: Pergamon, 1989.

Ball, Terence. "Marxian Science and Positivist Politics." In *After Marx*, edited by Terence Ball and James Farr, 235-60. Cambridge: Cambridge University Press, 1984.

Barbalet, Jack. "Moral Indignation, Class Inequality and Justice: An Exploration and Revision of Ranulf." *Theoretical Criminology* 6.3 (2002): 279-97.

Bauman, Zygmunt. *Modernity and the Holocaust*. Ithaca NY: Cornell University Press, 1989.

Birnbaum, Pierre. *Jewish Destinies, Citizenship, State, and Community in Modern France*. New York: Hill and Wang, 2000.

Breuilly, John. "Eduard Bernstein and Max Weber." In *Max Weber and His Contemporaries*, edited by Wolfgang J. Mommsen and Jürgen Osterhammel, 345-54. London: Allen & Unwin, 1987.

Bruch, Rüdiger vom, ed. *Weder Kommunismus noch Kapitalismus, bürgerliche Sozialreform in Deutschland vom Vormärz bis zur Ära Adenauer*. Munich: Beck, 1985.

Bruch, Rüdiger vom, Friedrich Wilhelm Graf, and Gangolf Hübinger, eds. *Kultur und Kulturwissenschaften um 1900: Krise der Moderne und Glaube an die Wissenschaft*. Stuttgart: Steiner, 1989.

Burrin, Philippe. *La dérive fasciste: Doriot, Déat, Bergery 1933-1945*. Paris: Editions du Seuil, 1986.

Clark, Evelyn A. "Adolf Wagner: From National Economist to National Socialist." *Political Science Quarterly* 55.3 (1940): 378-411.

Claussen, Detlev. *Grenzen der Aufklärung: Die gesellschaftliche Genese des modernen Antisemitismus*. Frankfurt am Main: Fischer, 1994.

Cunliffe, John, and Andrew Reeve. "Exploitation: The Original Saint Simonian Account." *Capital and Class* 59 (1996): 61-80.

Debray, Regis. *Critique of Political Reason*. London: Verso, 1983.

Dohm, Christian Wilhelm. "Über die bürgerliche Verbesserung der Juden." 1781. Deutsch-Jüdische Publizistik Steinheim-Institut, http://www.deutsch-juedische-publizistik.de/dohm.shtml (accessed February 17, 2013).

Durkheim, Emile "La science positive de la morale en Allemagne." *Revue Philosophique* 24 (1887): 33-284.

Falasca-Zamponi, Simonetta. "A Left Sacred or a Sacred Left? The Collège de Sociologie, Fascism, and Political Culture in Interwar France." *South Central Review* 23.1 (2006): 40-54.

Gane, Mike. *Auguste Comte*. London: Routledge, 2006.

Geary, Dick. "Max Weber, Karl Kautsky and German Social Democracy." In *Max Weber and His Contemporaries*, edited by Wolfgang J. Mommsen and Jürgen Osterhammel, 355-66. London: Allen & Unwin, 1987.

Gerhardt, Uta, ed. *Talcott Parsons on National Socialism*. New York: Aldine de Gruyter, 1993.

Gorges, Irmela. *Sozialforschung in Deutschland 1872-1914: Gesellschaftliche Einflüsse auf Themen-und Methodenwahl des Vereins für Sozialpolitik*. Königstein im Taunus: Anton Hain, 1980.

Grimmer-Solem, Erik. "'Every True Friend of the Fatherland': Gustav Schmoller and the "Jewish Question" 1916-1917." *Leo Baeck Institute Year Book* 52.1 (2007): 149-63.

———. *The Rise of Historical Economics and Social Reform*. Oxford: Oxford University Press, 2003.

Hawthorn, Geoffrey. *Enlightenment and Despair: A History of Social Theory*. Cambridge: Cambridge University Press, 1987.

Horkheimer, Max. "Traditional and Critical Theory." 1937. In *Critical Theory: Selected Essays*, 188-243. New York: Continuum, 1982.

Käsler, Dirk. "Das 'Judentum' als zentrales Entstehungs-Milieu der frühen deutschen Soziologie." In *Rassenmythos und Sozialwissenschaften in Deutschland*, edited by Carsten Klingemann, 50-79. Opladen: Westdeutscher Verlag, 1987.

Klingemann, Carsten, ed. *Rassenmythos und Sozialwissenschaften in Deutschland*. Opladen: Westdeutscher Verlag, 1987.

Kuhn, Bärbel. *Pierre Leroux: Sozialismus zwischen analytischer Gesellschaftskritik und sozialphilosophischer Synthese*. Frankfurt am Main: Peter Lang, 1988.

Levine, Donald N. "Simmel as Educator: On Individuality and Modern Culture." *Theory, Culture and Society* 8 (1991): 99-117.

Liebersohn, Harry. *Fate and Utopia in German Sociology, 1870-1923*. Cambridge, MA: MIT Press, 1988.

Lindenlaub, Dieter. *Richtungskämpfe im Verein für Sozialpolitik: Wissenschaft und Sozialpolitik im Kaiserreich vornehmlich vom Beginn des "Neuen Kurses" bis zum Ausbruch des 1. Weltkrieges (1890-1914)*. Wiesbaden: F. Steiner, 1967.

Loader, Colin. "Puritans and Jews: Weber, Sombart and the Transvaluators of Modern Society." *Canadian Journal of Sociology/Cahiers canadiens de sociologie* 26.4 (2001): 635-53.

Love, Joseph L. *Crafting the Third World: Theorizing Underdevelopment in Rumania and Brazil*. Stanford CA: Stanford University Press, 1996.

Manuel, Frank Edward. *The Prophets of Paris*. Cambridge MA: Harvard University Press, 1962.

Marx, Karl. "Zur Judenfrage." In *Marx Engels Werke*, 1: 347–77. Berlin: Dietz, 1964.

Mitchell, Marion. "Emile Durkheim and the Philosophy of Nationalism." *Political Science Quarterly* 46.1 (1931): 87–106.

Mommsen, Wolfgang J. *Max Weber and German Politics 1890–1920*. Translated by Michael S. Steinberg. Chicago: University of Chicago Press, 1984.

Peal, David. "The Politics of Populism: Germany and the American South in the 1890s." *Comparative Studies in Society and History* 31.2 (1989): 340–62.

Pickering, Mary. "Auguste Comte and the Saint-Simonians." *French Historical Studies* 18.1 (1993): 211–36.

Pilbeam, Pamela. "Fourier and the Fourierists: A Case of Mistaken Identity?" *French History and Civilization: Papers from the George Rudé Seminar* 1 (2005): 186–96.

Ranulf, Svend. "Scholarly Forerunners of Fascism." *Ethics* 50.1 (1939): 16–34.

Rehmann, Jan. *Max Weber: Modernisierung als passive Revolution. Kontextstudien zu Politik, Phiosophie und Religion im Übergang zum Fordismus*. Hamburg: Argument, 2013.

Repp, Kevin. *Reformers, Critics, and the Paths of German Modernity, Anti-Politics and the Search for Alternatives, 1890–1914*. Cambridge MA: Harvard University Press, 2000.

Rürup, Reinhard. *Emanzipation und Antisemitismus: Studien zur "Judenfrage" der bürgerlichen Gesellschaft*. Frankfurt am Main: Fischer, 1987.

Sartre, Jean-Paul. *Antisemite and Jew*. New York: Schocken Books, 1948.

Silberner, Edmund. "Pierre Leroux's Ideas on the Jewish People." *Jewish Social Studies* 12 (1950): 367–84.

Simmel, Georg. "Money in Modern Culture." 1896. In *Simmel on Culture: Selected Writings*, edited by David Frisby and Mike Featherstone, 243–55. London: Sage, 1997.

———. *The Philosophy of Money*. 1900. London: Routledge, 2004.

Stoetzler, Marcel. "Sociology." In *Writing the Holocaust*, edited by Jean-Marc Dreyfus and Daniel Langton, 41–61. Writing History series. London: Bloomsbury Academic, 2011.

———. *The State, the Nation and the Jews: Liberalism and the Antisemitism Dispute in Bismarck's Germany*. Lincoln: University of Nebraska Press, 2008.

Sutton, Michael. *Nationalism, Positivism and Catholicism: The Politics of Charles Maurras and French Catholics 1890–1914*. Cambridge: Cambridge University Press, 1982.

Szajkowski, Zosa. "The Jewish Saint-Simonians and Socialist Antisemites in France." *Jewish Social Studies* 9 (1947): 33–60.

Szporluk, Roman. *Communism and Nationalism: Karl Marx versus Friedrich List*. New York: Oxford University Press, 1991.

Toussenel, Alphonse. *Les Juifs, Rois de l'époque: Histoire de la Féodalité financière.* Paris: La Librairie de l'Ecole Sociétaire, 1845.

Turner, Stephen P. "Sociology and Fascism in the Interwar Period: The Myth and Its Frame." In *Sociology Responds to Fascism*, edited by Stephen P. Turner and Dirk Käsler, 1–13. London: Routledge, 1992.

Turner, Stephen P., and Dirk Käsler, eds. *Sociology Responds to Fascism.* London: Routledge, 1992.

Vörös, Kati. "The 'Jewish Question': Hungarian Sociology and Normalization of Antisemitism." *Patterns of Prejudice* 44, no. 2 (2010): 137–60.

Wallerstein, Immanuel. *After Liberalism.* New York: New Press, 1995.

Wernick, Andrew. *Auguste Comte and the Religion of Humanity: The Post-Theistic Program of French Social Theory.* Cambridge: Cambridge University Press, 2001.

Wiehn, Erhard R., ed. *Juden in der Soziologie.* Konstanz: Hartung Gorre Verlag, 1989.

Wilson, Stephen. *Ideology and Experience: Antisemitism in France at the Time of the Dreyfus Affair.* Rutherford NJ: Fairleigh Dickinson University Press, 1982.

Zumbini, Massimo Ferrari. *Die Wurzeln des Bösen, Gründerjahre des Antisemitismus: Von der Bismarckzeit zu Hitler.* Frankfurt am Main: Klostermann, 2003.

Part 1

The Antisemitic Contexts of Sociology's Emergence

1

Durkheim's Sociology and French Antisemitism

CHAD ALAN GOLDBERG

"The fundamental ideas of European sociology," Robert Nisbet has argued, "are best understood as responses to the problem of order created at the beginning of the nineteenth century by the collapse of the old regime" under the impact of the Industrial Revolution and the French Revolution.[1] Much the same could be said about nineteenth-century European antisemitism. Antisemitism, the historian Stephen Wilson has suggested, was "a rejection of modern society, as antisemites conceived and experienced it," which offered a "mythical explanation and a scapegoat" to account for and exorcise poorly understood processes of social change.[2] But even when modernity was interpreted in less threatening and more positive terms as an emancipatory and progressive development, the Jews could serve equally well to signify the threat of restoration and reaction. Moreover this function of the Jews as symbols of modernity or its antithesis was not unique to antisemitism; within classical sociological theory too, the Jews were identified, for example, with capitalist modernization (Marx, Sombart) or, conversely, with a traditionalistic economic ethos (Weber). All of this suggests that European sociology emerged not only alongside of and within the same milieu as nineteenth-century European antisemitism but also in relation to it. This would mean that the ideas of European sociology and antisemitism were not only responses to the same revolutions; they were also responses to each other.

This chapter investigates the relationship between European sociology and nineteenth-century European antisemitism through a case study of one sociologist, Émile Durkheim, in a single country, France. The importance of Durkheim to the emergence of European sociology and the importance of France to the history of European antisemitism make them well suited for this investigation. The interplay between Durkheim's sociology and French antisemitism was sometimes explicit, as in the remarks that Durkheim published about antisemitism during the Dreyfus affair,[3] but it was more often implicit, requiring careful exegesis to reconstruct it. I seek to accomplish this below, focusing on one side of this relationship—Durkheim's response to antisemitism—and one of the two revolutions that Nisbet identified: the French Revolution.[4]

The chapter proceeds in four steps. I begin by distinguishing and briefly sketching reactionary and radical forms of antisemitism in nineteenth-century France. While this dichotomous conception admittedly simplifies French antisemitism, eliding a variety of nuances, overlapping themes, and ambiguities, it usefully captures the elements that are most essential for the purposes of this study. I then discuss how Durkheim's sociology responded to each form of antisemitism. I suggest that his remarks about the Jews directly addressed antisemitic claims about them, their role in French society, and their relationship to modernity. At the same time, Durkheim was engaged in a reinterpretation of the French Revolution and its historical legacies that indirectly challenged other tenets of French antisemitism. In other words, he also challenged antisemitism in a roundabout way by showing that its tenets were derived from and rested upon a fundamentally flawed understanding of the Revolution to which it was, in part, a response. In sum I argue that Durkheim's work contains direct and indirect responses to reactionary and radical forms of antisemitism, and together these responses form a coherent alternative vision of the relationship between modernity and the Jews. The chapter concludes with a discussion of the broader implications of these findings.

A few caveats are in order. To provide a comprehensive account of Durkheim's ideas about the Jews and Judaism, one would need to describe fully both the development of his sociological work in general, including its various phases and changes in direction, as well as his social and historical milieu. Among the pertinent aspects of this milieu would be the history and composition of the heterogeneous Jewish population in France, the changing and contested definitions of Jewish identity in nineteenth-century Europe, and the critical events that raised Durkheim's awareness of antisemitism and shaped the development of his thinking. These events would undoubtedly include the 1892 Panama scandal in France and the antisemitic reaction to it; the Dreyfus affair between

1894 and 1906, in which Durkheim was involved as an active Dreyfusard; Durkheim's work during World War I on behalf of Jewish immigrants from Russia; and developments in Russia itself, including pogroms in 1903 and 1905 and the emancipation of Russian Jewry in 1917. Although I allude to some of these events, it is not my aim to provide this sort of comprehensive account here. The development of Durkheim's sociological work and the broader social context in which he formulated his ideas have been well documented by others and cannot be adequately addressed in the scope of this chapter.[5] Instead I focus more narrowly on one aspect of Durkheim's cultural and discursive milieu: I seek to understand his ideas about the Jews and Judaism as, at least in part, a dialectical response to opposing ideas that could be found in the public sphere in nineteenth-century France.

Reactionary Antisemitism: The Jews as Symbols of Revolutionary Modernization

Although the French Right was by no means monolithic or always unified, antisemitism found expression across both its old and new elements. In France, as elsewhere in Europe during the nineteenth century, antisemitism was often linked to anxiety about and reactions against modernization, in all of its disruptive manifestations.[6] Not every element of the French Right opposed all of these changes, but each could find aspects of modernity that threatened its particular ideals and interests. Insofar as the Jews came to be seen as a symbol of modernity and one of its governing factors, as both the sign and cause of a "world gone wrong,"[7] they became a lightning rod for the anxieties that modernization provoked. Furthermore because reactionary antisemites in France traced many of these same changes to the French Revolution of 1789, they also associated the Jews with the Revolution. Wilson notes that "association of the Jews with sedition, disruption and Revolution had long been a commonplace of antisemitic writing" in France, and the historian Esther Benbassa points out that in the late nineteenth century right-wing opinion continued to consider the Jew "the architect of revolution and anticlericalism, the persecutor of the clergy, and the destroyer of Christian religion and civilization."[8] Charles Maurras, for instance, a leader and theoretician of the Action Française, referred to the French Revolution as "the Jewish Revolution."[9] According to this view, the Jews orchestrated the French

Revolution out of self-interest and were its principal beneficiaries. As the jurist Edmond Picard put it, the "fearsome Semitic invasion dates only from 1789 and from the reforms realized by the Revolution."[10] Likewise for the journalist Edouard Drumont, the Jew was "the most powerful agent of turmoil that the world has produced." "Wherever the Jews appear," he insisted, "they spread disorder and ruin in their wake"; "the Semites excel in the politics of dissolution."[11] The Catholic clergy expressed similar views. The abbé Chabauty wrote that "the Revolution in all its reality is the Jewish nation, acting throughout the entire world, under the orders of its leaders, in several army corps and under several banners, inside, outside, and against Catholic and Christian society"; the abbé Lémann, who was himself a Jewish convert, denounced the Declaration of the Rights of Man as "a war machine in the hands of the Jews"; and the Catholic newspaper *La Croix*, referring to the centenary of the French Revolution as "the Semitic centenary," informed its readers that the Jews brought about the Revolution not only to emancipate themselves but to conquer France.[12] Catholic antisemites, in short, held the Jews responsible for all the tribulations that had afflicted the Church since 1789. French antisemitism, the writer Bernard Lazare concluded, was "the creed of the conservative class, of those who accuse[d] the Jews of having worked hand in hand with the Jacobins of 1789."[13]

If the Jews were identified with the Revolution in the discourse of reactionary antisemitism, "the rejected modern world was contrasted with an imagined 'Old France,'" and "'Old France' was set in explicit opposition to the Jews."[14] Antisemites like Drumont contended that the old regime had subordinated the Jews in order to protect itself from them: "If ancient France had been happy and glorious for many centuries, it was because it carefully guarded itself against the Jew."[15] Moreover reactionary antisemites tended to view Jewish influence as a cause or, alternatively, a consequence of the collapse of the old regime. Drumont tried to show "how, little by little, under the Jewish influence, old France was dissolved."[16] As the literary critic Ferdinand Brunetière put it in his review of Drumont's *La France juive*, if modern France "scarcely resembles that of Louis XIV and even less that of St. Louis, the fault, or rather the crime, lies with the Jews."[17] Reversing this reasoning, the monarchist Maurras insisted that it was the revolutionary destruction of the old regime—the "fall of the national dynasty," the "disorganization of the nobility and the clergy," the "persecution of Catholicism," the destruction of intermediary corporate bodies and the "achievement of centralization"—that explained the "rise to power" of the Jews and their allies: Freemasons, Protestants, and foreigners. By transforming France into "a dust of individuals, a desert of atoms," he argued, the Revolution had made it vulnerable to Jewish domination. What was needed, Maurras wrote in 1899, was to treat the Jews as foreigners and restore them to an inferior civil and legal status, "the precaution taken in the Middle Ages," as if one could undo the destruction of the old regime by striking at those whom, in his estimation, its destruction had most benefited.[18]

While this aspiration to restore the old regime and its clearly ordered social hierarchy united reactionary forms of antisemitism, this aspiration expressed itself in different ways, most notably in religious and racial terms. On the one hand, "antisemitism overlapped with the traditional Catholic view" to the extent that the latter was associated with "a backward-looking hierarchical view of the social order." Indeed "there was a tendency . . . to regard the Church itself as a paradigm of the general social order which antisemites yearned for" and Catholicism as "a necessary bulwark of the social order."[19] On the other hand, the language of racism provided a new and different way of reasserting social order, one that had the advantages of putative scientific credibility and broad public appeal (even to some socialists), though it existed in uneasy tension with Catholic theology (which stressed, after all, the possibility and duty of converting the Jews). As Wilson explains, racism sought to organize society "as a static hierarchy" and "to justify a kind of 'caste' system." "Late nineteenth-century French society was one in which the hierarchical classification in terms of orders, which had obtained under the Ancien Régime, was obviously inoperative, even in its modified postrevolutionary form." Although postrevolutionary France did not lack a status system, it was "shifting, based . . . to an increasing degree on 'merit' and wealth." If the Jews came to epitomize "uncertainty about social categorizations and ranking" by virtue of their social mobility, then "racial terminology provided an anti-solvent, a new form of absolute and binding classification."[20] In sum the Christian anti-Judaism expressed in clerical circles sought to reestablish a hierarchical social order modeled on the Church itself, while racial antisemitism revived in a new form the aristocratic principle of hereditary inequality.

Radical Antisemitism: The Jews as Symbols of the Old Regime

While the counterrevolutionary type of antisemitism just described may be its most familiar expression, it would be a mistake to conclude that antisemitism was confined exclusively to reactionaries who rejected the legacies of 1789. In addition there existed a radical and left-wing variant, the exponents of which—including some of the principal fathers of French socialism—saw themselves as the Revolution's most "faithful and uncompromising heirs."[21] Certainly not all French socialists were antisemitic, but "at the beginning of the Third Republic, the most important anti-Semitic writings came from the pens of socialists such as Albert Regnard, Gustave Tridon, and Auguste Chirac," and there were socialists across the movement's ideological and organizational divisions who mixed anticapitalism with antisemitism into the 1890s.[22] In contrast to the language of reactionary antisemitism, which tended to associate the Jews with the Revolution and with the disruptive modernizing processes it had unleashed, the discourse of radical antisemitism tended to identify the Jews with the old regime or, more precisely, a neofeudal social order.[23] For example, at a rally in the town of Suresnes in 1898, Georges Thiébaud and Lucien Millevoye "made declarations of antisemitic revolutionary Socialism, declaring that 'all the principles of 1789 are threatened by the Jewish conspiracy.'"[24] This view was a continuation of the sort of anti-Jewish views expressed during the Revolution itself by the antisemitic Jacobin Jean-François Rewbell, who prominently opposed the extension of citizenship rights to the Jews.[25] It harkened back to eighteenth-century perceptions of the Jews, characteristic of the French Enlightenment and subsequently revived in the writings of some nineteenth-century socialists, as archaic, ignorant, superstitious, traditionalistic, particularistic, clannish, and backward—in short, the very antithesis of the modern society that the French Revolution ushered in.

Identification of the Jews with the old regime took different forms, depending on which aspect of the Revolution was stressed. Most commonly the Jews were denounced as a new royalty or nobility. This view was summed up in the title of Alphonse Toussenel's popular book, *The Jews, Kings of the Epoch: A History of Financial Feudalism*, first published in 1845 and reissued in 1847, 1886, and 1888. Toussenel was a self-described disciple of Charles Fourier, whose book likely influenced Pierre-Joseph

Proudhon. "The French people," Toussenel argued, "supposedly freed by the revolution of '89 from the yoke of the feudal nobility, has only changed masters"; they were now "enfeoffed to the domination of Israel."[26] Using similar language, Proudhon denounced the Jews as "the rulers of the day," "indifferent . . . to the progress and freedom of the people they oppress," and he condemned as "counter-revolutionary . . . all the lenders of money and instruments of labor . . . who recognize the Jews as their leaders."[27] According to this view, the Jews matched and even exceeded the worst traits of the old feudal nobility; they were rapacious, greedy, parasitic, exploitative, and unwilling to engage in productive labor. This perception was common in French socialist circles, articulated by, among others, Fourier, Proudhon, and Chirac.[28] As Proudhon put it, "The Jew is by temperament an anti-producer, neither a farmer nor a manufacturer nor even truly a merchant"—in short, no part of the Third Estate.[29] Toussenel's identification of the Jews with the dominant forces of the old regime was echoed in Proudhon's declaration that "the reign of the Jews" was "the triumph of industrial feudalism" and the title of Chirac's own book, *The Kings of the Republic: History of the Jews*.[30] Although attacks on the Jews as agents of usury, speculation, exploitation, and profiteering were not confined to the Left, denunciation of the Jews as a new royalty or nobility issued frequently from radical quarters as a means of defining the problems of French workers, assigning blame, suggesting remedies, and motivating collective action.

In addition the discourse of radical antisemitism frequently associated the Jews with the Catholic Church. "While certain early socialists confused Jews and Jewish bankers with capitalism, others became anti-Semites owing to their anti-religious convictions."[31] This kind of hostility emerged from the French Enlightenment and was especially conspicuous in the work of Voltaire;[32] it reappeared in the anticlericalism of the Revolution, particularly during the Terror and its accompanying persecution of religion; and it resurfaced in the nineteenth century in the language of antisemitic socialists like Proudhon and Tridon. These figures opposed the Jews in part because they understood Christianity to be derived from Judaism.[33] As Proudhon put it, the Jews were the "first authors of that evil superstition called Catholicism in which the furious, intolerant Jewish element always prevailed over the other Greek, Latin, barbarian, etc. elements and served to torture humankind for so long."[34] Whether as symbols of feudal nobility or religious obscurantism, the Jews were consistently identified in the discourse of radical antisemitism not with the destructive consequences of revolutionary modernization but with the most oppressive and backward aspects of the old regime.

Durkheim's Sociology in Relation to Reactionary Antisemitism

If the discourse of reactionary antisemitism set the Jews in opposition to the traditional social order in Europe and identified them with the forces of revolutionary modernization that were rapidly dissolving that order, then Durkheim repeatedly inverted that representation. Again and again he portrayed the Jews as traditionalistic and backward. Far from constituting the advance guard of a dangerous and disruptive modernity, he suggested, they were in fact laggards in the process of social development.

Durkheim postulated that societies develop over time from simple forms of organization with few or no component parts to highly complex forms of organization with many internal parts.[35] In *The Division of Labour in Society* he repeatedly suggested that the Jews, by virtue of their segmentary organization based on clans, constituted a relatively simple and primitive social type. "These [segmentary] societies," he pointed out, "are the home *par excellence* of mechanical solidarity"—in other words, the form of solidarity that is the hallmark of the simple societies of the past, based on sameness, uniformity, and conformity, indicated by the prevalence of repressive law, which punishes dissimilarity from the group and precludes the emergence of the "individual personality" and "individual reflection." These characteristics—the distinguishing features of segmentary organization and mechanical solidarity—were in Durkheim's view exemplified by the Jews. "Among the Jews," he noted, "the most abominable crimes are those committed against religion." Since "religion is something essentially social," he inferred that among the Jews it is primarily attacks upon society or the group (rather than the individual) that are punished. Jewish law, as codified in the Pentateuch, thus exemplified the "wholly repressive" form of law characteristic of "the very lowest societies."[36]

In *The Division of Labour* the Jews were said to exemplify another feature of segmentary organization as well: a caste system or "fixed" division of labor that is "passed on by heredity." After pointing to the Indian caste system as "the most perfect model of this organization of labor," Durkheim noted that it was also found among the Jews in the form of the division among *kohanim* (priests), Levites, and Israelites. He suggested that both the low level of functional specialization among the Jews and the role of heredity in the distribution of the priesthood indicated the relatively simple and primitive nature of Jewish society.[37]

While these references to Jews in *The Division of Labour* were generally historical in nature, *Suicide* referred clearly to the Jews of modern Europe and yet characterized them in similar terms. Here too the Jews were described as a community held together by a premodern mechanical solidarity in which "everyone thought and lived alike" and "individual divergences were made almost impossible," which in turn accounted for their low suicide rate. "Judaism," he explained, "like all early religions, consists basically of a body of practices minutely governing all the details of life and leaving little room to individual judgment."[38]

Even Durkheim's observations about the high levels of modern education among European Jews did not lead him to depart significantly from this interpretation of Jewish social life. In *Suicide* he argued that education was associated with low social integration, high individuation, and free inquiry, all characteristics that are antithetical to traditional forms of solidarity based on the authority of custom and tradition. Once the authority of custom and tradition is destroyed, he argued, "they cannot be artificially reestablished; only reflection can guide us in life, after this."[39] Thus in modern societies mechanical solidarity must be replaced by a new and different sort of solidarity in which greater scope is allowed for individuality and "authority is rationally grounded."[40] In this new form of solidarity, which Durkheim termed organic, "reflection" and "criticism" would "exist next to faith, pierce that very faith without destroying it, and occupy an always larger place in it."[41] The Jews would seem to exemplify this possibility because they combined high levels of education (enrollment in *Gymnasien* and universities) with high levels of social integration. But Durkheim drew a different conclusion, namely that Jewish solidarity remains "primitive" and "ancient" in nature and that Jewish learning and "reflective thought" are merely superimposed upon their traditional form of solidarity without affecting or altering it in any way.[42]

In summary *The Division of Labour* and *Suicide* refer to Jews in different historical periods and places, but both works similarly invert the depiction of Jews in the discourse of reactionary antisemitism as symbols and agents of modernization. In Durkheim's writings mechanical solidarity—the very form of solidarity that reactionary antisemites wished to restore in France—is ironically epitomized by the very group whom the antisemites held responsible for its destruction. Likewise the Jews represent not money, mobility, and the dissolution of the old regime's rigid status system, as reactionary antisemitism would have it, but rather the permanent, fixed, and hereditary inequalities that characterized the old regime. In both respects Durkheim's Jews symbolize the past rather than the dominant trends of modern society.

Durkheim's challenge to reactionary antisemitism did not rest here, however. Even if the French Revolution had been a "Jewish Revolution"—a notion belied by Durkheim's characterization of the Jews—reactionary antisemitism fundamentally misconstrued its nature and consequences. The Revolution, he insisted, was not primarily or at least not only a source of social dissolution. Properly understood, it was a moment of "collective effervescence" through which social solidarity might be reestablished.[43] He agreed with Catholic reactionaries that "religion alone" could produce the "moral unity" that society needed.[44] However, he suggested, the postrevolutionary secular world was not so irreligious as they might think. The "principles of '89" were themselves "articles of faith," "a religion which has had its martyrs and apostles," and even though their "work miscarried," "everything leads us to believe that the work will sooner or later be taken up again."[45] Elsewhere Durkheim indicated what that work entailed: "it is a matter of completing, extending, and organizing individualism," the system of beliefs "which the Declaration of the Rights of Man attempted . . . to formulate" and which had "become the basis of our moral catechism." Catholic opposition to this "religion of the individual" was misguided, in Durkheim's view, because individualism provided "the only system of beliefs which [could] ensure the moral unity of the country" in the modern age. "To take it away from us when we have nothing else to put in its place," he declared, was to promote precisely what Catholic reactionaries most feared: "moral anarchy."[46]

Durkheim also took aim at reactionary antisemitism in its racial form. He challenged the scientific pretensions of racial antisemitism indirectly in *Suicide* by demonstrating that race did not adequately explain variation in the suicide rate. Moreover he denied that antisemites would find in race a model for the sort of stable and unambiguous social order they desired. Far from eliminating uncertainty about social categorizations and ranking, race exemplified confusion and uncertainty. "Due to crossings in every direction, each of the existing varieties of our species comes from very different origins," and consequently "no one could say with accuracy where they [races] begin and end."[47] The Jews were a case in point; through assimilation they "lose their ethnic character with extreme rapidity. Only two generations and it's gone."[48] Last, Durkheim understood that racial antisemitism sought to revive the sort of hereditary caste system he criticized in *The Division of Labour*, which he argued was not only incompatible with the heritage of the French Revolution (a point that reactionary antisemites would have readily acknowledged) but that was also destined to disappear as the division of labor advanced and society became more complex.[49]

Durkheim's Sociology in Relation to Radical Antisemitism

Like the radical antisemites, Durkheim saw himself as a champion and faithful heir of the Revolution, and his characterization of the Jews as traditionalistic and backward dovetailed with their view of the Jews as symbols of the old regime. However, despite these affinities, and despite his sympathetic stance toward socialism, Durkheim never succumbed to the socialism of fools. I suggest this contrast had less to do with his Jewish background than with fundamentally different conceptions of the French Revolution and what it would mean to complete it.

Radical antisemites wanted to dispossess society's privileged class, which they identified with the Jews, and to overturn what they imagined as a neofeudal social order based on Jewish domination and exploitation. In contrast, Durkheim sought to build socialism without class—or ethnic—warfare. "The problem," he wrote, "is not simply a question of diminishing the share of some so as to increase that of others, but rather of remaking the moral constitution of society." This formulation, he added, would divest socialism of its "aggressive and malevolent character."[50] Although these remarks were directed against class warfare rather than antisemitism, they make clear Durkheim's objections to both. While radical antisemites could only imagine a socialist society built on the dispossession and exclusion of the Jews, Durkheim envisioned a more universalistic socialism that would resolve social conflicts in a positive-sum manner. This approach, he stressed, would present "the social question...

in an entirely different manner. . . . It no longer opposes rich to poor, employers to workers"—or, he might have added, Semites to Aryans—"as if the only possible solution consisted of diminishing the portion of one in order to augment that of the other."[51] "However future society is organized," he insisted, "there will be a place for all."[52]

While Durkheim was averse to all attempts to resolve the social question through the dispossession of one group by another, he regarded the demand for the dispossession of the Jews as especially misguided because it was a form of scapegoating. He argued that such scapegoating strengthened solidarity by uniting society around hatred of the Jew, but he regarded this kind of solidarity as pathological in the context of late nineteenth-century France because it was narrow and exclusionary—a revival of the mechanical form of solidarity that in his view was unsuitable for complex, modern societies.[53] Thus just as reactionary antisemites ironically promoted social dissolution by their rejection of individualism, the radical antisemites, despite their pretensions to be the most faithful heirs of the Revolution, were in fact profoundly reactionary in their commitment to a premodern form of solidarity deeply at odds with the individual autonomy that the Revolution promoted.

Durkheim's preference for "remaking the moral constitution of society" over class (or ethnic) warfare flowed directly from his interpretation of the French Revolution. Like the radical antisemites, he saw fundamental continuities between the Revolution and the socialist movement of the nineteenth century, and he considered the Revolution to be unfinished business.[54] But he differed sharply with them over what it would mean to complete the work of the Revolution. While radical antisemites saw that work in negative terms (finishing or reiterating the destruction of the old regime), Durkheim emphasized the need to consolidate, extend, and institutionalize the "principles of '89," and he praised Claude Henri de Saint-Simon in particular for having recognized that need.[55] Durkheim indicated in a variety of places how this was to be done: revive occupational groups; "complete, organize and extend individualism"; promote greater equality of opportunity; "introduce more justice into contractual relations"; provide "all possible means of developing [individual] faculties without hindrance"; and "make a reality of the famous precept: 'to each according to his work.'"[56] By realizing a healthy, organic form of social solidarity appropriate to a complex society with a highly developed

division of labor, these measures would obviate the need for the pathological substitutes generated by scapegoating.

A discussion of Durkheim's response to radical antisemitism would
not be complete without addressing the anticlerical aspects of the latter.
Viewing Judaism with deep distrust as a corrupting influence that rendered its adherents unfit for citizenship, radical antisemites envisioned
a world emancipated from Judaism (and Catholicism). In this respect
too radical antisemitism was destructive rather than constructive, intent
primarily on negating the past. Durkheim's interpretation of the French
Revolution as a religious regeneration posed a double challenge to radical
antisemitism: it contested the conventional view (shared by reactionaries
and radicals alike) that the Revolution was fundamentally an assault on
religion, and (in contrast to both reactionary and radical antisemitism)
it held out the promise of an expanded solidarity in which the Jews could
be included. Here too Durkheim's response to radical antisemitism was
indebted to the ideas of Saint-Simon.[57] Saint-Simonianism had attracted considerable interest and support from French Jews in the first half of
the nineteenth century, in part because it held out the promise of Jewish
integration within the movement's new universalist religion.[58] Similarly
Durkheim's sociology held out the promise of Jewish integration within the "religion of the individual" propagated by the Revolution, a new,
modern, and universalistic civil religion that would transcend the religious divisions of the past.[59]

Summary

"To understand major contributions to the history of social thought,"
Nisbet suggested in his study of Durkheim,

> one must understand the setting in which these were made [includ-
> ing] . . . the ideas and social currents against which Durkheim's
> thought was directed. . . . Ideas are dialectical responses, caught up
> in the logic and circumstance of antithesis. . . . This is not to mini-
> mize the importance of data, of fact and experience, which the ideas
> of social scientists seek to synthesize and clarify. . . . Nevertheless,
> the genesis of thought is not fact, but idea, that most often provides
> the challenge, the thesis against which any major idea may be seen
> as antithesis.[60]

In line with this perspective, I have attempted to reveal the interplay of Durkheim's sociology with nineteenth-century French antisemitism. This endeavor has been fruitful in a variety of ways.

First, the findings presented here advance previous scholarship on Durkheim's relationship to the Jews and Judaism. Although Birnbaum and Strenski previously examined antisemitism as part of Durkheim's milieu, neither treated it fully. Birnbaum concentrated more narrowly on the Dreyfus affair and right-wing antisemitism, and he provided no sustained analysis of the discourse, themes, and motifs of French anti-semitism. Likewise Strenski's focus on genteel scholarly antisemitism did not permit a thoroughgoing investigation of antisemitic intellectuals outside the academy to whom Durkheim also reacted. This study builds upon their pioneering work but also goes beyond it in these respects.[61]

In addition to deepening our understanding of Durkheim, this chapter also has implications for our understanding of the emergence of socio-logical theory more generally. In a prominent critique, Raewyn Connell has challenged what she calls the "conventional foundation story" of sociology, exemplified by Nisbet's thesis of the two revolutions, accord-ing to which sociology was created in response to the dramatic "internal transformation of European society." Connell suggests that sociology emerged instead from colonial encounters with the non-European world. "The enormous spectrum of human history that the sociologists took as their domain," she argues, "was organized by a central idea: difference between the civilization of the metropole and an Other whose main fea-ture was its primitiveness."[62] However, as this chapter has demonstrat-ed, European sociology did not need to look beyond the civilization of the metropole to find such an Other. Furthermore the study of this Other was, in an indirect fashion, study of the metropole itself.

This last point becomes more apparent when we turn to the implica-tions of this chapter for nineteenth-century social thought more broadly. What French antisemitism and Durkheim's sociology had in common was that they understood modernity, in part, by reference to the Jews. "Religion," wrote Marx in his discussion of the Jewish question, "is sim-ply the recognition of man in a roundabout fashion; that is, through an intermediary."[63] Durkheim, substituting *society* for *man*, made a simi-lar point. This chapter has attempted to show that representations of the Jews in nineteenth-century social thought played an analogous role.

In the context of a social order undergoing revolutionary changes, the Jew served as the intermediary through which European thinkers could discern—and contest—the image of their own past and future. In the words of Yirmiyahu Yovel, "Jews were not only the targets and victims of modern European upheavals; they also provided Europeans with a mirror, a crooked, passion-laden mirror, in which to see a reflection of their own identity problems. The 'Jewish problem' was . . . not only a problem for Europe but a reflection of Europe's own problem with itself, of how, in an age of rapid transformation, Europeans were understanding their own identity, future, and meaning of life."[64]

Finally, this chapter has implications for the analysis of contemporary social relations in light of the resurgence of antisemitism at the turn of the millennium.[65] As Laqueur notes, "Antisemitism is a historical topic, but because it has not yet ended, it is not solely of historical interest." As in Durkheim's time, antisemitism is found on both the Right and the Left, and hostility to Jews continues to be tied to very different orientations to modernity. On the one hand, antisemitism has reemerged in conjunction with movements that oppose what are decried—and not without basis— as negative, disruptive, and destructive forms of social change, most notably the antiglobalization movement.[66] On the other hand, Jewish solidarity in the form of Jewish nationalism is decried as backward and anachronistic.[67] In this context Durkheim's work may provide inspiration and insight for formulating an alternative view that rejects identification of the Jews with the most threatening and destructive aspects of modernity while promoting a genuine universalism in which Jews and Jewish concerns may be fully integrated.

Notes

This chapter is an abridged version of an article previously published as "The Jews, the Revolution, and the Old Regime in French Anti-Semitism and Durkheim's Sociology," Sociological Theory 29.4 (2011): 248-71. The author is grateful to the American Sociological Association for permission to reprint it.

1. Nisbet, "The Two Revolutions," 21.
2. Wilson, *Ideology and Experience*, 613, 635.
3. Pickering and Martins, *Debating Durkheim*, 174-79. Goldberg, "Introduction to Émile Durkheim's 'Antisemitism and Social Crisis.'"

4. On sociology and the French Revolution, see Nisbet, "French Revolution and the Rise of Sociology in France." On Durkheim and the two revolutions, see Nisbet, *Émile Durkheim*, 19–23.

5. See Alexander, introduction; Birnbaum, "French Jewish Sociologists between Reason and Faith"; Clark, "Durkheim and the Institutionalization of Sociology in the French University System"; Clark, *Prophets and Patrons*; Collins, "Durkheimian Movement in France and in World Sociology"; Fournier, "Durkheim's Life and Context"; Fournier, *Émile Durkheim*; Gross, "Durkheim's Pragmatism Lectures"; Jones, "On Understanding a Sociological Classic"; Jones, "Durkheim, Frazer, and Smith"; Jones, "The Positive Science of Ethics in France"; Jones, "Ambivalent Cartesians"; Jones, "The Other Durkheim"; Jones, *Development of Durkheim's Social Realism* ; Jones and Kibbee, "Durkheim, Language, and History"; Lukes, *Émile Durkheim*; Pickering, "The Enigma of Durkheim's Jewishness"; Strenski, *Durkheim and the Jews of France*; Vogt, "Political Connections, Professional Advancement."

6. Wilson, *Ideology and Experience*; Benbassa, *Jews of France*, 137–38.

7. Vital, *A People Apart*, 188.

8. Wilson, *Ideology and Experience*, 349–50; Benbassa, *Jews of France*, 138.

9. Maurras, *Les vergers sur la mer*, xi. All translations from French are by the author.

10. Picard, *Synthèse de l'antisémitisme*, 85.

11. Drumont, *La France juive*, 1: 323; Drumont, *La France juive*, 2: 247, 329.

12. Chabauty, *Les juifs, nos maîtres!*, 247–48; Lémann, *La prépondérance juive*, 62; Wilson, *Ideology and Experience*, 515; Sorlin, *"La Croix" et les Juifs*, 92, 164–67.

13. Lazare, *Antisemitism*, 182.

14. Wilson, *Ideology and Experience*, 613, 615.

15. Drumont, *La fin d'un monde*, 37.

16. Drumont, *France juive*, 1: xii.

17. Brunetière, "Revue Littéraire, *La France juive*," 693.

18. Maurras, *Quand les Français ne s'aimaient pas*, 192–93; Roudiez, *Maurras jusqu'à l'Action Française*, 304.

19. Wilson, *Ideology and Experience*, 560–61.

20. Wilson, *Ideology and Experience*, 491–93.

21. Vital, *People Apart*, 198; see also 199–205.

22. Benbassa, *Jews of France*, 139. See also Silberner, "French Socialism and the Jewish Question."

23. Though reacting to modern capitalism, radical antisemites resorted to the language of 1789, much like the 1848 revolutionaries described by Marx: "Just when they seem engaged in revolutionising themselves and things, in creating something entirely new, precisely in such epochs of revolutionary crisis they anxiously conjure up the spirits of the past to their service and borrow from them names, battle slogans and costumes in order to present the new scene of world history in this time-honoured disguise and this borrowed language" (Tucker, *The Marx-Engels Reader*, 595).

24. Wilson, *Ideology and Experience*, 329; see 341.

25. Hertzberg, *The French Enlightenment and the Jews* , 314–68.

26. Vital, *People Apart*, 203–4; Toussenel, *Les Juifs, rois de l'époque*, 256, 122.

27. Proudhon, *De la justice dans la révolution et dans l'église*, 277; Proudhon, *Résumé de la question sociale*, 36.

28. Silberner, "Charles Fourier on the Jewish Question"; Silberner, "Proudhon's Judeophobia"; Wilson, *Ideology and Experience*, 265.

29. Proudhon, *Césarisme et christianisme*, 139. See also Wilson, *Ideology and Experience*, 267–79.

30. Proudhon, "Si les traités de 1815 ont cessé d'exister?," 423; Chirac, *Les rois de la république*.

31. Benbassa, *Jews of France*, 139.

32. Hertzberg, *French Enlightenment and the Jews*, 268–313.

33. Wilson, *Ideology and Experience*, 562–63.

34. Proudhon, *Carnets*, 23.

35. Durkheim, *Rules of Sociological Method*, 108–18.

36. On the segmentary organization of the Jews, see Durkheim, *Division of Labor in Society*, 128, 134–35, 204–5; on mechanical solidarity, 129, 24–29, 142, 106; on crime, religion, and Jewish law, 49–50, 92–93.

37. Durkheim, *Division of Labor*, 247.

38. Durkheim, *Suicide*, 159–60.

39. Durkheim, *Suicide*, 169.

40. Durkheim, "Individualism and the Intellectuals," 49.

41. Durkheim, *Socialism and Saint-Simon*, 215.

42. Durkheim, *Suicide*, 167–68.

43. Durkheim, *The Elementary Forms of Religious Life*, 213.

44. Durkheim, "Individualism and the Intellectuals," 50.

45. Durkheim, "The Principles of 1789 and Sociology," 34–35; Durkheim, *Elementary Forms of Religious Life*, 430.

46. Durkheim, "Individualism and the Intellectuals," 56, 45, 54, 50, 55.

47. Durkheim, *Suicide*, 83.

48. Durkheim, "Antisemitism and Social Crisis," 322.

49. Durkheim, *Division of Labor*, 246–68.

50. Lukes, *Émile Durkheim*, 320–30; see 323–24 for Durkheim's remarks.

51. Durkheim, *Socialism and Saint-Simon*, 204.

52. Durkheim, quoted in Lukes, *Émile Durkheim*, 324.

53. Birnbaum, "French Jewish Sociologists," 5; Goldberg, "Introduction to Émile Durkheim's 'Antisemitism and Social Crisis.'"

54. Durkheim, *Socialism and Saint-Simon*, 68–69; Lukes, *Émile Durkheim*, 545.

55. Durkheim, *Socialism and Saint-Simon*, 120, 122.

56. Lukes, *Émile Durkheim*, 326–27; Durkheim, "Individualism and the Intellectuals," 56. See also Durkheim, *Professional Ethics and Civic Morals*; Durkheim, "Individualism and the Intellectuals"; Durkheim, *Division of Labor*.

57. Durkheim, *Socialism and Saint-Simon*.

58. Benbassa, *Jews of France*, 120.

59. Moore, "David Émile Durkheim and the Jewish Response to Modernity." How precisely would the Jews be integrated into the "religion of the individual" propagated by the Revolution? Was it, like socialism for some European Jewish intellectuals, "a program of *assimilation by other means*," an abstract and universal movement in which "the handicap of Jewishness could be shed" and Jews could turn into "men as such" (Bauman, "Exit Visas and Entry Tickets," 75)? Or did Durkheim understand the "principles of '89" and the cult of the individual in dialectical terms as a form of collective consciousness that transcended but also preserved particularistic identities and attachments? His remark that the Jews were losing their "ethnic character" suggests the former interpretation. However, the latter interpretation is more consistent with his argument that mechanical solidarity based on sameness was giving way to an organic form of solidarity that allowed for pluralism and difference.

60. Nisbet, *Émile Durkheim*, 9.

61. For an overview of previous scholarship on Durkheim, the Jews, and Judaism, see Fournier, "Durkheim's Life and Context," 46–47; Birnbaum, "French Jewish Sociologists"; Strenski, *Durkheim and the Jews*, 9, 84–85, 97, 100, 104, 113–14, 124–25, 127–29, 142.

62. Connell, "Why Is Classical Theory Classical?," 1515, 1513, 1516–17.

63. Tucker, *Marx-Engels Reader*, 32.

64. Durkheim, *Elementary Forms of Religious Life*, 227; Yovel, *Dark Riddle*, xi.

65. Taguieff, *Rising from the Muck*; Cohen, "Auto-Emancipation and Antisemitism"; Harrison, *The Resurgence of Antisemitism*; Hirsh, "Anti-Zionism and Antisemitism"; Markovits, *Uncouth Nation*, 150–200.

66. Laqueur, *Changing Face of Antisemitism*, 207, 182–89. See also Postone, "History and Helplessness."

67. See, e.g., Judt, "Israel."

References

Alexander, Jeffrey C. Introduction to *Durkheimian Sociology*, edited by Jeffrey C. Alexander, 1–21. New York: Cambridge University Press, 1988.

Bauman, Zygmunt. "Exit Visas and Entry Tickets." *Telos* 77 (Fall 1988): 45–77.

Benbassa, Esther. *The Jews of France*. Translated by M. B. DeBevoise. Princeton NJ: Princeton University Press, 1999.

Birnbaum, Pierre. "French Jewish Sociologists between Reason and Faith." *Jewish Social Studies* 2.1 (1995): 1–35.

Brunetière, Ferdinand. "Revue Littéraire, *La France juive*." *Revue des deux mondes* 75 (June 1, 1886): 693–704.

Chabauty, Emmanuel. *Les juifs, nos maîtres!* Paris: Victor Palmé, 1882.

Chirac, Auguste. *Les rois de la république*. 1883–86. 2 vols. Paris: Éditions du Trident, 1987.

Clark, Terry Nichols. "Émile Durkheim and the Institutionalization of Sociology in the French University System." *European Journal of Sociology* 9 (1968): 37–71.

———. *Prophets and Patrons*. Cambridge MA: Harvard University Press, 1973.

Cohen, Mitchell. "Auto-Emancipation and Antisemitism (Homage to Bernard-Lazare)." *Jewish Social Studies* 10 (Fall 2003): 69–77.

Collins, Randall. "The Durkheimian Movement in France and in World Sociology." In *The Cambridge Companion to Durkheim*, edited by Jeffrey C. Alexander and Philip Smith, 101–35. New York: Cambridge University Press, 2005.

Connell, Raeywn. "Why Is Classical Theory Classical?" *American Journal of Sociology* 102.6 (1997): 1511–57.

Drumont, Édouard. *La fin d'un monde*. Paris: Albert Savine, 1889.

———. *La France juive*. Vol. 1. 1886. Paris: Éditions du Trident, 1986.

———. *La France juive*. Vol. 2. 1886. Paris: Éditions du Trident, 1986.

Durkheim, Émile. "Antisemitism and Social Crisis." 1899. Translated by Chad Alan Goldberg. *Sociological Theory* 26.4 (2008): 321–23.

———. *The Division of Labor in Society*. 1893. Translated by W. D. Halls. New York: Free Press, 1984.

———. *The Elementary Forms of Religious Life*. 1912. Translated by Karen E. Fields. New York: Free Press, 1995.

———. "Individualism and the Intellectuals." 1898. In *Émile Durkheim on Morality and Society*, edited by Robert N. Bellah, 43–57. Chicago: University of Chicago Press, 1973.

———. "The Principles of 1789 and Sociology." 1890. In *Émile Durkheim on Morality and Society*, edited by Robert N. Bellah, 34–42. Chicago: University of Chicago Press, 1973.

———. *Professional Ethics and Civic Morals*. Translated by Cornelia Brookfield. New York: Routledge, 1957.

———. *The Rules of Sociological Method*. 1895. Edited by Steven Lukes. Translated by W. D. Halls. New York: Free Press, 1982.

———. *Socialism and Saint-Simon*. Edited by Alvin W. Gouldner. Translated by Charlotte Sattler. Yellow Springs OH: Antioch Press, 1958.

———. *Suicide*. 1897. Edited by George Simpson. Translated by John A. Spaulding and George Simpson. New York: Free Press, 1951.

Fournier, Marcel. "Durkheim's Life and Context." In *The Cambridge Companion to Durkheim*, edited by Jeffrey C. Alexander and Philip Smith, 41–69. New York: Cambridge University Press, 2005.

———. *Émile Durkheim*. Paris: Fayard, 2007.

Goldberg, Chad Alan. "Introduction to Émile Durkheim's 'Antisemitism and Social Crisis.'" *Sociological Theory* 26.4 (2008): 299–321.

———. "The Jews, the Revolution, and the Old Regime in French Anti-Semitism and Durkheim's Sociology." *Sociological Theory* 29.4 (2011): 248–71.

Gross, Neil. "Durkheim's Pragmatism Lectures." *Sociological Theory* 15.2 (1997): 126–49.

Harrison, Bernard. *The Resurgence of Antisemitism*. Lanham MD: Rowman & Littlefield, 2006.

Hertzberg, Arthur. *The French Enlightenment and the Jews*. New York: Columbia University Press, 1968.

Hirsh, David. "Anti-Zionism and Antisemitism." 2007. Yale Initiative for the Interdisciplinary Study of Antisemitism Working Paper Series, http://eprints. gold.ac.uk/2061/.

Jones, Robert Alun. "Ambivalent Cartesians." *American Journal of Sociology* 100 (July 1994): 1–39.

———. *The Development of Durkheim's Social Realism*. New York: Cambridge University Press, 1999.

———."Durkheim, Frazer, and Smith." *American Journal of Sociology* 92 (November 1986): 596–627.

———. "On Understanding a Sociological Classic." *American Journal of Sociology* 83 (September 1977): 279–319.

———. "The Other Durkheim." In *Reclaiming the Sociological Classics*, edited by Charles Camic, 142–72. Malden MA: Blackwell, 1997.

———. "The Positive Science of Ethics in France." *Sociological Forum* 9 (March 1994): 37–57.

Jones, Robert Alun, and Douglas A. Kibbee. "Durkheim, Language, and History." *Sociological Theory* 11 (July 1993): 152–70.

Judt, Tony. "Israel: The Alternative." *New York Review of Books* 50.16 (2003): 8–10.

Laqueur, Walter. *The Changing Face of Antisemitism*. New York: Oxford University Press, 2006.

Lazare, Bernard. *Antisemitism*. 1894. London: Britons, 1967.

Lémann, Joseph. *La prépondérance juive. Première partie: Ses origines (1789-1791)*. Paris: Victor Lecoffre, 1889.

Lukes, Steven. *Émile Durkheim: His Life and Work*. New York: Harper & Row, 1973.

Markovits, Andrei S. *Uncouth Nation*. Princeton NJ: Princeton University Press, 2007.

Maurras, Charles. *Quand les Français ne s'aimaient pas*. 1916. 2d ed. Paris: Nouvelle Librairie Nationale, 1926.

———. *Les vergers sur la mer*. Paris: E. Flammarion, 1937.

Moore, Deborah Dash. "David Émile Durkheim and the Jewish Response to Modernity." *Modern Judaism* 6.3 (1986): 287–300.

Nisbet, Robert A. *Émile Durkheim*. Englewood Cliffs NJ: Prentice-Hall, 1965.

———. "The French Revolution and the Rise of Sociology in France." *American Journal of Sociology* 49.2 (1943): 156–64.

———. "The Two Revolutions." In *The Sociological Tradition*, 21–44. New York: Basic Books, 1966.

Picard, Edmond. *Synthèse de l'antisémitisme*. Paris: Albert Savine, 1892.

Pickering, W. S. F. "The Enigma of Durkheim's Jewishness." In *Debating Durkheim*, edited by W. S. F. Pickering and H. Martins, 10–39. New York: Routledge, 1994.

Pickering, W. S. F., and H. Martins, eds. *Debating Durkheim*. New York: Routledge, 1994.

Postone, Moishe. "History and Helplessness." *Public Culture* 18.1 (2006): 93–110.

Proudhon, Pierre-Joseph. *Carnets*. Vol. 2. Paris: Marcel Rivière, 1961.

———. *Césarisme et christianisme*. Vol. 1. 2d ed. Paris: C. Marpon and E. Flammarion, 1883.

———. *De la justice dans la révolution et dans l'église*. Vol. 6. 1858. Brussels: A. Lacroix, Verboeckhoven, 1870.

———. *Résumé de la question sociale; banque d'échange*. Paris: Garnier Frères, 1849.

———. "Si les traités de 1815 ont cessé d'exister?" 1863. In *Oeuvres complètes*, 327–428. New ed. Paris: Marcel Rivière, 1952.

Roudiez, Léon. *Maurras jusqu'à l'Action Française*. Paris: Éditions André Bonne, 1957.

Silberner, Edmund. "Charles Fourier on the Jewish Question." *Jewish Social Studies* 8 (1946): 245–66.

———. "French Socialism and the Jewish Question, 1865–1914." *Historia Judaica* 16, pt. 1 (April 1954): 3–38.

———. "Proudhon's Judeophobia." *Historia Judaica* 10.1 (1948): 61–80.

Sorlin, Pierre. *"La Croix" et les Juifs (1880–1899)*. Paris: Éditions Bernard Grasset, 1967.

Strenski, Ivan. *Durkheim and the Jews of France*. Chicago: University of Chicago Press, 1997.

Taguieff, Pierre-André. *Rising from the Muck*. 2002. Translated by Patrick Camiller. Chicago: Ivan R. Dee, 2004.

Toussenel, Alphonse. *Les Juifs, rois de l'époque*. Vol. 1. Paris: Gabriel de Gonet, 1847.

———. *Les Juifs, rois de l'époque*. Vol. 2. Paris: Gabriel de Gonet, 1847.

Tucker, Robert C., ed. *The Marx-Engels Reader*. 2d ed. New York: Norton, 1978.

Vital, David. *A People Apart*. New York: Oxford University Press, 1999.

Vogt, W. Paul. "Political Connections, Professional Advancement, and Moral Education in Durkheimian Sociology." *Journal of the History of the Behavioral Sciences* 27 (January 1991): 56–75.

Wilson, Stephen. *Ideology and Experience*. London: Associated University Presses, 1982.

Yovel, Yirmiyahu. *Dark Riddle*. University Park: Pennsylvania State University Press, 1998.

2

Sociology's Case for a Well-Tempered Modernity

Individualism, Capitalism, and the Antisemitic Challenge

MARCEL STOETZLER

In this chapter I begin by arguing that in the very text that constitutes one of the finest moments of classical sociology's commitment and struggle for progressive, liberal society, Durkheim's 1898 intervention in the Dreyfus affair, "Individualism and the Intellectuals," ambivalences are operative that undermine this commitment and point instead to contradictions at the heart of modernity itself. Then I turn to another canonical text and argue that Max Weber wrote *The Protestant Ethic and the Spirit of Capitalism* as a pro-capitalist challenge to German nationalist denunciations of the capitalist, or the American spirit, as mere utilitarianism, while maintaining intact the rejection of utilitarianism that Weber himself inherited from such nationalism. I suggest that Weber's specific argument on capitalism and (national) culture and its strategic aim of delegitimizing reactionary (typically also antisemitic) nationalism also underpins his conception of "the Jews" in *The Protestant Ethic*. Durkheim's and Weber's rejections of egotistic, economistic utilitarianism contain elements of the reactionary and antisemitic discourses that these two founding fathers of the discipline of sociology aimed to oppose. In the concluding section I argue that these ambivalences can be understood only by reference to the larger sociopolitical framework that classical sociology inherited from nineteenth-century liberalism.

Durkheim: Defending Nonegotistical Individualism against Spencer and the Economists

Perhaps Durkheim's most famous essay is "Individualism and the Intellectuals," his 1898 intervention into the Dreyfus affair.[1] This short but iconic text marked the end of the decade in which he had published three of his major works, *Division of Labour in Society* (1893), *Rules of Sociological Method* (1895), and *Suicide* (1897), and it stood at the beginning of the period that would result in his fourth major work, *Elementary Forms of Religious Life* (1912). That year also marked the turning point in the Dreyfus affair (1894–1906): in January 1898 Emile Zola had published his crucial text "J'accuse," emerging therewith as a key defender of the captain's case, and in March the leading anti-Dreyfusard, Ferdinand Brunetière, a literary historian and member of the Académie Française, had published his widely read reply, "Après le Procès." It is as a response to Brunetière that Durkheim wrote "Individualism and the Intellectuals."

Brunetière had formulated his reply to Zola and other high-profile defenders of Captain Dreyfus as a general attack on intellectuals and the beliefs they, in his point of view, typically held. Chief among these intellectual beliefs was Herbert Spencer's individualism. Spencer, wrote Brunetière, "argued that the military profession was an anachronistic survival of barbarism in the age of industry and commerce," an element of classic bourgeois enlightenment critique (such as in Adam Ferguson) that survived in Spencer's writings. Individualism was for Brunetière "the great sickness of the present time." The "self-infatuation" of intellectuals who arrogantly "rise above" laws and the statements of army generals in order to judge them by their scientific methods and logic, which is indeed what those who defended Dreyfus against his detractors in state and army (quite rightly) did, are "truly anti-social."[2]

Brunetière's concern was that the cohesion of a society under attack from corrosion by individualism needed to be defended, and this in turn required the defense of the authority of state and army. This conservative (i.e., compared to his full-blown racialist colleagues, relatively moderate) anti-Dreyfusard represents thus a significant aspect of the zeitgeist of the period against which Durkheim posited the new discourse of sociology. It is of course one of the fundamental questions of the discipline of sociology whether modern society produces its cohesion spontaneously through the division of labor, the invisible hand of the market (Adam Smith), or "the law of differentiation and integration" (Spencer), or whether it needs robust moral, cultural, religious framing by intentionally created institutions and consensus. Comte for example, "had no confidence whatever in the possibility that the cross-national and even intranational social ties necessary to cement the highly differentiated and specialized activity of industrial society would spontaneously emerge." Even when "industrial society" will have been "properly reorganized," the "social humanity" or "voluntary cooperation" will have to be "reproduced at every moment . . . because it rests on an (unnatural) preponderance of 'sociability over personality' and on a subjective consensus of mind, heart and body which likewise requires a reproductive—in Comte's terminology, 'rebinding', i.e. religious—practice."[3] Only in *Division of Labor* Durkheim had argued that the developed, modern division of labor gave rise to strong ("organic") solidarity that made remaining elements of "mechanical solidarity," based on likeness, less relevant and necessary—an argument that can be read as a critique of ethnic nationalism. When Durkheim increasingly (and surely under the impression of various social conflicts that erupted in the 1890s, not least the Dreyfus affair) abandoned this rather optimistic position, he seems to have repeated a shift that others had executed before him (Saint-Simon and Comte included) and that many more would repeat after him.[4] The constant repetition of this shift is, to no small extent, the history of sociology.

The wider historical background for this ambivalence is that the version of liberalism that trusted social harmony will emerge spontaneously and naturally if only no one interferes with the market learned throughout the nineteenth century to doubt its own wisdom, most prominently perhaps in the 1848 revolutions.[5] The market economy itself produces fragmentation rather than harmony (not least in the form of a dissonant working class), which needs to be attended to by (national) culture and the state.[6] The paradox that the totality of economy, society, state, and culture as under the dominance of capital produces unity only by way of producing fragmentation is one of the fundamental contradictions of modernity that the social sciences grapple with. All practitioners of the discipline of sociology in its classical period seem to share, though, the notion that the moral, cultural, religious code, if needed at all, must reflect and accommodate modern society as it presents itself, namely as based on individualism, rational-choice market exchanges, and the division of labor. Therefore one cannot simply aim to reimpose old-time religion: modern times call for the creation of new religions, such as the "religion of humanity" (Comte) or the "cult of the individual" (Durkheim) or charismatic political leadership underpinned by ethically driven capitalism (Weber), as well as at the margins of the discipline, for example the celebration of "effervescence" by the hyper-Durkheimians Bataille and Caillois.[7] It is significant that Durkheim's "Individualism and the Intellectuals" pivoted on his suggestion that modern society cannot but reject challenges to the rights of the individual as sacrileges. Anti-individualism is sacrilegious because, according to Durkheim, individualism is the new religion, and the only religion modern society produces. Durkheim's notion that the cult of the individual is now the religion that holds society together is in this essay undergirded by a polemic against Spencer, utilitarianism, and "egotistical individualism": he calls utilitarian individualism "a ferment of moral dissolution" (a choice of words that is rather close to a conservative, typically antisemitic *critique* of modern society) and contrasts it to "eighteenth-century liberalism" that he claims has penetrated French institutions and "our whole moral organization." He claims that the "idealists" (including Rousseau, Kant, Fichte, and Hegel) fought against the utilitarian ethic because "it appeared to them incompatible with social necessities" (although in fact utilitarianism knew of social utility). The "utilitarian egoism of Spencer and the economists" equals "crass commercialism which reduces society to nothing more than a vast apparatus of production and exchange," while Kant based his ethics on "faith and submission."[8] The strange and surprising point is that Durkheim's celebrated liberal republican rejection of Brunetière's attack on the Dreyfusards overlaps in the core of its argument with that of the enemy. Against Durkheim *and* Brunetière, I would like to suggest, "Spencer and the economists" need in the present context to be defended, as Durkheim seems to have been driven to caricature and demonize Spencer—whose thought occupies the area between liberalism and positivism that is also, for example, Durkheim's—by the same impulse that drove the antisemites.[9] This antimodernist impulse inhabits, of course, in Durkheim's case the subtext, not the manifest center of the text.

Durkheim agrees with his opponents that only religion can produce "the moral unity of the country" but holds against them that "we know today that a religion does not necessarily imply symbols and rites, properly speaking, or temples and priests." "'Essentially, it is nothing other than a body of collective beliefs and practices endowed with a certain authority." If religion should be defined in such a generic way, most late nineteenth-century observers (as well as still many early twenty-first-century contemporaries) would probably consider nationalism to be the strongest candidate for being the religion of contemporary society; yet Durkheim argues that the "religion of humanity, of which the individualistic ethic is the rational expression, is the only one possible." "To the extent that societies become more voluminous and expand over vaster territories" (an argument earlier proposed by Spencer), situations become more diverse and circumstances more mobile, to the effect that "traditions and practices" need to "maintain themselves in a state of plasticity and inconstancy." At the center of Durkheim's argument for the inevitability of individualism is a non sequitur: because of "more developed division of labor," everybody's "contents of consciousness" become increasingly differential. This leads toward "a state, nearly achieved as of now, where the members of a single social group will have nothing in common among themselves except their humanity, except the constitutive attributes of the human person in general"—a rather unsociological argument that omits the nation and all other structures of societal mediation.[10] As Durkheim himself had argued earlier, the division of labor itself creates interdependence, society, and shared structures of consciousness, but unfortunately it does not produce *automatically*, in and of itself, cosmopolitanism and selfless humanitarianism. Durkheim continues with the equally dubious claim that communion of spirits can no longer be based on definite rites and prejudices because modern society has overcome rites and prejudices. Consequently, according to Durkheim, "nothing remains which men can love and honor in common if not man himself. That is how man has become god for man and why he can no longer create other gods without lying to himself." None of this is plausible. It is on these grounds, however, that Durkheim believes that individualism is a "necessary doctrine": "in order to halt its advance it would be necessary to prevent men from differentiating themselves more and more from each other" and "to lead them back to the old conformism of former times" (including mechanical solidarity), that is, to contain the general evolutionary tendencies of societies to become ever more extended, centralized and differentiated. "Such an enterprise," namely halting or containing the course of societal evolution, "whether desirable or not, infinitely exceeds all human capability," wrote Durkheim in a rather Spencerian, teleological, deterministic moment; history has shown meanwhile that there is no lack of "definite rites and prejudices" in modern societies. The liberal (and socialist) belief in the irreversibility and linearity of progress, though, as paraded by Durkheim here, has proven to be a major liability to the struggles to stop disaster.[11]

Weber: When Capitalism Was a Good Thing

Weber's *The Protestant Ethic and the Spirit of Capitalism* is fundamentally a book about how capitalism turned from a good thing into a bad one, providing some hesitant implications about how the process could at least partially be reversed. From the history and actuality of capitalism Weber constructs a conceptual dichotomy between what he defines as essential and specific about modern, Western, bourgeois capitalism, and what is not so: essential, authentic, modern capitalism is contrasted with not specifically modern, or non-Western, forms or characteristics of capitalism, including the "pariah capitalism" of "the Jews."[12] Among the characteristics of the former (the "ideal-type" capitalism) is most prominently the drive for accumulation for its own sake, that is, neither for utility nor for enjoyment. Famously Weber credited Puritan Christian sects in the context of the English Revolution with having invented the "spirit of capitalism" in its specific, genuine form, while his narrative suggests that once it was "invented" and out there, it gained its own momentum, turned into an objective culture, became independent of its Puritan roots, and lost its "spirit," and the concern with material goods turned from a "light cloak" into a "casing hard as steel."[13] Weber describes this process in which capitalism lost what—ideal-typically— should be its spirit, its being bounded, framed, and directed by a religious (Christian, Protestant, Calvinist) ethic, as a degeneration or regression toward "pure utilitarianism."[14] Utilitarianism (or rather a caricature of it) was of course also one of the principal targets of nineteenth-century antisemites, as well as of Durkheim's specific effort at defending individualism against its detractors.

Weber gives few hints of the general discourse from which and into which his search for genuine as opposed to utilitarian capitalism was feeding, but they are clear enough: on one of the first pages of the first chapter he invokes Thomas Carlyle, perhaps the most influential author of a "cultural" or "ethical critique" of capitalism. Weber (mis)quotes Carlyle's formulation in the introduction to his 1845 edition of the letters and speeches of Cromwell that Puritanism was "the last of all our heroisms." (Weber quotes the original English but leaves out the word *all*.)[15] He refers a few times to Matthew Arnold, and the famous formula describing the personality type produced by decadent (post-Puritan) capitalism seems to be an amalgam or paraphrase of bits from Goethe, Nietzsche, Stefan George, plus perhaps other turn-of-the century *Kulturkritiker* (critics of civilization): "specialists without spirit, sensualists without heart."[16] Most prominently, however, Weber uses Ferdinand Kürnberger's 1855 novel, *Der Amerikamüde*, "the one who got tired of America," as a sounding board for his own project.

In the second chapter of *Protestant Ethic* Weber develops his "ideal-typical" concept of the "spirit of capitalism" out of a reading of two texts by Benjamin Franklin (of 1736 and 1748), which Weber quotes from Kürnberger's novel.[17] (Weber notes that he corrected Kürnberger's translation according to the English original.) In the novel by the Austrian writer (one of the cohort of "disappointed" 1848 democrats that includes many key figures in nineteenth-century National Liberalism as well as radical antisemites like Richard Wagner) Franklin's texts represent the spirit of America and are the contrasting foil against which the "German," humanistic values of the novel's protagonist, Dr. Moorfeld, are developed. Newly arrived in America, full of idealism and high expectations, the German emigrant Moorfeld is treated to a reading of Franklin's texts right away in the first chapter of the novel, the starting point of the process that leaves him increasingly disillusioned with and indeed "tired of America." (Moorfeld is appalled by New York's mammonism and soon goes to Pennsylvania. However, the backwoods disappoint him too; they turn out to be neither pleasant nor romantic, i.e., quite different from German forests. He finds that the farmers are dependent on bankers and speculators in New York, Baltimore, and Philadelphia, who must have been the ancestors of those who in contemporary populist discourse are referred to as the East Coast.) The gist of Franklin's texts that represent the spirit of America for Kürnberger and the capitalist spirit for Weber is, in Weber's words, the celebration of "the honest man of recognized credit" (in the German version, literally "the credit-worthy man") and the "duty of the individual to the increase of his capital which is assumed as an end in itself."[18] Weber correctly describes Kürnberger's novel as a "document of the (now long since blurred-over) differences between the German and the American outlook [*Empfinden*], one may even say of the type of spiritual life, which, in spite of everything, has remained common to all Germans, Catholic and Protestant alike, since the German mysticism of the Middle Ages, as against the Puritan capitalistic valuation of action [*Tatkraft*]."[19] This national framing of the question of a noncapitalist Empfinden shows that the main thrust of Weber's argument is indeed not a defense of Protestant against, as one might have expected, Catholic "spirits" but Anglo-Saxon Calvinist against German Lutheran *as well as* Catholic spirits. Weber surely saw the Calvinist spirit also active in Germany, though, and helping to strengthen it for the better of the German nation was the whole point of the book.[20]

Kürnberger's text was a contribution to the debate that after 1848 aimed to redefine German nationalism under conditions of capitalist modernization. Weber published (and finished writing) *The Protestant Ethic* just after returning from a visit to America in 1904, where he had observed that in certain Puritan sects "in the midst of modern capitalism the personal ethic of individual responsibility . . . had survived and was the basis for social action." This, the admirable version of the spirit of capitalism, was thus not "utilitaristic."[21] Whereas Kürnberger's America had been a (mid-nineteenth-century) vision of how Germany might but ought not develop, Weber's argument constitutes a critique of "the illusions of modern romanticists" within the field of competing conceptions of German nationality as it had developed in German post-1848 liberalism.[22] What Weber found in the United States he also found at home, although, regrettably, overshadowed by the more powerful cultures ("spirits") of Lutheranism and Catholicism. As Barbalet writes, in *The Protestant Ethic* Weber aimed to answer questions that he had raised in his 1895 inaugural lecture about the German middle class's (lack of) ability to satisfy national aspirations. *The Protestant Ethic* was in this sense "an instrument of political education." When Weber complained in the 1895 lecture about "the hackneyed yelping of the ever-growing chorus of amateur politicians . . . [who] believe it is possible to replace 'political' with 'ethical' ideas," and subsequently fail to do what Realpolitik demands must be done, then *The Protestant Ethic* seems to suggest a type of ethics that makes amateurish, hackneyed, moralistic, romantic yelping unnecessary.[23] (Seeing *The Protestant Ethic* as an "instrument of political education" also solves the puzzle of why it has survived a century of scholarly refutations that have shown that Weber got many of his facts and interpretations wrong.[24]

Like any other powerful ideological construction, the text is immune to factual refutation—although the latter is always a good starting point of critique—but can be challenged only at the level at which it actually operates, namely the level of asking what kind of modern bourgeoisie can, or should, govern what kind of modern society.)

The Protestant Ethic is in this sense a polemic *against* the German nationalist denunciation of the (American) capitalist spirit as mere utilitarianism that nevertheless maintains the rejection of utilitarianism intact.[25] Weber, who inherits the legacy of German nineteenth-century National Liberalism (of which his father, Max Weber Sr., had been a functionary), continues its characteristic struggles to negotiate a place within German nationalism for "the capitalist spirit," or to be precise, a politically and ethically attractive version of that spirit that would be compatible with what for German National Liberals were the specific values of the German nation. This ongoing renegotiation, the necessity to square capitalism with national culture, the search for culturally mediated and therefore benign, not so utilitarian, not so American, and, sometimes, not so Jewish capitalism, of which Kürnberger's novel was a classic expression, is the general foundation of the ambivalence characteristic of nationalist liberalism. It was this ambivalence that made some National Liberals receptive also to antisemitism (Heinrich von Treitschke is the best-known example) and prevented others from consistently opposing it.[26] It would appear that *The Protestant Ethic*, a foundational text of the discipline of sociology, is part of that same general discourse; although it comes out *against* romantic nationalism and *for* the capitalist spirit, ambivalence remains.[27]

The text's location in this wider context also lends significance to the scattered remarks it contains on Jews, their characteristics and their alleged role in history. The connection to antisemitic anticapitalism is hinted at when Weber notes, apparently with sympathy, that asceticism condemned "covetousness, Mammonism, etc." *Mammonism* is another keyword of late nineteenth-century *Kulturkritik*, criticism of modern civilization or culture, including its antisemitic variety. Weber also mentions Dutch Synods that excluded usurers.[28] Excluding usurers (however anyone may have defined that highly contentious term) does of course not make them antisemitic, but it signals an affinity between the discourse on asceticism and that on "Jewish capitalism."[29] Weber also points out that "Calvinism opposed organic social organization in the fiscal-monopolistic form which it assumed in Anglicanism under the Stuarts,"[30] a stance that he seems to sympathize with. He similarly opposed the state-socialist conceptions of leading members of the Verein für Sozialpolitik such as the antisemite Adolph Wagner.[31] It is in these ways that Weber's (typically National Liberal) ambivalences are woven into the text of *The Protestant Ethic*.

Jews and Jewish Capitalism

Weber's position evolved in a protracted dialogue with his colleague Werner Sombart. Both had emerged from the tradition of German "national economists," most of whom had a more or less state socialist inclination, meeting in a milieu where National Liberalism and (state-) "socialist" monarchism mixed, and it was in this specific context that they wrote their respective texts on what the spirit of capitalism was, who was responsible for it, and what was bad and what was good about it. Their positions primarily differ in where exactly they locate the dismal side of capitalism that endangers Western civilization, individualism, personality, and the amount of societal cohesion necessary to warrant civilization, individualism, and personality . For Sombart, trading and monetarization, summed up in the Jewish spirit, were to blame, while Weber was more original and pertinent in pointing at rationalization processes in the organization of labor, and, perhaps following Simmel's analysis in this point, the wider social sphere.[32] The cliché of the Jewish "commercial people" appears in this context as a reference to a group that was relevant merely at an early stage of the modernization process. In this sense, in Weber's account, the Jews are excused. While Sombart's critique of capitalism increasingly constructs a dichotomy between good, heroic, productive, martial capitalism and bad, money-minded, narrowly utilitarian, pacifist, parasitical Jewish capitalism, Weber arrives at a more dialectical view where the same historical force is responsible for the fantastic wealth and potential liberation (of the individual) produced by the modern economy but also for the "casing hard as steel" that suffocates individuality, personality, and *Kultur* (a dialectic that, again, is close to Simmel's account and also a distant relative of Marx's). Weber's disagreement with Sombart's emerging antisemitism did not translate, though, into a defense of Jewishness; liberals (like socialists as well) in the period took good care to avoid being suspected of "philosemitism."

In this sense Weber wrote (in a footnote added to the text of *The Protestant Ethic* in the edition of 1920) that in the opinion of English Puritans, "Jewish capitalism was speculative, pariah-capitalism, Puritan capitalism the bourgeois organization of labour." This (actually Weber's, not so much the English Puritans') argument is premised on a distinction between speculation and productive labor. According to this myth (or, as Weber might have put it, ideal-type), Jewish capitalism "looked to war, supplies from the state, state monopolies, commercial speculations, and the financial and construction projects of princes," all, so Weber seems to imply, bad premodern habits that capitalism has since overcome.[33] Puritan-driven, proper modern capitalism, however, comes, according to Weber, with the peace-bringing *doux commerce* as sketched out (as an enlightened hope) by Hume, Smith, and Kant.[34]

For Sombart, by contrast, the commercialization of economic life is the problem; trading is necessary but should not dominate and suffocate the creativity of heroic entrepreneurism. Sombart's historical hero, the entrepreneur, shared "the freebooting, martial element that Weber had dismissed as a traditional form of capitalism," i.e., as irrelevant and alien to modern capitalism.[35] Weber, in turn, tarred the Jews with the brush of what Sombart would have considered the heroic, un-Jewified, martial means of building the modern world while making a healthy profit.

The fact that Weber was sufficiently familiar with the reality of modern capitalist society to let the Jews off the hook in that respect does not mean that he was any fonder of them than Sombart was. The necessities involved in creating a coherent national culture that can salvage capitalist modernity both from its enemies and from itself remains the overriding value that would always trump sympathies for "minority cultures," just as it made the National Liberals of Weber's father's generation dislike the good old Jewish stubbornness, the refusal to shed that annoying anachronistic remaining bit of "cultural difference."[36] On the other hand, though, commitment to the humanistic education of the old-fashioned *Bürgertum* of which he declared himself so proudly a member made Weber also claim that the Puritan ethic that he expected should inspire the salvation of modern, Western, capitalist civilization owed a lot to the spirit of the ancient Hebrews (a "philosemitic" but historically dubious claim).[37] Furthermore Weber and Sombart reflected in their disagreement a specific divergence within nineteenth-century antisemitism: whereas antisemites of a liberal background (and also many socialists) had tended to see Jews as backward elements unfit for integration in a modern, bourgeois society, conservative antisemites (and also quite a few socialists) had blamed them for ushering in capitalist, liberal modernity. It was only the more radical antisemitism that emerged as an increasingly robust, though then still marginal ideology toward the end of the nineteenth century that combined and synthesized these two aspects in varying ways.[38] These two complementary main lines of nineteenth-century antisemitism seem to resonate in the subtexts of Weber's and Sombart's respective arguments about the Jews as too modern and therefore malignant, and as representatives of an outmoded, premodern economic mentality.[39]

Sociology, Capitalism, Liberalism

In the process of proposing nonegotistical individualism, Durkheim revoked the more dialectical conception of individual and society that had underpinned his first works, including *The Division of Labour in Society* (written under the influence of and in conversation with Spencer, contemporary German moral philosophy and "socialism of the lectern").[40] Weber's and Durkheim's discourses are similar in that both defend the modern spirit by distinguishing it from utilitarianism. Durkheim argues against Brunetière and the antisemites in this respect very much like Weber argues against Kürnberger and German "romantic" nationalists (who were often enough also antisemites): the proper, modern (in Weber's case, National Liberal; in Durkheim's case, republican) spirit (Weber: Protestant-inspired capitalism; Durkheim: the religion of the individual) must be strictly distinguished from the base thinking of Spencer and the economists. Weber defends capitalism as nonutilitarian just as Durkheim defends individualism as nonegotistical. Both ignore that the antisemites whom Durkheim challenges head-on, Weber more between the lines, engage in a not entirely dissimilar project: trashing a straw man called Spencer or some equivalent and proposing a scheme of collective morality or quasi-religion (sometimes more, sometimes less openly national) by which the alleged dissolution of society in the modern age can be halted.

Why does any of this matter?

Part of the thrust of my argument is that Spencer and the economists need to be defended against the wrong kind of critique. Nineteenth-century antisemites, but also liberal opponents of antisemitism like Durkheim, hardly give Spencer and the economists a fair hearing: they attack straw men, while at the same time reproducing some of the basic assumptions they pretend to challenge. The critique of false critiques is, though, the precondition of any emancipatory critique.[41] The latter, informed by (self-)awareness of the "limits of enlightenment,"[42] must therefore undertake to salvage and develop the Enlightenment elements of the doctrines of Spencer and the economists; this is the case even when, or especially when, it remains committed to the critique of the capitalist political economy whose apologists "the economists" are. The difficulty of the task consists in challenging the limits of Enlightenment and liberal modernity without betraying the humanity and individualism it has brought about for some and promised for all. The study of the liberal response to and involvement with antisemitism, including that of classical sociology, the "scientific" version of liberal and positivist social thought, is part of the analysis and critique of liberal modernity's self-destruction.

The formation of sociological theory and that of (modern) antisemitism are related, partly cosubstantial, while at the same time competing, sometimes antagonistic phenomena, as sociology responded to, but in responding also followed, antisemitism, or rather followed some shared impulses. Sociological theory emerged as a liberal response to crisis phenomena at several points in the nineteenth century, while modern antisemitism is likewise a "travesty of a social theory" that offers in its phantasmagorias of "the Jew" and "Jewification" an explanation of the same society's deficiencies and crises.[43] Modern sociology and modern antisemitism took their definite forms in the last quarter of the nineteenth century when both responded to phenomena (in Germany and France, to be sure) that can be described as a mixture of the final crisis of traditional society under regimes of intense modernization and early manifestations of a crisis of modern, capitalist, liberal society itself (overlapping but distinct phenomena). Several of the most influential antisemitic texts in the nineteenth century were written in France by writers who came from "early socialism," in particular the field that resulted in France from the disintegration of the Saint-Simonian movement led by Barthélemy Prosper Enfantin (whose actual basis in Saint-Simon, however, is rather dubious) and its merger with the Fourierist school in the 1830s, in Germany from the left-Hegelian school (which likewise was only to an extent based in Hegel's philosophy).[44] Both of these traditions were significantly parts of the wider liberal, democratic, and socialist currents of the time, inherited elements of the Enlightenment and had been produced by the era of bourgeois revolution. As such they are also fully part of the intellectual background of the formation of the discipline of sociology. One implication of this historical ambiguity is that the (according to some antisemites) allegedly Jewish science of sociology, like the wider traditions of liberalism, individualism, and rationalism (also sometimes connoted as Jewish), share some of their roots and lineages with their mortal enemy, modern antisemitism.[45]

Durkheim and Weber, to be sure, were aware of antisemitism as a problem and reacted against it. The specific content of their reactions shows, however, an implicit—probably unconscious—acknowledgment that antisemitism reacted to perceived problems that were also their own concerns as sociologists: on the one hand, the atomization and disintegration of society; on the other hand, the suffocation of individual freedom and personality by that same society. The sociological concepts of the "thingness" of society, its "anomies," the "casing hard as steel," and, more abstractly, the predominance of structure over agency, society over community, commerce over sheer life, are also at the basis of what antisemites saw (and still see) as the "Jewification" of society. This allows us to ask to what extent sociologists proposed, consciously or not, sociology as an alternative, liberal competitor to antisemitism (as well as to revolutionary Marxism).[46]

Saint-Simon and, at least initially, his followers had thought of Judaism as a crucial ingredient of the prospective religion of the future and also esteemed bankers highly as organizers of modern credit and thereby crucial for the industrialization and pacification of the world. According to Enfantin, the Jews in the past "exploited, by usurious money-lending, not the peasant—that was the privilege of the nobles—but the nobles themselves, a work of great social usefulness."[47] In the present, Jewish, like any other bankers, promoted peace. Likewise a text by Auguste Colin (a Fourierist) stated that God had sent the Jews "everywhere to be apostles of peace and industry. They are the industrial and political *tie* between the nations; they are the bankers of the kings, and hold in their hands [the power to decide over] peace or war."[48] Sweet commerce seemed to be promoted by God-sent Jews. These "philosemitic," "utopian-socialist" appraisals of the beneficial effects of, as it were, the Judaization of society from the first half of the nineteenth century were reflected in the emerging tradition of modern antisemitism by turning them into warrants for genocide. Such reversal gained currency when bourgeois thought lost the optimism characteristic of Saint-Simonianism and early, post–French Revolution liberalism, after the unbridgeable contradictions at the basis of liberal society had to be taken account of. Saint-Simon had seen human history as "marked by the constant decline of 'parasitism' and the rise of peaceful industry," governed by "the producers" under the leadership of the most important merchants and manufacturers.[49] This account was proven wrong by actual nineteenth-century history: "parasitism" had not disappeared, nor was industry as peaceful, commerce as sweet as expected. The conviction that parasites were to be destroyed, though, stuck.

The antagonism to unproductive, parasitic eaters and those unable to "improve" the productive forces (in the first place, the warrior nobility and other savages) has, since Locke and Sieyes, remained at the heart of bourgeois thought and tends to provide it with its more revolutionary impulses.[50] Deep as this notion is built into the structure of bourgeois thought, it is reasonable to assume that subjects of bourgeois society who are by and large in agreement with its fundamental structures will be receptive to any argument that targets any group, including "the Jews," as unproductive eaters or as endangering the productive power of society and the cohesion that warrants its reproduction (be that because this group is too savage and backward or too modern and cosmopolitan or too savage *by way of* being too modern). This specific ideological context of modern antisemitism is crucial, I argue, for an explanation of liberal society's receptiveness to antisemitism and allows us to refer to it as the index of a more general and fundamental problem.

To the extent that sociology is an offshoot of the (lowercase) liberal tradition (as is socialism, generally speaking), it is also implicated in this problem.[51] The crux of the matter is the question of who the parasites are: the nobility? traders and bankers? the Jews? the bourgeoisie? the capitalists? international finance capital? Wall Street? the East Coast? freemasonry? The question of which box (or boxes) the antiparasitist will tick depends on what political alliance he or she is in and who or what this alliance is supposed to be fighting. The bottom line is this: those to be denounced, and perhaps persecuted, as parasites are those who do not contribute to creating and reproducing society, whereby one's own specific understanding of what that society is, or ought to be, is crucial. As formulating such understandings is one of the professional tasks of sociologists, they are crucially implicated in this mechanism.[52] A social theory that would be a reliable tool in the struggle against antisemitism, or at least immune to it, would need to radically sever the link between a person's worth, or right to live, belong, and reproduce, from that person's contribution to the production and reproduction of society, let alone her or his compatibility with the cultural and political forms (including nation, state, gender) of that society. It would not know the concept of parasites.

Notes

Some sections of this article were previously published in my article 'Antisemitism, capitalism and the formation of sociological theory' in Patterns of Prejudice, *44:2, 2010, pages 161–94.*

1. Durkheim, "Individualism and the Intellectuals," in *On Morality and Society*. An alternative (sometimes superior) translation with a useful introduction is Lukes, "Durkheim's 'Individualism and the Intellectuals.'". On the context, see Goldberg, "Introduction."
2. Lukes, "Durkheim's 'Individualism and the Intellectuals,'" 17–18.
3. Wernick, *Auguste Comte and the Religion of Humanity*, 215, 211.
4. Barbalet (in the context of his critical discussion of Weber) points to Adam Smith as the original modernist sociologist who based the capitalist spirit in "social processes rather than religious doctrinal subscription" (*Weber, Passion and Profits*, 12). Giddens suggests that Durkheim synthesized the opposing positions of Saint-Simon and Comte; according to Durkheim according to Giddens, "Comte was mistaken in supposing that the condition of unity in traditional societies, the existence of a strongly formed *conscience collective*, is necessary to the modern type of society," while Saint-Simon went too far when he suggested authority in modern society merely needed to be the "administration of things" (Giddens, *Studies in Social and Political Theory*, 239). However, it is questionable whether either Saint-Simon or Comte held the respective views in such one-sided form in the first place.
5. Stoetzler, *The State, the Nation*, chapter 9; Langewiesche, *Liberalism in Germany*.
6. See Lloyd and Thomas, *Culture and the State*.
7. On Bataille and Caillois, see Falasca-Zamponi, "A Left Sacred"; Stone, "Georges Bataille and the Interpretation of the Holocaust"; Weingrad, "The College of Sociology and the Institute of Social Research"; Wolin, *The Seduc-*

tion of Unreason. Bataille and Caillois started out on their exploration of "the sacred" as constitutive of politics and as part of an effort to understand and fight fascism, but the solutions they came to recommend were so vehemently and undialectically opposed to utilitarianism and democracy that they ended up in the vicinity of fascism (at least temporarily and without thereafter having been able to account for the problem satisfactorily). The fact that radical but undialectical rejections of democracy and utilitarianism remain the principal inroad for fascism into emancipatory antihegemonic movements is what lends urgency and contemporary relevance to the otherwise 'academic' discussion of whether it was wise for Durkheim and his students to join into the reactionaries' polemics against 'Spencer and the economists'. What is at stake here is the old question of whether the Left can afford even the slightest ambiguity about its stance toward the Right while struggling against liberalism. It cannot.

8. Durkheim, "Individualism and the Intellectuals," 47, 48, 45, 47. This would also seem like a rather dubious interpretation of Kant.

9. A recent, revisionist work on Spencer is Francis, *Herbert Spencer and the Invention of Modern Life.* For a restatement of utilitarianism from within sociology, see Camic, "The Utilitarians Revisited."

10. Durkheim, "Individualism and the Intellectuals," 51. Durkheim added, as if he wanted to reach out to his Christian fellow citizens, that Christianity was already just another, somewhat disguised form of individualism anyway (53).

11. Durkheim, "Individualism and the Intellectuals," 51–52. Perrin has written on Durkheim's relation to Spencer, "While Durkheim misinterprets or misrenders much of Spencer's theory, he appropriates, with little or no acknowledgement, many of its essential features" ("Emile Durkheim's *Division of Labor* and the Shadow of Herbert Spencer," 793). What Spencer, perhaps unhelpfully, called the "organic" conception of society meant that society "naturally" evolves toward a state of minimal government and maximal extent of communal life and voluntary cooperation, thereby performing "a change from an incoherent homogeneity to a coherent heterogeneity," which latter term is meant to denote a synthesis of community and individuality (Hiskes, "Spencer and the Liberal Idea of Community," 600, 601). All this is in a register of liberalism not far from Durkheim's.

12. Weber developed the notions of "pariah-people" and "pariah-capitalism" in the course of his ongoing exchange with Sombart (Ghosh, "The Place of Judaism in Max Weber's *Protestant Ethic*").

13. These formulations are from the famous and inspirational last few pages of *The Protestant Ethic.* On the problem of how to translate "stahlhartes Gehäuse," see Baehr, "The 'Iron Cage' and 'Shell as Hard as Steel.'" Weber writes already earlier in the text (*Protestantische Ethik*, 43) that the capitalistic order is (for the individual) a "faktisch unabänderliches Gehäuse" (Parsons translated this phrase as "an unalterable order of things"; *Protestant Ethic*, 54).

14. "The religious roots died out slowly, giving way to utilitarian worldliness" (Weber, *Protestant Ethic*, 176). A similar formulation can be found on 177.

15. Weber, *Protestant Ethic*, 37; Weber, *Protestantische Ethik*, 27. I am not aware of evidence that Weber was influenced by Carlyle beyond using some of Carlyle's works as sources for his research on the English Revolution, but there are strong parallels that make Weber seem rather akin to Carlyle. Carlyle, a Scottish Puritan, had hoped, indeed like Weber, to infuse an unheroic present with some of the spirit of the English Revolution by, among other things, editing Cromwell's writings (Young, *The Victorian Eighteenth Century*, 22). There he praises English Puritanism as "a practical world based on belief in God" (quoted on 22). In his last work (six volumes on the history of Frederick the Great, 1858–65) he praised virtues in Prussian history such as (Puritan-inspired) thrift (18) and "Reformation sobriety" (37). Carlyle's crucial suggestion that the modern world is an age of machinery "in every outward and inward sense of that word" (in "Signs of the Times" [1829], quoted in Murphy, "Carlyle and the Saint-Simonians," 101), in which the individual can no longer accomplish anything out of individuality but only as a part of various "machineries" and institutions and with the help of mechanical aids, surely is close enough to Weber's view (as well as to Simmel's).

16. Weber, *Protestantische Ethik*, 169n28, 268n379, 161; Weber, *Protestant Ethic*, 191n23, 280n96, 182. Although this seems to be Weber's own formulation, he put it in quotation marks as if it were an unreferenced quotation; it might also be an actual quotation that he could assume contemporaries would have recognized.

17. The passage Weber uses is in book 1, chapter 1 of the novel. Parsons obscures in his translation the reference to Benjamin Franklin by mistakenly referring to "Benjamin Ferdinand" instead (Weber, *Protestant Ethic*, 50).

18. Weber, *Protestant Ethic*, 48–54; Weber, *Protestantische Ethik*, 37–42.

19. Weber, *Protestant Ethic*, 192n3.

20. Weber's mother, Helene, was a Calvinist of (on the maternal line) Huguenot background (Liebersohn, *Fate and Utopia in German Sociology*, 83). Lawrence Scaff notes that eleven-year-old Max was given a copy of Benjamin Franklin's autobiography in translation by Friedrich Kapp, a political ally of Max Weber Sr. Kapp had written an introduction to the German edition wherein he recommended that German fathers should teach their sons Franklin's practical maxims (Scaff, *Max Weber in America*, 12).

21. Loader, "Puritans and Jews," 639. Weber also contrasted to the American sects "the bureaucratic structure of the European 'church,' which offered no hope for the future" (Loader, "Puritans and Jews," 639). Bureaucratic domination is thus, next to utilitarianism, the other mortal enemy of a viable, modern, capitalist culture.

22. Weber, *Protestant Ethic*, 56. He discusses the contrast between German and Anglo-Saxon spirit also (127–28).

23. Barbalet, *Weber, Passion and Profits*, 19, 25, 27.
24. Most recently, for example, Steinert, *Max Webers unwiderlegbare Fehlkonstruktionen*.
25. Weber grants that Franklin's discourse is "already" overdetermined by utilitarianism; the ideal-type has to be constructed by mindful exegesis out of a less than ideal-typical empirical reality (the actual Franklin who still was a carrier of the genuine Puritan spirit but already affected by its degeneration; *Weber, Protestant Ethic*, 52). In fact Weber, like Kürnberger, seems to have misconstrued Franklin considerably. Joachim Radkau quotes Mark Stoll (*Protestantism, Capitalism, and Nature in America*, 86), who calls Franklin "one of the most secular Americans of the 18th century," and Eduard Baumgarten (in his 1936 study of Benjamin Franklin as "the chief instructor of the American Revolution") who emphasized Franklin's hedonism and Epicureanism (Radkau, *Max Weber: A Biography*, 600).
26. I have developed this problem in *The State, the Nation, and the Jews* and in "Cultural Difference in the National State." Kürnberger's "anti-Yankeeism" does not seem to contain any explicitly antisemitic elements (at least judging from quickly looking through his six hundred rather dull pages), but its general conception is in line with, for example, Gustav Freytag's "Debit and Credit," also of 1855 (see Achinger, *Gespaltene Moderne*): German Christian moral values, and indeed German ways of doing business could provide a socially sustainable form of capitalism that is contrasted to its rapacious and pathological (American, English, Jewish) forms. This liberal anticapitalism is quite different from, for example, Richard Wagner's antisemitism, but both discourses bear a family resemblance. For a comparative analysis of Freytag and Treitschke, see Stoetzler and Achinger, "German Modernity, Barbarous Slavs and Profit-seeking Jews."
27. The interrelatedness of the question of asceticism with that of the nation is also evident in a famous quote from a letter Weber wrote in February 1906: "That our nation never went through the school of harsh asceticism, in *any* form, is . . . the source of everything I find hateful in it (as well as in myself)" (quoted in Radkau, *Max Weber: A Biography*, 317).
28. Weber, *Protestant Ethic*, 172, 260n7.
29. It is instructive to note that Weber's friend Simmel emphasized (especially in *The Philosophy of Money*) the double character—with benign and malign aspects inseparably, namely "tragically," interwoven—of the modern "money economy," thereby delegitimizing opposition to capitalism (antisemitic or otherwise), but nevertheless legitimated attacks on "Mammonism" when he defined in a text from 1914 Mammonism as obsessive and single-minded money making (Simmel, "Mammonismus," 312–13). Especially in the 1914 context of Simmel's supporting militaristic patriotism, Simmel adopts with this remark an element of antisemitic nationalism.
30. Weber, *Protestant Ethic*, 179.

31. Durkheim also thought society rather than the state should, in principle, bring about benign capitalism, although he might have welcomed a slightly more interventionist "visible hand" than Weber did.

32. Simmel and Weber addressed what Marx implied in the concept of "real subsumption" (Postone, *Time, Labor, and Social Domination*, 182); this is the ground on which some in the Marxist tradition (such as Sayer, *Capitalism and Modernity*) have aligned Marx and Weber.

33. Weber, *Protestant Ethic*, 270–71n58; Weber, *Protestantische Ethik*, 257–58n342.

34. Barbalet points to the ambiguity in Weber's attitude toward the Jews and antisemitism in these terms: "Weber's failure to contribute to a sociology of anti-Semitism is a significant omission . . . because he was aware of anti-Semitism and opposed to it when it touched him." Weber was aware of anti-semitism's "consequences on Jewish opportunities and aspirations. However, in his sociological treatment of the Jews he regards the pariah concept and its corollaries as not only necessary but sufficient in explaining Jewish economic marginalization. That is to say, in Weber's view, the conditions of the Jews are to be explained only by reference to the particulars and peculiarities of their religious beliefs" (*Weber, Passion and Profits*, 196). Weber constructs his ideal-types of Jews, Puritans, and others out of his "philosophical presuppositions" (in other words, prejudices) rather than coherent, empirically backed analysis (202).

35. Loader, "Puritans and Jews," 644.

36. Abraham, *Max Weber and the Jewish Question*.

37. Weber might have adopted this idea from the Jewish historian Heinrich Graetz (Ghosh, "The Place of Judaism in Max Weber's *Protestant Ethic*," 242). Weber's argument reflects here, as in many other ways, nineteenth-century National Liberalism that tended to defend Jews only when this could be instrumentalized for the apologetics of market capitalism. This is what prompted socialists like Mehring to equate all forms of defense of Jewish emancipation—what Mehring calls "philosemitism"-with the defense of capitalism and liberalism. In reality, of course, neither most Jews nor all defenders of Jews were particularly pro-capitalist. On Mehring, compare Fischer, *The Socialist Response to Antisemitism in Imperial Germany*.

38. Stoetzler, *The State, the Nation and the Jews*, chapter 8.

39. Radkau similarly concludes, "The attitude to Jews and Judaism is also one of Weber's great ambivalences, and there is much to suggest that it occupied him throughout his life" (*Max Weber: A Biography*, 427; *Max Weber: Die Leidenschaft des Denkens*, 673). On the concept of pariah capitalism, he notes that "many passages in Weber would have been at least as useful as Sombart's 'Jewish Book' for anti-Semites who distinguished between creative and predatory capital" (*Max Weber: A Biography*, 438).

40. Durkheim, "La science positive de la morale en Allemagne"; Jones, "The Positive Science of Ethics in France."

41. In other words, no emancipation without truth.

42. Adorno and Horkheimer, *Dialectic of Enlightenment*, 137.

43. Rürup, *Emanzipation und Antisemitismus*, 115.

44. Central to this process in Germany was the positivist reformulation of the concept of the *Volksgeist* that became a positive entity thereby, such as in Johann Herbart or Moritz Lazarus (Simmel's teacher) in social science, but also in nationalist and racist ideologies (Belke, Einleitung).

45. "Friedrich Gundolf, himself of Jewish origin, mockingly described sociology in 1924 as a 'Jewish sect'" (Radkau, *Max Weber: A Biography*, 431). Radkau quotes from Dirk Käsler.

46. The fact that Horkheimer and Adorno made understanding antisemitism a central aspect of their critical theory seems to reflect the conviction that the renewal of Marxism as an emancipatory theory—after it had been turned into an ideology of domination—needed to confront the issues at stake here.

47. Enfantin (1832), quoted in Silberner, "Pierre Leroux's Ideas on the Jewish People," 378.

48. Colin, quoted in Silberner, "Pierre Leroux's Ideas on the Jewish People," 378. Szajkowski quotes another Saint-Simonian writer (Barrault) with an almost identical statement ("The Jewish Saint-Simonians and Socialist Antisemites in France," 41); here the Jews are the "bankers of the angels."

49. Iggers, introduction, xxi.

50. I have developed this argument in "Antisemitism, the Bourgeoisie, and the Self-Destruction of the Nation-State." The notion that the nobility are a warrior caste, that is, savages (as in Sieyes, who suggested sending them back into the Frankish forests), is mirrored by the complementary idea that the savages are noble (as in Herder).

51. On lowercase liberalism, see Wallerstein, *After Liberalism*.

52. The discussion of the dialectic between sociology and antisemitism may help explain why sociology throughout the past one hundred years had so little to say on the subject of antisemitism; perhaps sociologists were reluctant to address antisemitism (or fascism) confidently because they had to fear to see in their portrayals distorted mirror images of their own discipline. (This suggestion was made by Nicole Asquith, University of Bradford, in the discussion of a presentation of an earlier version of this paper at the ESA conference in Glasgow, 2007.)

References

Abraham, Gary. *Max Weber and the Jewish Question: A Study of the Social Outlook of His Sociology*. Urbana: University of Illinois Press, 1992.

Achinger, Christine. *Gespaltene Moderne: Gustav Freytags Soll und Haben, Nation, Geschlecht und Judenbild*. Würzburg: Königshausen und Neumann, 2007.

Adorno, Theodor W., and Max Horkheimer. *Dialectic of Enlightenment: Philosophical Fragments*. Translated by Edmund Jephcott. Stanford CA: Stanford University Press, 2002.

Baehr, Peter. "The 'Iron Cage' and 'Shell as Hard as Steel': Parsons, Weber, and the *Stahlhartes Gehäuse* Metaphor in the *Protestant Ethic and the Spirit of Capitalism*." *History and Theory* 40.2 (2001): 153-69.

Barbalet, Jack. *Weber, Passion and Profits: "The Protestant Ethic and the Spirit of Capitalism" in Context*. Cambridge: Cambridge University Press, 2008.

Baumgarten, Eduard. *Benjamin Franklin: Der Lehrmeister der amerikanischen Revolution*. Frankfurt am Main: Klostermann, 1936.

Belke, Ingrid. Einleitung in *Moritz Lazarus und Heymann Steinthal: Die Begründer der Völkerpsychologie in ihren Briefen, mit einer Einleitung herausgegeben von Ingrid Belke*, xiii-cxxxviii. Tübingen: Mohr 1971.

Camic, Charles. "The Utilitarians Revisited." *American Journal of Sociology* 85.3 (1979): 516-50.

Durkheim, Emile. "Individualism and the Intellectuals." 1898. In *On Morality and Society*, edited by Robert N. Bellah, 43-57. Chicago: University of Chicago Press, 1973.

———. "La science positive de la morale en Allemagne." *Revue Philosophique* 24 (1887): 33-284.

Falasca-Zamponi, Simonetta. "A Left Sacred or a Sacred Left? The Collège de Sociologie, Fascism, and Political Culture in Interwar France." *South Central Review* 23.1 (2006): 40-54.

Fischer, Lars. *The Socialist Response to Antisemitism in Imperial Germany*. Cambridge: Cambridge University Press, 2007.

Francis, Mark. *Herbert Spencer and the Invention of Modern Life*, Ithaca NY: Cornell University Press, 2007.

Ghosh, Peter. "The Place of Judaism in Max Weber's *Protestant Ethic*." *Zeitschrift für Neuere Theologiegeschichte/Journal for the History of Modern Theology* 12.2 (2006): 208-61.

Giddens, Anthony. *Studies in Social and Political Theory*. London: Hutchinson, 1977.

Goldberg, Chad. "Introduction to Emile Durkheim's 'Anti-Semitism and Social Crisis.'" *Sociological Theory* 26.4 (2008): 299-323.

Hiskes, Richard P. "Spencer and the Liberal Idea of Community." *Review of Politics* 45.4 (1983): 595-609.

Iggers, Georg. Introduction to *The Doctrine of Saint-Simon: An Exposition. First Year, 1828-1829*, ix-xlvii. New York: Schocken 1972.

Jones, Robert Alun. "The Positive Science of Ethics in France: German Influences on *De la division du travail social*." *Sociological Forum* 9.1 (1994): 37-57.

Kürnberger, Ferdinand. *Der Amerikamüde, Amerikanisches Kulturbild*. 1855. Frankfurt am Main: Insel, 1986.

Langer, Ulrich. *Heinrich von Treitschke: Politische Biographie eines deutschen Nationalisten*. Düsseldorf: Droste, 1998.

Langewiesche, Dieter. *Liberalism in Germany*. Translated by Christiane Banerji. Houndmills, England: Macmillan, 2000.

Liebersohn, Harry. *Fate and Utopia in German Sociology, 1870–1923*. Cambridge MA: MIT Press, 1988.

Lloyd, David, and Paul Thomas. *Culture and the State*. London: Routledge, 1998.

Loader, Colin. "Puritans and Jews: Weber, Sombart and the Transvaluators of Modern Society." *Canadian Journal of Sociology/Cahiers canadiens de sociologie* 26.4 (2001): 635–53.

Lukes, Steven. "Durkheim's 'Individualism and the Intellectuals.'" *Political Studies* 17.1 (1969): 14–30.

Murphy, Ella M. "Carlyle and the Saint-Simonians." *Studies in Philology* 33 (1936): 93–118.

Perrin, Robert G. "Emile Durkheim's *Division of Labor* and the Shadow of Herbert Spencer." *Sociological Quarterly* 36.4 (1995): 791–808.

Postone, Moishe. *Time, Labor, and Social Domination: A Reinterpretation of Marx's Critical Theory*. Cambridge: Cambridge University Press, 1996.

Radkau, Joachim. *Max Weber: A Biography*. Translated by Patrick Camiller. Cambridge, England: Polity, 2009.

———. *Max Weber: Die Leidenschaft des Denkens*. Munich: Hanser, 2005.

Rürup, Reinhard. *Emanzipation und Antisemitismus: Studien zur "Judenfrage" der bürgerlichen Gesellschaft*. Frankfurt am Main: Fischer, 1987.

Sayer, Derek. *Capitalism and Modernity: An Excursus on Marx and Weber*. London: Routledge, 1991.

Scaff, Lawrence A. *Max Weber in America*. Princeton NJ: Princeton University Press, 2011.

Silberner, Edmund. "Pierre Leroux's Ideas on the Jewish People." *Jewish Social Studies* 12 (1950): 367–84.

Simmel, Georg. "Mammonismus." 1914. In *Georg Simmels Philosophie des Geldes, Aufsätze und Materialien*, edited by Otthein Rammstedt, Christian Papilloud, Natàlia Cantó i Milà, and Cécile Rol, 312–13. Frankfurt am Main: Suhrkamp, 2003.

Steinert, Heinz. *Max Webers unwiderlegbare Fehlkonstruktionen: Die protestantische Ethik und der Geist des Kapitalismus*. Frankfurt am Main: Campus Verlag, 2010.

Stoetzler, Marcel. "Antisemitism, the Bourgeoisie, and the Self-Destruction of the Nation-State." In: *Hannah Arendt and the Uses of History, Imperialism, Nation, Race, and Genocide*, edited by Richard King and Dan Stone, 130–46. Oxford: Berghahn, 2007.

———. "Cultural Difference in the National State: From Trouser-selling Jews to Unbridled Multiculturalism." *Patterns of Prejudice* 42.3 (2008): 245–79.

———. *The State, the Nation and the Jews: Liberalism and the Antisemitism Dispute in Bismarck's Germany*. Lincoln: University of Nebraska Press, 2008.

Stoetzler, Marcel, and Achinger, Christine. "German Modernity, Barbarous Slavs and Profit-Seeking Jews: The Cultural Racism of Nationalist Liberals." *Nations and Nationalism* 19.4 (2013): 739–60.

Stoll, Mark. *Protestantism, Capitalism, and Nature in America.* Albuquerque: University of New Mexico Press, 1997.

Stone, Dan. "Georges Bataille and the Interpretation of the Holocaust," In *Theoretical Interpretations of the Holocaust*, edited by Dan Stone, 79-101. Amsterdam: Rodopi, 2001.

Szajkowski, Zosa. "The Jewish Saint-Simonians and Socialist Antisemites in France." *Jewish Social Studies* 9 (1947): 33-60.

Treitschke, Heinrich von. "Der Socialismus und seine Goenner." 1874. In *Zehn Jahre Deutscher Kämpfe, Theil 2: Von 1871-1879, Dritte Auflage*, 112-222. Berlin: Reimer, 1897.

Wallerstein, Immanuel. *After Liberalism.* New York: New Press, 1995.

Weber, Max. *The Protestant Ethic and the Spirit of Capitalism.* 1930. Translated by Talcott Parsons. Introduction by Anthony Giddens. London: Allen and Unwin, 1978.

———. *Die protestantische Ethik und der Geist des Kapitalismus.* Erfstadt: Area verlag, 2006.

Weingrad, Michael. "The College of Sociology and the Institute of Social Research." *New German Critique* 84 (2001): 129-61.

Wernick, Andrew. *Auguste Comte and the Religion of Humanity: The Post-theistic Program of French Social Theory.* Cambridge: Cambridge University Press, 2001.

Wolin, Richard. *The Seduction of Unreason: The Intellectual Romance with Fascism from Nietzsche to Postmodernism.* Princeton NJ: Princeton University Press, 2004.

Young, Brian W. *The Victorian Eighteenth Century: An Intellectual History.* Oxford: Oxford University Press, 2007.

3

Fairness as an Impetus for Objective, Scientific Social Research Methods

The Reports about Jewish Traders in the 1887 Usury Enquête *of the Verein für Socialpolitik*

IRMELA GORGES

This chapter deals with prejudices toward Jews among Germans in the mid-1880s and how these prejudices induced early social and economic scientists to take steps to develop objective methods of empirical social research. These prejudices became manifest in an *enquête* conducted in 1887 by the German Association for Social Policy (Verein für Socialpolitik, VfS), founded in 1872. Introductory remarks about the situation of Jews and the work of the VfS around 1880 in Germany may help to explain the circumstances.

The Situation of Jews in Imperial Germany around 1880

Until the establishment of Imperial Germany in 1871 German Jews struggled for their emancipation. In 1869 the Northern German Federation (Norddeutscher Bund) enacted a law that guaranteed civil rights and unhindered religious practice to all citizens of the German Reich, including the Jews.[1] The law was adopted in the Constitution of Imperial Germany in 1871. Mainly liberal politicians, but also Otto von Bismarck (1815–98), a conservative member of the Prussian Parliament and, later, the "architect" and first chancellor of Imperial Germany, supported legal emancipation.[2]

At the beginning of the Imperial German period, about two and a half million Jews lived in Germany, and about two-thirds of them, 640,000 to 1 million persons, lived in Berlin (Prussia). In spite of legal emancipation, Jews still suffered under prejudices and deprivations from the government and non-Jewish Germans. In spite of their on-average high level of education (compared to Christian Germans), Jews rarely were appointed to positions in the state administration; they were allowed to enter the technical service but not the military service or judicial positions. The majority of Jews therefore engaged in private businesses, mainly in the commercial and trade sectors. The small number of those who were elected to the German Parliament usually were nominated by the Liberal Party. Only a few Jews had become full professors at universities; some had founded, for instance, medical bureaus or became librarians; and very few reached the position of judge.[3] When the economic boom of the early 1870s ended and, at the same time, the demands of the socialist workers movement became stronger and seemed to endanger Imperial Germany, Bismarck returned to a conservative authoritarian policy. In 1878 he used two assassination attempts on the emperor to push through a law against all social democratic activities (Sozialistengesetze) that stopped short of banning the party itself, due to strong resistance by Liberal Party members. The law required being extended every two and a half years. In the course of these antiliberal politics Jews lost Bismarck's support, and antisemitic voices became stronger. A prominent Protestant may serve as an example: Adolf Stoecker (1835–1909), a Protestant priest and founder of the Christian Socialist Workers Party, who had become a member of Parliament for the German Conservative Party in the Reichstag (Imperial Parliament) in 1880, agitated against Jews as well as against the Social Democratic Party. From 1881 onward no Jewish member was to be found among the members of the German Imperial Parliament.[4]

A sophisticated conception of society that offered a theoretical explanation for the outsider position of Jews within Bismarckian society was provided by the political economist and politician Leon Zeitlin (1876–1967), who suggested that Bismarck saw the state as an organic functioning community in which all parts should work with and profit from one another and in accordance with the goals of the state's leadership. Thereby even the poorest German should preserve his dignity with the aid of the state and be protected whenever he was not able to help himself.[5] Bismarck was convinced that state aid should be linked with self-help in an organic way.[6] He found that the Social Democratic Party as well as the Jews instead aimed at destroying the state and establishing a new order. The social legislation that Bismarck initiated in 1883, the year Karl Marx died, illustrated Bismarck's idea of an organic inclusion of the needy industrial workers into the state as well as his intention to exclude those who would not support the organic community. Zeitlin's interpretation suggests that this "organic approach" to society was widely accepted among Germans at the time.

It seems plausible that the idea of the need to defend society against intruders became more virulent during times of crisis, thereby causing resentment against those defined as outsiders. The first economic crisis in Imperial Germany that may have helped strengthen anti-Jewish prejudice started in 1873 and lasted until the mid-1890s. While Bismarck reacted in 1879 with protective duties, others, like the journalist Otto Glagau (1834–92), accused the Jews of being responsible for the crisis, thereby again stirring up antisemitic prejudice.[7]

It is an important characteristic of the history of the period that in Germany the peak of the Industrial Revolution coincided with an economic crisis. Between 1860 and 1914 about 16 million moved from the agrarian areas to the industrial centers in the western part of Germany.[8] Even if there was no decline of production until 1879, according to eyewitness reports unemployment became evident already, only a few years after the foundation of Imperial Germany. (The statistical bureaus of the time did not collect unemployment data.)[9] At the beginning of the 1870s, when industrialization started to reach its peak in Imperial Germany, nearly 25 percent of all inhabitants of Germany were counted as "industrial workers,"[10] although the process of regulating through legislation the work relations between industrial workers and entrepreneurs had not even begun. The founding statute of the Social Democratic Party, the Gothaer Program of 1875, included moderate socialist aims, such as the demand for workers' cooperatives, democratic franchise, an eight-hour workday, and the Marxian goals of fighting capitalism and establishing the union of industrial workers in an international workers movement.[11]

The Verein für Socialpolitik

Already since the mid-1860s the disadvantages of an unrestricted liberalism and the growing impoverishment of the working class became overt. Mostly national liberal academics, professors of the then so-called historical school of national economics, addressed "the social question" (*soziale Frage*), the situation of the working class under the conditions of the Industrial Revolution. Economists advocating free-market policies soon called them "socialists of the chair" (*Kathedersozialisten*).[12]

In July 1872 a group of professors of national economics, journalists, politicians, and others met in the city of Halle. They had begun to worry not only about the social, physical, and economic condition of the industrial workers but also about the whole of the German state and its "flourishing" in the future.[13] In a second, larger meeting in October 1872, the organization VfS was founded.[14] The VfS saw itself as open to members of any political orientation supporting a moderate amount of state intervention, believing that practical reform work should dominate theoretical analyses.[15]

Until the commencement of the first antisocialist legislation in 1878 the Verein für Socialpolitik successfully conducted enquêtes (empirical studies), which were presented and critically discussed in its biannual general meetings. The three dominating research subjects were (1) social policy issues aiming at improving the situation of industrial workers, (2) economic policy issues such as the reform of stock corporations and tax or trade issues, and (3) methodological issues, how the VfS could gather more valid information about its research issues.[16] At the beginning of the 1870s the method of enquête was still in its infancy. It was initially understood to mean a survey conducted by the state.[17] One member of the VfS by the name of Embden differentiated between enquêtes that could serve democratic and those that served administrative political goals.[18] The VfS adopted the term *enquête* for the information-gathering process of its own studies. On the basis of the results of these enquêtes the VfS passed resolutions about what should be done to improve the situation that was described and analyzed during the meetings. The resolutions then were handed over to members of Parliament.[19]

Soon after the first antisocialist law (*Sozialistengesetz*) was passed by Parliament in 1878, the VfS ceased to conduct enquêtes about problems of the industrial workers. Since the early 1880s, without justifying this turn in any detail, the VfS concentrated on enquêtes about "the rural problem," mainly the problems of the peasants. At the same time the members decided not to formulate and pass resolutions to Parliament anymore. It was clear that this shift was due to the new political situation. This was made more explicit when in 1884 the chair of the general meeting stated that the Verein was henceforth to provide the scholarly research that Parliament, administration, and government relied on for the sufficiently detailed preparation of new legislation but lacked the time to undertake. He emphasized that the VfS was thereby following a higher goal than party politics, "occupying a loftier ground than the political parties" and "like the choir in Greek tragedy" remaining in the background, pleading for moderation, advocating "what is true and good, right and just."[20] Besides this shift toward a more scientific orientation, he was sure that the VfS would also be able to solve its "other most important" task.[21] It can be assumed that he wanted to indicate that the VfS should continue to pursue the practical implementation of enquête results into day-to-day political decisions, but he did not want to emphasize a practical political engagement due to the restrictions of activities the new antisocialist act prescribed. The shift toward agrarian themes relieved the VfS from suspicion that it was supporting Social Democratic Party goals. The VfS's research interest and practical concern now turned to the needy peasants of Germany. The consequences of rural usury, the subject of the enquête that will be discussed in the following pages, was identified as one of the most urgent problems peasants faced. The enquête on rural usury was planned in 1885, when it became obvious that the anti-usury law of 1880 had not decisively diminished usury in Germany.

The Predecessors of the VfS Usury Enquête in the 1880s

Already in 1882 the VfS had published a volume on the results of an enquête about "the inheritance laws and the distribution of landowners in Imperial Germany (the distribution of agricultural real estate and the common inheritance laws.)"[22] This enquête was discussed in the regular meeting of the VfS in the same year. It was found that the owners of large farms in the northeast were better off than the owners of the very small farms in the southwest of the Reich. The different inheritance laws were responsible for the common problem that farms became too big or too small to be profitable; in the northeast a single heir inherited an entire property, while in the southwest the inherited land had to be divided into equal parts between all heirs. In addition these landowners lost their competitiveness with producers from other countries; consequently, it was argued, smallholders as well as rural workers became susceptible to socialist agitation.[23]

When two years later the results of another enquête on the "situation of peasants in Germany" were discussed during the 1884 meeting of the VfS, it became clear that primarily the debts caused by enormous communal taxes put pressure on the peasants rather than the inheritance laws.[24] Also professional usury was found to be responsible for the poor financial situation of the peasants. The members of the VfS suggested that in order to protect especially the small peasantry from too high indebtedness, professional usury should be counteracted by founding farmers' cooperative credit institutes and consumer and sales organizations.[25] Other aspects of the overall agrarian problem were tackled in further enquêtes. The enquête on "inner colonization in Germany,"[26] for instance, dealt with the problem of how to maintain the profitability of large estates mainly in eastern Germany, when many of the best rural workers moved to the big industrial cities. The members of the VfS suggested that these properties should be divided into medium and small-scale farms because these would stay in a more profitable and healthy economic condition than big farms. It seemed that the VfS defined the "agrarian problem" mainly as the financial situation of the peasants. Another enquête, dealing with the impact of retail trade on the prices for consumers, discussed in the regular meeting of the VfS in 1886, looked into the financial problems of peasants as well as consumers.[27] The enquête examined the differences between wholesale and retail prices, suspecting that retail shops were making undue profits. However, the unanimous statistical analyses of the prices of different sizes of basic food products did not result in any relevant criticism of retail trade prices. More detailed investigations could not be conducted, mainly because it seemed too difficult to measure the exact differences between the wholesale and retail prices. However, the statistical analyses seemed to indicate that it was not necessary to look for possible social factors or responsible parties in order to detect unfair prices paid by consumers.[28]

The only "agrarian problem" that apparently could not be solved by statistical analyses of objective facts was the problem of rural usury. Even though usury was forbidden by the Anti-Usury act in March 1880, and even though the statistical numbers of usury were diminishing and the cooperative banks, like the Schulze-Delitzsch cooperative banks or Raiffeisenbanken, offered acceptable interest rates, there still were rumors and complaints about a great number of peasants who lost their mostly small or medium-size farms due to usury. The definition of usury was ambiguous: while the Anti-Usury Act of 1880 defined usury as an unduly high interest rate, the state of Baden defined usury as one contractor taking advantage of the foolishness or misery of another.[29]

The Enquête on Rural Usury in Imperial Germany

In 1885 the working committee of the VfS decided to conduct an enquête on rural usury in Germany in order to "complete" earlier studies on the agrarian issue.[30] The relevance of the issue became obvious when the first few answers were discussed in 1886 in the Prussian Landesökonomierath, an administrative body consisting of members of the Agrarian Ministry of Prussia and elected members of the Chamber of Agriculture, which represented the interests of farmers and foresters. As the information seemed to reveal an overall critical situation, it was decided to systematically gather information in all federal lands of Germany. The final results of the enquête, reports from twenty-seven experts, were published as a book and handed over to the Deutsche Landwirtschaftsrath even before the enquête was discussed in a general meeting of the VfS. The Deutsche Landwirtschaftsrath was a committee consisting of representatives of the German Landwirtschaftskammern, an association acting in the interests of all farmers, and was authorized to directly contact the chancellor or Parliament in order to present to them their experts' statement on any relevant issue. August von Miaskowski (1838–99), a professor of national economy and himself a member of the Prussian Landesökonomierath, reported on the results of the enquête in the 1888 general meeting of the VfS and informed the VfS members that the Reichstag had already presented a petition to Bismarck in which he was asked to decide upon suitable measures against usury.[31]

The enormous interest in the results of the enquête on the part of government and the agrarian organizations even before the VfS had finally discussed it can partly be explained by the fact that the enquête had highlighted a kind of usury that aroused shock and resentment. This usury was not a mere matter of too high interest rates but of cheating and outwitting poor peasants not very well versed in business matters. In all the reports in which usury was diagnosed the peasants lost their property by way of deception.

"Typical" Examples of Usury

Three examples of "typical" usury will suffice to describe how the usurers proceeded.

First example: A peasant buys a cow but does not have to pay the full price immediately. The seller allows him to pay the rest at some point in the future when the peasant will have had a good harvest. However, even after a good harvest the seller might choose not to ask for the money. Only when the peasant finds himself short of money or without any money at all does the seller suddenly want to have all the money at once. When in this situation the peasant is not able to pay all the money, the seller threatens him to bring the case to court. The peasant reacts in panic and finally loses his farm. The usury occurred when the peasant was able to afford to pay the money but was persuaded by the seller not to do so.[32]

Second example: A peasant wants to buy either a piece of land or cattle in an auction. The day before the auction takes place the seller invites the peasant to a pub and, offering free beers, makes him drunk. Sometime during the evening the seller tempts the peasant to sign a contract at unfavorable conditions. Or the seller earlier paid money to some other people and offered them free beer under the condition that they would convince the peasant to buy the seller's products during the auction the next day.[33] The usury occurred when the seller invited the peasant or the "advertisers" to the pub the day before the auction.

Third example: A seller offers a young cow to a peasant to purchase on credit. The peasant takes the cow, but the seller remains the owner as long as the full price is not paid. Usually the price will be above the cow's value, and the payment deadlines are chosen so that the peasant probably will not be able to keep them. When the cow has gained weight and is worth more than when it was sold to the peasant, the seller asks the peasant to pay the rest of the price at a time when he knows that the peasant will not be able to pay. The peasant does not see another way out but to give the well-fed cow back without being refunded the money he has already paid, or the seller offers to replace the well-fed cow with a younger one and the procedure begins anew.[34] The intended usury started when the peasant took the cow and began feeding it.

There are numerous variations of usury to be found in the enquête reports in which peasants were cheated and found themselves trapped in a financial predicament. The reports provoked resentment and outrage not only because of the ways the usurers circumvented legal requirements such as written contracts and caps on interest rates but also because in nearly all reports those accused of committing usury were said to be Jews.

Mentions of Jews as Usurers in the Reports and the VfS Debate on the Rural Usury Enquête

The enquête on rural usury was discussed during the general meeting of the VfS in 1888. Mentions of Jews as usurers in the discussion and in the written reports differed according to the speaker's or reporter's aspiration to be objective and to commit himself to the scientific method.

First, there were those who did not mention Jews as usurers at all, such as Erwin Nasse (1829-90), a professor of national economy and president of the VfS since 1873. Nasse summarized the discussions on the enquête in the general meeting of the VfS in 1888. He pointed out that measures to prevent usury seemed to have been considered more important than putting pressure on usurers. It had become obvious that the peasants, mainly those with small farms in middle and southwest Germany, were unable to "resist" the advances of usurers because of their "low intellectual state of mind, their lack of independence in making decisions, their lack of sense for commercial issues and their inability to control the whole commercial process," "in short their [lack of] overall cultural abilities with regard to the farm business."[35] Even if there were more cooperative banks and better legal regulations, the peasants would still not be able to handle the borrowing process properly.[36] Nasse did not mention Jews as usurers a single time.

Second, a slightly higher number of references to Jews as usurers occurred when the attendees discussed the enquête results in the VfS general meeting of 1888. There was only one discussant who, intentionally or not, moved from referring to usurers as "traders" to claiming without proof that Jews were guilty of usury. A Dr. Heitz from Hohenheim asked how the traders were able to gain knowledge of the peasants' financial situation so that they could tempt them into unfair business. Heitz answered his own question by identifying these traders as Jews who would not have any problem accessing information from the real estate register, thereby learning about the financial situation of nearly all peasants in a village. He claimed that he had often heard that one only had to ask the "Israelite So-and-So" if one wanted to be informed about the general circumstances in a community; they were said to be better informed than the local pub owner or priest.[37] Heitz then continued his argument without further references to Jews. All other speakers talked about "traders" when criticizing usurers. Ministerialrath (a position in a government department) Buchenberger from Karlsruhe, who had gathered the information for and had written the report on the state of Baden, stated he wished that the reports had not exaggerated the issue of religious denomination of the usurers and that reporters had remained more objective in the face of the misery they had observed during their investigations.[38]

A much higher frequency of mentions of Jews as usurers is evident in the original reports that constituted the basis of the enquête. Even though most of those who reported about usury in the enquête volume were academics (e.g., they held a high position in the state administration, in the Christian Church, or in peasant organizations, or they were lawyers), they did not refrain from blunt accusations. More than half of the twenty-seven reports named Jews as the main usurers. Already in the second sentence of the first report, written by a Ministerialrath Metz about usury in Alsace-Lorraine, Jews were blamed as "natural" usurers. Metz started his report by saying, "Already in 1779 an anonymous paper was published with the title 'Observations d'un Alsacien sur l'affaire present des Juifs en Alsace' . . . in which the Jews were accused of being responsible for usury."[39] In the paper the author went on to describe how the peasants were urged to follow the usurers' advice. His description was nearly representative of the examples of usury given in subsequent enquête reports. In each case of usury the peasant was cheated because he did not understand the usurer's tactics. Metz and all the other authors seemed eager to make Jews responsible for all kinds of usury, whether when selling cattle, real estate, or consumer goods.[40] It seemed that for many authors *Jew* and *usurer* were synonyms. Some referred to an "Israelite element," as did Dr. Franz from Weimar, who reported on the state of Thuringia.[41] Some claimed that usury had a "direct relation to religious issues," meaning the Jewish religion, or that usurers were "mostly Jews" hiding their organized activities under the profession of "traders."[42] Still others wrote about the social and political power of the Jews, as, for example, when a day for the cattle market coincided with a Jewish religious holiday, the business would either be very poor or the Jews would move the market to another day.[43] Regierungsrath Fritz Schade found for the Großherzogtum Hessen that the most dangerous traders were "the hawker-Jews" (even if it was commonly acknowledged that hawking was not a form of usury). He described the hawker-usurer as initially poor but clever, moderate, and hardworking until he had reached his goal of becoming rich, while the fortunes of those he did business with, the peasants, were diminishing to the same extent.[44] But some reporters also found that some of the peasants were able to learn. Freiherr von Cetto reported from Bavaria that a peasant was able to free himself from "the Jewish usurer" in spite of being broke: he borrowed money from one of the cooperative credit banks when "the Jew" asked him to pay a contractual penalty.[45] Chaplain Georg Friedrich Dasbach (1846–1907), a Jesuit, social reformer, editor of a Catholic newspaper, and a recent member of the VfS, emphasized his opinion of the Jews as usurers when he printed in boldface a sentence about a Jew who was said to have planned to earn a fortune (50 Thaler) by way of usury in only fifty days.[46]

Very few authors conceded that usurers came from different professions and religions. For example, J. Schneider wrote about the state of Brandenburg that in some regions there were more Christian than Jewish usurers.[47] There were only two reports on usury (written by an advocate named Mahla on Bavaria and by a Landrath Knebel) in which the usury problem was outlined in detail without mention of the usurers' religion.[48] Other reports, mainly on the northeast regions of Germany such as Western Prussia, did not observe any usury and therefore no Jewish usurers.

Close reading of the texts suggests that the higher his position within the VfS, the less likely was an author to mention Jews as responsible for usury in the rural areas. The reason for this seems to have been the notion of scientificity. As president of the VfS, Nasse knew very well that the mandate of the VfS was to conduct enquêtes that met the demand for objective and adequate research methods. As the different frequencies of mentioning Jews indicate, most attendees of the VfS meeting seemed to have agreed that accusing Jews of being usurers was not based on methods that mirrored reality in an exact way and that most reports failed to describe the usurers objectively. Being "objective" meant being "scientific" in terms of method.[49]

One report that mentioned Jews implied still another dimension that went beyond the lack of objectivity. During the general meeting of the

VfS in 1888, the statistician Gottlieb Schnapper-Arndt, who will be dealt with in the next section, criticized authors who wrote their report without signing their name.[50] Hugo Thiel, the responsible coordinator of the usury enquête, explained that one author had asked him for anonymity. He had accepted this request because "in these times no one in this country can write anything that even looks from a distance as if it would be said against Jews without the author being dragged through the newspapers in a most unpopular way."[51] However, the only anonymous report, the one on Kassel, did not exceed the level of unfair comment on Jews found in those already cited except that the reporter explicitly denied being an "antisemite."[52] Thiel seems to be referring to a phenomenon that is discussed today as the quasi-censorship by "political correctness."[53] It may well have been the case that Jewish owners of newspapers used their clout to delegitimize anti-Jewish prejudice. However, Thiel's statement on the author's reasons for wishing to stay anonymous can also be interpreted as an expression of his own resentment against Jewish publishers.

The Critique of the Usury Enquête from a Scientific Point of View

The discussion about prejudices toward Jews shown in the reports of the usury enquête already had begun before the 1888 general meeting of the VfS. One of the main critiques came from Dr. Gottlieb Schnapper-Arndt (1846–1904), a statistician and private lecturer on social statistics who, in 1901, became a lecturer at the Akademie für Sozial-und Handelswissenschaften in Frankfurt am Main, the forerunner of Frankfurt University that was founded in 1914.[54] In spring 1888 Schnapper-Arndt presented his critique in a lecture held at the Freies Deutsches Hochstift, an association founded to preserve the cultural ideas of the revolution of 1848.[55] Schnapper-Arndt criticized the usury enquête from two angles: the way reporters accused Jews of being usurers and the questionnaire Thiel had developed.

The questionnaire for the enquête on rural usury had been developed by Hugo Thiel (1839–1918), privy counselor and assistant secretary of state in the Prussian Ministry of Agriculture since 1879. He had also been responsible for recruiting the men who were to report about usury in each federal state of Germany.[56] Before the discussion about the enquête on usury in 1888, the members of the VfS had never discussed how to develop a questionnaire. Like the questionnaires used in earlier enquêtes, the one on usury contained open-ended questions, to each of which Thiel added examples of what the reporter may be able to observe. For instance, question 4 asked if an extensive usury with goods could be observed: if peasants, for instance, received seed on credit and had to pay the credit with a part of their crop, or if the peasants received an inferior quality of goods in exchange for their rural products.[57] Question 5 asked whether the reporters observed that usurers "take over the entire business of a peasant, or if the usurers left peasants uninformed about their real financial situation ... if the traders could act like this because the peasant did not understand accountancy ... if usury was combined with a defiance of laws, if a promissory note could be executed in only one payment, or if the debtor is forced to sign a receipt for a cash loan even though he only agreed to share the future profit of some rather dubious business."[58] Some questions ran to half a page. They implied that the reporters would be able to identify usury when it occurred. It is important to add that no question Thiel formulated asked for the religious denomination of the usurers.

Schnapper-Arndt, for the first time in the history of empirical social research, argued that the questions were not detailed enough, that the reporters failed to try hard enough to get at the truth, and that reporters interpreted what they found in accordance with what the formulation of the questions suggested.[59] He proposed that each question should be answerable with a yes or no in order to neutralize its underlying tendentiousness. This and other proposals by Schnapper-Arndt have since been developed further and have become routine aspects of contemporary methodology in empirical social research. For instance, the questionnaire should not ask questions about the consequences of a social fact before it was clear that the social fact was indeed existent. Furthermore Schnapper-Arndt criticized suggestive questions, such as "Do peasants depend on usurers in a way that by necessity will impoverish them?" If the main aim of the enquête was to discover the forms, extent, and causes of usury in order to determine countermeasures, it would have to present "truthful" and "objective" answers.[60] Schnapper-Arndt also suggested trying to interview both the peasant and the usurer. This method had already been discussed by the VfS in the 1870s.[61] Schnapper-Arndt argued that the best way to achieve objectivity would have been to conduct a statistical survey in which pure numbers would describe the range of usury. However, he admitted that the subject of usury was too complex to be translated into statistics.[62] At the time statistical surveys and critical comments on the objectiveness of statistics were not common.

Schnapper-Arndt's other important criticism of the enquête was that generalizations from single cases were made in an inadmissible manner.[63] The theory of probability, which could determine the probability of the existence of a general phenomenon, had been discovered more than two hundred years earlier by Blaise Pascal (1623–60) and Pierre de Fermat (1608–65) and developed further by Pierre Simon Laplace (1749–1827) but had not yet found its way into the research practice of the VfS.[64]

Criticism of the Enquête from a Human Point of View

Schnapper-Arndt's critique of the questionnaire of the usury enquête as well as of the analysis contained in the individual reports could be evaluated as a decisive but not spectacular step forward in the development of scientific social research methodology. However, it seems that he attacked the usury enquête not only for its lack of objectivity. Schnapper-Arndt was himself Jewish (he was buried at the "old Jewish cemetery" in Frankfurt am Main,[65]) although he mentioned his religion neither in the VfS discussion on usury nor in his publication on the methods of the usury enquête. However, he concluded his presentation on the methodology of social enquêtes before the Freies Deutsches Hochstift with regret at having to mention what he described as a painful and ugly issue, namely the presence of "a whole anthology of insulting comments on Jews" as well as the fact that reporters seem to have felt they had to literally reproduce only "the Jewish jargon," although all reports were based on data collected from rural populations, all of whom obviously spoke a variety of dialects.[66] He refrained from enumerating the whole range of malicious slanders against Jews in the reports; instead he referred to an article by Julius Platter (1844–1923) in which all passages against Jews were quoted verbatim. However, Schnapper-Arndt emphasized that Platter's comment on the usury enquête was not written the way he would have done. Platter was a national economist who taught in Zurich and commented on the usury enquête from a socialist point of view, a political position that Schnapper-Arndt would not have dared to adopt while the antisocialist law was in effect.[67] Schnapper-Arndt merely pointed to the reports by Freiherr von Cetto, owner of a big farm, and by Chaplain G. F. Dasbach, who was the secretary of a peasants' association in southwest Germany, as examples of unfair and biased statements on Jews.[68] They would have consistently identified usurers as Jews and generalized from single cases to usury in general. Schnapper-Arndt urged his audience not to look for "race" as a cause of problems but to try to detect the true causalities behind the surface of phenomena. It was dangerous to assign general human characteristics to only one particular "race."[69] He furthermore warned the VfS not to use enquêtes to slander a whole professional or religious group.[70] He ended his presentation with a remarkable plea for humaneness. He argued that social problems could not be solved by accusing any social group for behaving in a bad way; instead he was convinced that only all-embracing love for humankind would lead to social reforms carried out successfully.[71] The VfS had always joined efforts to improve the lives of all human beings, and it should be spared from tendencies found in the usury enquête.[72] Finally, he quoted Francis Bacon (1561–1626): "We must solemnly and firmly resolve to renounce all prejudices forever, so as to cleanse and liberate our minds."[73]

Schnapper-Arndt repeated his (ultimately rather moderate) critique during the general meeting of the VfS in 1888. The members accepted his criticism, at least partly. Most of his suggested methodological innovations became routine in subsequent empirical social research, and no future enquête of the VfS was similarly accused of reproducing prejudice.

Summary

The 1887 enquête on rural usury conducted by the Verein für Socialpolitik produced a most controversial result due to its members' lack of sophisticated methods of empirical social research. Because of the missing expertise the enquête produced prejudicial results on two sociopolitically sensitive subjects: the situation of Jews within society and usury in poor rural areas of Germany. The tight interrelation between the two phenomena in combination with the lack of objectivity of the research results caused a broad but retort-free reaction within the academic and political community concerned with social reforms at the time. In the face of the difficult societal background of Jews since the foundation of Imperial Germany in 1871 and under the critical political position of the VfS during the antisocialist laws in the 1880s, Gottlieb Schnapper-Arndt, a member of the VfS, an expert in statistics, and himself a Jew, presented a critical analysis and, at the same time, gave valuable advice on how to conduct scientific and objective empirical social research. His plea for scientific research methods that would produce objective results implied fairness to the research subjects—in the case of rural usury, to Jews in Imperial Germany.

Notes

1. "Gesetz betreffend die Gleichberechtigung der Konfessionen in bürgerlicher und staatsbürgerlicher Beziehung."
2. Rürup, "Emancipation and Bourgeois Society," 84–86.
3. Hamburger, "One Hundred Years of Emancipation," 18.
4. Hamburger, "One Hundred Years of Emancipation," 20.
5. Zeitlin, *Fürst Bismarcks social-, wirtschafts- und steuerpolitische Anschauungen*, 14.
6. Zeitlin, *Fürst Bismarcks social-, wirtschafts- und steuerpolitische Anschauungen*, 15.
7. Weiland, *Otto Glagau und "Der Kulturkämpfer."*
8. Köllmann, "Bevölkerungsgeschichte," 20.
9. Borchardt, "Wirtschaftliches Wachstum und Wechsellagen," 264.
10. Briefs, "Das gewerbliche Proletariat," 149–52.
11. Born, *Von der Reichsgründung bis zum Ersten Weltkrieg*, 36.
12. Kersten-Conrad, *Der Verein für Sozialpolitik und seine Wirksamkeit*, 34.
13. *Schriften des Vereins für Socialpolitik*, 1872, 6. All volumes were published in Leipzig by Duncker & Humblot.
14. Gorges, *Sozialforschung*, 53–55.
15. Gorges, *Sozialforschung*, 36, 58.
16. Gorges, *Sozialforschung*, 58.
17. Gorges, *Sozialforschung*, 109–14 .
18. Gorges, *Sozialforschung*, 58.
19. Gorges, *Sozialforschung*, 58.
20. Literally, the VfS stood for "auf einer höheren Zinne . . . als auf der Zinne der Partei"). *Schriften des Vereins für Socialpolitik* 28 (1884): 2; 47: 4.
21. *Schriften des Vereins für Socialpolitik* 28 (1884): 2.
22. "Das Erbrecht und die Grundeigentumsverteilung im Deutschen Reich. [Die Verteilung des landwirtschaftlich genutzten Grundeigentums und das gemeine Erbrecht]." *Schriften des Vereins für Socialpolitik* 20 (1882).
23. Gorges, *Sozialforschung*, 161.
24. "Bäuerliche Zustände in Deutschland," *Schriften des Vereins für Socialpolitik* 22–24 (1883); *Schriften des Vereins für Socialpolitik* 28 (1884).
25. Gorges, *Sozialforschung*, 162.
26. *Schriften des Vereins für Socialpolitik* 32 (1886).
27. *Schriften des Vereins für Socialpolitik* 36 (1888); *Schriften des Vereins für Socialpolitik* 38 (1888).
28. *Schriften des Vereins für Socialpolitik* 36 (1888): 2.

29. Liebner, *Wucher und Staat*, 14, 314.

30. *Schriften des Vereins für Socialpolitik* 35 (1887): iii.

31. *Schriften des Vereins für Socialpolitik* 36 (1888): 5.

32. See, for example, *Schriften des Vereins für Socialpolitik* 35 (1887): 22.

33. See, for example, *Schriften des Vereins für Socialpolitik* 35 (1887): 99.

34. See, for example, *Schriften des Vereins für Socialpolitik* 35 (1887): 312.

35. *Schriften des Vereins für Socialpolitik* 36 (1888): 110, translated by the author; Gorges, "Usury and Social Exclusion in Imperial Germany," 240.

36. *Schriften des Vereins für Socialpolitik* 36 (1888): 111.

37. *Schriften des Vereins für Socialpolitik* 38 (1888): 97; Gorges, "Usury and Social Exclusion in Imperial Germany," 240.

38. *Schriften des Vereins für Socialpolitik* 35 (1887): 17–52; *Schriften des Vereins für Socialpolitik* 38 (1888): 92.

39. The reference is to the pamphlet's second edition, Neuchatel 1790; *Schriften des Vereins für Socialpolitik* 35 (1887): 1.

40. See, for instance, *Schriften des Vereins für Socialpolitik* 35 (1887): 194, 216, 219, 227, 248, 253, 262, 285, 304.

41. *Schriften des Vereins für Socialpolitik* 35 (1887): 272.

42. *Schriften des Vereins für Socialpolitik* 35 (1887): 19, 54.

43. *Schriften des Vereins für Socialpolitik* 35 (1887): 55.

44. *Schriften des Vereins für Socialpolitik* 35 (1887): 74.

45. *Schriften des Vereins für Socialpolitik* 35 (1887): 89.

46. "Der Jude rechnete sich also einen Gewinn von 50 Thalern für die Zeit von 50 Tagen." *Schriften des Vereins für Socialpolitik* 35 (1887): 154. The Mark replaced the Thaler in 1871 but was kept as the second currency until 1907. 1 Thaler or Taler = 3 Mark (Caspar, *Vom Taler zum Euro*).

47. *Schriften des Vereins für Socialpolitik* 35 (1887): 291.

48. *Schriften des Vereins für Socialpolitik* 35 (1887): 113, 121.

49. *Schriften des Vereins für Socialpolitik* 38 (1888): 79.

50. *Schriften des Vereins für Socialpolitik* 38 (1888): 83.

51. "Weil jetzt kein Mensch im Lande mehr irgend etwas schreiben kann, was nur entfernt so aussieht, als ob es gegen Juden gerichtet sei, ohne in der allermißliebigsten Weise durch die Presse geschleift zu werden." *Schriften des Vereins für Socialpolitik* 38 (1888): 105, translated by the author.

52. *Schriften des Vereins für Socialpolitik* 38 (1888): 218.

53. See, for instance, Noelle-Neumann, *Öffentliche Meinung*; Felsmann, *Mediale Tabubrüche*.

54. Zander, "Gründung der Handelshochschulen," 126–44; Gorges, "Usury and Social Exclusion in Imperial Germany," 241.

55. Schnapper-Arndt, *Zur Methodologie sozialer Enqueten*. The association's renowned successors were the Akademie zur Wissenschaftlichen Erforschung und Pflege des Deutschtums/Deutsche Akademie (Academy for Scholarly Research and Fostering of German Culture and Language/German Acad-

emy), founded in 1925 and, after it was closed down in 1945, reopened as the Goethe Institute in 1951.

56. *Schriften des Vereins für Socialpolitik* 35 (1887): iii.

57. *Schriften des Vereins für Socialpolitik* 35 (1887): vii.

58. *Schriften des Vereins für Socialpolitik* 35 (1887): vii.

59. Gorges, *Sozialforschung*, 178.

60. Schnapper-Arndt, *Zur Methodologie sozialer Enqueten*, 18.

61. Gorges, *Sozialforschung*, 104.

62. Schnapper-Arndt, *Zur Methodologie sozialer Enqueten*, 5.

63. Schnapper-Arndt, *Zur Methodologie sozialer Enqueten*, e.g., 27, 31.

64. Laplace, *Théorie analytique des probabilités*.

65. See "Grave of Dr. Gottlieb Schnapper-Arndt."

66. "Ich kann die Erörterung dieses Punktes nicht übergehen, soviel des Peinlichen, ich möchte sagen Unschönen, ihr auch innewohnt. . . . Eine ganze Blumenlese beleidigender, die Juden als solche verächtlich machender Äusserungen und Wendungen, ist aus zahlreichen dieser Berichte zusammenzustellen, und der jüdische Jargon ist der einzige Dialekt, den diese Berichte, die doch alle unter Bauernbevölkerungen spielen, zuweilen in Naturtreue glauben wiedergeben zu sollen." Schnapper-Arndt, *Zur Methodologie sozialer Enqueten*, 39.

67. Schnapper-Arndt, *Zur Methodologie sozialer Enqueten*, n40. Schnapper-Arndt referred to Julius Platter, "Der Wucher und die Bauern in Deutschland," *Deutsche Worte*, edited by Engelbert Pernerstorfer, April–May 1888. Unfortunately the article by Platter was not accessible to the author.

68. Schnapper-Arndt, *Zur Methodologie sozialer Enqueten*, 85–112, 151–212, 41–43.

69. Schnapper-Arndt, *Zur Methodologie sozialer Enqueten*, 44.

70. Schnapper-Arndt, *Zur Methodologie sozialer Enqueten*, 23.

71. "Nur von den Prinzipien allumfassender Menschenliebe ausgehend, dies ist wenigstens meine Überzeugung, werden die sozialreformatorischen Bestrebungen unserer Tage Erfolg haben können, wahren Erfolg." Schnapper-Arndt, *Zur Methodologie sozialer Enqueten*, 45.

72. The citation reads, "Möchten schöne Bestrebungen, wie diejenigen, deren Förderung der Verein für Sozialpolitik mit in die Hand nahm, fürderhin vor solchen Trübungen verschont bleiben." Schnapper-Arndt, *Zur Methodologie sozialer Enqueten*, 45.

73. "Allen Vorurteilen müssen wir strenge und feierlich für immer entsagen, den Verstand reinigen und frei machen." Schnapper-Arndt, *Zur Methodologie sozialer Enqueten*, 46. [This is from Bacon's *Novum Organum* (1620), aphorism 68; the original Latin passage from which this is taken reads, "Atque de idolorum singulis generibus, eorumque apparatu jam diximus; quae omnia constanti et solenni decreto sunt abneganda et renuncianda, et intellectus ab iis omnino liberandus est et expurgandus." The German version quoted by Schnapper-Arndt translates "idols" as *Vorurteile*, "prejudices."—Editor.]

References

Albrecht, Gerhard, et al., eds. *Grundriss der Sozialökonomik IX. Abteilung. Das soziale System des Kapitalismus, I. Teil. Die gesellschaftliche Schichtung im Kapitalismus.* Tübingen: J. B. Mohr (Paul Siebeck), 1926.

Aubin, Hermann, and Walter Zorn, eds. *Handbuch der deutschen Wirtschafts- und Sozialgeschichte.* Vol. 2. Stuttgart: Klett-Cotta, 1976.

Borchardt, Knut. "Wirtschaftliches Wachstum und Wechsellagen 1800–1914." In *Handbuch der Wirtschafts-und Sozialgeschichte*, edited by Herrmann Aubin and Walter Zorn, 2: 198–275. Stuttgart: Klett-Cotta, 1976.

Born, Karl Erich. *Von der Reichsgründung bis zum Ersten Weltkrieg: Handbuch der deutschen Geschichte.* Vol. 16. 2d ed. Edited by (Bruno) Gebhardt. Stuttgart: Klett, 1976.

Briefs, Götz. "Das gewerbliche Proletariat." In *Grundriss der Sozialökonomik IX. Abteilung. Das soziale System des Kapitalismus, I. Teil. Die gesellschaftliche Schichtung im Kapitalismus*, edited by Gerhard Albrecht et al., 124–240. Tübingen: J. C. B. Mohr (Paul Siebeck), 1927.

Caspar, Helmut. *Vom Taler zum Euro: Die Berliner, ihr Geld und ihre Münze.* 2d revised ed. Berlin: Story, 2006.

Felsmann, Klaus-Dieter, ed. *Mediale Tabubrüche vs. Political Correctness. Erweiterte Dokumentation zu den 12. Buckower Mediengesprächen.* Munich: Kopaed, 2008.

Gorges, Irmela. *Sozialforschung in Deutschland 1872–1914: Gesellschaftliche Einflüsse auf Themen und Methodenwahl des Vereins für Sozialpolitik.* 2d ed. Königstein im Taunus: Anton Hain, 1986.

———. "Usury and Social Exclusion in Imperial Germany during the 1880s." In *The World Economy: Contemporary Challenges*, edited by Irena K. Heijduk and Wieslaw M. Grudzewski, 231–44. Warsaw: Difin, 2011.

"Grave of Dr. Gottlieb Schnapper-Arndt (1846–1904)." http://www.flickr.com/photos/33784579@n05/5266127077/ (accessed November 6, 2013).

Hamburger, Ernst. "One Hundred Years of Emancipation." In *Leo Baeck Institute Yearbook xiv*, 3–66. London: Horovitz, 1969.

Kersten-Conrad, Else. *Der Verein für Sozialpolitik und seine Wirksamkeit auf dem Gebiet der Arbeiterfrage.* Halle: Fischer, 1906.

Köllmann, Wolfgang. "Bevölkerungsgeschichte 1800–1970." In *Handbuch der Wirtschafts-und Sozialgeschichte*, edited by Wolfgang Rubin and Walter Zorn, 2: 9–50. Stuttgart: Klett-Cotta, 1976.

Laplace, Pierre-Simon. *Théorie analytique des probabilités.* 1925. 4th ed. Paris: Gabay, 1995.

Liebner, Katrin. *Wucher und Staat: Die Theorie des Zinswuchers im Deutschland des 18. und 19. Jahrhunderts.* Berlin: Duncker und Humblot, 2010.

Noelle-Neumann, Elisabeth. *Öffentliche Meinung: Die Entdeckung der Schweigespirale.* Enlarged ed. Frankfurt am Main: Ullstein, 1989.

Rürup, Reinhard. "Emancipation and Bourgeois Society." In *Leo Baeck Institute Yearbook XIV: Publications of the Leo Baeck Institute*, 67–91. London: Horovitz, 1969.

Schnapper-Arndt, Gottlieb. *Zur Methodologie sozialer Enqueten: Mit besonderem Hinblick auf die Erhebungen über den Wucher auf dem Lande*. Frankfurt am Main: Franz Benjamin Auffahrt, 1888.

Weiland, Daniela. *Otto Glagau und "Der Kulturkämpfer": Zur Entstehung des modernen Antisemitismus im frühen Kaiserreich*. Berlin: Metropole, 2004.

Zander, Gunther Herbert. "Gründung der Handelshochschulen im deutschen Kaiserreich (1898-1919)." PhD dissertation, University of Cologne, 2004.

Zeitlin, Leon. *Fürst Bismarcks social-, wirtschafts-und steuerpolitische Anschauungen: Darstellung und Kritik*. Leipzig: Richard Wöpke, 1902.

4

Coldly Admiring the Jews

*Werner Sombart and Classical German Sociology
on Nationalism and Race*

Y. MICHAL BODEMANN

How did classical German sociology address the question of the nation
and of ethnonational solidarities? It might be argued that the founders of
German sociology—Weber, Simmel, Sombart, and Tönnies—institutionally
also among the founders of the German Sociological Society, together
with Robert Michels and Franz Oppenheimer had to deal with two different traditions, which in turn were at variance with their own bourgeois
nationalist German sociological tradition as it established itself around
the turn of the century. The first tradition they had to contend with was
what Werner Sombart later attacked as "proletarian socialism": an "anti-
national," "anti-German" and "rootless," "Jewish dominated" movement
best represented by Heinrich Heine's enthusiasm for republican France,[1]
Marx and Engels's internationalism, and the internationalism of much
of the early German labor movement, which originally used the "Mar-
seillaise" as its own anthem. This internationalism was in the tradition
of the Europeanist spirit of the Napoleonic period between about 1804
and 1814.[2] Marx and Engels's dismissal of the "peoples without history," a rejection of ethnonational bonds in favor of a (European-defined)
cosmopolitanism centering, however, around the "historical" peoples
of France, Germany, and England, was and still is the most noteworthy
expression of this internationalism.

A second tradition sociology had to contend with was that of racial
hygiene and a large and varied body of racial theories that had spread
throughout Europe, and Germany in particular, influenced by Gobineau

and H. S. Chamberlain.[3] These theories, however, especially the eugenic theories, were found across the entire political spectrum from right to left and among non-Jews and Jews alike.[4] German racialist thought found encouragement through three modern phenomena. The first was the experience of the breakdown of the old feudal order, the development of an industrial, ethnically diverse working class with its massive urbanization. The second phenomenon was the colonial experience, first indirectly via France and Britain as the major colonial powers, but later directly with the development of Germany's own colonies in Africa (1884) and China (1897). The German "discovery" in the nineteenth century of the United States plays a role here as well.[5] Gobineau's theories regarding the white, yellow, and black races as well as his theories about a French aristocracy, Frankish-Germanic in origin, ruling over inferior Celtic masses, relates to both these phenomena. Last but not least, racist thought was triggered by Jewish emancipation during the Napoleonic wars and, already much before the turn of the century, by steady and mounting Jewish immigration from the East and the new role of the Jew in modernity. The racist anti-Jewish theme was developed by Chamberlain and his admirers in Germany, most notably perhaps Richard and Cosima Wagner and their circle in Bayreuth.

The First Soziologentag

The first and the second German Soziologentage, meetings of the German Sociological Society in 1910 and 1912, were fully enmeshed in these issues, and its animated debates are a useful indicator of where the emerging community of academic sociology stood at the time. In light of the national debates in Germany, it was clearly no accident that the organizers of the First Soziologentag featured a long paper by the then leading racial biologist and editor of the *Archiv für Rassen-und Gesellschaftsbiologie*, Alfred Ploetz. At these meetings, Ploetz wanted to sketch the major issues concerning the polarity of race and society and of society as a unitary organism. When human society is seen as a unitary organism, however, a number of issues pertaining to the health of the "social body" become crucial. In Tönnies's apt summary of Ploetz's position, "There is this contrasting tendency: on one hand, the tendency of society that is expressed in the morality of altruism, to help and therefore to support the weak; on the other hand, the interest of the race, the enduring biological unit, to preserve itself. This latter interest demands the extermination of the weak, whereas society wants to preserve the weak."[6] The key issue here is undoubtedly the imagery of the social collectivity of race constituted as a unitary organism rather than as a collectivity consisting of interrelated but separate elements: an organism is by necessity affected in its entirety by deterioration from inside, by attacks from outside, by internal fission or by fusion with another organism. This imagery, then, addressed the key issues of the underclass in Germany—the emergence of the working class—and the apperception of the stranger. Accordingly Ploetz's imagery of race as an organism reverberated around a number of issues. First was the issue of racial mixture, which in his view—and that of other race theorists before him—might be of only short duration because of reduced fertility, or it would produce "culturally inferior" societies. This had occurred, Ploetz contended, in the case of the "republics of tropical America." The former, in his view, could be seen in North America, where "the Indians, and in the South Sea the Polynesians, faced by whites, melt like snow in the sun," and where in relation to blacks, segregation is increasingly severe. Since race/society—the distinction is in fact often blurred—is dealt with as an organism, medical nomenclatures apply, and Ploetz speaks of the physiology, the pathology, and the hygiene of race. Racial health may well be affected by such destructive external forces as industrialization or the importation of "alien bacteria and poisons" such as "intoxicating beverages."[7] Those societies in which solidarity of its members and mutual help are strong are a "weapon" in support of the race, whereas degeneracy loosens the social fabric.

In the introduction to the following discussion of Ploetz's contribution, a paper in which Ploetz had attempted to be very circumspect and scientific in his tone, Sombart as the session chair thanked the speaker for having introduced "tremendous ferment" into the gathering, and it is of interest how the audience had "read" the racial biologist. In the context of environmental and genetic factors, members of the audience sympathetic to racial biology challenged sociology to explain such phenomena as "vagabondage," "begging," "prostitution," "sexual perversity," and juvenile crime; they associated environmental explanations with the position of the social democrats and addressed racial biology in terms of the great questions of the day: Could modern industrial relations still be seen in terms of social solidarity, or were they exploitative relations instead? How could the glory of the German nation be attained for at least a short period of time, and to what extent was Ancient Greece a mirror of contemporary times? Ferdinand Tönnies, a strong critic of Ploetz, asked who were the societally and racially weak individuals. Are the physically strong to be given preference, and should those who were physically weak but of high intelligence not be maintained? The families of great minds, Tönnies contended, often became extinct with their deaths, such as in the case of Goethe, a "physiologically weak" individual. Similarly Moses Mendelssohn was a cripple, yet his family produced the composer Mendelssohn-Bartholdy and other able individuals until today; the "preservation of cripples might therefore be . . . of the highest value."[8]

The second half of this debate was taken up with Max Weber's debate of Ploetz. In contrast to Tönnies's critique, Weber seemed less radical. He accepted the thesis of the historical effects of racial selection such as the effects of negative selection of disadvantaged individuals in the Middle Ages, but often, he added, the wrong people were selected out. The societal principle of neighborly love, for example, often worked in the opposite direction by excluding, through celibacy, some of the brightest, most able members from procreation. One modern version of neighborly love, social policy, on the other hand, might select those who are economically weak but are strong "in terms of racial hygiene"; here neighborly love might in fact work to strengthen racial hygiene—evidently Weber's answer to some conservative critics of the welfare system.

Weber discounted the idea of racial instincts and of an inborn aversion of whites against blacks, claimed by "respected gentlemen in Dr. Ploetz's journal." Such racial instincts were expressed, for example, in the alleged aversion against the bodily odor of one race by the other: "I can take recourse to my own nose and in closest contact have not perceived anything of this sort."[9] Instead blacks even in the northern United States were treated with contempt and fear because, for reasons of tradition, they constituted a labor force that demanded little. Moreover the contemporary bourgeois American wanted to be an aristocrat in the European sense of the term and thus needed something to be contemptuous of.[10]

In response to his critics, Ploetz expressed the wish that the achievements of the ancient Greeks could have persisted until our days. This would have been possible only if the racial quality "present in the upper stratum of the Greek people" had persisted.[11] He conceded that, generally, some individuals were born into a situation without access to resources; yet "in the poorer classes, there are a large number of people who have been pushed into it on account of certain defects. You yourself know and you can observe every day how a person who lacks nothing else but the most simple drive to economise, who throws his money out the window, is finally forced to go to America to wash dishes or to perish [*verkommt*] in any other way."[12]

Ploetz finally returned to the "question of the Negroes." "Yankees" and other better inhabitants refused to interact socially with blacks because they felt embarrassed by the lack of moral inhibition, the more defective intelligence, and the "on average more silly behaviour of the Negroes," who are excluded "because of their inferiority in intellectual and moral terms."[13] Weber interjected that the most distinguished sociologist in the southern states, W. E. B. Du Bois, was black, and that Weber had had the chance to have breakfast with him in St. Louis, though a southern gentleman would have found it scandalous to be associated with him. In his own summation, toward the end of the session, Weber stated that he expected from the "Messrs. race biologists, . . . and what we surely will receive from them some day, is the exact proof of very specific causal relations [*Einzelzusammenhänge*], that is, the key significance of very concrete inherited qualities for concrete individual phenomena of social life. This, gentlemen, is missing so far."[14] Evidently in light of such hostile reaction, Ploetz resignedly concluded, "It does not matter to us racial biologists how sociology proceeds. We have [in our discipline] particular needs that we must fulfill."[15] Sombart, more sympathetically disposed to Ploetz, insisted in his final remarks as chair of the session, "also in the name of my friend Max Weber," that sociology did indeed have a mutual interest with biology, and he hoped, the apparent rejection by sociologists notwithstanding, that in future they would discuss these problems with Dr. Ploetz and his friends "very often."[16]

What were the major themes of this debate on race in Frankfurt am Main on the morning of Friday, October 21, 1910? Sombart, in the final remarks just mentioned, referred to the significance of biology for the decline of Greece and for the "Negro question in America." I would contend, however, that these two themes were displacements for very sensitive questions relating to the internal and external constitution of Germany, and of great concern in Germany itself. The first theme concerns the social upheavals created by capitalism, with the emergence of the working class as a threat to established order and bourgeois culture. The sociologists here discounted the social Darwinist explanation provided by racial biology. The superiority or inferiority of a particular social group had to be explained by the material resources available to these groups, by their respective traditions and cultures. Rather than eliminating inferior genetic stock, as the racial biologists suggested, the sociologists tended to advocate a social policy that would improve social conditions.

The second major theme was that of the status, and the superiority, of Germany in relation to other nations—a theme just as close to Ploetz as to the sociologists. In his paper Ploetz had repeatedly invoked the importance of solidarity and of mutual help for the strength of the race and of society. Solidarity was important in light of internal and external threats such as parasitism, miscegenation, and the threat from highly reproductive groups; elsewhere he had spoken of the high birth rate of the Poles at the eastern border of Germany "that is pushing us back."[17] Principally this second theme was dealt with not in relation to modern Germany but transposed to Ancient Rome and Greece instead. Weber more than the others rejected Ploetz's theories concerning biologically debilitated elites that were so clearly influenced by Gobineau and Chamberlain. Instead Weber suggested—for the case of Rome and Greece but with obvious reference also to modern Germany—that a historically significant nation would best survive by means of a strong and culturally rich elite that was firm in its tastes and traditions.

Remarkably, throughout this long debate there was no open discussion of the possible genetic inferiority of the German lower class,[18] nor a discussion of the Other/stranger in the German context. The discussion of ethnos and nation was bracketed for Germany. In the eyes of the majority of both the sociologists and the racial biologists, Germany seemed apparently ethnically homogeneous, and although the proliferative Poles were indeed recognized as a threat to the eastern border, the Danes and Frisians in the North, Belgians and Alsatians in the western part of the monarchy, and the influx of eastern Europeans into Germany, especially from the Balkans, and of such visible minorities as Ostjuden, were ignored. One important Jewish name, that of Moses Mendelssohn, was raised several times, as we have seen, by Tönnies and by Robert Goldscheid, a Viennese Jew. Should he have been "preserved" or "selected out"?[19] Despite the obvious relevance, Mendelssohn's Jewishness was not raised even once; his case was discussed as that of a cripple—arguably a metaphor for Jewishness, because bodily deformity was associated with the Jews.[20] Instead of discussing ethnonational diversity at home, the entire debate about the ethnic or racial stranger, and of his body odor, was transposed into a safer, exoticized terrain: the United States.

On other occasions, however, at least five major sociologists—Simmel, Sombart, and Tönnies, but also Weber and Michels—had addressed the phenomenon of the stranger. It is of interest to examine these discussions in some detail.

Three Strangers

The first of the three to write about the stranger was Georg Simmel. His essay "The Stranger" appeared first as "Exkurs über den Fremden" in his *Soziologie* (1908), but earlier brief tentative formulations can be found in his *Philosophy of Money* that appeared in 1900, and essays such as "The Metropolis and Mental Life" ("Die Grossstadt und das Geistesleben" [1903/1950]) address this issue obliquely as well.[21] It is important to see, then, that Simmel's interest in the stranger derives from his interest in modernity: the stranger is a product of the increasing division of labor, and in earlier times his domain was that of money; the stranger is neither friend nor foe but instead is utterly indifferent.[22] In Sombart, by contrast, the modernizing stranger is the Jew tout court rather than modernizers who might also be Jews.

Simmel's essay begins with the important observation that the stranger represents the "unity of two determinations": that of wandering, being detached from space, and that of being fixed in a particular space. In contrast to the wanderer who comes today and leaves tomorrow, the stranger, in Simmel's famous formulation, "comes today and stays tomorrow"; "he is the potentially wandering person who although he has not moved on also has not fully overcome the detachment of coming and going." He therefore represents the unity of nearness and distance, he is an "element of the group." The stranger appears in the development of the economy as the merchant for products produced outside one's own sphere, and he must be a stranger to one of these spheres. He is detached from the soil "and enters a sphere, so to speak, as 'supernumerary' in which all the economic positions are already occupied. The classical example is provided by the history of European Jews."[23]

The stranger, Simmel says, since he is not organically connected through fixities of kin, locale or profession, is characterized by objectivity. This requires not simply distance and noninvolvement but is a "particular formation made up of distance and nearness, indifference and engagement." Objectivity signifies freedom but has dangerous potentialities, because often outside emissaries and agitators are being blamed for rebellions of all sorts; the stranger is freer because he is not tied by habituation, piety, or precedents. It is important to see that he is always a member of the group; this distinguishes the stranger from the "inhabitant of Sirius," which is a nonrelation, or from the relationship of the Greeks to the Barbarians, people who are denied all general human characteristics. Strangers, on the other hand, have human characteristics, although they are not seen as individuals but rather represent a particular type, as evident in the medieval Jews' tax, which was levied irrespective of the individual income characteristics of the Jew.[24]

Sombart's phenomenology of the stranger, written only a few years later and contained in his *Die Juden und das Wirtschaftsleben* (*The Jews and Modern Capitalism* [1911]) shows some interesting parallels and telling differences. In order to understand the Jews' particular capitalist abilities, Sombart argues, one must examine their peculiar position within the national communities (*Volksgemeinschaften*) in which they were active. This position concerns especially their spatial dispersal, their character as semicitizens, their wealth, and their role as strangers. Precisely where the Jews were least at home, they were at their most effective. As new immigrants they had to keep their eyes open in order to quickly find their bearings in the new environment. "While the natives [*Alteingesessene*] still lie in their warm beds, they [the Jews] stand outside in the fresh morning air and first have to seek to build themselves a nest."[25] As strangers, as interlopers (*Eindringlinge*), they have to think practically about the kind of production or trade they want to pursue and whom to link up with; they therefore replace traditionalism with rationalism.

Social-psychologically, the Jews were also strangers because of the inner contrast between them and the surrounding population, due to "an almost caste-like separation from their host peoples." They were "segregated and therefore closed up together [*zusammengeschlossen*], or if you prefer, they were close together and therefore segregated." The Jews saw themselves as "something special" and in return were seen as such by their hosts. This has led among Jews "to types of action and mentalities that by necessity emerge in the contact with strangers"; it has loosened the bond of moral obligation and has eased one's conscience; the inter- action with strangers has always been more inconsiderate. Their segre- gation, in the last instance, is wanted by them; the hostile attitudes of the surrounding populations toward them are normally secondary. Even in antiquity, their dislike of others was noted, and they thank God in their prayers that he did not make them Gentiles.[26]

The differences between Sombart and Simmel are therefore readily apparent. Sombart's image of the stranger is absorbed entirely by his imagination of the Jew, whereas for Simmel the Jew is merely the pro- totypical or metaphorical stranger. While Simmel admits that the Jews are not organically connected to society at large, they nevertheless are members of the group and in contact with everyone. Sombart's Jew, on the other hand, is segregated, whereas Simmel's stranger/Jew is distant *and* close, indifferent *and* involved, which explains his objectivity. Som- bart's Jew is, like Simmel's stranger, nontraditional and rational, but while Simmel's stranger is engaged and involved, Sombart's stranger is indif- ferent toward the state and politically without color. Most important, however, while Simmel's stranger is distant *and* near, one who comes today and stays tomorrow, Sombart's Jew is the distant stranger, the in- terloper who comes today and leaves tomorrow: the wanderer, the me- dieval Ahasverus utterly indifferent to his environment.[27]

Tönnies writes about the stranger-as-merchant only two years af- ter Sombart, in 1913, in an essay entitled "Individuum und Welt in der Neuzeit" (Individual and world in the modern period), republished in a collection in 1926. Very much like Simmel, he finds that individualism and the individual evolve more fully in the modern period, and initial- ly in the economy: the merchant or trader assumes an increasingly im- portant role, more aware of his personal interest than the traditional es- tates; less sedentary, he travels as part of his profession; he moves from the narrow confines of his town into the large economic region that he sees spread out before himself. Similarly strangeness and the stranger in general encourage the growth of a businesslike spirit, that is, pursuing one's own advantage. Most apparent in Europe is the case of the Jews, "a dispersed remnant of the ancient urban civilisation," held together as a "homeless people of religion" through kin ties and the faith in their God.

Predestined as intermediaries, they assume an increasingly important role in the process of commodification. They are "hated, feared and persecuted the more medieval culture mobilises in its struggle against the forces that are its enemies." As this struggle progresses, tolerance begins first in the Protestant areas and eventually results in legal emancipation. Where Simmel virtually equated the merchant with the stranger, Tönnies equates the merchant with the Jew; their characteristics (*Wesen*) melt in with trade and capitalism to such a degree "that some characteristic traits that are considered to be Jewish describe trade, especially money and banking in general, although they are often intensified by Jewish idiosyncrasies. On the other hand, their alienness towards their host people is maintained or strengthened the more in modern life they are brought together in large numbers, that is, in the metropolis, and the more widespread in the modern world strangeness and the struggle of all against all become." Just as, "most clearly in the case of the Jews," other racial or religious strangers as well form among themselves a "community [*Gemeinschaft*], a type of conspiracy that tends towards inconsiderateness [*Rücksichtslosigkeit*] towards others."[28]

Here the positive aspects of the stranger that we found in Simmel's more optimistic analysis have disappeared completely; in Tönnies's *Kulturpessimismus* the Jew as stranger is a very distant figure; he is characterized neither by freedom nor by objectivity; he epitomized the modern merchant-stranger and, insofar as he is at the core of capitalism, promotes the war of all against all. We see, then, that in contrast to Simmel's Jew, who is always also involved and a member of the group, the stranger/Jew in Sombart and Tönnies, as in Weber, is segregated by his own free will, and his behavior toward his hosts is willfully calculative or even cunning. As strangers, Jews decompose the traditional ties of Gemeinschaft. None of the three sociologists, however, provides any sense of a Jewish community: no sense of their internal structuration and utterly unable to recognize Gemeinschaft structures in this community itself.

The Second Soziologentag, the *Archiv*, and the *Handwörterbuch*

Tönnies had proposed that the second sociology meetings in 1912 be devoted to the "concepts of people and nation in relation to race, state and language."[29] The theme of race, then, as we have seen, and not class, was a major issue in the early sociological debates in Germany; it was, however, the outcome of a diverse variety of interests and ideas. As indicated earlier, I agree with Friedrich Lenger, Sombart's biographer, that in these early debates the issue of race, and of ethnonational phenomena, was used in part at least to keep Marxist analyses at bay; the anti-Marxist sentiment had already been apparent when, in his paper at the first Soziologentag, Alfred Ploetz addressed the question of the working class from the perspective of racial hygiene. He pointed to the massive increase of social legislation being directed at an ever larger number of weaker members of society (*Volksgenossen*) that debilitated the genetic stock and also referred to British suggestions that industrialization might damage the quality of race.[30] This diversionary strategy, skirting the issue of class and dealing with race and the nation instead, was spelled out explicitly by Sombart, who apparently had turned away from his earlier work on modern capitalism and now stated, in the discussion during the Second Soziologentag, "But let us not underestimate the great merit of race theory: that it has freed us from the domination of the materialist conception of history, that it has provided us with a new point of view."[31] As it turned out, the Second Soziologentag did in fact not include any Marxist-oriented contributions; in part at least this had to do with the fact that, excluding the Austro-Marxist School, most Marxist-oriented scholars skirted the issue of ethnonational solidarities. The second question, however, that, often obliquely and in peculiar ways, played a role in shaping these sociological debates before the war, including the plans for the Second Soziologentag, concerned the Jews. Sombart, expressly supported by Weber, argued that the "concept or the essence of the phenomena under consideration—that is, nation, people, etc." must be clarified because "how else should we take a position regarding, after all, the most important nationalities question today—the Jewish one? We would skirt the issue if we did not admit into discussion in some form the question, so burning for millions of Jews: are we a people, are we a nation—and do we have the right to act as one?"[32] Sombart and also Weber, then, recognized that the Jewish question was an important issue that had to be addressed by sociologists. Nevertheless Tönnies opposed including this theme in the program of the Second Soziologentag, and Simmel opposed dealing with the issues of race, *Volk*, and nation altogether because "we should choose topics where the dilettante babblers have to shut up."[33] It might be surmised that Simmel himself could have been concerned about getting embroiled personally in the race issue and the issue of his Jewishness. This is suggested, for example, by Sombart's ad hominem remarks directed against Franz Oppenheimer, the strongest critic of race theory. Leading the discussion at the Second Soziologentag, for example, Sombart had attacked Oppenheimer with these words: "And if he is fighting race theory so bitterly, may he not himself be an interested party?"[34]

The Jewish question, then, the question of the Jewish nationality, not to speak of the question of antisemitism in Germany, was never made an issue at the sociology meetings before World War I if we exclude some minor comments by Weber on whether the Jews could be considered a nation,[35] or Tönnies's response to Ploetz at the First Soziologentag concerning Moses Mendelssohn.

What in fact was presented and discussed at the Second Soziologentag? The meeting attempted a systematic discussion of the idea of people and nation. Paul Barth addressed the question of "nationality in its sociological significance"; Ferdinand Schmid spoke about "nationalities and the law," Ludo Moritz Hartmann on "nation as a political factor," Franz Oppenheimer on "the racial philosophy of history," and Robert Michels on "the historical development of the idea of the fatherland." The result was remarkable: Barth's paper was a tedious discussion of the nation, which in his view appeared constant throughout history, from antiquity onward, and which he juxtaposed to a universalistic idea of humanity; it was replete with citations from Plato, Kant, and Fichte and found that sympathy to one's Volk was emotionally enriching. Predictably the discussion following this paper was thin, with dutiful but critical comments by Tönnies and Weber. The second paper, on nationalities and the law, even more tedious, brought no response at all, and the lackluster discussion took issue with Hartmann's definition of the nation as a "community of culture." Weber predictably wondered how much *Kulturgemeinschaft* there was between the aristocracy and the proletariat of a country and insisted on the German Sociological Association's statute of value neutrality; otherwise this would lead to a "chaos of mutual national recriminations" such as between Poles and Germans.[36] Hartmann's paper, influenced by the Austro-Marxist School, evoked slightly greater interest, although Weber took issue with Hartmann's mystical conception of immutable ethnogeographic boundaries between Germanic, French, and Slavic cultures in Europe. With Otto Bauer, Hartmann argued that intense contact between different ethnic groups would lead to assimilation.

This gathering picked up some excitement only with Oppenheimer's blistering polemical attack against race theory, which rejected its claim to scientific status completely and which evoked rather strong criticisms, beginning with Sombart, but even Weber felt obliged to maintain some distance from Oppenheimer by suggesting there might possibly be a link between race and artistic expression.[37] Even Robert Michels's very learned, encyclopedic survey of the idea of patriotism evoked very little response, and there were few new ideas emerging from the discussion; it was particularly remarkable that, Michels's encyclopedic journey through European patriotisms notwithstanding, Jewish patriotism, the Zionist movement, and the very pertinent writings of Moses Hess were not mentioned once.

In sum, then, one gains the impression that the discussion of nation, ethnos, and race was the idea of the sociological triumvirate of Weber, Tönnies,[38] and Sombart, but—with the exception of race—of virtually no interest to the rank and file of German sociology at the time, notwithstanding the virulent nationalisms all over Europe, only two years before the outbreak of the war. It is moreover remarkable that the Second Soziologentag did not, despite Sombart's suggestion, also raise the question of the Jewish minority in Germany or elsewhere in Europe, indeed one of the burning and relevant ethnonational issues in the prewar period. In its later years—the Third Soziologentag was held after a long war-time hiatus in 1922—questions on ethnonational solidarities receded further into the background in the overall sociological debates in Germany. The themes now discussed were revolution (1922), sociology of knowledge, social science, and social policy (1924), democracy, natural law, and sociological methods (1926). In 1928, at the Sixth Soziologentag, in a panel on migration, even Oppenheimer, who would have been most likely to do so, failed to address ethnonational issues. In 1930, at the last Soziologentag before World War II and the rise of fascism and antisemitism in Germany, ethnonational phenomena were indeed addressed: those of the German "tribes" such as Bavarians and Saxons. This panel was steeped in racial Germanic rhetoric and of course excluded any discussion of non-German minorities in Germany.

This indifference to questions of nationality, ethnic minorities, and the Other is similarly reflected, for example, in the tables of content of the *Archiv für Sozialwissenschaften und Sozialpolitik* under the editorship of Germany's most renowned sociologists, Weber, Sombart, and later Tönnies. There, in the years between 1910 and 1933, only a minuscule number of articles addressed the issues of nation, race, and people. Two of these, reports on the anti-Jewish pogroms and the status of the Jewish minority, were published anonymously, without any comment, in the *Archiv*.[39] How, finally, were these issues addressed in Alfred Vierkandt's *Handwörterbuch der Soziologie* (1931), which might be considered a compendium of German sociological knowledge before Nazism? As a systematic overview, the *Handwörterbuch* does indeed address these issues to some extent, with Michels on patriotism, Friedrich Hertz—critically—on race theories, and Waldemar Mitscherlich on Volk and nation. The entries by Tönnies on community and society, by Sombart on basic forms of social life, by Goetz Briefs on the proletariat, and by Oppenheimer on relations of power address these issues at least in passing as well. It is nevertheless indicative that Mitscherlich, a relative unknown, would write one of the key articles in this respect and that neither he nor the others— with the, albeit limited, exception of Briefs's discussion of the element of rural-urban and ethnically heterogeneous migration in the formation of the proletariat—addressed the issue of ethnonational minorities, not to speak of Jews as a key minority in Germany.

Only Sombart, once again, does directly address the issue in his entry of the *Handwörterbuch*, as part of an article on "basic forms of human social life." Sombart speaks here of the concept of "Volk next to nation, and distinct from it." He distinguishes "statistical groups," that is, groups that have particular ethnic characteristics in common without being conscious of these, such as language, political system, or the like, and common history, whereas "independent and intentional associations . . . have become conscious of their common characteristics." Volk is defined on the basis of common background (*Herkunft*), nation on the basis of a common future (*Hinkunft*). Jews all over the world, for example, are therefore a statistical group, allegedly unaware of their common characteristics, whereas orthodox Jews and Zionists form intentional associations; their tradition directs them to the future, and as such they assume the characteristics of nation. In short, a people (Volk) that has become conscious of itself and that is in the process of forming a state is also on the way to turning into a nation.[40] The anomaly for Sombart here are ethnonational groups that are conscious of their identity without having the will to become a nation. One example is the Germans in Brazil, the other the French Canadians, who say, "Vive le drapeau anglais et la langue francaise [*sic*]." This anomaly, which interestingly enough Sombart does not seem to find in Germany itself, defies further analysis in his view; it is the "notorious minorities problem."[41]

In short, we can say that ethnonational phenomena were dealt with to a minimal degree in classical German sociology, especially compared to early American sociology. The few contributions that emerged can be viewed as sociology's response to race theories on one hand (Weber) or were trying to integrate race theory into sociology on the other (Sombart). Race theories in turn were dealt with also in order to counter the impact of Marxist theory, and the socialists, with the exception of the Austro-Marxists, were obsessed with internationalism and failed to grasp the significance of ethnonational identities. Sociology was therefore theoretically utterly unprepared for the nationalist frenzy that was about to be unleashed with the outbreak of World War I, or with the ever more intense antisemitism and the rise of fascism after the war.

Werner Sombart

With this broader overview behind us, I would now argue that in the context under consideration there have been five outstanding early contributions to the discussion of ethnonational phenomena and in greater or lesser degree to the Jewish question: these are Sombart's discussion of Jews and modern capitalism (1911), Weber's *Ancient Judaism* and other writings on ethnonational solidarities (1917/1927), Oppenheimer's theory of ethnic domination and state structures (1907), Michels's writings on patriotism (1913), and, later, Carl Schmitt's conception of the friend/foe relation and national myths (1932). In this final section, I will resume my earlier discussion of Sombart and review what are the first major contributions of classical German sociology on modern Jewry, asking how they might be useful to us today.[42]

In essence Sombart's discussion of the Jews, originally intended as a mere chapter in his work on modern capitalism, must be seen as being a part of his debate with Weber, especially Weber's writings on the

Protestant ethic. That debate began with Weber's critique of Sombart's theses on the origins of modern capitalism in his massive *Der moderne Kapitalismus* (1902), in which the Jews were not seen as being a major driving force—a view he revised later. In his earlier work Sombart attributed the origins of capitalism to rationalized economic action and double-entry bookkeeping. As Sombart put it in his introduction to *The Jews and Modern Capitalism*:

> I hit upon the Jewish question completely by accident when I had embarked upon a fundamental revision of my *Modern Capitalism*. ... Max Weber's analyses in relation to the interconnections between Puritanism and capitalism forced me to pursue the influence of religion on economic life more than I had done so far, and here I encountered the Jewish problem first. Because, as a careful examination of Weber's argumentation demonstrated, all those components of the Puritan dogma that appear to me to be of real significance for the elaboration of the capitalist spirit were borrowings from the sphere of ideas of the Jewish religion.[43]

This is not the place to deal with all of Sombart's ideas concerning the role of the Jews in economic life. He argued that the Jews were principally responsible for the growth of capitalism and for economic growth in general: "We are astonished that the parallelism has not before been observed between the geographical mobility of the Jewish people and the economic fortunes of the different peoples and cities on the other. Israel passes over Europe like the sun: at its coming new life bursts forth, at its going, all falls into decay."[44] In the first section of his book, Sombart draws a portrait of the Jews from the time of pre-Inquisition Spain on to Holland; he then takes us to the Jews in Brazil and the United States and from there back to modern Western Europe. In the second section he discusses the significance of the Jewish religion for capitalism. In the third section he deals with the "evolution of the Jewish psyche" (*jüdische Wesen*)—the problem of race: the formation of the Jewish people from different "racial" stock in antiquity and the preservation of their "purity of blood" in subsequent history. He finally arrives back in Germany and in the "modern metropolis," which he sees as the fulfillment of Jewish existence. Throughout this work and some of his other writings, Sombart sees the Jews as arising from the starkness and barrenness of the desert: as the force of cold rationality, goal-orientedness, mobility, and adaptability. Jews constitute a stark contrast to the mysticalness of the German soul embedded in nature, especially the forest and walking on "steaming earth."

As we saw earlier, Sombart's Jews are also the epitome of strangeness, in a conception, despite the parallelisms, at variance with that of Simmel.[45] Sombart's Jews, however, *are* not only the perpetual strangers, they themselves *create* strangeness and anonymity: they more than anything are the component that has produced *Gesellschaft*, the society of strangers found in all that is opposed to German *Gemeinschaft*: America and especially the modern city. A number of character traits are responsible for this; the principal element, however, is the (alleged) Jewish practice of usury, which distinguishes between lending to one's own and lending to others. Due to this practice and a number of other innovative financial—impersonal—practices, the Jews not only had the major role in creating capitalism; they also engendered the impersonal nature of modern society. Whereas European nations and especially Germany retained much of Gemeinschaft-type mentality, the United States as a co-creation of the Jews lacks this spirit of tradition and Gemeinschaft altogether; it is therefore "in all its parts a land of Jews [*Judenland*]." "What we call Americanism is to a large part nothing other than congealed Jewish spirit."[46] This is so especially because of the settlement process in the United States, Sombart argues:

> A band of tough men and women, let us say twenty families, moved into the wilderness to start a new life. Among those twenty, nineteen were equipped with plough and scythe, ready to clear the forests, burn the steppe, and with the labour of their own hands earn a livelihood by tilling the soil. The twentieth family, however, opened a store to provide their companions quickly with the necessities of life that could not be produced on the land. Soon this twentieth family also began to arrange the distribution of the products which the other nineteen won from the soil. . . . Very often, the store had a kind of agricultural credit bank as an adjunct. Often also perhaps a real estate agency or similar. . . . Accordingly, it may be said that American economic life was from the beginning impregnated with

capitalist organisation and capitalist spirit. . . . And who built this "New World" of capitalist imprint? The twentieth family in each village. Need we add that this twentieth family was in each case a Jewish family that joined a band of settlers or soon sought them out on their homesteads?[47]

Sombart's stereotyping of the Jewish character had a strong racial coloring. He was at pains to demonstrate that among Jews intermarriage was virtually absent for over two thousand years and that until today Jews have preserved the purity of the ethnic/racial stock. He hoped furthermore that the recent development of intermarriage would cease and that the separateness would continue. His strongest plea for a separate (and unequal) position of the Jews in Germany can be found in *The Future of the Jews* (1912), very positively received by the German Zionist movement and later translated into Hebrew by David Ben Gurion. Here, Sombart insisted once again on the separateness of the Jews; he supported the Zionist goal of a homeland in Palestine and proposed a numerically diminished, individualized rather than collective ethnic presence of Jews in Germany. One of the many parallels to Gobineau and other racial theorists like Ploetz was Sombart's idea that racial mixing would lead to a deterioration of the people involved.[48] For this reason Germans and Jews needed to remain separate, but the presence of a limited number of Jews— perhaps as in the case of the American settlers—was to be of great benefit to Germany. Despite these apparent racial ideas, Sombart strenuously denied any racist bias—a bias, however, that can be found quite similarly in other authors of the time, including Jewish authors such as Arthur Ruppin, whom Sombart referred to repeatedly.[49] *Semites*, for example, was for him a "purely linguistic term." Especially in later years Sombart found the Jewish spirit also quite well outside the bounds of Jewish bodies. His characterization not only of America but also of the English in his war pamphlet *Händler und Helden* (Merchants and heroes [1915]) is a subterranean representation of his ideas of the Jewish spirit, and in his *Deutscher Sozialismus*, published when the Nazis were already in power, he most explicitly rejected any biological racist implications. The "spirit had left the body," in these ominous words: "Now, however, another point is more important: the Jewish spirit is in no way tied to the person of the Jew, and it could well continue to exist even when the last Jew and descendant of Jews [*Judenstämmling*] would have been exterminated."[50] Finally, while Sombart had a great deal to say about the Jewish collective psyche, there is virtually no sociological conception here of the Jews as a corporate group at least rudimentally conjugated by internal normative or institutional structures. While Sombart accepts the important role of rabbis and of religious instruction, he fails to see or is unable to convey any sense of ethnic Jewish community, of its leadership, its internal policing, and its traditions and memories. Jews are instinctual nomads, and only the Zionist project promises to turn them into a normal people.

Just as Sombart was influenced by Simmel's *Philosophy of Money*, so Sombart's work unquestionably had an important influence on Weber's *Ancient Judaism*: the idea of a *Jewish* ethic, that is, an ethic as the inherent trait of a people; the immutability of the Jewish character, especially in its negative traits; and, finally, the downplaying of oppression and the insistence by both Sombart and Weber that the ghetto was principally not imposed from without but built from within. It was the great merit of Weber and his significant difference from Sombart that he located Jewish character traits not in an assumed nomadic past and in the desert but in institutions and elites that not only produced a Jewish ethic but also shaped the Jews into a people.

Notes

A different version of this chapter was previously published as "Ethnos, Race and Nation: Werner Sombart, the Jews and Classical German sociology," Patterns of Prejudice 44.2 (2010): 117-36.

1. Sombart, *Der proletarische Sozialismus*, 45.
2. Michels, "Zur historischen Analyse des Patriotismus," 396.
3. Mosse, *Towards the Final Solution*, 79; Arendt, *The Origins of Totalitarianism*. See also Ruppin, *Die Juden der Gegenwart*.
4. Mosse, *Towards the Final Solution*, 156; Ruppin, *Die Juden der Gegenwart*.
5. Diner, *Verkehrte Welten*.
6. *Verhandlungen des Ersten Deutschen Soziologentages*, 148.
7. *Verhandlungen des Ersten Deutschen Soziologentages*, 121.
8. *Verhandlungen des Ersten Deutschen Soziologentages*, 149.
9. *Verhandlungen des Ersten Deutschen Soziologentages*, 154.
10. *Verhandlungen des Ersten Deutschen Soziologentages*, 155.
11. *Verhandlungen des Ersten Deutschen Soziologentages*, 159.
12. *Verhandlungen des Ersten Deutschen Soziologentages*, 160.

13. *Verhandlungen des Ersten Deutschen Soziologentages*, 164.

14. *Verhandlungen des Ersten Deutschen Soziologentages*, 156.

15. *Verhandlungen des Ersten Deutschen Soziologentages*, 164.

16. *Verhandlungen des Ersten Deutschen Soziologentages*, 165.

17. *Verhandlungen des Ersten Deutschen Soziologentages*, 163.

18. With some telling exceptions, however. In the course of the discussions at the Second Soziologentag, Sombart makes the following comment, directed at Oppenheimer: "Oppenheimer simply seems to want to explain everything from the environment; he seems to believe any worker could head a large factory just as well as the capitalist entrepreneur who with the help of the environment has worked himself up into that position; that talent and predisposition might have contributed their part does not enter his mind" (*Verhandlungen des Zweiten Deutschen Soziologentages*, 185).

19. *Verhandlungen des Ersten Deutschen Soziologentages*, 149, 160.

20. Gilman, *The Jew's Body*, 303.

21. *Verhandlungen des Ersten Deutschen Soziologentages*, 155; Simmel, *Philosophie des Geldes*, 290.

22. Simmel, *Philosophie des Geldes*, 290. Since the three sociologists discussed here use only the masculine pronoun, I have maintained this usage here. This is indeed a very male-centered discourse, and the absence of a discussion of women and strangeness and Jewish women as strangers is an additional weakness that deserves a separate analysis.

23. The idea of the supernumerary recalls the idea of Sombart's "twentieth family" in the United States (Sombart, *Die Juden und das Wirtschaftsleben*, 44).

24. Simmel, "The Stranger,".

25. Sombart, *Die Juden und das Wirtschaftsleben*, 205.

26. Sombart, *Die Juden und das Wirtschaftsleben*, 206, 283, 282, 283, 282.

27. An example of Sombart's image of the Jew, rootless, as a stranger who comes today and leaves tomorrow, is an episode he relates in the context of his characterization of Jews as antimystical and without sensibility for nature and the environment. One day, he notes, a Jewish student came to him in Breslau from eastern Siberia for the sole purpose of studying the works of Marx with him. "It took him three weeks for this long journey, and already on the day following his arrival, he visited me and asked me for one of Marx's writings. A few days later, he returned, spoke to me about what he had read, returned the book and took a new one. This went on for a few months. Then he returned to his Eastern Siberian village. He had not taken notice of his environment, not met anyone, did not take walks at all, hardly knew where he had been staying. He passed through the world of Breslau without seeing it, just as he had gone through his previous world, and how in future years he will go through the world without having any sense of it, only with Marx in his head. A typical case? I do think so" (*The Jews and Modern Capitalism*, 317/246).

28. Tönnies, "Individuum und Welt in der Neuzeit," 23–24.

29. Lenger, *Werner Sombart*, 204.

30. *Verhandlungen des Ersten Deutschen Soziologentages*, 112, 116.

31. *Verhandlungen des Zweiten Deutschen Soziologentages*, 186.

32. Sombart, quoted in Lenger, *Werner Sombart*, 204.

33. Simmel, quoted in Lenger, *Werner Sombart*, 204.

34. *Verhandlungen des Zweiten Deutschen Soziologentages*, 185. To be fair, this comment was triggered in part by Oppenheimer's polemical and polarizing presentation, which to some degree sought to contrast German and Jewish positions. Oppenheimer ridiculed "Germanomania," which he "thought was a term [he] had coined" until he discovered that the German Jewish writer Saul Ascher had already used this term in 1815 (100). Alluding to H. S. Chamberlain's theory of different brain structures, "plis de la pensée," of Jews and Germans and his scientifically untenable theories, Oppenheimer remarks elsewhere, "Luckily for me I find that serious critique . . . has arrived at the same result with astonishing consensus, that [Chamberlain's] *Grundlagen* are scientifically completely worthless. Otherwise I would have to ask myself if not my own specific brain structure would stop me permanently from grasping the *plis de la pensée* of the pure Germanic man" (119). Moreover Oppenheimer in his paper directly dismissed, if not ridiculed, Sombart's idea of the racial purity of the Ancient Israelites. Oppenheimer's remark and Sombart's response give us a good sense of the antisemitic atmosphere at the time.

35. *Verhandlungen des Zweiten Deutschen Soziologentages*, 49.

36. *Verhandlungen des Zweiten Deutschen Soziologentages*,72, 74.

37. *Verhandlungen des Zweiten Deutschen Soziologentages*,189.

38. Tönnies favored discussing these themes but, in contrast to the others, resisted the influence of racial hygiene on sociology. He made use here of the statute of value-free science in the charter of the Deutsche Gesellschaft für Soziologie. See Lenger, *Werner Sombart*, 205.

39. "Der Allgemeine Jüdische Arbeiterbund zur Zeit der russischen Revolution."

40. This is dealt with similarly, partly even verbatim, in Sombart's *Deutscher Sozialismus*. This distinction between Volk and nation-state was, however, fairly commonplace in the contemporary discussion. See, e.g., Stoelting, *Akademische Soziologie in der Weimarer Republik*, 348; Michels, "Zur historischen Analyse des Patriotismus."

41. Vierkandt, *Handwörterbuch der Soziologie*, 229.

42. For a comprehensive analysis of Sombart's work, see the masterly biography by Lenger, *Werner Sombart*.

43. Sombart, *Die Juden und das Wirtschaftsleben*, v. Translated into English by M. Epstein imprecisely as *The Jews and Modern Capitalism* (1951). The translation omits many sections and is inaccurate throughout. The redeeming value of the English-language edition of 1951 is the introduction by Bert F. Hoselitz, which also cites a variety of critiques of this work, including the contemporary ones.

44. Sombart, *Die Juden und das Wirtschaftsleben*, 35; Sombart, *The Jews and Modern Capitalism*, 157.

45. In Simmel's view, in contrast to that of Sombart, Jews are not inherently strangers; instead their strangeness is explained by their structural position. In a brilliant passage in his *Philosophy of Money* that prefigured the "Exkurs über den Fremden," Simmel wrote, "Scattered people that penetrate more or less closed cultural spheres can develop roots or can find a free place in production only with difficulty. They are therefore at first dependent on intermediate trade that is far more flexible than primary production. Its space [*Spielraum*] can almost limitlessly be expanded by means of purely formal combinations and can therefore most easily absorb external elements that have not grown up into the group from its roots. The deep trait of Jewish intellectuality that moves far more in logical-formal combinations rather than in substantive and productive production stands in an interdependent relationship with this situation of economic history" (*Philosophie des Geldes*, 287).

46. Sombart, *Die Juden und das Wirtschaftsleben*, 31, 44.

47. Sombart, *Die Juden und das Wirtschaftsleben*, 44–45; Sombart, *The Jews and Modern Capitalism*, 62–63.

48. Mosse, *Towards the Final Solution*, 79.

49. Sombart, *Die Juden und das Wirtschaftsleben* , e.g., 353. In a language almost interchangeable with that of Sombart, Ruppin writes, "The mixing of Jews and non-Jews by means of baptism and mixed marriage must be considered to be detrimental from the point of view of maintaining the higher racial quality [*Erhaltung ihrer hohen Rassebegabung*]. The demand that arises therefrom is to prevent this mixing and to maintain the Jews as a separate people [*Sondervolk*]. This, however, is only possible once not only the mixing has been brought to a stop, but when the entire process of assimilation as well has been halted; its beginning was the de-nationalisation, and its end the [racial] mixing. Combatting the mixing alone means to try to deal with the symptoms in the manner of quacks, instead of tackling the disease at its roots. Once the process of assimilation has set in and has proceeded to the de-nationalisation, that is, to the extinction of all Jewish characteristics, then the complete mixing and absorption of the Jews can no longer be stopped" (*Die Juden der Gegenwart*, 230).

50. Sombart, *Deutscher Sozialismus*, 194.

References

Abraham, Gary. *Max Weber and the Jewish Question: A Study in the Social Outlook of His Sociology*. Urbana: University of Illinois Press, 1991.

———. "Max Weber on 'Jewish Rationalism' and the Jewish Question." *Politics, Culture and Society* 1.3 (1988): 358–91.

————. "Modernist Anti-Pluralism and the Polish Question." *New German Critique* 53 (Spring/Summer 1991): 33–66.

"Der Allgemeine Jüdische Arbeiterbund zur Zeit der russischen Revolution." *Archiv f. Sozialwissenschaften und Sozialpolitik*, 1913.

Anderson, Benedict. *Imagined Communities*. London: New Left Books, 1978.

Arendt, Hannah. *The Origins of Totalitarianism*. 1950. New York: Harcourt, Brace, Jovanovich, 1966.

Aschheim, Steven E. *Brothers and Strangers: The East European Jew in German Jewish Consciousness, 1800–1923*. Madison: University of Wisconsin Press, 1982.

Baumgarten, Eduard. *Max Weber: Werk und Person*. Tübingen: J. C. B. Mohr (Paul Siebeck), 1964.

Bodemann, Y. Michal. "Priests, Prophets, Jews and Germans: The Political Basis of Max Weber's Conception of Ethno-national Solidarities." *Archives européennes de sociologie* 34 (1993): 224–47.

————. "Staat und Ethnizität: Der Aufbau der Jüdischen Gemeinden im Kalten Krieg" (State and ethnicity: The reconstruction of Jewish communities in the cold war). In *Jüdisches Leben in Deutschland seit 1945*, edited by Micha Brumlik et al., pages 49-69. Frankfurt: Athenaeum Verlag, 1986.

————. "The State in the Construction of Ethnicity and Ideological Labour: The Case of German Jewry." *Critical Sociology* 17.3 (1991): 35–46.

Boehlich, Walter, ed. *Der Berliner Antisemitismusstreit*. Frankfurt am Main: Insel, 1965.

Brentano, Lujo. *Der wirtschaftende Mensch in der Geschichte*. Leipzig: Felix Meiner, 1923.

Brocke, Bernhard vom. *"Sombarts Moderner Kapitalismus": Materialien zur Kritik und Rezeption*. Munich: DTV, 1987.

Diner, Dan. *Verkehrte Welten: Antiamerikanismus in Deutschland. Ein historischer Essay*. Frankfurt am Main: Eichborn, 1993.

Fleischmann, Eugène. "Max Weber, die Juden und das Ressentiment." In *Max Webers Studie über das antike Judentum: Interpretation und Kritik*, edited by Wolfgang Schluchter, 263–88. Frankfurt: Suhrkamp, 1981.

Gellner, Ernest. *Nations and Nationalism*. Ithaca NY: Cornell University Press, 1983.

Gilman, Sander. *The Jew's Body*. London: Routledge, 1991.

Guttmann, Julius. "Die Juden und das Wirtschaftsleben." *Archiv f. Sozialwissenschaften und Sozialpolitik* 36 (1913).

Hintze, Otto. "Rasse und Nationalität und ihre Bedeutung für die Geschichte." 1903. In *Soziologie und Geschichte, Gesammelte Abhandlungen*, 46–65. Göttingen: Vandenhoek und Ruprecht, 1982.

Hobsbawm, Eric J. *Nations and Nationalism since 1780: Programme, Myth, Reality*. Cambridge: Cambridge University Press, 1990.

Lenger, Friedrich. *Werner Sombart, 1863–1941: Eine Biographie*. Munich: Beck, 1994.

Leon, Abram. *The Jewish Question: A Marxist Interpretation*. New York: Pathfinder Press, 1970.

Liebeschütz, Hans. "Max Weber's Historical Interpretation of Judaism." *Leo Baeck Institute Year Book*, 1964, 41–68.

Manasse, Ernst Moritz. "Max Weber on Race." *Social Research* 14 (1947): 191–221.

Marx, Karl. "On the Jewish Question." In *Early Writings*, edited by T. B. Bottomore, 27–43. New York, McGraw-Hill, 1963.

Michels, Robert. *First Lectures in Political Sociology*. Minneapolis: University of Minnesota Press, 1949.

———. "Zur historischen Analyse des Patriotismus." *Archiv für Sozialwissenschaft und Sozialpolitik*, 1913, 14–43, 394–449.

Mosse, George L. *Towards the Final Solution: A History of European Racism*. 1978. New York: Howard Fertig, 1990.

Oppenheimer, Franz. *Der Staat*. Frankfurt am Main: Die Gesellschaft, 1907

Papcke, Sven. *Vernunft und Chaos: Essays zur sozialen Ideengeschichte*. Frankfurt am Main: Fischer, 1985.

Rehberg, Karl-Siegbert. "Das Bild des Judentums in der frühen deutschen Soziologie: Fremdheit und Rationalität als Typusmerkmale bei Werner Sombart, Max Weber und Georg Simmel." In *Juden in der Soziologie*, edited by Erhard R. Wiehn, 127–74. Konstanz: Hartung-Gorre Verlag, 1989.

Rex, John, and David Mason, eds. *Theories of Race and Ethnic Relations*. Cambridge: Cambridge University Press, 1986.

Rose, Paul Lawrence. *Revolutionary Anti-Semitism in Germany: From Kant to Wagner*. Princeton NJ: Princeton University Press, 1990.

Roth, Guenter. "Between Cosmopolitanism and Ethnocentrism: Max Weber in the Nineties." *Telos* 96 (1993): 148–62.

Ruppin, Arthur. *Die Juden der Gegenwart: Eine sozialwissenschaftliche Studie*. 1904. Köln: Jüdischer Verlag, 1911.

Schluchter, Wolfgang, ed. *Max Webers Studie über das antike Judentum: Interpretation und Kritik*. Frankfurt: Suhrkamp, 1981.

Schmitt, Carl. *Der Begriff des Politischen: Text von 1932 mit einem Vorwort und drei Corollarien*. 1932. Berlin: Duncker und Humblot, 1963.

———. *Verfassungslehre*. Berlin: Duncker und Humblot, 1928.

Simmel, Georg. "The Metropolis and Mental Life." In *The Sociology of Georg Simmel*, edited by Kurt H. Wolff, 409–24. New York: Free Press, 1950.

———. *Philosophie des Geldes*. 1900. Frankfurt am Main: Suhrkamp, 1989.

———. *Soziologie: Untersuchungen über die Formen der Vergesellschaftung*. 1908. Frankfurt am Main: Suhrkamp, 1992.

———. "The Stranger." In *The Sociology of Georg Simmel*, edited by Kurt H. Wolff, 402–8. New York: Free Press, 1950.

Sombart, Werner. "Artvernichtung oder Arterhaltung." in: *Gegen die Phrase vom jüdischen Schädling*, edited by Heinrich Mann, 249–53. Prague: Amboss Verlag, 1933.

———. *Der Bourgeois: Zur Geistesgeschichte des modernen Wirtschaftsmenschen.* Munich: Duncker und Humblot, 1920.

———. *Deutscher Sozialismus.* Berlin: Buchholz und Weisswange, 1934.

———. *Händler und Helden: Patriotische Besinnungen.* Munich: Duncker und Humblot, 1915.

———. *The Jews and Modern Capitalism.* New York: Free Press, 1951.

———. *Die Juden und das Wirtschaftsleben.* Munich: Duncker und Humblot, 1911.

———. *Luxury and Capitalism.* Ann Arbor: University of Michigan Press, 1967.

———. *Luxus und Kapitalismus.* Munich: Duncker und Humblot, 1913.

———. *Der moderne Kapitalismus.* Leipzig: Duncker und Humblot, 1902.

———. "Nationale Eigenarten im sozialen Kampf." *Neue Deutsche Rundschau (Freie Bühne)* 7.2 (1896): 1037–51.

———. *Der proletarische Sozialismus.* 10th revised edition of *Sozialismus und soziale Bewegung.* Jena: Fischer, 1924.

———. *Warum gibt es in den Vereinigten Staaten keinen Sozialismus?* Tübingen: Mohr, 1896.

———. *Die Zukunft der Juden.* Munich: Duncker und Humblot, 1912.

Stoelting, Erhard. *Akademische Soziologie in der Weimarer Republik.* Berlin: Duncker und Humblot, 1984.

Tal, Uriel. *Christians and Jews in Germany: Religion, Politics and Ideology in the Second Reich, 1870–1914.* Ithaca NY: Cornell University Press, 1975.

Tönnies, Ferdinand. "Individuum und Welt in der Neuzeit." 1913. In *Fortschritt und Soziale Entwicklung,* Karlsruhe: G. Braun, 1926.

Verhandlungen des Ersten Deutschen Soziologentages in Frankfurt/M. Tübingen: J. C. B. Mohr, 1911.

Verhandlungen des Zweiten Deutschen Soziologentages vom 20.–22. Oktober in Berlin. Tübingen: J. C. B. Mohr, 1913.

Vierkandt, Alfred, ed. *Handwörterbuch der Soziologie.* Stuttgart: Ferdinand Enke Verlag, 1931.

Volkov, Shulamit. *Jüdisches Leben und Anti-Semitismus im 19. und 20. Jahrhundert.* Munich: C. H. Beck,1990.

Weber, Max. *Ancient Judaism.* Edited and translated by H. H. Gerth and D. Martindale. New York: Free Press, 1952.

———. *Gesammelte Aufsätze zur Religionssoziogie III.* Tübingen: J. C. B. Mohr (Paul Siebeck), 1927.

———Weber, Max. *Gesammelte Aufsätze zur Sozial-und Wirtschaftsgeschichte.* Tübingen: J. C. B. Mohr (Paul Siebeck), 1924.

———. *Gesammelte Aufsätze zur Soziologie und Sozialpolitik.* Tübingen: J. C. B. Mohr (Paul Siebeck), 1924.

———. *Gesammelte Aufsätze zur Wissenschaftslehre.* Tübingen: J. C. B. Mohr (Paul Siebeck), 1922.

———. *Gesammelte Politische Schriften.* Tübingen: J. C. B. Mohr (Paul Siebeck), 1921.

———. *Wirtschaft und Gesellschaft.* 1956. Köln: Kiepenheuer und Witsch, 1964.

Part 2

Sociology's Reaction to Antisemitism

5

Rereading Marx on the "Jewish Question"

Marx as a Critic of Antisemitism?

ROBERT FINE

Two views prevail concerning Karl Marx's alleged antisemitism. The disparaging view is that Marx, notwithstanding his Jewish origins, was himself an antisemite *avant la lettre* or at least made use of antisemitic tropes and reproduced antisemitic stereotypes in his own work. This view is present among some commentators on Marx and firmly entrenched among students of modern antisemitism.[1] It is based in particular on a reading of the second of Marx's two 1843 essays, "On the Jewish Question," where he appears to link Judaism to huckstering and global financial power and to equate human emancipation with emancipation of society from Judaism. His representation of Jews is said to inherit a long tradition of radical anti-Jewish hostility and to prefigure the more virulent, political, and sometimes "socialist" antisemitism to come. Marx is portrayed in this literature as a progenitor of what is today labeled the "antisemitism of the Left."

By contrast, the apologetic view adopted by most Marxist commentators tends to ignore the whole issue of antisemitism in Marx's own writings. If confronted, it either trivializes it as a passing personal prejudice that did not enter into Marx's scientific writings or it normalizes it as a sign of his times. In some cases it translates Marx's negative typifications of Jews and Judaism into the more acceptable language of anticapitalism, for example, by translating the word *Judentum* into the more neutral *commerce*.[2] In other cases it may even endorse the negative typifications of Jews it finds in Marx's writings, on the grounds that it is necessary to understand what is true in the antisemitic imagination in order to combat it and on the assumption that Marx's negative typifications of Jews derive in part from empirically verifiable Jewish phenomena. If we put these strategies together, we too often find in Marxist scholarship on Marx a propensity to bypass or dissolve the question of antisemitism.[3]

The problem I have with the first of these interpretations, the disparaging view that Marx was in some significant sense antisemitic, is that beyond the second essay on the Jewish question there is scant evidence of antisemitic thinking in his published works. Marx was known to deploy racist and antisemitic epithets in some of his private correspondence with Engels.[4] A frequently cited case is his depiction of fellow socialist Ferdinand Lassalle as *Jude Itzig* in letters to Engels (July 30, 1862 and May 29, 1863). However, such private correspondence was not intended for public consumption, the name Itzig seems to have been in regular use among Jews as a deflator of grandiose pretensions by a fellow Jew, and the remark should be read as a facetious mockery of Lassalle's own predilection for the pseudo-science of physiognomy.[5] In further private correspondence with Engels Marx made fun of Lassalle's "smooth, self-important, vainglorious, deceitful charlatan's physiognomy" (June 6, 1853) and expostulated that Lassalle "proved by his cranial formation and hair" that he "descends from the Negroes who had joined Moses' exodus from Egypt" (July 30, 1862). We may wish to accuse Marx of bad taste or chuckle at his acerbic wit, which I am more inclined to do, but there is no evidence that he had any interest in or truck with the pseudo-science of physiognomy. There is plenty of evidence that he became increasingly infuriated by Lassalle's authoritarian and antiliberal form of socialism.

There is occasional use of anti-Jewish epithets in Marx's political articles. The best known is an article titled "The Russian Loan," published under Marx's name on January 4, 1856, in the *New York Daily Tribune*. One offending passage runs thus: "We find every tyrant backed by a Jew, as is every Pope by a Jesuit. In truth, the cravings of oppressors would be hopeless, and the practicality of war out of the question, if there were not an army of Jesuits to smother thought and a handful of Jews to ransack pockets. . . . The real work is done by the Jews, and can only be done by them . . . as they monopolise the machinery of the loan-mongering mysteries." This article was probably written by Engels, though Marx put his name to it, and attacked the role of *Jewish* finance alongside that of *Jesuit* ideology.[6] It is noteworthy, however, that a couple of years earlier, on

April 15, 1854, Marx wrote an article about Ottoman-ruled Jerusalem in which he commented, "Nothing equals the misery and the sufferings of the Jews at Jerusalem, inhabiting the most filthy quarter of the town . . . the constant objects of Mussulman oppression and intolerance."[7] Marx's attack on Jewish loan-mongering was arguably in a tradition of radical Jewish critiques of the "economic Jew"—not unlike, say, Irene Nemirovsky's radical critique of a rich Jewish merchant modeled on her father in her 1929 novel *David Golder*. Whether or not we consider Marx's critique of Jewish finance antisemitic, it was compatible with sympathy for the suffering of the great majority of poor Jews.[8]

Perhaps the more telling objection to the antisemitic representation of Marx lies in the support he gave to the emancipation of Jews, that is, to the movement in Germany to remove all civil and political restrictions on Jews and grant them equal civil and political rights alongside other citizens. Marx and Engels were consistently critical of socialist and radical thinkers who opposed Jewish emancipation or made support for the emancipation of Jews conditional on Jews giving up their Judaism or in some other way "improving" themselves. It is noteworthy that many of the socialists and radicals Marx and Engels attacked in their writings did have antisemitic leanings. These included Bruno Bauer, to whom Marx's double-essay "On the Jewish Question" was a response, the anarchist Pierre-Joseph Proudhon, the cooperative socialist Charles Fourier, the radical philosopher Eugen Dühring, the insurrectionist socialist Louis-Auguste Blanqui, and the revolutionary anarchist and pan-Slavist Mikhail Bakunin.[9]

Consider, for instance, the case of Bakunin, a leading opponent of Marx in the First International. He put the existence of a Jewish conspiracy to control the world at the center of his political thinking. In his *Appeal to Slavs* (1848) he wrote that the "Jewish sect" was a "veritable power in Europe," reigning despotically over commerce and banking and invading most areas of journalism. "Woe to him who makes the mistake of displeasing it!" he wrote.[10] In letters to the Bologna section of the *International* Bakunin was equally graphic:

This whole Jewish world, which constitutes a single exploitative sect, a sort of bloodsucker people, a collective parasite, voracious, organised in itself, not only across the frontiers of states but even across all the differences of political opinion—this world is presently,

> at least in great part, at the disposal of Marx on the one hand and of the Rothschilds on the other. . . . In all countries the people detest the Jews. They detest them so much that every popular revolution is accompanied by a massacre of Jews: a natural consequence.[11]

Conspiracy thinking, cult of violence, hatred of law, fecundity of destruction, Slavic ethnonationalism and antisemitism—these elements were inseparable from Bakunin's revolutionary anarchism. Marx's own interest was less in the anti-Jewish prejudices of these authors than in the cognitive and normative limitations of which these prejudices were symptomatic. Still, Marx's consistent criticism of those on the "Left" who displayed antisemitic tendencies places a big question mark by the proposition that Marx himself was antisemitic or espoused antisemitic views.

If we turn to the second of the prevailing views on Marx's relation to antisemitism, the apologetics found especially within Marxism, this is no more solidly grounded than the denigration of Marx as an antisemite. It tends to work on the assumption that antisemitism is an ideology of nationalists, while Marxism is a universalist way of thinking opposed to all forms of racism, including antisemitism. Marxists consequently downplay or deny antisemitism within their own ranks, including Marx himself. As Lars Fischer argues, leading members of the pre-1914 German Marxist movement were prone to defend Marx's essays on the Jewish question on the dubious grounds that he was facing up to the truth-content of antisemitic representations of Jews.[12] They read Marx's essays on the Jewish question as support for the argument that Jews had to *earn* the right to legal and political equality by overcoming their own exclusivism and by confronting the hypocrisy of demanding their own emancipation while not standing up for the general cause of emancipation. According to this interpretation, Marx's own reading of the Jewish question was that the demand of Jews for equal rights was incompatible with their indifference to the rights of others.[13]

The Marxist scholar Franz Mehring offered a case in point when he approvingly cited a passage from the work of Bruno Bauer as if it were Marx's own view. The passage in question was critical of "defenders of Jewish emancipation" for privileging Judaism and exempting it from criticism: "The same people . . . who watch with pleasure when Christianity is subjected to criticism are capable of condemning anyone who also wants to subject Jewry/Judaism to criticism. . . . The defenders of Jewish emancipation have hence appropriated the odd position of fighting against privileges and at the same time granting Jewry/Judaism the privilege of immutability, invulnerability and unaccountability."[14] Eduard Bernstein wrote in a similar vein that "Marx favoured postponement of the question of equal rights for Jews . . . until the coming socialist revolution." Karl Kautsky appealed to Marx as authority for the prescription that "the sooner Judaism disappears, the better for society and for the Jews themselves."[15] As Enzo Traverso put it, "The Marxism of the Second International . . . welcomed the idea of Jewish assimilation as the inevitable and desirable culmination of the 'path of history,'" and cited Victor Adler's desire for "the death of the wandering Jew".[16] When Marx's texts on the Jewish question were republished by the German Social Democrats in 1881, only the bulk of the second essay, the section that contains the most problematic statements about Jews and Judaism, was reproduced. Bernstein justified this selection on the grounds that the entire text was too long and the most important passages were those that dealt with "the social significance of Jewry."[17] Marxists in this period (with Rosa Luxemburg as an exception) were wont to focus on the second of Marx's essays on the Jewish question because they read it as resonating with their own preconceptions and concurred with the view they associated with Marx that Jews had to overcome their antisocial instincts if they were to become worthy of equal rights.[18]

The legacy of this Marxist reading of Marx was to encourage Marxists to embrace the Jewish question uncritically and to encourage scholars of antisemitism to treat Marx and Marxism as part of the problem, not as a critical resource. The proposition I wish to put forward is that both disparaging and apologetic representations of Marx offer deeply problematic frameworks for reading Marx's texts and for reconstructing his contribution to our understanding of the Jewish question. The aim of this chapter, then, is to return to Marx without the weight of this ideological baggage. What is at stake in this project is not just what we think of Marx himself, but the reconstruction of a critical theory in which the critique of antisemitism is afforded the centrality it deserves.

The Origins of the Marx-Bauer Debate

In the European Enlightenment there was no shortage of anti-Jewish prejudice on show, but there was also a strong thread of support for the emancipation of Jews.[19] Most Enlightenment writers denounced the conditions under which Jews were forced to live and championed civil and political reform—either as a road to the "improvement" of Jews or more radically as a right of Jews.[20] In the last decades of the eighteenth century German reformers and French revolutionaries alike appealed to the universality of rights to combat the persecution of Jews. For example, Clermont-Tonnerre famously wrote, "We must refuse everything to the Jews as a nation and accord everything to Jews as individuals."[21] His argument was directed against the prerevolutionary status of Jews in France, which designated Jews a separate "nation" that could profess its own religion and have its own institutions of self-government, including its own courts, but remained subject to fiscal, occupational, and residential restrictions.[22] He called for the abolition of the subordinate status of Jews in the old order and for the granting of equal civil and political rights to Jews in the new order. However, his words could also be interpreted as a demand that Jews should be refused civil and political rights as long as they maintained their Judaism, and it was this demand that was endorsed by some of Marx's contemporaries but not, I suggest, by Marx himself.

In the Enlightenment one of the key debates around the Jewish question was between assimilationists, who looked to the reform or disappearance of Judaism as the desired effect of emancipation, and anti-assimilationists, who argued that Judaism need not and ought not to be suppressed in the course of building an inclusive and universal civil life. Among the latter Moses Mendelssohn famously wrote, "Adopt the mores and constitution of the country in which you find yourself . . . but be steadfast in upholding the religion of your fathers, too. Bear both burdens as well as you can."[23] Among the former Abbé Gregoire supported emancipation on the grounds that it would lead to "the moral and physical regeneration of Jews."[24] Similarly, in his 1781 essay "Concerning the Amelioration of the Civil Status of Jews" the Prussian reformer Christian von Dohm held that Judaism as it existed contained antisocial principles that prevented Jews from "keeping faith with the community." He demanded that Jews be granted civil and political rights precisely to enable them to overcome their "deficiencies."[25] In his 1791 letter to the Jews of Alsace, Isaac Berr (himself Jewish) presented the emancipation of Jews as the start of a process in which Jews must "work a change in our manners, in our habits, in short, in our whole education . . . and divest ourselves entirely of that narrow spirit of Corporation and Congregation in all civil and political matters."[26] We should not overstate the distinction between assimilationists and anti-assimilationists in the Enlightenment period, since Mendelssohn also looked to the autonomous self-reformation of Judaism as a complement to emancipation—one that would do away with its backward-looking, messianic excesses and reconstruct it as a religion "within the bounds of reason," to use Kant's phrase.

In the postrevolutionary period the links connecting the emancipation of Jews to the Jewish question broke apart and shifted to an opposition between emancipationists on one side and ideologues of the Jewish question on the other. Citing the universalistic ideals embodied in the Declaration of the Rights of Man and Citizen, emancipationists espoused the inclusion of Jews as equal citizens. Ideologues of the Jewish question tallied up the negative qualities of Jews and expressed deep distrust at the prospect of granting them equal rights they did not deserve. A holding position was that Jews might be granted equal rights once they abandoned their Judaism.

The shifting nature of this debate may be illustrated by the polemics between the older Hegel and the radical Jacob Fries. Jews were largely excluded from Fries's category of "the people." In a pamphlet titled *On the Danger Posed to the Welfare and Character of the German People by the Jews* (1816) Fries maintained that Jews should be prohibited from establishing their own educational institutions, marrying Gentiles, employing Christians as servants, and entering Germany. Fries added for good measure that Jews should be forced to wear a distinctive mark on their clothing and be encouraged to emigrate.[27] Hegel was highly critical of Fries's radical populism, which he characterized thus: "In a people among whom a genuine communal spirit prevails, all business relating to public affair would gain its *life from below, from the people itself*." Hegel argued that this populist philosophy reduced "the complex inner articulation of the ethical, i.e. the state, the architectonics of its rationality . . . to a mush of 'heart, friendship and enthusiasm.'" Fries, he wrote, substituted feeling for the work of understanding, expressed contempt for science on the grounds that truth cannot be known while at the same time declaring this truth to be incontrovertible, and reduced ethics to subjective conviction with the result that the most criminal of principles could be accorded the same status as the most democratic and ethical.

Hegel described the hatred of right and law Fries displayed as "the chief shibboleth whereby false friends of 'the people' give themselves away."[28] He declared it a matter of "infinite importance" that "a human being counts as such because he is a human being, not because he is a Jew, Catholic, Protestant, German, Italian, etc." He added that when we speak of Jews as *human beings* "this is not just a neutral and abstract quality . . . for its consequence is that the granting of civil rights gives those who receive them a *self-awareness* as recognised *legal* persons in civil society." He dismissed those who sought to deny civil and political rights to Jews on the pretext that Jews belonged to a "foreign nation," arguing, "If they had not been granted civil rights, the Jews would have remained in that isolation with which they have been reproached, and this would rightly have brought blame and reproach upon the state which excluded them."[29]

Two decades later the legacies of Hegel and Fries split into yet more polarized extremes. Bruno Bauer, a radical theologian and member of the Young Hegelian circle, published a monograph, *The Jewish Question* (*Die Judenfrage*), in 1843, and three further articles in 1843 and 1844. Bauer's argument was that for Jews to become full Prussian citizens on an equal footing with other citizens, they first had to surrender their Judaism. He characterized Jews as an ahistorical people in the sense that while history called for evolution, the Jews always wished to stay the same.[30] He declared that the Jewish spirit lacks the historical capacity to evolve and the basic resources for the elevation of morality. Indeed Bauer displayed a well-worn litany of anti-Jewish prejudices: Jews pride themselves on being the only true people but are indifferent to the happiness of other peoples; Jews claim discrimination at the hands of Christian society but possess prodigious influence over the destiny of Europe through their financial power; Jews call for their own emancipation but not for the emancipation of others; Jews are hated in the Christian world but provoke this treatment since they have no interest in the progress of humanity at large; Jews derive no universal moral principles from their own suffering. Bauer concluded that there could be no Jewish emancipation as long as Jews clung to their Judaism. The civil equality of Jews could be implemented only where "Jewry no longer exists."

In response to Bauer's refurbishment of the Jewish question, Marx picked up on the emancipatory promise of the Enlightenment project. In 1843 and 1844 he wrote in quick succession two essays "On the Jewish Question" and then coauthored with Engels *The Holy Family*. The first essay contained a strong defense of Jewish emancipation, the right of Jews to equal civil and political rights, and the end of all restrictions on movement, residence, professional activities, and access to the civil service. The second essay addressed and seems to bristle with anti-Jewish economic stereotypes. Finally, the monograph *The Holy Family* offered a scathing critique of the "holy criticism" or "critical criticism" of Bauer and like-minded German radicals who resurrected the Jewish question and opposed Jewish emancipation. These writings were part of the young Marx's larger critique of the Young Hegelian and early socialist movements.[31]

Marx's criticisms of Bauer turned from an initial tone of respect for Bauer's "dash, perception, wit and thoroughness" to heavy sarcasm directed against "Saint Bruno's holy criticism." Marx began his first essay "On the Jewish Question" by paraphrasing Bauer's opposition to the legal emancipation of Jews:

> You Jews are egoists if you demand a special emancipation for yourselves as Jews. You should work as Germans for the political emancipation of Germany and as men for human emancipation and you should look upon the particular form of oppression and shame which you experience not as an exception to the rule but rather as a confirmation of it. . . . The Jew by his very nature cannot be emancipated. . . . The Jew himself can behave only like a Jew towards the state, i.e. treat it as something foreign, for he opposes his chimerical nationality to actual nationality, his illusory law to actual law, he considers himself entitled to separate himself from humanity, he refuses in principle to take any part in the movement of history, he looks forward to a future which has nothing in common with the future of mankind as a whole and he sees himself as a member of the Jewish people and the Jewish people as the chosen people.

According to Bauer's view of the world, the natural inclination of Jews was to betray the "universal cause" for the sake of their own Jewish interests. For Jews to demonstrate their commitment to the cause of universal human emancipation, they had to abandon their Judaism: "As long as he is a Jew, the restricted nature that makes him a Jew will inevitably gain the ascendancy over the human nature which should join him as a man to other men."

To Bauer's rhetorical question—Why should the German be interested in the liberation of the Jew if the Jew is not interested in the liberation of the German?—Marx responded with unconditional support for Jewish emancipation: "We do *not* tell the Jews that they cannot be emancipated politically without radically emancipating themselves from Judaism, which is what Bauer tells them." Bauer asked of Jews, "Do you from your [restricted] standpoint have the right to demand political emancipation?" Marx inverted the question: "Does the standpoint of political emancipation have the right to demand from the Jews the abolition of Judaism and from man the abolition of religion?"[32] Bauer maintained that "the Christian state . . . cannot allow adherents of another particular religion . . . complete equality with its own social estates." Marx replied that as a matter of fact in France and North America "the Jews (like the Christians) are fully politically emancipated," and added in relation to Germany, "States which cannot yet politically emancipate the Jews must be rated by comparison with the perfected political state and shown to be underdeveloped."[33]

For Marx the Jewish question was really a German question. It was not about the nature of Jews but about the Prussian state: "Criticism . . . becomes criticism of the political state."[34] The real subject matter of the Jewish question was political emancipation.[35] Freedom of religion, the right to be religious or not in any way one wishes, is not the same thing as freedom *from* religion. In the United States there was no state religion, and yet it was "the land of religiosity *par excellence*."[36] Political emancipation signifies that religion becomes a private right and the state becomes a secular state. It does not signify the abolition of religious distinctions but their transformation into nonpolitical matters. Since political emancipation grants freedom of religion and does not demand freedom from religion, there is no reason to demand of Jews that they free themselves from the Jewish religion.

Marx argued that Bauer's opposition to Jewish emancipation was symptomatic of an inability to come to terms with modern political life more generally. By attributing to political movements a *social* significance more fundamental than their *political* significance, Bauer translated the exclusion of Jews from citizenship into the self-exclusion of Jews from society: "Only those exclude themselves who do not wish to take part in its development."[37] Bauer devalued rights and representation as the "illusion of the masses" and bemoaned the thoughtlessness of the "representatives of the mass" who sowed these illusions. In *The Holy Family* Marx and Engels jibed in response, "How low 'the mass' is in comparison with holy criticism."[38] For Bauer the social was everything; the political was nothing. He put the overcoming of Judaism at the center of the revolutionary endeavor of political life to "constitute itself as the real harmonious species-life of man."[39] Bauer offered the vista of human emancipation *in opposition to* the rights of man and citizen and on the grounds that political emancipation falls short of human emancipation devalued political emancipation. The contrast with Marx could not be stronger. Marx characterized the Declaration of the Rights of Man and Citizen as a "great step forward" that marked the difference between "the modern representative state and the old state of privileges" and turned the affairs of state into the affairs of the people.[40] Marx acknowledged the limits of political emancipation: "The fact that you can be politically emancipated without ... renouncing Judaism shows that political emancipation *by itself is not human emancipation*."[41] However, he drew the opposite conclusion to that drawn by Bauer. The point was not to devalue civil and political rights but, on the contrary, to revalue them. The critique of the limits of rights is not the same thing as the trashing of rights.

In a passage often cited out of context to prove that Marx was a "critic" of rights, Marx observed, "Not one of the so-called rights of man goes beyond egoistic man, man as a member of civil society, namely an individual withdrawn into himself, his private interest and his private desires, and separated from the community."[42] The grammar of Marx's argument is, I would suggest, quite simple and runs along these lines. It is true that none of the rights of man goes beyond egoistic man, but then it makes no sense to exclude the Jews on the grounds of their alleged egoism and separation from the community. As David Seymour writes, "The situation Bauer attributes solely to the Jews as a consequence of their particularistic 'restricted nature' is in fact attributable to members of civil society *as* members of civil society."[43] The radicalism of Marx's essay lay in liberating the emancipation question from the Jewish question.

The Notorious Second Essay

Let me now turn to the second of Marx's essays on the Jewish question. The language of the second essay is troubling. Let me quote at some length from the Penguin translation to give a flavor of how troubling it is:

What is the secular basis of Judaism? Practical need, self-interest. What is the secular cult of the Jew? Haggling. What is his secular God? Money. Well then! Emancipation from haggling and from money, i.e. from practical, real Judaism, would be the same as the self-emancipation of our age. . . .

We therefore recognise in Judaism the presence of a . . . contemporary anti-social element whose historical evolution—eagerly nurtured by the Jews in its harmful aspects—has arrived at its present peak, a peak at which it will inevitably disintegrate. The emancipation of the Jews is in the last analysis the emancipation of humankind from Judaism. . . .

Money is the jealous God of Israel before whom no other God may stand. . . . Exchange is the true God of the Jew. His God is nothing more than illusory exchange. . . . What is present in an abstract form in the Jewish religion—contempt for theory, for art, for history, for man as an end in himself—is the actual and conscious standpoint, the virtue, of the man of money. . . . The chimerical nationality of the Jew is the nationality of the merchant, of the man of money in general. . . .

The ungrounded and unfounded law of the Jew is only the religious caricature of . . . the purely formal rites with which the world of self-interest surrounds itself. Here too the supreme relation of man is the legal relation, the relation of laws which apply to him not because they are the laws of his own will and nature but because they dominate him and because breaches of them would be avenged. . . .

As soon as society succeeds in abolishing the empirical essence of Judaism—the market and the conditions which give rise to it— the Jew will have become impossible. . . . The social emancipation of the Jew is the emancipation of society from Judaism.[44]

How are we to understand the tension between Marx's unequivocal defense of the political emancipation of Jews in his first essay and his deployment of this mouthful of anti-Jewish economic stereotypes in the second essay?

One interpretative strategy is to normalize it. We could observe that the use of *Jew* as a synonym for *usurer* was eminently respectable and that similar economic stereotypes of Jews were found widely within the radical milieu of which the young Marx was part.[45] We could point out that Moses Hess (a pioneer of Zionism) wrote of the special role of Jews in the bourgeois "huckster world" and regarded Jews as the prototype of the "man of money"; or that Heinrich Heine wrote in an attack on Jewish bankers that he did not believe that "Israel ever gave money, save when its teeth were drawn by force"; or that the Hegelian scholar Eduard Gans, whose lectures Marx attended at university and who founded a society for Jewish studies, declared in the society's journal that Jewish life reflected a "double aristocracy whose component parts . . . are . . . money and rabbis."[46] These instances may illustrate how widespread anti-Jewish economic criticism was among radical intellectuals, Jewish and non-Jewish, but they do not address why Marx used language in the second essay that seems to cross any boundary between social criticism of certain Jewish classes and proto-antisemitism.

Perhaps Marx was more Bauerite than I have suggested? The difference between Bauer and Marx could on this reading be reduced to the difference between one who demands that Jews give up their noxious Judaism *prior* to being granted equal rights, and the other who advances equal rights for Jews as a prequel for Jews giving up their Judaism. If we followed this line of interpretation, we could read Marx as at once an advocate of equal rights for Jews and a critic of their secular attachments to money. We could say that Marx was chastising the Jews: "You take your rights but offer nothing in return." This reading of the text turns Marx into a pale reflection of Bauer, but it does not explain the discontinuity with the first essay, in which support for emancipation of Jews is radically dissociated from anything to do with the Jewish question.

Let me put forward, then, an alternative reading of the text. It is that the grammar of Marx's response to Bauer in the second essay is meant to be the same as the grammar of his response in the first essay. While Bauer represents the Jew as "moneyman," Marx responds that in the modern world "money has become a world power." While Bauer imagines that money is "the practical spirit of the Jews," Marx responds that money has become "the practical spirit of the Christian peoples." While Bauer insists that Jews play a clandestine and destructive role in the financing of the modern state, Marx responds that the power of money has become as pervasive as nation-states. While Bauer says that money is the "jealous God of Israel" before whom no other god may stand, Marx responds that the God of the Jews has become the God of the world. In short, the second essay turns the anti-Jewish economic stereotypes Bauer expressed on their head.

Articulated in an intensely facetious style, Marx's strategy was not to challenge the veracity of antisemitic representations of Jews but to reveal their irrelevance. The association of Judaism with global financial power was not Marx's but Bauer's; it was the common sense of the evolving antisemitism that Bauer represented. We may speculate that Marx used Bauer's proto-antisemitic language in the second essay to express his growing disgust with this whole way of thinking. Marx's tone certainly became harsher and more sarcastic the more he saw through the shallowness of Bauer's "radicalism." This reading of the text may also help explain why Marx never returned to the proto-antisemitic thematics sometimes attributed to him. However, if I am right in this interpretation, we still have to ask why Marx did not make it plain that he did not endorse the anti-Jewish stereotypes he was mocking.

The distinction between the grammar of Marx's response to Bauer and that of Bauer's other (Jewish and non-Jewish) critics is that Marx refused to engage with Bauer on the terrain of whether his depiction of Jews was empirically grounded.[47] Some of Bauer's other critics had amply demonstrated that "the Jews" were a more complex, differentiated, and class-divided category of people than Bauer could possibly acknowledge. Hess pointed out that Bauer's association of *Judentum* with egoism exposed a woeful ignorance of Jewish society on the part of its author: "Nothing is more foreign to the spirit of Judaism than the egoistic salvation of the isolated individual. . . . No nation refutes egoism more strongly than the Jewish."[48] Heine declared wittily, "Some think they know the Jews because they have seen their beards."[49] Marx has often been criticized for not dwelling on the inaccuracy of Bauer's representation of "the Jews," but we may treat this as a mark of recognition that no amount of evidence about the true nature of Jewish life is going to change the mind of those who choose to go down an antisemitic path. As Sartre observed a century later, the antisemitic outlook is effectively resistant to empirical criticism of this sort. In *Antisemite and Jew* (1946) Sartre described antisemitism as a "passion" that is not caused or refutable by experience: "The essential thing here is not a 'historical fact' but the idea that the agents of history formed for themselves of the Jew."[50] There is a sense in which the antisemite can never lose the argument. If we point out that most Jews are not powerful financiers or that most powerful financiers are not Jews, the antisemitic imagination remains no less fixed on the Jewish financier. Marx's refusal to challenge Bauer on empirical grounds may be read as an intuitive understanding that antisemitism is not simply a prejudice that can be dispelled by evidence.

The radicalism of Marx's response to Bauer lay in breaking from the whole perspective of the Jewish question.[51] His defense of Jewish emancipation broke from any assumption of the goodness of Prussian or Christian civil society. It refused to attribute the uncivil traits of civil society to the exclusivism of Jews. It had no truck with the idea that Jews had to earn their right to rights by throwing off their allegedly harmful Jewish characteristics. It repudiated the idea that the humanity of Jews—like the humanity of criminals in Bentham's panopticon—was an abstraction whose realization required penitence, reform, education, and self-punishment. Marx detached the emancipation of Jews from all such qualifications.[52]

The Jewish Question and Human Emancipation

If divergent readings of Marx's second essay are possible, how are we to decide which is the most accurate? It may be indicative of how we should read these essays on the Jewish question that Bauer went on to play with the idea of shipping German Jews to "the land of Canaan" and to paint the Jews as "white Negroes" incapable of conversion to Christianity,[53] while Marx went on to develop a universalistic critique of value, money, and capital. We cannot enter into the young Marx's mind, but let us imagine that Marx himself was at the time of writing uncertain of what he meant. This may allow us to work out another interpretative strategy, one that relates Marx's words to his wider conception of human emancipation.

Marx's retention of the distinction between political and human emancipation proved prescient not because he wanted to devalue the rights of man and citizen but, on the contrary, because equal rights for Jews (which for the most part were achieved in western Europe by the 1870s) proved to be a prelude not for human emancipation but for political antisemitism. Legal recognition of Jews turned out to be no guarantee of social recognition. Indeed it was when Jews achieved equal legal status that antisemitism became an organized political movement, and it was in the name of antisemitism that a wave of *ressentiment*, nurtured by a sense of injustice that Jews were treated as equal human beings, was directed at Jews and at states that recognized Jews.

Marx's critique of capitalism was guided by humanist concerns and based on a universalistic idea of humanity. His aim was to comprehend the fate of humanity in the modern capitalistic world.[54] In a society dominated by the dull compulsion of economic forces, in which humanity is enslaved to the movement of things, Marx's goal was the emancipation of humanity by humanity, a "real humanism," as he put it. What content did Marx give to the idea of "real humanism"? According to Karl Löwith's account, Marx's idea of human emancipation signified "emancipation from every kind of particularity in human life as a whole; from the specialisation of occupations just as much as from religion and privatisation."[55] This conception of human emancipation as emancipation from every kind of particularity receives support from those sections of the *Communist Manifesto* in which Marx and Engels pay homage to the dissolving effects of bourgeois society: "All fixed, fast frozen relations, with their train of ancient and venerable prejudices and opinions, are swept away. . . . All that is solid melts into air. . . . All that is holy is profaned." Marx and Engels attributed the power of dissolving all particulars to the demonic energy of the bourgeoisie: "The bourgeoisie . . . has left no other bond between man and man than naked self-interest. . . . The bourgeoisie has resolved personal worth into exchange value. . . . The bourgeoisie has drowned . . . religious fervour . . . in the icy waters of egoistical calculation. . . . The bourgeoisie has stripped of its halo every occupation hitherto honoured. . . . The bourgeoisie has torn away from the family its sentimental veil."[56] The bourgeoisie created a proletariat lacking in name, individuality, place, and all particular qualities. Nothing could be taken from them because all had already been taken. They had been made into commodities bought and sold in the marketplace. Marx was soon to recognize that wageworkers in capitalist society are not commodities but owners of commodities, beginning with their own capacity to labor. They therefore have more to lose than their chains.[57] In the *Manifesto*, however, communism appeared as the movement of the proletariat whose aim was to abolish particularity for all—property, family, independence, marriage, religion, and nationality—while the bourgeoisie had abolished them only for some.

If this were Marx's conception of human emancipation, then it would be hard to imagine what place there could be for Judaism or Jews in the communist future. The specter of capitalism Marx and Engels put forward so forcibly appears uncomfortably close to the premonition Nietzsche had of a barbarism-to-come: "The waters of religion are ebbing and are leaving behind swamps or ponds; the nations are again separating from one another in the most hostile manner and are trying to rip each other to shreds.... Never was the world more a world, never was it poorer in love. . . . Everything . . . serves the coming barbarism."[58] If Jews appear, as they do in the antisemitic imagination, as the particularized people par excellence, then it is but a short step to see emancipation from Judaism as a first step in the emancipation of humanity from all particulars. Did Marx as a young man, like Nietzsche after him, have a brief sojourn in the infected territory of antisemitic thought? It is doubtful. In the *Communist Manifesto* Marx and Engels wrote of the "barbarism" into which capitalist society was regressing and poured scorn on the "foul and enervating literature" of so-called German true socialism—a form of socialism capable only of "hurling the traditional anathemas against liberalism, against representative government, against bourgeois competition, against bourgeois freedom of the press, bourgeois legislation, bourgeois liberty and equality, and of preaching to the masses that they had nothing to gain, and everything to lose," by all of these. One of the key aims of "true" German socialism, as Marx and Engels called it, was to dissolve the fiction of equal rights for Jews and present the Jews as "a secret world power which makes and unmakes governments."[59] Marx's disgust with this political philosophy was palpable.

For Bauer and those who followed in his footsteps, human emancipation was premised on particularizing the Jews and then imagining a "world without Jews." The vista of human emancipation Marx put forward was quite different. He does not say much about it, but in the final paragraphs of the first essay on the Jewish question he introduces this formulation: "Only when real individual man resumes the abstract citizen into himself and as an individual man has become a species-being in his empirical life, only when man has recognised and organised his *forces propres* as *social forces* so that social force is no longer separated from him in the form of *political* force, only then will human emancipation be completed."[60] In this singular utopian moment Marx offered a conception of human emancipation that was based not on overcoming the achievements of political emancipation but on overcoming the dominance of abstractions over individual lives—a dominance exemplified in its most irrational form in the abstraction of "the Jews." The real humanism Marx reached out for was not about excluding Jews for failing the test of universality but about recognizing the humanity of all human beings, including Jews. For Marx, recognition of the right of *all* human beings to have rights, as Hannah Arendt later put it,[61] is the beginning of a long and arduous journey of human self-emancipation.

This humanist Marx is not the only Marx we can find, and in order to uncover it we have to shake off "the pulviscular cloud of critical discourse" that has surrounded Marx's work.[62] We have to reconstruct for ourselves Marx's own writings. However, one advantage of this reading of Marx is to recover a tradition of critical theory, which understands that the Jewish question is fundamentally a non-Jewish question and that resistance to antisemitism is a core component of critical theory and practice. This approach may not solve the puzzle of the second essay to everyone's satisfaction, but it is to my mind what is most important.

Notes

1. See, e.g., Silberner, "Was Marx an Anti-Semite?"; Carlebach, *Karl Marx and the Radical Critique of Judaism*; Poliakov, *Histoire de l'Antisémitisme*, 227–37; Kaplan, *Marx Antisemite?*; Rose, *Revolutionary Antisemitism in Germany from Kant to Wagner*, 296–305; Johnson, *A History of the Jews*, 350–52.

2. See Wheen, *Karl Marx*, 56.

3. See Fischer, *The Socialist Response*; Postone, "History and Helplessness"; Postone, "'Anti-Semitism and National Socialism"; Traverso, *The Marxists and the Jewish Question*.

4. Léon Poliakov argues, "Un coup d'oeil sur la correspondance de Karl Marx suffit pour nous apprendre qu'il se complaisait à des pointes antisémites jusqu'à la fin de ses jours." While we must take seriously a man of Poliakov's scholarship, I do not share this view. Poliakov comments on Marx: "On peut croire aussi que les Juifs, qu'il ne connaissait qu'à travers quelques bourgeois, lui paraissaient aussi condamnables que ce monde" (*Histoire de l'Antisémitisme*, 233–34). Poliakov was convinced that Marx was in a long line of radicals who identified bourgeois society with Judaism.

5. See Draper, *Karl Marx's Theory of Revolution IV*, 60.

6. Anderson, *Marx at the Margins*, 262n18.

7. Quoted in Anderson, *Marx at the Margins*, 51.

8. Traverso records that in Germany in 1780 nine-tenths of Jews belonged to the poorest strata of the population and that a century later the proportion had been reversed: the poor constituted no more than a tenth (Traverso, *The Jews in Germany*, 14). At the time of Marx's writing, in 1843, Julius Carlebach records that small traders and hawkers constituted 66 percent of the Jewish working population in Prussia and most of the Jewish working population in Eastern Europe. Marx recognized that the historic role of Jews in commerce and usury in precapitalist commercial society was being replaced by the more systematic processes of national capital (Carlebach, *Karl Marx and the Radical Critique of Judaism*, 56).

9. Engels wrote of Dühring's "hatred of Jews, exaggerated to the verge of absurdity." Engels went on, "That same philosopher of reality who has a sovereign contempt for all prejudices and superstitions is himself so deeply imbued with personal crotchets that he calls the popular prejudice against the Jews, inherited from the bigotry of the Middle Ages, a 'natural judgment' based on 'natural grounds,' and he rises to the pyramidal heights of the assertion that 'socialism is the only power which can oppose population conditions with a strong Jewish admixture.' (Conditions with a Jewish admixture! What 'natural' German language!) Enough of this. . . . He cannot produce his philosophy of reality without dragging in his repugnance to tobacco, cats and Jews as a general law valid for the whole of the rest of humanity, including the Jews themselves" (Engels, *Anti-Dühring*, 126, 161).

10. Quoted in Draper, *Karl Marx's Theory of Revolution*, 3: 293.

11. Quoted in Draper, *Karl Marx's Theory of Revolution*, 3: 296.

12. Fischer, *The Socialist Response*, 13.

13. Fischer, *The Socialist Response*, 39.

14. Cited in Fischer, *The Socialist Response*, 53.

15. Cited in Carlebach, *Karl Marx and the Radical Critique of Judaism*, 265–66.

16. Traverso, *The Marxists and the Jewish Question*, 4.

17. Fischer, *The Socialist Response*, 58.

18. Even Luxemburg is quoted as saying in 1910 that Marx arrived at an understanding of the "social base" of the Jewish problem, namely, that Judaism was nothing other than the "spirit of the usurer and the trickster" (Traverso, *The Marxists and the Jewish Question*, 16).

19. See Hertzberg, *The French Enlightenment and the Jews*, 269–368.

20. Gottlieb, "Between Judaism and German Enlightenment"; Mendelssohn, *Moses Mendelssohn*; Mirabeau, *Sur Moses Mendelssohn*.

21. Quoted in Hunt, *Inventing Human Rights*, 155–58.

22. Gershom Scholem's comment that emancipation costs the Jews "the formal disavowal of Jewish nationality—a price that the outstanding writers and the spokesmen of the Jewish vanguard were only too happy to pay," should be read in the light of the restrictions "nationality" implied in the prerevolutionary context (cited in Traverso, *The Marxists and the Jewish Question*, 22).

23. Mendelssohn, *Jerusalem or on Religious Power and Judaism*, quoted in Alexander, *The Civil Sphere*, 477.

24. Quoted in Traverso, *The Jews and Germany*, 5.

25. Quoted in Alexander, *The Civil Sphere*, 466–71. See also Robert Fine, "Cosmopolitanism and Antisemitism."

26. Quoted in Alexander, *The Civil Sphere*, 477.

27. Avineri, *Hegel's Theory of the Modern State*, 119–20.

28. Hegel, *The Elements of the Philosophy of Right*, 15–19.

29. Hegel, *The Elements of the Philosophy of Right*, §209R, §270n.

30. Engels once characterized Jews as one of the ahistorical and residual peoples who were once suppressed by the more historic nations and then became "fanatical standard-bearers of counter-revolution." He also described Polish Jews as "the dirtiest of all races." However, Engels also denounced antisemitism as a reactionary form of "feudal socialism" with which social democracy could have nothing in common (Traverso, *The Marxists and the Jewish Question*, 23–26).

31. Colletti's introduction to Marx, "On the Jewish Question," 7–56.

32. Marx, "On the Jewish Question," 213, 212–13, 227, 216.

33. Marx and Engels, *The Holy Family*, 137–38. See also Marx, "On the Jewish Question," 214–17.

34. Marx, "On the Jewish Question," 216.

35. Marx and Engels, *The Holy Family*, 112–13.

36. Marx, "On the Jewish Question," 217.

37. Quoted in Marx and Engels, *The Holy Family*, 119.

38. Marx and Engels, *The Holy Family*, 118.

39. Marx, "On the Jewish Question," 222.

40. Marx and Engels, *The Holy Family*, 143.

41. Marx, "On the Jewish Question," 226.

42. Marx, "On the Jewish Question," 230.

43. Seymour, *Law, Antisemitism and the Holocaust*, 11.

44. Marx, "On the Jewish Question," 236–41.

45. Draper, *Karl Marx's Theory of Revolution*, 1: 591–608.

46. Draper, *Karl Marx's Theory of Revolution*, 1: 593–95 .

47. Carlebach, *Karl Marx and the Radical Critique of Judaism*, 353.

48. Quoted in Carlebach, *Karl Marx and the Radical Critique of Judaism*, 195.

49. Quoted in Carlebach, *Karl Marx and the Radical Critique of Judaism*, 190.

50. Sartre, *Antisemite and Jew*, 15.

51. I do not see the evidence for the contention of Jeffrey Alexander that "Marx continues to insist, as other Jewish reformers had before him, that Jews must change to achieve the emancipation promised by civil society" (*The Civil Sphere*, 486). The change Alexander thinks Marx insisted upon was that Jews could achieve "real emancipation only by abandoning religion and working for revolutionary transformation" (487). Keen as Marx was for Jews and non-Jews

to take the road of revolution, there is no evidence in Marx's works that he made the emancipation of Jews *conditional* upon their joining the revolutionary cause. Such a scenario would have gone directly against the spirit of Marx's actual insistence on distinguishing political from human emancipation.

52. This interpretation diverges from Traverso's comment that Marx took up themes already present in Ludwig Feuerbach, that Judaism was the religion of egoism, and more generally in the Young Hegelians that the Jew was equated with money (Traverso, *The Marxists and the Jewish Question*, 18). Marx in his youth was immersed in the thinking of the Young Hegelians but was also involved in a critical appraisal of the "radical extremes" (Löwith, *From Hegel to Nietzsche*) into which the Hegelian synthesis was split. Marx learned to reject both the Christian theological critique of Judaism and its secularized derivatives.

53. Carlebach, *Karl Marx and the Radical Critique of Judaism*, 147.

54. See Löwith, *Max Weber and Karl Marx*, 42–43; Löwith, *From Hegel to Nietzsche*, 102–30.

55. Löwith, *Max Weber and Karl Marx*, 106.

56. Marx and Engels, *Communist Manifesto*, 38.

57. Marx and Engels, *Communist Manifesto*, 64–65.

58. Nietzsche, *Untimely Meditations*, 148–49. Nietzsche foresaw a spiritless radicalism arising from these swamps, full of hostility to rights, law, culture—and Jews. "I have not met a German yet who was well disposed toward the Jews," he wrote, and did not exempt himself as a young man: "During a brief daring sojourn in very infected territory, I too did not altogether escape this disease" (cited in Yovel, *Dark Riddle*, 119). In *Genealogy of Morals* Nietzsche described antisemites as "*men of ressentiment*, physiologically unfortunate and worm-eaten, a whole tremulous realm of subterranean revenge, inexhaustible and insatiable in outbursts against the fortunate and happy" (111 §14). Mealy-mouthed he was not.

59. Marx and Engels, *Communist Manifesto*, 57.

60. Marx, "On the Jewish Question," 234.

61. Arendt, *The Origins of Totalitarianism*. 298.

62. Calvino, *Why Read the Classics?* 6.

References

Alexander, Jeffrey. *The Civil Sphere*. Oxford: Oxford University Press, 2006.

Anderson, Kevin. *Marx at the Margins: On Nationalism, Ethnicity, and Non-Western Societies*. Chicago: University of Chicago Press, 2010.

Arendt, Hannah. *The Origins of Totalitarianism*. New York: Harvest, 1976.

Avineri, Shlomo. *Hegel's Theory of the Modern State*. Cambridge: Cambridge University Press, 1974.

———. "Marx and Jewish Emancipation." *Journal of the History of Ideas* 25.3 (1964): 445–50.

————. "A Note on Hegel's Views on Jewish Emancipation." *Jewish Social Studies* 25.2 (1963): 145–51.

Bauer, Bruno. "Die Fähigkeit der heutigen Juden und Christen, frei zu werden" (The capacity of present-day Jews and Christians to become free). 1843. In *Einundzwanzig Bogen aus der Schweiz*, edited by Georg Herwegh, 136–54. Leipzig: Reclam 1989.

————. *Die Judenfrage* (The Jewish question). Braunschweig: Friedrich Otto Verlag, 1843.

————. "Neueste Schriften über die Judenfrage." *Allgemeine Literatur—Zeitung*, March 1844.

Calvino, Italo. *Why Read the Classics?* Translated by Martin McLaughlin. London: Jonathan Cape, 1999.

Carlebach, Julius. *Karl Marx and the Radical Critique of Judaism*. London: Littman Library of Jewish Civilisation, Routledge and Kegan Paul, 1978.

Draper, Hal. *Karl Marx's Theory of Revolution*. Vol. 1: *State and Bureaucracy*. New York: Monthly Review Press, 1977.

————. *Karl Marx's Theory of Revolution*. Vol. 3: *The Dictatorship of the Proletariat*. New York: Monthly Review Press, 1986.

————. *Karl Marx's Theory of Revolution*. Vol. 4: *The Critique of Other Socialisms*. New York: Monthly Review Press, 1990.

Engels, Frederick. *Anti-Dühring*. London: Lawrence and Wishart, 1943.

Ezra, Michael. "Karl Marx: Radical Antisemitism." *Harry's Place*, May 12, 2009, http://hurryupharry.org/2009/05/12/karl-marx-radical-antisemitism/. (Accessed November 2013.)

Fine, Robert. *Democracy and the Rule of Law*. London: Pluto, 1985.

————. *Political Investigations: Hegel, Marx, Arendt*. London: Routledge, 2001.

————. "Cosmopolitanism and Antisemitism: Two Faces of Universality." In *On Cosmopolitan Modernity*, edited by Anastasia Marinopoulou. London: Continuum, forthcoming.

Fischer, Lars. "The Non-Jewish Question and Other 'Jewish Questions' in Modern Germany (and Austria)." *Journal of Modern History* 82 (December 2010): 876–901.

————. *The Socialist Response to Antisemitism in Imperial Germany*. Cambridge: Cambridge University Press, 2007.

Gottlieb, Michah. "Between Judaism and German Enlightenment: Recent Work on Moses Mendelssohn in English." *Religion Compass* 4.1 (2010): 22–38.

Hegel, Georg. *The Elements of the Philosophy of Right*. Cambridge: Cambridge University Press, 1991.

Hertzberg, Arthur. *The French Enlightenment and the Jews: The Origins of Modern Anti-Semitism*. New York: Columbia University Press, 1990.

Hunt, Lynn. *Inventing Human Rights: A History*. New York: Norton, 2007.

Johnson, Paul. *A History of the Jews*. London: Phoenix, 1994.

Kaplan, Francis. *Marx Antisemite?* Paris: Berg International, 1990.

Löwith, Karl. *From Hegel to Nietzsche*. Garden City NY: Doubleday Anchor, 1967.

———. *Max Weber and Karl Marx*. London: Routledge, 1993.

Marx, Karl. "On the Jewish Question." In *Marx's Early Writings*, edited by Lucio Colletti, 211–41. Harmondsworth: Penguin, 1992.

———. "Wage Labour and Capital." In Karl Marx and Friedrich Engels, *Selected Works in One Volume*, 64–93. London: Lawrence and Wishart, 1970.

Marx, Karl, and Friedrich Engels. *The Communist Manifesto*. In *Selected Works in One Volume*, 31–63. London: Lawrence and Wishart, 1970.

Marx, Karl, and Friedrich Engels. *Letters*. http://www.marxists.org/archive/marx/letters/date/.

Marx, Karl, and Friedrich Engels. *The Holy Family or Critique of Critical Criticism: Against Bruno Bauer and Company*. Moscow: Progress, 1980.

McLellan, David. *Marx before Marxism*. London: Penguin, 1972.

Mendelssohn, Moses. *Moses Mendelssohn: Selections from His Writings*. Edited and translated by Eva Jospe. Introduction by Alfred Jospe. New York: Viking Press, 1975.

Mirabeau, Honore-Gabriel. *Sur Moses Mendelssohn, sur la reforme politique des Juifs*. 1853. Whitefish MT: Kessinger, 2009.

Nietzsche, Friedrich. *Untimely Meditations*. 1876. Translated by R. J. Hollingdale. Cambridge: Cambridge University Press, 1997.

Nietzsche, Friedrich. *On the Genealogy of Morals: A Polemic*. 1887. Translated by Douglas Smith. Oxford: Oxford University Press, 2009.

Poliakov, Léon. *Histoire de l'Antisémitisme: 2 L'Age de la Science*. Paris: Seuil, 1981.

Postone, Moishe. "Anti-Semitism and National Socialism." In *Germans and Jews since the Holocaust*, edited by Anson Rabinbach and Jack Zipes, 302–14. New York: Holmes and Meier, 1986.

———. "History and Helplessness: Mass Mobilisation and Contemporary Forms of Anticapitalism." *Public Culture* 18.1 (2006): 93–110.

Rose, Gillian. *Hegel contra Sociology*. London: Athlone, 1981.

Rose, Paul. *Revolutionary Antisemitism in Germany from Kant to Wagner*. Princeton NJ: Princeton University Press, 1990.

Sartre, Jean-Paul. *Antisemite and Jew*. New York: Schocken, 1965.

Seymour, David. *Law, Antisemitism and the Holocaust*. London: Glasshouse, 2007.

Silberner, Edmund. "Was Marx an Anti-Semite?" *Historia Judaica* 11.1 (1949): 3–52.

Traverso, Enzo. *The Jews and Germany*. Translated by Daniel Weissbort. Lincoln: University of Nebraska Press, 1995.

———. *The Marxists and the Jewish Question: The History of a Debate 1843–1943*. Translated by Bernard Gibbons. Amherst MA: Humanity Books, 1994.

Wheen, Francis. *Karl Marx*. London: Fourth Estate, 1999.

Yovel, Yirmiyahu. *Dark Riddle: Hegel, Nietzsche, and the Jews*. University Park: Pennsylvania State University Press, 1998.

6

From Assimilationist Antiracism to Zionist Anti-antisemitism

Georg Simmel, Franz Boas, and Arthur Ruppin

AMOS MORRIS-REICH

This essay delineates three responses to antisemitism by social scientists of Jewish descent: Georg Simmel (1858-1918), one of the founders of academic sociology; Franz Boas (1858-1942), the founder of American cultural anthropology; and Arthur Ruppin (1876-1943), the founder of Jewish sociology and demography. Simmel and Boas were both staunch supporters of Jewish assimilation; Ruppin, a prominent Zionist leader, was an opponent of assimilation. All three thinkers recognized the reality of modern antisemitism and viewed it as a set of cognitive and social practices that were irreducible to Christian animosity toward Jews. Their responses to antisemitism diverge, though, with regard to the epistemic and ontological status of antisemitism and regarding the question of what should be done about it. My principal proposition in this chapter is that the reactions of these three thinkers were shaped by a generational difference, namely whether they had grown up in a historical context when the ideal of assimilation was still intact, as did Simmel and Boas, or in a somewhat later context when this ideal had already been destroyed by the renewed antisemitism of the 1870s, as was the case with Ruppin. Continuing allegiance to assimilation made it difficult for the two representatives of the older generation directly to challenge antisemitism, whereas the replacement of this ideal by Zionism made it easier to do so for the younger Ruppin; however, the assimilationist perspective prompted the former two to develop social science perspectives that were designed to be more or less immune to race thinking, whereas the anti-assimilationist perspective was capable of accommodating a certain conception of race.

Simmel, Boas, and Ruppin were at one stage or another objects of direct antisemitism. Simmel's academic career was impeded by antisemitic sentiments within the German academy.[1] In 1908 an antisemitic letter by Dietrich Schäffer effectively blocked Simmel's appointment to a professorship in the Philosophy Faculty at Heidelberg University. Boas was the subject of antisemitic insults from his childhood in Minden, throughout his student years in Berlin and Kiel, and after he moved to the United States, within the academic milieu. Boas arrived in the United States in 1887 with visible scars on his face, the result of duels that he had initiated in defense of his honor against antisemitic insults. In his childhood home in Magdeburg, Ruppin suffered from antisemitic insults from his schoolmates.[2] In his diary Ruppin monitored with great sensitivity changes in the social antisemitism he encountered. Countering antisemitism as well as collecting statistics on contemporary Jewry was clearly at the root of his establishing the Berliner Büro für jüdische Statistik und Demographie.

A wave of antisemitism swept German society in the 1870s. This wave peaked in the Berlin antisemitism dispute of 1879-80. In modern antisemitism, Christian, secular, and anti-Christian ideas and images, racial categories, and the politics of the newly united Germany were intimately mixed. Antisemitism became a social and cultural phenomenon so widely spread that it could not be avoided, a fact that affected individual Germans, both Jewish and Gentile. Simmel and Boas encountered the antisemitic wave of the 1870s as young men, when they were already deeply committed to ideas of integration and assimilation. Ruppin, however, grew up in a society marked by the presence of social and intellectual antisemitism from a much earlier age. Simmel and Boas chose an indirect strategy of response to antisemitism, whereas Ruppin responded to it directly.

Their specific forms of response cannot be understood without reference to the role of race in the development of anthropology and sociology as disciplines. As academic disciplines in German universities, sociology and anthropology are both developments of the latter half of the nineteenth century. Both sociology and anthropology were greatly influenced by similar conceptual tendencies such as Spencer's theory of differentiation and Darwin's theory of evolution. Concepts of race, however, developed differently in each discipline. In the German case, anthropology was conceptually, if not always empirically, differentiated from *Ethnologie*, *Volkskunde*, and *Völkerkunde* and referred to the natural scientific study of man and the species' biological history. *Anthropologie* (physical anthropology) almost inherently entailed concepts of race—in the plural, though, as concepts of race ranged from racial determinism to race as at least in part a social construct. Leaving aside the complex question of whether a discipline based on notions of race is inherently racist or not, it should be noted that in Germany up until the turn of the twentieth century anthropology was led by politically liberal luminaries such as Rudolf Virchow, who viewed themselves, and were viewed by their environment, as staunchly antiracist and anti-antisemitic. Virchow was a vocal opponent of political antisemitism. In retrospect, however, his anthropological surveys of German schoolchildren were more ambiguous and may have inadvertently contributed to the antisemitic racialization of Jews.[3]

In German sociology by the end of the nineteenth century, the status of biology in general and of race in particular was fiercely disputed. This controversy had appeared and had already been resolved on the institutional level before World War I. With the support of the most prominent members of the guild, including Ferdinand Tönnies, Max Weber, and Simmel, race, at least officially, was expelled from the sociological discipline.[4]

Furthermore it is important to keep in mind that the genealogy of antisemitism is different from that of race, and, while historically related, the two should be clearly distinguished. Key antisemites of the period, including Richard Wagner and Wilhelm Marr, were not primarily preoccupied with the concept of race, whereas prominent figures in the genealogy of racism such as Count Joseph Gobineau, Ernst Haeckel, Francis Galton, and William Ripley viewed Jews as racially inferior but were much more focused on race as a general organizing principle. While race and antisemitism are historically entangled in this period, their interplay allowed appropriation or rejection of both, as well as the possibility of rejecting one and adopting the other.

Anti-Jewish themes and stereotypes played a complex role in social science of the period. Even a socially influenced person such as Gustav Schmoller, a monarchist historian of economics who greatly influenced the development of sociology and who had published the works of Jewish authors (including an early essay by Simmel) in the yearbook he edited, expressed anti-Jewish ideas. Wilhelm Dilthey, to take another prominent example, developed a strictly individualist notion of the *Geisteswissenschaften* that excluded "race." While Dilthey impeded Simmel's appointment in Berlin University, he was not viewed as antisemitic and in fact supported several Jewish scholars. His historical account of Germany, however, emphasized the central role of the Church and the army, a common perception of Germany that not only excluded Jews but was also closely associated with antisemitic views. Equally complex is Weber's case. His sociological work could hardly be seen as antisemitic. Weber, as is well known, supported Simmel's (failed) appointment at Heidelberg University and was known to be a supporter of Jewish students. But comments made in *Economy and Society* and his conception of "Jewish rationalism" nonetheless reconnected with contemporary antisemitic themes or stereotypes.[5]

In the history of the social sciences there existed also direct links between antisemitic ideology and specific branches of knowledge. The Americans William Ripley and Madison Grant relied on racialist concepts that represented Jews as inferior, expressing explicitly antisemitic arguments and images. Grant also established the Galton Society in 1918 as an antisemitic alternative to the American Anthropological Association, after Boas was elected as its president.[6] Ernst Haeckel's stance with regard to Jews and antisemitism has been a matter of much historical debate.[7] Yet it is clear that his philosophical-anthropological theoretical framework played a key role in the generation of racist antisemitic literature.

Albeit employing different strategies, Simmel's and Boas's responses to antisemitism are closely tied to their repudiation of principles of fundamental racial difference. In contrast, certain other scholars of Jewish descent rejected antisemitic claims but did not reject racial categories as such. This is demonstrated in Ignaz Zollschan's *Das Rassenproblem*, which appeared in Vienna in 1912, and in Ludwik Gumplowicz's earlier *Der Rassenkampf*.[8] Authors of Jewish background responded to antisemitism differently and according to their dissimilar conceptual presuppositions. Significantly, therefore, the different biographical, intellectual, and institutional aspects do not necessarily coincide. In this multifaceted and complex historical context, which includes personal, intellectual, and institutional aspects, we must place Simmel, Boas, and Ruppin.

The generation of German Jews born in the 1850s and early 1860s obtained their entire schooling in the German educational system. The German language was its principal and often sole language, and, as a rule, this generation was deeply committed not only to German culture and values but to the idea of Jewish integration into German society and culture. Antisemitic ideas were not disseminated solely by writers of pamphlets, ideologues, and politicians,[9] but after the renowned historian Heinrich von Treitschke legitimized the term *antisemitism* in his 1879 article "Our Prospects," even to liberal Jews who had admired Treitschke for his liberal nationalism it became clear that intellectual antisemitism had become established and could no longer be disregarded. But members of this generation were faced with a dilemma: a direct response to antisemitism undermined their own commitment to assimilation by calling it into question. Indeed many Jews of this generation responded only indirectly to antisemitism. In contrast, a younger generation that had matured in a society marked by antisemitism experienced rejection by large segments of German society. This younger generation was sometimes better equipped to respond candidly to antisemitism. The paradox, however, exemplified in the case of Ruppin, is that such direct responses were often interlocked with racial concepts. They were grounded in biological categories and impinged on the antisemitic categories that were becoming increasingly prevalent in branches of German social science, particularly within anthropology after 1900. Responses to antisemitism were balanced between ideas of Jewish separation at one ideological end, mainly associated with the Zionist idea, and ideas that focused on the transformation of German society at large, tied to socialist or Marxist universalistic ideologies. This generational dimension is important for the comparative analysis.

Georg Simmel: A Methodology Immune to Race Thinking

Simmel never referred to antisemitism as a circumscribed social phenomenon or even employed the word *antisemitism* in his publications. This does not reflect lack of interest on Simmel's behalf, or his failure to notice the existence of antisemitism in German society, but rather is a sign that he viewed it as particularly sensitive matter that necessitated great caution.[10] Simmel supported Jewish integration into German society and culture and, as Köhnke has observed, viewed any public allusion to antisemitism by individuals of Jewish descent as a potential obstacle to that integration. Substantiation for this interpretation can be found in the fact that in his private correspondences Simmel refers more than once to antisemitism in Germany and Austria.[11]

Simmel's response to antisemitism can be examined through separate but interconnected perspectives, ranging from general epistemic considerations to more specific allusions to race or Jews. He does not deny the reality of markers of Jewish difference but, based on a specific set of sociological principles, attempts to undermine the antisemitic claim that these markers are biologically innate or racially determined. But his strategy is to circumvent the definition of antisemitism as a separate object or set of social interactions with distinctive characteristics. This can be demonstrated through the way theoretical presuppositions condition references to Jews or to racial difference.

Throughout his career Simmel created an elaborate sociological theory that circumvented and made redundant the category of race, its imagery and markers. Two of his central sociological notions—"social form" and "social type"—directly impinge on the interpretation of Jewish difference. Specifically these notions transform differences commonly conceived as racial into socially constituted differences.

Simmel developed the notions of social form and social type from the bottom up, in terms of individual "interaction." In his choice he was well aware that the principal alternative to interaction throughout the history of philosophy and in contemporary physics was "substance." His insistence that social forms and social types were the result of individual interaction undermined common conceptions of society and culture as preexisting entities, deriving directly from "nature," "Volk," or "race."

The history of the notion of social form, which Simmel developed in his early monograph *On Social Differentiation* (1881-82), demonstrates the composite history of antisemitism in German social science, which involves the delicate interrelationship between conceptual and biographical considerations.[12] Social form was in fact a reformulation of Simmel's German Jewish teacher Moritz Lazarus's notion of *Verdichtung*, or condensation, which Lazarus viewed as the foundation of collective psychology. Lazarus, however, came under the attack of Dilthey, who rejected Lazarus's concepts as based on a collectivistic epistemology. To comply with neo-Kantian individualist epistemology, as well as to withstand Dilthey's criticism, Simmel reframed Lazarus's Verdichtung as a social form on the strictly individualist grounds of individual interaction. Social forms are the result of gradual solidification of individual interactions into stable, persisting forms. Such forms gain an "existence," according to Simmel, and a certain amount of coercive power, though they do not exist in the ontological sense. Yet individuals in any society confront social forms in their daily lives and must grapple with them in order to achieve their individual intentions or goals.

Social form is at the core of Simmel's sociological theory. Simmel employed the notion of individual interaction throughout his career and, as shown by David Frisby, made use of interaction to gradually radicalize his definition of society. In fact in his later work he made interaction between individuals the sole criterion for the existence of society.[13] Any social form therefore is secondary and results from individual interaction. The antisemitic view that Jews are racially different from and inferior to non-Jews was, to follow Simmel's definitions, a social form, an example of the solidification of individual social and cognitive practices into forms that gained a certain "life" or "existence" of their own. Significantly such an interpretation does not necessarily deny the existence of individual differences or differences between groups; it places them, however, in a strictly individualist sociological framework.

Simmel's later notion of social type runs parallel to his idea of social form in certain respects. In contrast to social form, however, which aims for the solidification of relations, social type seeks to account for individual identities. Simmel develops this notion in his programmatic essay "How Is Society Possible?" and employs it for the analysis of numerous such types. The notion of social type is developed through the discussion of three "sociological apriorities." The first principle is that the picture of another person is distorted in principle.[14] This is because every person has a core of individuality that cannot be subjectively reproduced by another. As a result, we think of the individual with his or her singularity under universal categories. In order to recognize that individual, we subsume him or her under a general type.

This sociological a priori principle is closely connected to an additional consideration, namely that the other person is never "entirely himself" but only a fragment of himself. Yet humans cannot grasp fragments, only wholes. As a result, the other man is typed according to the idealization of his personality from given fragments. Simmel's second sociological a priori consideration is that "each element of a group is not a societary part, but beyond that something else." This "constitutes the positive condition for the fact that he is such a group member in other aspects of his being." Simmel's third principle is that "society is a structure of unequal elements," but the possibility of belonging to a society rests on the *assumption* that each individual "is automatically referred to a determined position within his social milieu, that this position ideally belonging to him is also actually present in the social whole."[15] Particular social types are conceived as cast by the specifiable reactions and expectations of others. Yet the latter a priori principles deny the possibility of complete identity between individual and type and between individual and social role.

These sociological principles are at the root of Simmel's entire sociological work, but they also form a response to antisemitism. Simmel maintains that the creation of social types rests on an intimate dialectics between individuals and others. Types therefore are to a great extent "negative," that is, imposed from without, by way of interaction. The relations are with others who assign an individual a particular position and expect him to behave in specific ways. Furthermore this is not entirely an individual matter in the sense that his characteristics are seen as attributes of the social structure. The gist of this interpretation is that an individual assigned to a certain type, be it that of the poor, the whore, the stranger, or any other, has his individual features completed into more general categories of types. In other words, types are socially mediated categories rather than naturally classified differences. Simmel, however, discusses only individual differences and categories he conceives as universal, avoiding the intermediate case of "specific differences," including racial difference. He does not deny the reality of differences but rather subjects them to a strictly individualistic analytical framework. Simmel discusses Jews, as we will see shortly, in terms of the type of the stranger. But, based on the above principles, the very category of the Jew lends itself to analysis as a social type. Jews are individual humans who are classified as "Jews" following the sociological a priori principles elucidated above.

Both social form and social type establish the sociological method on methodological and ontological individualism and view social relations and social identities in individual terms. While Simmel's motivations cannot be reduced to countering antisemitism, these principles clearly contest biological, racial, and historical collectivistic accounts of Jews, Jewish difference, and antisemitic sentiments or social forms.

Simmel's few references to Jews or Jewish difference, when read within the theoretical framework elucidated above, read as part of a strategy to undermine antisemitic representations of Jews. I will illustrate Simmel's strategy of sociologically explaining Jewish difference through two references he makes to the Jews in "The Stranger" and "The Sociology of the Senses."

Simmel was very restrained in his allusions to race. "The Sociology of the Senses," which appeared as an *Exkurs* in the 1908 *Soziologie*, is one of the few places in which he relates to this topic. In this text he alludes to the Jews in a carefully constructed discussion of the sociology of the senses. Simmel analyzes the effect of differences conceived as being racial. He confronts racial differences through a discussion of the sense of smell, presenting it as the lowest and most primitive of the senses. The sense of smell stands in complete opposition to the higher faculties of thought and volition. Furthermore he does not refer to the smell of people but to the smells arising from the environment, which adhere to people.[16] Simmel gives three examples of this phenomenon:

> The reception of the Negro in higher social circles of North America is out of the question by reason of the body odour of the Negro, and the mutual dark aversion between Germanic people [*Germanen*] and Jews has been ascribed to the same cause. Personal contact between educated people and workers often so vigorously advocated for the social development of the present, the *rapprochement* of the two worlds of which the one does not know how the other lives also advocated by the educated classes as an ethical ideal, fails simply because of the insuperability of impressions of smell.[17]

In this passage Simmel juxtaposes three pairs, bringing together social and racial frames of reference: black and high-class North Americans; Jews and Germanic peoples; the proletarian class and the educated. Based on his individualist framework, both "races" as well as "classes" are secondary social constructs. Yet Simmel stages the three pairs in a specific way that implicitly undermines the racist asymmetries underlying these pairs of oppositions. In the American example, for instance, the aversion implied is the aversion of *white* people to Negroes' smell. Simmel, however, speaks only of the "higher social circles of North America" rather than referring to race characteristics. Even in the only pair in which both sides of the opposition are explicitly stated in racial terms, he translates the racial antagonism into terms of class. Through this replacement he implies that the German-Jewish example could also be translated into socially mediated rather than racial frames of reference. Simmel casts racial differences as social constructs, thereby undermining the claim that the difference is natural, inherent, permanent, and unalterable.[18]

Simmel's most famous allusion to Jews is in his Exkurs on the stranger. Different commentators have observed that Simmel's description of the stranger greatly resembles descriptions of Jews.[19] In this text there are two important aspects that are often overlooked. The first aspect I wish to emphasize is that Simmel's stranger, as noted by Otthein Rammstedt, is identifiable by a specific form of interaction. That is, it is cast in sociological categories of individual interaction. The second point is that a close reading of his description reveals that Simmel does not deny the reality of Jewish difference: "[The stranger's] position within [society] is fundamentally affected by the fact that he does not belong in it initially and that he brings qualities into it that are not, and cannot be, indigenous to it."[20] Simmel does not deny the reality of Jewish difference, but the coordinates of his sociological method render Jewish difference and antisemitic sentiments secondary social constructions.

Simmel's sociological theory postulates that social forms are constituted through the gradual solidification of individual interactions. This theory implies that both markers of Jewish difference or identity as well as antisemitic sentiments are ultimately secondary results of individual interactions. Simmel's social theory offers itself as an alternative to theories of society grounded on collectivistic categories in general and to racial categories in particular. His radical epistemological individualism attempts to rule out, in practice if not in theory, the possibility that individual essence can be racially determined.

Simmel's rhetorical strategy is that of circumvention, that is, dealing with antisemitism without circumscribing it as a particular social phenomenon. His implicit interpretation of antisemitism, in this respect, opposed widespread late nineteenth-century views that antisemitism was a natural or a biological phenomenon, constituting the racially determined asymmetric aversion of non-Jews toward Jews.

Franz Boas: Antisemitism as a Form of Prejudice

Boas was a student in Kiel, in northern Germany, when antisemitism became a recognized, institutionalized student movement. Letters to his parents testify to his firsthand encounter with antisemitism.[21]

Similarly to Simmel, Boas wrote voluminously, but only rarely on Jews. Also like Simmel, Boas's strategy was not to isolate antisemitism as a specific social phenomenon but rather to treat it within broader categories of human diversity and prejudice. Unlike Simmel, who attempted to free sociological discourse from racial categories altogether, Boas aimed not at eliminating race from anthropology but at changing its grounding and diminishing its significance. In particular he aimed at undermining deterministic notions of race from within a discourse that was founded on and permeated by "race." He gained his reputation as an anthropologist and scientist from within his anthropological discipline, a fact that endowed his alternative explanations with scientific authority.

Boas's writings address antisemitism on three different, interconnected but separate scientific registers. The first register can be found in his contributions to the field of physical anthropology, most notably his 1911 study of immigrants' children, the subtext of which was to contest political and scientific antisemitism.[22] The second is found in his articles that addressed antisemitism or racism directly. The third register is found in his works that systematically undermined racist scientific methodologies.

The status of race in Boas's earlier work is ambivalent, an ambivalence that is essential for understanding the trajectory of his career with regard to racism and, in a different way, to antisemitism as well. Boas's most important physical anthropological study directly combated antisemitism but was carried out, to a great extent, in racial categories. In the political context of a fierce controversy over the immigration of eastern European Jews and Asians to the United States, Boas studied changes in body form among children of immigrants in New York. Racial theory of the time viewed the skull as the most stable part of the body, racially determined, and least susceptible to change. Proponents of racial determinism used differences in cranial index to argue that differences between races are biological and innate. Opponents of immigration of Jews and

Asians to the United States viewed the inferiority of Jews and Asians as innate and opposed their admittance into the country on racial grounds.

Within this highly polemical context, Boas studied 17,821 individuals of seven ethnonational groups, including a large group of Jewish immigrants. He discovered that the average measures of cranial size of children born within ten years of their mother's arrival were significantly different from those of children born more than ten years after their mother's arrival. Boas did not deny that physical features were inherited but argued that over time the environment has an influence on these features. The unmistakable subtext of this study was the adaptability of populations conceived as racially inferior. The political implications of this study were immediate.[23]

Within the scientific community this study implied that differences between races were not immutable. The status of race in this study, however, is ambivalent. Its ambivalence stems from the fact that Boas chose to operate within a field immersed in race. In order to speak with scientific authority, he attempted to modify the meaning and extension of race rather than to reject it altogether.

The subject of some of Boas's work from the 1920s and 1930s is racist and antisemitic literature in both the United States and Europe. Two essays, published in 1923 and 1934 for a wide readership, directly counter racist, antisemitic, and Nordic racial theories: "Are the Jews a Race?" and "Aryans and Non-Aryans." In both essays Boas deconstructs claims of the existence of Jewish and Aryan races and racial types. He attempts to counter existing literature in which Jews are conceived as a race or a group with specific racial characteristics and argues that Jews are already deeply assimilated in their surroundings. He claims that they display a variety of types and that they were never, even in their pre-Diaspora past, racially homogeneous.

While Boas's essay discusses Jews, his goals transcend those of the "Jewish question." He tackles definitions of race: "Numerous attempts have been made to give a scientific status to the feeling of racial difference and particularly to the claim of Nordic superiority. . . . In none of these discussions, however, do we find a concise and definite answer to the question of what constitutes a race."[24] Rather than move deductively, from the general to the individual case of the Jews, Boas deconstructs racist accounts of Jews in order to discard antisemitic conceptions of race as unscientific. The deconstruction of the Jews' case epitomizes his conception of race: "In practically every nation there is a mixture of different types that in some cases intermingle and scatter through the whole country."[25] Boas's argument concerning the Jews is backed by his perception that peoples are necessarily composed of various racial types and that one should not confuse peoples and racial types. In terms of the specific response to antisemitism, however, Boas, like Simmel, does not deny the existence of Jewish difference but rejects the meaning accorded to it by antisemitic writers. Even in his short article on Jews Boas does not lose sight of his wider anthropological and theoretical goals.

The most important aspect of Boas's response to antisemitism is found in his methodological criticism of racist anthropology. I will briefly exemplify this form of criticism with two cases from which one can learn about his form of argumentation.[26]

The essay "On Alternating Sounds" (1889) illustrates how Boas employed methodological grounds in order to counter racist anthropology. The article was a response to a paper presented a year earlier by the anthropologist and linguist Daniel Garrison Brinton. Brinton had observed that in the spoken languages of many Native Americans, certain sounds regularly alternated. Based on evolutionary theory, he interpreted this as a sign of linguistic inferiority, claiming that Native Americans were at a lower stage of evolution. In his response Boas argued that "alternating sounds" was not a feature of Native American languages but rather a reflection of the culturally determined nature of human perception. What Brinton conceived as alternating sounds did not reflect how the Inuit might pronounce a word but rather how one phonetic system (the English) was unable to accommodate another (the Inuit). Employing a form of neo-Kantian critique, Boas made a unique contribution to the methods of descriptive linguistics. Yet his ultimate goal was to show that the perceptual categories of Western researchers risked systematically misperceiving a meaningful element in another culture. What appeared to be evidence of cultural inferiority was in fact the consequence of unscientific methods and reflected Western beliefs as to their perceived superiority. This essay did not touch on antisemitism directly but bore on Jews, who in Europe were marked as primitive remnants of an inferior life form that inexplicably had survived into modern society.[27]

Boas was famous for his negative form of argumentation: rather than making positive claims, he argued against the methods and empirical findings of the writers he opposed. In the first footnote to *Anthropology and Modern Life*, he lists the names of the most important American and German racist and antisemitic writers and then, in the body of the text, proceeds to systematically undermine each and every point of their methodological and epistemic underpinnings. He claims that the definitions of the racist theorists were weak and untenable and that their analyses were gross simplifications of complex empirical situations. He also questions their form of inductive procedure, which connects arbitrary phenomena that are in fact genetically disparate. Boas employs a radical form of realism in order to criticize their scientific realism and ultimately attacks the "Nordic Idea."[28] He argues against these racist and antisemitic writers by showing that reality does not conform to their definitions of "races," "racial types," or "racial traits."

Bringing these perspectives together, the "bigger picture" of Boas's response to antisemitism emerges. His major contribution was his "normalizing" of antisemitism. Aligning Jews with other minorities, he transformed antisemitism into a subcase of "racism" and "prejudice." This attempt has been so successful within branches of the social sciences that it goes almost unnoticed. Jews are objects of prejudice and hate not because Jews enjoy a special status in Western, Christian civilization or imagination, and certainly not because anything specifically "Jewish" triggers prejudice against them, but because of a human tendency to ostracize members of minority groups. Boas subordinated antisemitism to racism. He could achieve this only by ignoring those traits that were specific to antisemitism, such as the role of Christianity and the historical continuity of anti-Jewish sentiment. Recall that in his cultural and physical anthropology Boas systematically employed historical particularism to undermine comparative evolutionist accounts of culture and race. In ignoring the particular aspects of antisemitism, therefore, rhetorical and epistemic considerations were closely intertwined. The crux of Boas's response to antisemitism, in the end, was that there is nothing specifically anti-Jewish in antisemitism.

Arthur Ruppin: Antisemitism Is a Danger Not Devoid of Advantages

"Anti-Semitism cannot be overcome by opposing its arguments alone," Ruppin states in *The Sociology of the Jews*.[29] Unlike Simmel or Boas, Ruppin wrote extensively on antisemitism throughout his career, both in his diary and in his professional writings. Although his tools were universal, Ruppin declined to view antisemitism as part of some general social phenomenon. In contrast to Simmel and Boas, he viewed social scientific responses as a means not only to refute antisemitic notions of Jewish inferiority but also to enhance Jewish pride and self-esteem.[30]

We have much information about Ruppin's encounter with antisemitism because he addressed the topic in his diary from his youth in the 1890s onward. In Rawicz (a small town in what was then part of the German Reich, today Poland), where he spent his early years, a mixed city of Germans, Poles, and Jews, he professed that he had encountered no antisemitism. But in Magdeburg, a bigger German city to which the family later moved, Ruppin suffered from antisemitic insults from his schoolmates.[31] His diary entries have been said to "view Jews through an antisemitic lens."[32] In his youth there is evidence that Ruppin professed a strong aversion for his Jewish body, Jews in general, and in particular Jewish women. According to Yehoiakim Doron, he also expressed admiration for the blond Nordic body.

Ruppin's curiosity led him to acquire and read antisemitic literature. His immediate response to the Loewe and Dreyfus affairs, as well as to other accusations made against Jews, was harsh. He did not doubt the veracity of the allegations leveled against the Jews in question and hoped their punishment would be severe, as he believed that such individuals incriminated the Jewish collectivity. He connected antisemitism and class. He did not believe that antisemitism was aimed at all Jews; he believed it was aimed at rich Jews.[33] In contrast to Simmel and Boas, Ruppin's self-identification as a Jew was explicit and central to his identity. With the radicalization of antisemitism toward the end of the nineteenth century, Ruppin's views on the subject gradually transformed. Disapproving judgments of Jews, for instance, disappeared from his diary. Alarmed by what he termed the "snowball" of antisemitism in the 1890s, Ruppin referred to the possibility that the Jews would be expelled from Germany.[34] He became not only the target of antisemitic incidents but also their conscientious observer.[35] He never reflected on his early diary entries, but his later analyses can be read as reflexively attempting to explain them. The study of antisemitism became a cornerstone of his academic project, crucial to his model for the sociological and demographic study of contemporary Jewry, from *Die Juden der Gegenwart* (1904) through *Soziologie der Juden* (1930), *The Jews in the Modern World* (1935) and *The Jewish Fate and Future* (1940), which was published after Germany had invaded Poland, with its huge Jewish population, and the outbreak of World War II. Ruppin's basic view of antisemitism as a permanent feature of European society, culture, and history strongly resembles views of slightly earlier proto-Zionist and Zionist leaders such as Moses Hess, Leon Pinsker, Max Nordau, Theodor Herzl, and Ahad Ha'am.[36] He does not refer to them as scientific authorities, however, but grounds his conviction on sociological arguments.

If we compare Ruppin's earliest Jewish study with his later work, crucial changes are evident in his response to antisemitism. *Die Juden der Gegenwart* (1904, revised edition 1911) centers on the dangers of assimilation to Jewish existence. The discussion of antisemitism is subject to that of assimilation, antisemitism viewed as an "insufficient obstacle" against assimilation.[37] A certain minimal amount of antisemitism, Ruppin is implying, is necessary for Jewish national survival.

Ruppin differentiates between political, social, and economic antisemitism, describes antisemitism in different countries, and identifies its origin in Germany. He then analyzes modern antisemitism as being closely connected to the legal emancipation of Jews, and he emphasizes the discrepancy their legal emancipation created between their legal and social situation. He suggests that contemporary antisemitism is aimed at the Jews' race rather than their religion. The idea that antisemitism is intent on "declassing" Jews (*Deklassierung*) becomes a touchstone of his interpretation, to which he returns in his later publications. A deep ambivalence is built into Ruppin's interpretation of antisemitism, which is present already in this early publication. Jews are trapped in modern societies between threats from opposite directions. Beyond a certain threshold, antisemitism is in itself a danger. However, social antisemitism alone cannot stand in the way of assimilation, which is an even more serious threat to Jewish survival in modern conditions. The legal emancipation of Jews cannot be reversed, and their legal disenfranchisement (*Entrechtung*) is unlikely.[38]

Some of the fundamental elements of Ruppin's interpretation of antisemitism are already present in this publication, but in light of his later works, his interpretation is only partial; the deeper or more primitive anthropological aspect of antisemitism is absent from his discussion. While he continues to view antisemitism as an obstacle, a counterforce to as-similation, in his later publications Ruppin gradually comes to see anti-semitism as a constant factor in Jewish history, in itself independent of as-similation, and develops scholarly means for its study and representation.

Ruppin's perspective on antisemitism is intertwined with his Zionist convictions. In his later publications he refers to antisemitism as a mul-tilayered phenomenon. At its most primitive, fundamental level, anti-semitism flows from a "group instinct," an anthropological, permanent feature of human nature: "Any person who is not born within the group but enters its territory as a migrant, or as a member of subjugated group, is regarded an alien."[39] Ruppin is adamant about the irrational nature of this anthropological feature; rational justification follows hatred that is born of the heart, not the other way around.[40] Strangers ultimately are admitted to the group, according to Ruppin, but only contingent on their consent to assimilate, leaving no trace of their difference. This anthropo-logical feature is the source of the Jews' peculiar situation.

The Jews' peculiarity is that despite their dispersion, they resisted such assimilation: "If the Jews had pursued the path of *connubium* from the be-ginning of their dispersion, there would have been no hatred of the Jews today, but there would also have been no Jews."[41] In this sense Ruppin concurs with Boas, who believed, like many anthropologists, that with the disappearance of the Jews as such, the "Jewish question" too would disappear. Yet unlike Boas, Ruppin opposed that solution. Modern soci-ety, according to Ruppin, brought about a fundamental change in Jew-ish existence. In the modern period Jewish existence was "being ground up"—this is Ruppin's image—between the erosive effects of assimilation on the one hand and the dangers of antisemitism on the other. A minimal rate of antisemitism therefore is necessary for Jewish survival, as long as Jews live as a minority in modern societies.

In his publications after 1933 Ruppin treats Nazi, state-sponsored an-tisemitism separately, paying particular attention to the role of Hitler and to racial theory.[42] He views it as a "new stage," a radical form of an-tisemitism and, in cultural terms, an enormous regression.[43] Yet he does not indicate that it is categorically different from or more violent than earlier phases of antisemitism. He differentiates between Christian anti-Jewish sentiment and racial antisemitism and criticizes, in particular, the Aryan racial theory of the "spiritual Judaization" of culture. He opposes the view that antisemitism is a specifically modern phenomenon and in practice views its expressions as manifestations of one and the same phenomenon. Ruppin's historical account differs therefore from Simmel's and Boas's, as Ruppin is not driven to separate "objective" and "subjective" features of antisemitism, nor does he attempt to follow the role of the subjective in constituting the "objective." His rejection of a "general theory" of prejudice of which antisemitism is only a subcase is at the core of his concepts and rhetorical strategy. Even when countering antisemitic accusations, his categories do not fundamentally differ from those of his antisemitic opponents. For instance, when he criticizes racial antisemitism, he attempts to refute its allegations based on what he asserts to be the superior standard for the measurement of interracial hatred: the rate of intermarriage.[44] Rather than moving from a specific social phenomenon to a general category, his direction is the opposite: from universal categories of analysis to the specific features of antisemitism as a phenomenon. Indeed from descriptions of the antisemitic accusations Ruppin moves directly to a detailed discussion of statistical rates of Jewish criminality in order to repudiate antisemitic allegations. He responds to antisemitic accusations on the grounds of reality, empirically, and based on the same categories.

Ruppin often claimed that he was not led to Zionism by antisemitism. Zionism, according to Ruppin, enabled the Jews to escape from both assimilation and antisemitism. Jews suffered from antisemitism because the inferiority inflicted on them stemmed from the very peoples to whom they wish to assimilate.[45] Once a majority society of Jews or, more precisely, a society not subordinate to a non-Jewish majority would come into existence, antisemitism would no longer be necessary for Jewish survival. Antisemitism therefore is not a necessary condition for Jewish existence as such but only as long as Jews are a minority.

Summary: Science History versus Jewish History

From the perspective of the conceptual history of the social sciences, Simmel, Boas, and Ruppin belonged to opposing paradigms. Their respective responses to antisemitism were founded on competing social science concepts, and they differed in their scientific and extrascientific goals. While with regard to their respective responses to antisemitism, Boas and Ruppin seem to have undergone far greater changes throughout their careers than Simmel, in epistemic terms the principal opposition remains between Simmel and Boas, on the one side, and Ruppin on the other. Simmel believed from the outset that social reality was a construction composed of the more elemental individual interaction. Boas, especially after his "cultural turn," gradually moved in a similar direction: antisemitism too was not a natural response to Jewish difference but rather a socially constructed phenomenon. Indeed Boas and Simmel were crucial in shifting the attention to the construction of such social forms, thereby transforming antisemitism into a phenomenon pertaining to society rather than to the Jews as such. In other words, they were instrumental in transforming the social science discussion of the "Jewish question" to the discussion of antisemitism. Ruppin, on the other hand, viewed antisemitism, at least in part, as a natural response to innate and real differences between non-Jews and Jews. Opposing antisemitism more directly than did Simmel or Boas, conceptually Ruppin was also far more integrated into the racial discourse than they were.

But if we shift our perspective from that of the conceptual history of modern social science to the history of responses to antisemitism within the German cultural sphere (and in Boas's case, the American too), a different picture comes to light. Despite their conceptual differences, Simmel, Boas, and Ruppin are part of one shared movement, that which grappled with and responded to antisemitism within science and outside of it, albeit in different forms and with different discursive strategies. Here the most important dividing line is that between antisemites and their opponents. From this perspective, Simmel's, Boas's, and Ruppin's responses differ in their ideological, political, and intrascientific goals, as well as their rhetorical strategies and forms of argumentation, while they share in the attempt to respond to and fight back against the rising tide of social, political, and scientific antisemitism.

Notes

A different version of this chapter was previously published as "Circumventions and confrontations: Georg Simmel, Franz Boas and Arthur Ruppin and their responses to antisemitism," Patterns of Prejudice 44.2 (2010): 195–215.

1. On the role of antisemitism in Simmel's academic career, see Birnbaum, "In the Academic Sphere."

2. Goren, *Arthur Ruppin*. All translations of Goren are mine.

3. Zimmermann, "Anti-Semitism as Skill."

4. For a concrete reconstruction of the debate, see Bodemann in this volume.

5. Weber's relationship to Jews has been a matter of intense dispute. For a comprehensive yet controversial account of Weber in this respect, see Abraham, *Max Weber and the Jewish Question*. More recently, see Barbalet, "Max Weber and Judaism."

6. Spiro, "Nordic vs. Anti-Nordic."

7. See Wikart, *From Darwin to Hitler*.

8. On Zollschan, see Gilman, "Smart Jews in Fin-de-siècle Vienna." On Gumplovicz, see Adamek, "Ludwik Gumplowicz." On Jews who wrote on race, see Lipphardt, *Biologie der Juden*.

9. For a comprehensive discussion, see Stoetzler, *The State, the Nation, and the Jews*. See also Lindemann, *Esau's Tears*, 131.

10. Köhnke, "Simmel als Jude," 145. Köhnke quotes several of Simmel's letters in which he reports having warned younger Jewish colleagues considering an academic career in German universities of the insurmountable difficulties they were to expect (145, 145n217, 379n91, 146).

11. Köhnke, "Simmel als Jude," 147.

12. Simmel, *Über sociale Differenzierung*, in particular 115–38.

13. Frisby, "The Study of Society."

14. Simmel, "How Is Society Possible?," 9.

15. Simmel, "How Is Society Possible?," 10, 18.

16. Simmel, *The Philosophy of Money*, 118; Simmel, *Soziologie*, 733.

17. Simmel, "Sociology of the Senses," 118; Simmel, *Soziologie*, 733–34.

18. Stepan and Gilman, "Appropriating the Idioms of Science," 99.

19. Mendes-Flohr, "The Berlin Jew as Cosmopolitan," 23.

20. Rammstedt, "L'étranger de Georg Simmel," 143.

21. Cole, *Franz Boas*, 58–59.

22. Boas, "Changes in Bodily Form in Descendants of Immigrants."

23. It should be noted that Boas's study appeared before Mendelian genetics established itself in physical anthropology. Opponents of the immigration of eastern European Jews and Asians to the United States such as Madison Grant ridiculed Boas's findings as absurd. Several years ago Corey Sparks and Richard Jantz reevaluated Boas's study and questioned his use of statistics. Sparks and Jantz, "A Reassessment." Three prominent statisticians then responded to Sparks and Jantz by reevaluating and validating Boas's statistics. See Gravlee, Bernard, and Leonard, "Heredity, Environment, and Cranial Form."

24. Boas, "Race: What It Is," 22–23.

25. Boas, "The Jews," 39.

26. Stocking, "The Critique of Racial Formalism."

27. Steinberg, "Aby Warburg's Kreuzlingen Lecture."

28. Boas, *Anthropology and Modern Life*, 19–20, 29, 44, 80.

29. Ruppin, *The Sociology of the Jews*, 41 (all translations are mine); Ruppin, *The Jewish Fate and Future*, 207.

30. For a discussion, see Hart, *Social Science and the Politics of Modern Jewish Identity*.

31. Goren, *Arthur Ruppin*, 24.

32. Goren, *Arthur Ruppin*, 33. See his diary entries of November 23, 1894; March 7, 1892; June 12, 1893. On the relationship between young Ruppin and anti-semitism, see Doron, "Classical Zionism and Modern Anti-Semitism," particularly 91.

33. It is interesting to compare Ruppin's analysis with Nachman Syrkin's (*Nachman Syrkin Socialist Zionist*), who also integrated a Zionist and a Marxist interpretation.

34. Goren, *Arthur Ruppin*, 33, from Ruppin's diary, August 4, 1893.

35. Goren, *Arthur Ruppin*, 100.

36. See their respective entries in Herzberg, *The Zionist Idea*.

37. Ruppin, *Die Juden der Gegenwart*, 197.

38. Ruppin, *Die Juden der Gegenwart*, 198, 199, 204.

39. Ruppin, *The Jewish Fate and Future*, 207. These statements greatly resemble statements made by Boas, yet Boas viewed them as remnants of a primitive organization of humanity, and Ruppin, it seems, thought that they were constant and immutable. See also Ruppin, *Sociology of the Jews*, 30.

40. Ruppin, *Sociology of the Jews*, 30.

41. Ruppin, *The Jewish Fate and Future*, 208.

42. Ruppin, *The Jewish Fate and Future*, 233–43, 233–34; Ruppin, *Sociology of the Jews*, 33–36.

43. Ruppin, *The Jewish Fate and Future*, 225.

44. Ruppin, *Sociology of the Jews*, 34. Conversely, he criticizes Aryan race theory for working under the false assumption of pure racial types (35).

45. Ruppin, *Sociology of the Jews*, 40.

References

Abraham, Gary A. *Max Weber and the Jewish Question: A Study of the Social Outlook of His Sociology*. Urbana: University of Illinois Press, 1992.

Adamek, Wojciech. "Ludwik Gumplowicz: A Forgotten Classic of European Sociology." *Journal of Classical Sociology* 6.3 (2006): 381–98.

Barbalet, Jack. "Max Weber and Judaism: An Insight into the Methodology of *The Protestant Ethic and the Spirit of Capitalism*." *Max Weber Studies* 6.1 (2006): 51–67.

Birnbaum, Pierre. "In the Academic Sphere: The Cases of Emile Durkheim and Georg Simmel." In: *Jewish Emancipation Reconsidered: The French and German Models*, edited by Michael Brenner, Vicki Caron, and Uri R. Kaufmann, 169–96. Tübingen: Paul Mohr, 2003.

Boas, Franz. *Anthropology and Modern Life.* New York: Dover, 1936.

———. "The 'Aryan.'" In *Race and Democratic Society*, 43–53. New York: Biblo and Tannen, 1945. Originally "Aryans and Non-Aryans," *Mercury*, June 1934.

———. "Changes in Bodily Form in Descendants of Immigrants." In *Race, Language, and Culture*, 60–75. Chicago: University of Chicago Press, 1982.

———. "The Jews." In *Race and Democratic Society*, 39–42. New York: Biblo and Tannen, 1945. Originally "Are the Jews a Race?," *The World Tomorrow*, January 1923.

———. "Race: What It Is." In *Race and Democratic Society*, 22–23. New York: Biblo and Tannen, 1945.

Cole, Douglas. *Franz Boas: The Early Years, 1858–1906.* Seattle: University of Washington Press, 1999.

Doron, Yehoiakim. "Classical Zionism and Modern Anti-Semitism—Comparisons and Influences (1883–1914)." *Hatzionut*, 1983, 57–101 (in Hebrew).

Frisby, David. "The Study of Society." In: *Simmel and Since: Essays on Georg Simmel's Social Theory*, 15–19. London: Routledge, 1992.

Gilman, Sander L. "Smart Jews in Fin-de-siècle Vienna: 'Hybrids' and the Anxiety about Jewish Superior Intelligence—Hofmannsthal and Wittgenstein." *Modernism/Modernity* 3.2 (1996): 45–58.

Goren, Yaacov. *Arthur Ruppin: His Life and His Work.* Jerusalem: Yad Tabenkin, 2005 (in Hebrew).

Gravlee, Clarence C., H. Russell Bernard, and William R. Leonard. "Heredity, Environment, and Cranial Form: A Reanalysis of Boas's Immigrant Data." *American Anthropologist*, n.s., 105.1 (2003): 125–38.

Gumplovicz, Ludwig. *Der Rassenkampf.* Innsbruck: Wagner'sche Univ.-Buchhandlung, 1883.

Hart, Mitchell B. *Social Science and the Politics of Modern Jewish Identity.* Stanford CA: Stanford University Press, 2000.

Herzberg, Abraham, ed. *The Zionist Idea: A Historical Analysis and Reader.* Philadelphia: Jewish Historical Society, 1997.

Köhnke, Klaus Christian. "Simmel als Jude." In *Der junge Simmel in Theoriebeziehungen und sozialen Bewegungen.* Frankfurt: Suhrkamp, 1996.

Lindemann, Albert S. *Esau's Tears: Modern Anti-Semitism and the Rise of the Jews.* Cambridge: Cambridge University Press, 1997.

Lipphardt, Veronika. *Biologie der Juden: Jüdische Wissenschaftler über "Rasse" und Vererbung 1900–1935.* Göttingen: Vandenhoeck & Ruprecht, 2008.

Mendes-Flohr, Paul. "The Berlin Jew as Cosmopolitan." In *Berlin Metropolis: Jews and the New Culture 1890–1918*, edited by Emily Bilski, 14–31. Los Angeles: University of California Press, 1999.

Rammstedt, Otthein. "L'étranger de Georg Simmel." *Revue des Sciences Sociales de la France de l'est* 21 (1994): 146–53.

Ruppin, Arthur. *The Jewish Fate and Future.* Translated by E. W. Dickes. London: Macmillan, 1940.

————. *Die Juden der Gegenwart*. Berlin: Jüdischer Verlag, 1911.

————. *The Sociology of the Jews*. Vol. 2. Berlin: Stiebel, 1930 (in Hebrew).

Simmel, Georg. "How Is Society Possible?" In *Georg Simmel on Individuality and Social Forms*, edited and translated by Donald N. Levine, 6-22. Chicago: University of Chicago Press, 1971.

————. *The Philosophy of Money*. Translated by David Frisby and Tom Bottomore. London: Routledge, 1978.

————. "Sociology of the Senses." In *Simmel on Culture*, edited by David Frisby and Mike Featherstone, 118. London: Sage, 1997.

————. *Soziologie: Untersuchungen über die Formen der Vergesellschaftung*. Frankfurt am Main: Suhrkamp, 1992.

————. *Über sociale Differenzierung*. In *Aufsätze 1887-1890. Über sociale Differenzierung. Die Probleme der Geschichtsphilosophie*. 1892. Frankfurt am Main: Suhrkamp, 1989.

Sparks, Corey S., and Richard L. Jantz. "A Reassessment of Human Cranial Plasticity: Boas Revisited." *Proceedings of the National Academy of Sciences of the United States of America* 99. 23 (2002): 14636-39.

Spiro, Jonathan P. "Nordic vs. Anti-Nordic: The Galton Society and the American Anthropological Association." *Patterns of Prejudice* 36.1 (2002): 35-48.

Steinberg, Michael P. "Aby Warburg's Kreuzlingen Lecture: A Reading." In *Aby M. Warburg: Images from the Region of the Pueblo Indians of North America*, translated by Michael P. Steinberg, 59-114. Ithaca NY: Cornell University Press, 1995.

Stepan, Nancy L., and Sander Gilman. "Appropriating the Idioms of Science: The Rejection of Scientific Racism." In *The "Racial" Economy of Science: Toward a Democratic Future*, edited by Sandra G. Harding, 170-93. Bloomington: Indiana University Press, 1993.

Stocking, George W., Jr. "The Critique of Racial Formalism." In *Race, Culture, and Evolution: Essays in the History of Anthropology*, 161-94. Chicago: University of Chicago Press, 1968.

Stoetzler, Marcel, *The State, the Nation, and the Jews: Liberalism and the Antisemitism Dispute in Bismarck's Germany*. Lincoln: University of Nebraska Press, 2008.

Syrkin, Mary, ed. *Nachman Syrkin Socialist Zionist: A Biographical Memoir and Selected Essays*. New York: Herzl Press, 1961.

Treitschke, Heinrich von, *A Word about Our Jewry*. 1879. Edited by Ellis Rivkin. Translated by Helen Lederer. Cincinnati: Hebrew Union College, n.d.

Wikart, Richard. *From Darwin to Hitler: Evolutionary Ethics, Eugenics and Racism in Germany*. New York: Palgrave Macmillan, 2004.

Zimmermann, Andrew. "Anti-Semitism as Skill: Rudolf Virchow's Schulstatistik and the Racial Composition of Germany." *Central European History* 32.4 (1999): 409-29.

Zollschan, Ignaz. *Das Rassenproblem unter besonderer Berücksichtigung der theoretischen Grundlagen der jüdischen Rassenfrage*. 4th ed. Vienna: Wilhelm Braumüller, 1920.

7

The Rise of Sociology, Antisemitism, and the Jewish Question

The American Case

RICHARD H. KING

Where and to what degree antisemitism existed, flourished, and even diminished in the United States between the 1890s and the 1960s is an important issue, but it is not one I want to pursue here directly. Nor am I interested in whether antisemitism has been worse or less bad than in Europe. Rather I want to explore the way the "Jewish question" was posed in America in the first two-thirds of the twentieth century, chiefly among sociologists, anthropologists, and even historians as they sought to analyze antisemitism and to conceptualize the position of Jews in the United States. This necessarily involves some discussion of the relationship between the study of the "Jewish question" and of the "race question," specifically between antisemitism and so-called color-coded racism.[1] I will conclude by identifying several different lines of inquiry about the position of Jews in the United States from the end of World War II to the end of the 1960s, the period in which the Jewish question was answered in the United States in a quite different way than it had been earlier in Europe.

Disciplinary Inquiry and Antisemitism

If one seeks to answer the question of when and where the Jewish question was explored systematically, the newly emerging discipline of sociology in the late nineteenth century is one place to look. Racial and ethnic tensions were at their peak in America between 1890 and World War I, the period in which sociology and anthropology emerged as academic disciplines.[2] The first sociology department in the United States was founded at the University of Kansas in 1890, while the departments at Chicago and Columbia were preeminent in the years leading up to World War I. (Émile Durkheim founded the first department of sociology in France in Bordeaux in 1896.) The *American Journal of Sociology* began publication in 1895, and the American Sociological Association was formed in 1905.

It is surprisingly difficult to find any great empirical or theoretical concern with antisemitism in the work of sociological pioneers such as Lester Frank Ward and William Graham Sumner, who represented the liberal and conservative tendencies in the new discipline. Both thinkers were concerned with working out the proper relationship between state and civil society. Whereas Ward's thought focused on an evolutionary ethic of cooperative action in the form of state regulation of the economy, Sumner famously contended that "stateways cannot change folkways," thus favoring social and economic self-regulation over the application of state power to regulate these spheres. His stateways/folkways dictum was also used to justify racial segregation in the South, but he also warned in *Folkways* (1907) that "modern scholars have made the mistake of attributing to race much which belongs to the ethos," that is, national character.[3] Ward himself contended that Negroes were different from whites, but he thought that with sufficient opportunities "they too would become civilized," while Ward's student, the feminist thinker Charlotte Perkins Gilman, "thought Jews and African Americans examples of arrested evolution."[4] But in neither case were such concerns central to Ward's or Gilman's thought. About the same time, Thorstein Veblen's *The Theory of the Leisure Class* (1899), with its critique of the society and culture of the newly rich in America, could easily have picked out American Jews as symbols of the rampant materialism of the time, but, as we shall see, Veblen championed rather than condemned the influence of Jews in contemporary society. What linked all three of these leading sociologists was an evolutionary view of society and culture, thus giving testimony to the influence of Charles Darwin and Herbert Spencer, the two figures who seem to have most clearly shaped the discipline in America. Indeed the paucity of entries on antisemitism in Dorothy Ross's *The Origins of American Social Science* (1991) is probably a good indication of the marginal nature of antisemitism or the Jewish question in general among American academic sociologists in these early years.

The relative absence of systematic studies or theoretical probes dealing with the Jewish question is not, however, a claim about the extent
or depth of antisemitism in America. The ideology of Anglo-Saxonism
reinforced nativist suspicion of immigrants particularly from southern
and eastern Europe and included strong components of antisemitism.[5]
If Sumner and Ward had no particular interest in Jews in American society, the fifth president of the ASA, E. A. Ross, who was a political progressive like Ward, racialized and stereotyped Jews in his work—along
with the other usual suspects. He was a devotee of what Franz Boas called
"the Nordic nonsense" and feared white racial suicide and cultural decline, while being active in the eugenics movement. Sociologist Henry
Pratt Fairchild's *The Melting Pot Mistake* (1926) made it clear that Jews—
and also Catholics and other foreigners—were viewed with considerable
suspicion by some professional sociologists, even if they were Marxists.
Thus racially and ethnically inflected discussions of the problems of the
new industrial capitalism could come from the Left as well as from the
Right, though not, I think, as frequently.

But though Ross and Fairchild were atypical of the mainstream of the
profession, long-term but unequal relationships with Native Americans
in North America and the presence of recently freed slaves in the South,
combined with pro-imperialist and colonialist tendencies among European nations, meant that most white Americans, including academic
sociologists, were predisposed to assume the racial or, at least, cultural
superiority of white, Protestant American and northern European cultures. Still, historian Hasia Diner has suggested that there was perhaps
less antipathy to Jews among sociologists than among the patricians of
the English and history departments of American universities.[6] The market for racially inflected master narratives of decline was more often sup-
plied by gentlemen historians such as Madison Grant. His *The Passing of
the Great Race* (1915) was vastly influential, as was the work of Lothrop
Stoddard, who was similarly involved in the eugenics movement and
offered a racialized and Aryanized vision of history in *The Rising Tide of
Color against White World-Supremacy* (1920).[7]

The absence of special concern with the Jewish question among academic sociologists in America contrasts with the case of Germany, especially before World War I. Though Michal Bodemann has claimed that
"the 'Jewish question'—the question of Jewish nationality, not to men-

tion the question of antisemitism in Germany—was never made an issue at *Soziologentagen* before World War I,"[8] the concern of German sociology with questions of nation, people, ethnicity and race, including some discussions of antisemitism, seems surprisingly much stronger than in American sociology at the same time. Georg Simmel and Franz Oppenheimer were Jewish, and the latter was particularly outspoken in his rejection of racial antisemitism. Max Weber's sociology of religion took up the importance of ancient Judaism in developing the concept of prophecy, while his historical sociology of capitalism contrasted the pariah capitalism of traditional Judaism with Protestant-shaped modern capitalism. In addition Weber tried to avoid racial explanations in his work on the rise of modern capitalism. This cannot be said of his colleague Werner Sombart, who contended that the ethics of Judaism mandated different treatment for Gentiles than for Jews in the taking of usury. What Sombart meant to show was that Jews had been responsible for undermining the spiritual, communal basis of the West through commercial capitalism. Interestingly Sombart also referred to America as *Judenland*, a culture and society made for and in part by commercially minded Jews.[9] Beyond that Sombart attributed Jewish power and influence to racial, not just cultural differences. There was a direct causal relationship between the impersonal, instrumentalist social ties of *Gesellschaft* and Jewish influence.

Why wasn't there more concern with Jews in American sociology and social science generally? Anthropologist Franz Boas indirectly suggested an answer in the address W. E. B. Du Bois invited him to give at Atlanta University in 1906. There Boas noted that the proper comparison to make was "the position of Negroes in America to that of Jews in Europe."[10] Thus Boas was suggesting that African Americans had the same crucial importance in American life and social sciences that Jews did in Europe but that the Jewish question had relatively less salience in America. For all the racialization of Jews around the turn of the century, they were, as Seymour Martin Lipset once put it, "never defined as the largest visible out-group," and antisemitism was only "one of many competing prejudices." Overall, American sociology was historically more preoccupied with the race question than the Jewish question, more concerned with alleged obstacles to modernity presented by African Americans than the dangers presented by the carriers of the modern spirit, the Jews of America.[11]

It is also easy to forget that neither the study of American race relations nor the conceptualization of the Jewish question took off until African Americans and Jewish Americans entered into higher education as students and teachers; moreover American higher education was largely segregated in most of the country until after World War II. Du Bois and Boas were exceptions that proved the rule here. Even at that, Jews were admitted, albeit with quota restrictions, to elite private institutions (i.e., the Ivy Leagues) and thronged to public institutions such as the much heralded City College of New York much earlier and in greater numbers than African Americans, who were largely confined to historically black colleges in the South and border states. Graduate education at, for example, the University of Chicago was particularly important in training an emerging black academic elite in the 1930s, after the predominantly black Howard University had taken up the challenge in the 1920s and before.

Some interesting wrinkles begin to emerge here in the sociology of institutional life and sociology of knowledge. Boas, a German Jewish émigré, was perhaps the most important figure in the American effort to discredit theories of inherited racial differences. But several of his students who worked on American topics neglected or deflected the Jewish question. To be sure the empirical evidence about the variability of types that Boas used in his pioneering studies was in part drawn from studies of the urban Jews of New York. But besides that, Amos Morris-Reich has noted that Boas wrote (only) two articles, one in 1923 and the other in 1934, on Jews and race, and then later he developed a critique of racial hierarchy, while not absolutely denying differences among groups. Even more interestingly Morris-Reich suggests that Boas ended by subsuming antisemitism under the category of racism and thus never linked the treatment of Jews with the supposed persisting traits of Jews: "The crux of Boas's response to antisemitism, in the end, was that there was nothing specifically Jewish about it."[12] Most of his work as an anthropologist, along with that of several of his most prominent students—Ruth Benedict and Margaret Mead, to name two—was concerned with cross-cultural issues and cultural relativism. In the Boasian ambit, then, a theoretical universalism and a cultural cosmopolitanism led to a certain neglect of Jewish identity and thus underplayed the specific workings of antisemitism.

It is also fascinating to speculate why several of Boas's Jewish students, including Melville Herskovits, Otto Klineberg, and Ashley Montagu, chose to focus their work on African Americans rather than Jewish Americans. After all, the general pattern is that members of a minority group initially are most interested in studying their own group, a pattern that can be seen in the career of Zora Neale Hurston, one of Boas's best-known students, and that of Abram Harris, an economist at Howard. Writing in 1970, Lipset was struck retrospectively by the fact that most Jewish social scientists "have also abstained from writing about American Jews" because of their "desire to be perceived as American rather than Jewish intellectuals."[13] There was of course a strong element of altruism and political progressivism, even radicalism, among American-born Jewish sociologists of race relations. Where earlier (Protestant) sociologists were often linked to social and settlement house work that derived from their moral and religious orientation (or that of their parents), in the interwar years many younger Jewish intellectuals, including social scientists, were also socialists or at least political radicals. In moving from socialism to sociology (or in combining socialism with sociology), however, they did not jettison the universalism that led them to reject their own particularistic loyalties, and they generally supported political and legal equality.

Significantly in the 1960s the African American intellectual Harold Cruse spoke out on what he remembered as the tendency of Jewish radicals in the Communist Party in the 1930s to discourage group cultural consciousness among African Americans, while continuing to identify themselves as Jews.[14] Yet with Boas's students or black academics and intellectuals in general, it was not so simple. A universalist emphasis can be seen in Klineberg's important work on intelligence testing, which attacked the idea of different intellectual capacities between the two "races," and in Montagu's analysis of racial prejudice. But Herskovits devoted his intellectual career to uncovering the carryovers from African cultures that became part of black Caribbean and African American culture; that is, he laid the groundwork for talking of a still existing *African* American culture. The novelist Richard Wright's rejection of black nationalism as an ideology was clear-cut, but the setting and subject matter of his fiction remained the black community, south and north. The Trinidadian Trotskyist C. L. R. James wrote a major history of the Haitian Revolution in 1938, *The Black Jacobins*, and also claimed that black Americans would have to be organized around race rather than class, at least in the short run. Du Bois moved to something approaching a nationalist position by the late 1930s, and with that questioned the possibility of black assimilation. Thus though Cruse had been talking primarily from his experience in CPUSA circles in Harlem, his 1967 pronouncement on these topics considerably overstated the case he was trying to make about the 1930s. Many African American intellectuals did emphasize racial and cultural particularism over universalism in the 1930s. What Cruse's claim did signify in the overheated atmosphere of the 1960s were the fraying ties, even breakdown of the "special relationship" between African Americans and Jewish Americans.

Overall the number and quality of black social scientists who advanced the study of the race question in the interwar years was quite remarkable. Charles Johnson, E. Franklin Frazier, St. Clair Drake, Horace Cayton, and Allison Davis were all associated with or products of the Sociology Department at the University of Chicago, while Ira D. Reed, Rayford Logan, Ralph Bunche, and Abram Harris were based at Howard University in Washington DC. After the war the radical sociologist Oliver C. Cox offered a powerful critique from the Left of the liberal assumptions of Gunnar Myrdal's *An American Dilemma* (1944), and Kenneth and Mamie Clark published research on the effects of race on young children all throughout the 1940s and early 1950s. This work was referred to in the 1954 *Brown v. Board of Education* decision that ruled segregation unconstitutional. In fact Myrdal's Carnegie Foundation–funded project that produced *An American Dilemma* played a huge role in supporting a whole cadre of black social scientists and intellectuals in their efforts to advance or consolidate their careers. Though by no means a homogeneous group, most of them were wary of, even hostile toward racial nationalism. Ironically, for instance, it was an African American sociologist, E. Franklin Frazier, who challenged Herskovits's claim that there was a strong African component in black American culture. The important thing here is to see that the often bitter debate about the complex relationship between the Jewish question and the race question in the 1960s was already a point of contention in the 1930s.[15]

If Boas and his students played a major role in challenging racial and cultural categorizing, the Chicago School of sociology, led by Robert Park, a former student of Georg Simmel and one-time assistant to Booker T. Washington, also pioneered the study of race and ethnicity in the interwar years. Obviously Louis Wirth's *The Ghetto* (1928) was an important landmark in the study of Jewish assimilation and antisemitism, and much of the Chicago School's empirical research was as focused on European immigrants as it was on southern blacks who were arriving in Chicago and other northern cities. But though not obvious at first glance, Chad Alan Goldberg has pointed out that Park's innovative work on the "marginal man" as a "general social type" actually "regarded Jews as the prototype of the marginal man," along with African Americans who exhibited what Du Bois had earlier referred to as "double consciousness." From this perspective, Lipset later observed that for Park the Jews were "the most American of all groups in the nation" and, for that reason alone, should be a "major topic of research."[16] Still, the sociological profession looked with suspicion at works by Jews on Jewish topics and used terms such as *objectivity* and *dispassion* to signify the desired (Gentile) detachment toward such phenomenon.[17] In addition many Jewish academics and intellectuals seemed burdened by a past they wanted to escape and thus tended to avoid studying Jewish Americans until after the war, while African Americans were fascinated by a past they wanted to rediscover and thus to investigate and then change, sometimes radically. It remained to a Gentile, Robert Park, to enshrine modern Jews, albeit in veiled fashion, as the prototypical modern type, the marginal man.

A further assumption in the study of marginality was that those members of the minority group who suffered most psychological stress were those who were closest in appearance and status to the dominant social group. The analysis of the sociology of marginality also led to a concern with individual and group "damage" and was much debated, especially during the 1960s when the effects of antisemitism and color-coded racism were compared.[18] Moreover Park's four-stage model of minority-majority interaction, involving competition, conflict, accommodation, and assimilation, privileged assimilation both descriptively and normatively. In this sense it was a sophisticated version of the melting pot thesis. Yet in *The Ghetto* Wirth also focused on the return of second- and third-generation Jews to the earlier ghetto cultural values or at least some updated version of them.[19] Ironically in light of Sombart's emphasis upon the destructive effects of Jewish-inspired capitalism on communal ties within the dominant Christian society, what Wirth portrayed in his study was the process by which the *Jewish Gemeinschaft* dispersed into the broader *Gesellschaft*. This meant that the Chicago School had no way to explain the limits to

Jewish assimilation. From that perspective, the four-stage model could be accommodated to the melting pot but not the cultural pluralist model.

The four-stage model also relatively underplayed prejudice as the main factor in the study of ethnic and racial conflict; instead it suggested that group conflict is part of what it means to be a group and need not be based on race or ethnicity. The minority group is not necessarily inferior, only different. The Chicago model also tended to neglect the specifically political and legal obstacles to assimilation. African American sociologists of the Chicago School knew very well the importance of political and legal obstacles to assimilation. But though a discussion of these obstacles was not totally absent from Wirth's study of the Jewish ghetto, the book made it easy to overlook the historical importance of legal restrictions on where African Americans could play or work or live in general, since living in the Jewish ghetto had presumably had a large voluntary component.

From Sociology to Social and Cultural Thought

During the interwar years there was a third cluster of intellectuals, philosophers, and social scientists who were concerned with race, ethnicity, and national culture, but from a less value-free and more committed political and cosmopolitan perspective. Often referred to as cultural pluralists, they were represented by two former students of philosopher William James, Horace Kallen and Du Bois, along with publicist Randolph Bourne and the controversial economist and social theorist Thorstein Veblen. Approaching the matter from various perspectives, they rejected the melting-pot and "Anglo-Conformity" models of assimilation,[20] while tending to think in broader terms than the closely focused models of the Chicago School. In fact they were close to the Boasians in adopting a broadly cultural relativist stance that challenged the superiority of white, Christian, Northern European culture and were more inclined to be skeptical about inherited racial differences or the fixity of types. There were remnants of race thinking in their work, but where present it tended to be of the "romantic racialist" sort.[21]

In terms of our major concern, these thinkers were, if not exactly philosemitic, certainly favorably disposed toward Jews. The cultural pluralism implied by Du Bois's idea of African American double consciousness, which of course anticipated the concept of marginality by several decades, led him to later speak out forthrightly against Nazi racial theorizing in the 1930s, and he supported the establishment of Israel after the war. Kallen, a Jew, and Bourne, a Protestant, saw Jews neither as a "misfortune" (Treitschke) nor as marginal but as representative Americans. Whereas Kallen saw America as a "nation of nations" in which each national group was able to preserve its own culture, Bourne's emphasis fell more upon the exchange and mixing of cultures, what much later was called "hybridity." Of Norwegian descent, Veblen wrote a remarkable essay in 1919, "The Intellectual Pre-eminence of Jews in Modern Europe," which traced the preeminence back both to their social marginality and their racial-cultural hybridity. The strategic shrewdness of Veblen's essay consisted in his identification of what most people understood as group weaknesses (marginality and impurity) to be sources of strength, even superiority. Thus both he and Du Bois anticipated and helped shape the Chicago School's emphasis on marginality.[22]

A fascinating chapter in the story of cultural pluralism and philosemitism can be seen in the close relationship that grew up in the interwar years between the eminent WASP jurist Oliver Wendell Holmes Jr. and several bright young progressive Jewish lawyers and/or intellectuals. In exploring the "de-Christianization of American public culture" in the first half of the twentieth century, the historian David Hollinger has observed that these lawyer-intellectuals—Felix Frankfurter, Morris Cohen, Jerome Frank, and Max Lerner—chose Holmes, with his "tough-mindedness," his secular worldview, and his jurisprudential realism *cum* pragmatism, as a role model. These Jewish intellectuals did not simply assimilate into the existing legal and political culture but "also helped to reconstitute American intellectual life." In fact what was true for Holmes was also true for a younger WASP intellectual, Edmund Wilson, who psychoanalyzed this cross-ethnic and cross-generational transference with the question "Were they . . . looking for a fully American father"?[23] Indeed the mature Wilson showed how the process was reciprocal: WASPs might also find Jewish culture and tradition attractive. His essay "The Jews" and a long review in 1953 of the correspondence between Justice Holmes and an Anglo-Jewish intellectual, Harold Laski, gave ample testimony to the way Wilson's sensibility had been profoundly shaped by the Hebraism of the New England Puritan and his immersion in the Old Testament vision. Wilson thought that his own intellectual attraction to Marx and Marxism had to do with his own affinity with "the great modern Jewish thinkers or leaders whose position has something of the rabbinical."[24] Though interrupted by World War II, such interwar intellectual and cultural alliances across ethnic lines were to emerge with full force after the war.

The Jewish Question in the Postwar World

Not surprisingly the end of World War II represented a watershed in the way the Jewish question, particularly antisemitism, was dealt with publicly and privately.[25] Casual racial and religious prejudice took on a more ominous shape in the wake of the Holocaust. Moreover Jews in general moved from a position of marginality in American intellectual and cultural life to one of considerable power after the war, as witness the emergence of what became known as the New York (Jewish) intellectuals and also the growing importance of Jews in popular and middle-brow culture.[26] The postwar years also witnessed the use of the term *Judeo-Christian* with increasing frequency to describe a supposedly existing interfaith consensus uniting the country, while one of the most influential of postwar works in the sociology of religion, Will Herberg's *Protestant-Catholic-Jew* (1951), suggested that ethnicity had faded while religion had emerged as the vehicle for Americans of these three "faiths" to join the "democratic consensus," which encompassed Jew and Gentile, Protestant and Catholic.[27] What was remarkable was that American Jewry, only 3 percent of the population, was accorded coequal religious-cultural status with the two dominant branches of Christianity. Thus having escaped the Holocaust and enjoying unprecedented affluence, American Jews identified themselves even more strongly as American. At the same time the heightened sense of the precariousness of Jewish identity created by the Holocaust meant there was a stronger connection between American Jews and Jews outside the United States. All this fed into and was augmented by the creation of the state of Israel in 1948. Thus American Jewish identity looked very different, was more complexly structured and inflected, after the war than it had been before.

This newly emergent Jewish consciousness manifested itself by more open concern with Jewish life and culture.[28] The *Menorah* journal, founded in 1915, and *Jewish Social Studies*, founded in the 1930s, were joined by *Commentary*, a publication of the American Jewish Committee, after the war. Between 1947 and 1952 somewhere around 170 articles dealing with aspects of the Holocaust appeared in these three publications, along with the *Chicago Jewish Forum*, the *Jewish Spectator*, and the *Reconstructionist*.[29] Many of the authors of these essays and articles were clearly refugees who had begun arriving from Germany and Central Europe in America in the 1930s. Thus the postwar American Jewish community had the publishing outlets to allow voices to be heard within that community and also with increasing frequency in general circulation publications.

Nor was the scholarly world silent during and after the war about the Jewish question, a term that was less frequently heard after the war. Two books on antisemitism were published during the war, while Theodor W. Adorno, Max Horkheimer, and their associates from the Frankfurt School and also the psychoanalytic community worked on several projects funded by the American Jewish Committee under the rubric Studies in Prejudice. The best known was the massive *The Authoritarian Personality* (1950). Erich Fromm's prewar *Escape from Freedom* (1941) and Erik H. Erikson's long essay "The Legend of Hitler's Childhood" (1942) marked major contributions of the psychoanalytic tradition-in-exile to the study of fascism and antisemitism.[30] Thus post-1930s American sociology in a broad sense was enriched (some would also say distorted) by the psychoanalytically derived questions and concerns advanced by European émigré intellectuals.

Overall the first quarter-century after the war saw the emergence of four large areas of sociological, cultural, and historical concern that constitute the postwar version of the Jewish question.

The Holocaust: One of the obvious crucial areas for the study of Jews in postwar America, the study of the Holocaust, was given impetus by émigré scholars such as Hannah Arendt, Bruno Bettelheim, and Raul Hilberg. But by the 1960s American Jewish scholars such as historian Stanley Elkins had advanced a provocative, and controversial, claim in *Slavery* (1959) that there were analogies between the experience under slavery and in the concentration camps, thus carrying on the black-Jewish comparisons from the prewar period. In *The Feminine Mystique* (1963) Betty Friedan famously referred to middle-class suburbia as a kind of "air-conditioned" concentration camp for women. And later in the 1960s the social psychologist Stanley Milgram designed scientific experiments to shed light on the "obedience to authority" that explicitly followed on the revelations of the Eichmann trial in Jerusalem in 1961.[31]

The most important and perhaps earliest non-Jewish contribution to the study of the Holocaust came in Dwight Macdonald's long essay "The

Responsibility of Peoples" (1945). Among other things Macdonald rejected the notion of collective German guilt, while suggesting that if such an
idea were accepted, the people of Britain and the United States should also
be called to task for passively accepting the mass saturation bombing of
German cities. (Later versions of the essay referred to the dropping of the
atomic bomb on Japan and the displacement of the Arab population in Palestine by the Israelis.) By the 1960s the concept of totalitarianism had become a common working assumption in the social sciences, and totalitarianism, according to Arendt, was erected on the camp system in Germany
and the gulag in the Soviet Union. Moreover the controversy over Arendt's
Eichmann in Jerusalem (1963) was hardly confined to the American Jewish
community since the book itself was first serialized in the *New Yorker* magazine. The debate about both Eichmann and the bureaucratic mentality that
contributed to mass murder created a new level of Holocaust consciousness in America and to a degree in Europe. Arendt's *The Origins of Totalitarianism* (1951) had already underlined the modernity of the Holocaust, the
application of industrial methods to the extermination of millions of people justified by secular, pseudo-scientific racial theories. Overall the question as to whether the Holocaust should be seen as a creation of modernity
or was some horrible atavism or aberration underlay much of the inquiry.

Prejudice (Racism, Antisemitism): The scholarship on the Holocaust was
paralleled by a huge increase in systematic studies of antisemitism and
other forms of prejudice, all of which were usually assumed to be similar in nature. Indeed the answer to the prevention of another Holocaust
was seen to be study of prejudice in all its manifestations. In contrast
with *The Authoritarian Personality* and most studies of prejudice, Bruno
Bettelheim and Morris Janowitz's *The Dynamics of Prejudice* (1950) *contrasted* antisemitism and color-coded prejudice in terms of origins and
dynamics. Their approach challenged the broad assumption that there
was a general theory of prejudice that could explain both antisemitism
and white racism and then provide suggestions on how to prevent prejudice in the future. Arendt's *Origins*, like Fromm's *Escape from Freedom*, adopted a historical perspective on a *modern* antisemitism that was secular
rather than religious in origins and goals. Indeed racially based prejudice,
including antisemitism and racism, was increasingly seen as a modern
phenomenon, by no means the same sort of phenomenon as religious
hostility to Judaism and Jews.

Interestingly the familiar tendency to study antisemitism by study-ing other ideas similar to it was also evident in *The New American Right* (1955) and its expanded version, *The Radical Right* (1963). Edited by the sociologist Daniel Bell, the collections sought to identify the origins of a new kind of "pseudo-conservatism," the term borrowed by historian Richard Hofstadter from Adorno in *The Authoritarian Personality*. Along with Hofstadter, at least three of the major contributors were Jewish so-ciologists: David Riesman, Lipset, and Bell. Specifically the central ques-tion was whether the new Radical Right was covertly antisemitic, since the mind-set marking it echoed the conspiratorial, often quasi-paranoid worldview associated with antisemitism. The surprising answer was "not apparently" or "not particularly." Even Senator Joe McCarthy kept his distance from antisemitism. There were no pogroms, no camps, no purg-es of Jews emerging in the McCarthy era.[32]

As was the case with early postwar studies of the Holocaust, the contri-butions of Gentiles to the study of prejudice were relatively small but not unimportant. Talcott Parsons's 1942 essay "The Sociology of Modern An-tisemitism" has had no major influence, but Gordon Allport's *The Nature of Prejudice* (1954), a work of synthesis, was an important contribution, which escaped the exclusive focus on psychoanalytic understandings of antisemitism. Studies of white racism and its effects on black Americans flourished in the 1940s and later. Two of the best known—Myrdal's *An American Dilemma* and the articles by the Clarks on the damaged self-image of young black children—scarcely mentioned antisemitism at all. Nor was it any different with the "caste and class" school of sociology that studied black southerners in the 1930s, which was spearheaded by John Dollard and Allison Davis, a white and black sociologist with psy-choanalytic orientations.[33]

Contemporary Jewish Life: Sociologists and historians took up the study of American Jews fairly quickly after the war by focusing on topics such as immigration, assimilation, and of course the relations between Jews and African Americans. Harvard historian Oscar Handlin's *The Uprooted* (1951) sought to recapture the experience of Eastern European immigrants to the United States in the second wave of immigration but without foot-notes or a conventional scholarly apparatus. The postwar years also saw a vast expansion of higher education and, with that, the increase of Jews in higher education as students and faculty. Thus when in 1970 Lipset observed that American Jewish social scientists were reluctant to study Jewish topics, his generalization was already out of date and had been since the mid-1940s. Indeed the presence of Lipset, Bell, and Riesman in the study of the antisemitic potential of the Radical Right was a testament to its inaccuracy. Gary Marx's *Protest and Prejudice* (1967) explored the increasingly ambivalent relationship between blacks and Jews, while Milton M. Gordon's *Assimilation in American Life* (1964) and Nathan Glazer and Daniel Patrick Moynihan's *Beyond the Melting Pot* (1964) challenged both the simplistic melting pot and the idealized cultural pluralist models of ethnicity in America. Though it appeared after the historical focus here, Irving Howe's *World of Our Fathers* (1976), a broadly conceived exploration of the history and social experience of Jews in America, came closest to being the major study of American Jewish experience to match Myrdal's *An American Dilemma* or Horace Cayton and St. Clair Drake's *Black Metropolis* (1945). But Howe's focus on the experience of *Ostjuden* in New York was finally too narrowly conceived and lacked the conceptualizing orientation of sociology and social theory at their best.

Aside from the polemical contributions of black intellectuals such as Cruse, the most prominent scholarly contribution to the history of American ethnicity by a non-Jew was John Higham's *Strangers in the Land* (1955). It located antisemitism and the experience of American Jews within a broader nativist tradition in American life and culture. Interestingly Higham's emphasis, like that of most students of Jewish history at the time, focused on Jews and other European ethnics as religious-cultural rather than racial groups and thus was part of the general swerve away from race that was also reflected across the board after the war. The peculiarly American distinction between ethnicity and race, nativism (under which antisemitism was placed) and racism, never looked stronger.[34] If this literature, and much like it, was still too detached and scholarly, the postwar years saw the emergence of a talented cadre of Jewish fiction writers—Saul Bellow, Bernard Malamud, Norman Mailer, and Philip Roth—who explored with particular relish and power what it meant to be a Jew in America in the postwar world, not to mention popular studies such as Stephen Birmingham's *Our Crowd* and Leo Rosten's *The Joys of Yiddish* (1968).

Modern Culture and the Self: A final component of the postwar version of the Jewish question avoided a direct engagement, by and large, with antisemitism but was a response to the problem of the marginality of the self to society, as addressed by several sociologists who were Jewish. For example, Benjamin Nelson's *The Idea of Usury* (1949, 1969) explored the origins of the modern world by examining the difference between Christian and Jewish ideas of how the "other" was to be treated in economic terms. He concluded that the Deuteronomic distinction between those who might and might not be charged interest was a way station on the road to modernity in which society was constructed on the principle of universal "otherhood." But contrary to Sombart, Jews were not the sole creators of modern capitalism, nor were they totally traditional, as claimed by Weber. But their economic ethic—charge Jews no interest; charge Gentiles interest—foreshadowed the impersonal *gesellschaftlich* rather than the more intimate *gemeinschaftlich* ties that link people in modern society. Erving Goffman's *The Presentation of the Self in Everyday Life* (1959) offered a dramaturgical model of the self as a set of roles and thus echoed David Riesman's "other-directed" self in *The Lonely Crowd* (1950), while Goffman's *Asylums* (1961) drew upon some of the concentration camp literature to discuss the sociological nature of total institutions such as prisons, asylums, and monasteries. Was there a self to which or to whom one might be true? And what sort of room for agency and autonomy exists in such places? One lesson was clear: modern men and women did not have to wait to be sent to concentration camps to experience something of the threat to self and sociality brought to completion in the camp systems of the totalitarian states.

An analysis of the contemporary cultural revolution was offered by Philip Rieff in *The Triumph of the Therapeutic* (1966). There he analyzed the transition from an older normative, "creedal" (i.e., religious) culture to a remissive culture in which self-realization as dictated by a therapeutic ethic and ideal were central. Where a previous generation of Jewish intellectuals had been profoundly influenced by Marx, Rieff placed Freud's pervasive influence at the heart of the postwar cultural revolution, even though his ethic was one of adjustment to rather than emancipation from repression. Against all this, Rieff held out a faint hope that the figure of "the Jew of Culture" could at least survive. And as though testing out Rieff's claim, as well as foreshadowing the postmodern, Robert Jay Lifton's essay, "Protean Man" (1967) suggested an emerging global type of sensibility/self that was not defined by final commitments but by the range of experiences, not by deep relationships but by their variety.

What these examples suggest is that by the end of the turbulent decade of the 1960s, the experience of American Jewry seemed to have taken on the representative status that Robert Park had once attributed to it in his analysis of marginality. In particular these works by contemporary sociologists of Jewish birth suggested a sea change not only in American Jewish culture but in the culture of modernity in America. One of the most stimulating studies focusing on the contemporary Jewish question was John Murray Cuddihy's *The Ordeal of Civility* (1974), a work of cultural sociology written by an ex-Catholic about how ex-Jews have tried to become ex-Protestants. Cuddihy's thesis was that Jews in modern Europe and America were deeply ambivalent about adopting/ adapting to the ethic/ethos of bourgeois civility, manners, and mores that assimilation into modern Gentile society entailed. For this he turned to high European thought, particularly Freud, and imaginative literature (mostly Jewish and African American fiction) to explore the vicissitudes of modernity. Interestingly three decades later, when Yuri Slezkine asserted in *The Jewish Century* (2004) that "modernization, in other words, is about everyone becoming Jewish," he was turning Cuddihy's "ordeal of civility" thesis on its head.

It is fitting that Philip Roth, America's greatest modern novelist of the travails of assimilation, returned in *American Pastoral* (1996) to the theme that had linked much of his work: the vicissitudes of post-1930s middle-class Jewish life in modern America. *American Pastoral* is perhaps American literature's most powerful exploration of the postwar Jewish experience in America. (It is also something like a strong re- or misreading of Cuddihy's *The Ordeal of Civility* some twenty years later.) What *American Pastoral* managed to do was to force readers, Jews and Gentiles alike, to face the question of what the costs of becoming an American actually were.

We are left with two somewhat contradictory conclusions. On the one hand American sociologists and historians of race and ethnicity have presented a complexly positive answer to the Jewish question in America, which is particularly striking in the first quarter-century after the Holocaust. Yet more pessimistic and troubled renderings of modern American Jewish experience can be found in the fiction of Roth and many of his contemporaries. How the two positions can be reconciled remains to be answered. The history of the efforts to understand Jewish life in America, beginning at least with the emerging social sciences around the turn of the twentieth century, dictates no confident answer. But from a topic that was touched on only in disguised form or received merely polemical treatment to one that made claims for the representative status of American Jews and culminating in the watershed decade of the 1960s when the post–World War II consensus seemed to dissolve before the eyes of the country, the Jewish question has always been *there* waiting to be explored.

Notes

Special thanks to Stephen J. Whitfield, Lawrence J. Friedman, and Chad Alan Goldberg for reading earlier drafts, as well as to David Hollinger, Howard Brick, and Daniel Geary for answering questions I posed to them.

1. Put another way, the "Jewish question" asks how Jews fit into a Gentile society and particularly the nature of the hostility to their becoming a part of it. In *Race: A Short History* George Fredrickson uses the term "color coded racism" to refer to white racism. See also King, *Race, Culture and the Intellectuals* for similarities and differences in the two types of prejudice.
2. That the founding figures in the history of sociology, e.g., Durkheim and Weber, or earlier Tocqueville and Marx, were not sociologists by training meant ironically that their work had an intellectual richness lacking once the discipline became professionalized.
3. Sumner, *Folkways*, 75. See also Woodward, *The Strange Career*, 103–4 for the way Sumner was used by defenders of segregation.
4. Calhoun, introduction, *Sociology in America*, 8. There are two chapters dealing with race in Calhoun's valuable volume, but neither deals at all with antisemitism nor with the Jewish question in America. In fact antisemitism is listed only once in the index.
5. The literature on modern antisemitism in America is vast, but the place to begin is still Higham, *Strangers in the Land*. But see also Jacobson, *Whiteness of a Different Color*; Guterl, *The Color of Race in America*; Dinnerstein, *Antisemitism in America*; Lindemann, *The Race Accused*; Goldstein, *The Price of Whiteness*; and, more generally, Gerstle, *American Crucible*.
6. Diner, introduction to *The Ghetto*, xxxviii.
7. For the racial consensus circa the beginning of World War I—and on into the 1920s—see Fredrickson, *The Black Image in the White Mind*, 320–22.
8. Bodemann, "Ethnos, Race and Nation," 129. See also Mitzman, *Sociology of Estrangement*, 251–56. *Patterns of Prejudice* 44.2 (2010), edited by Marcel Stoetzler, is devoted to the theme "Modern Antisemitism and the Emergence of Sociological Theory," itself the title of a conference at the University of Manchester organized by Stoetzler and held November 2–3, 2008. My paper here developed out of the paper I gave at that conference.

9. Bodemann, "Ethnos, Race and Nation," 133–36.

10. Pierpont, "The Treasure of America," 55. For more on Boas and the context of his thought, see Stocking, *Race, Culture and Evolution*; Williams, *The Social Sciences and Theories of Race*, chapter 2; Whitfield, "Franz Boas."

11. Lipset, "The American Jewish Community in a Comparative Context," 151. See Frederickson, *Race* for the contrasting analysis of Jews and blacks in relation to modernization.

12. Morris-Reich, "Circumventions and Confrontations," 206–9.

13. Lipset, "The American Jewish Community," 149.

14. See Cruse, *The Crisis of the Negro Intellectuals*; see also King, *Race, Culture and the Intellectuals*, 268–77.

15. See King, *Race, Color and the Intellectuals*, 132–36 for a discussion of Frazier's critique of Herskovits and black cultural particularism.

16. Wirth, *The Ghetto*; Lipset, "The American Jewish Community," 148. For the general point about the Jewish link to marginality, see Goldberg, "Robert Park's Marginal Man."

17. Hasia Diner makes this point several times in her introduction to the reprint of *The Ghetto*, ix–lxiii. For the point about "objectivity" and "dispassion," see xxviii.

18. Daryl Scott in *Contempt and Pity*, 21–26 stresses the damaging effects of marginality as seen in the work of the Chicago School, while Fred H. Matthews in *Quest for an American Sociology* claims Park treated it in a positive sense too (171). Stressing damage in his "Self-Hatred among Jews," Kurt Lewin also commented on this phenomenon among black Americans based on skin color.

19. Wirth, *The Ghetto*, chapter 13. Amitai Etzioni, "*The Ghetto*: A Reevaluation" notes that the pluralist rather than assimilationist model fits Wirth's data better.

20. See Gordon, *Assimilation in American Life*, chapter 4.

21. Horace Kallen in particular believed in racial differences that were more than circumstantial, as in fact did Du Bois and Veblen. Both Kallen and Du Bois later took their distance from these positions.

22. Brackman, "'A Calamity Almost Beyond Comprehension'"; Kallen, *Culture and Democracy in the United States*, ix–lxix; Bourne, *War and the Intellectuals*, chapters 8 and 9; Veblen, "The Intellectual Pre-eminence of the Jews in Modern Europe."

23. Hollinger, "The 'Tough Minded' Justice Holmes," 43, 51, 53.

24. Wilson, "Holmes-Laski Correspondence," 100.

25. In "A Critique of Leonard Dinnerstein's *The Origins of Black Anti-Semitism in America*," Stephen J. Whitfield suggests that World War II saw a break in the history of African American antisemitism, a claim that I want to make for American antisemitism in general.

26. Heinze, *Jews and the American Soul*.

27. Silk, "Notes on the Judeo-Christian Tradition in America."

28. Indeed already in 1936 Archibald McLeish, writing for the editors of *Fortune* magazine, was generally optimistic about the prospects for Jews in America,

even though the 1930s saw a disturbing rise in antisemitism in America. See *Jews in America*.

29. Myers, *Annotated Bibliography*.

30. Erik H. Erikson, "The Legend of Hitler's Childhood," in *Childhood and Society*.

31. See Fermaglich, *American Dreams and Nazi Nightmares* for discussion of these three texts.

32. The Internal Security Act of 1950, also known as the McCarren Act, did provide for camps to be set up in so-called emergency situations.

33. Dollard, *Caste and Class in a Southern Town*; Davis, *Children of Bondage*.

34. See Jacobson, *Whiteness of a Different Color* for a study that focuses much more on the racialization of European ethnics than Higham and thus minimizes the American distinction between race and ethnicity.

References

Adorno, T. W., et al. *The Authoritarian Personality*. New York: Harper and Row, 1950.

Allport, Gordon. *The Nature of Prejudice*. Reading MA: Addison-Wesley, 1954.

Arendt, Hannah. *Eichmann in Jerusalem*. 2d ed. New York: Viking Press, 1965.

———. *The Origins of Totalitarianism*. 2d ed. Cleveland OH: Meridian Books, 1958.

Bell, Daniel, ed. *The Radical Right*. Garden City NY: Doubleday Anchor Books, 1964.

Bettelheim, Bruno, and Morris Janowitz. *The Dynamics of Prejudice*. New York: Harper and Brothers, 1950.

Birmingham, Stephen. *Our Crowd*. New York: Harper and Row, 1967.

Bodemann, Y. Michal. "Ethnos, Race and Nation: Werner Sombart, the Jews and Classical German Sociology." *Patterns of Prejudice* 44.2 (2010): 117–36.

Bourne, Randolph. *War and the Intellectuals*. Edited by Carl Resek. New York: Harper Torchbooks, 1964.

Brackman, Harold. "'A Calamity Almost Beyond Comprehension': Nazi Anti-Semitism and the Holocaust in the Thought of W. E. B. Du Bois." *American Jewish History* 88.1 (2000): 53–93.

Calhoun, Craig, ed. Introduction to *Sociology in America*. Chicago: University of Chicago Press, 2007.

Cayton, Horace, and St. Clair Drake. *Black Metropolis*. New York: Harper and Row, 1962.

Cruse, Harold. *The Crisis of the Negro Intellectuals*. New York: Morrow, 1967.

Cuddihy, John Murray. *The Ordeal of Civility: Freud, Marx, Levi-Strauss, and the Jewish Struggle with Modernity*. New York: Basic Books, 1974.

Davis, Allison. *Children of Bondage: The Personality Development of Negro Youth in the Urban South*. New York: Harper and Row, 1964.

Diner, Hasia. Introduction to *The Ghetto*, ix–lxiii. New Brunswick NJ: Rutgers University Press, 1997.

Dinnerstein, Leonard. *Antisemitism in America*. New York: Oxford University Press, 1994.

Dollard, John. *Caste and Class in a Southern Town*. Garden City NY: Doubleday Anchor, 1957.

Erikson, Erik H. *Childhood and Society*. 2d ed. New York: Norton, 1963.

Etzioni, Amitai. "*The Ghetto*: A Reevaluation." In *The Chicago School: Critical Assessments*, edited by Ken Plummer, 73–85. New York: Routledge, 1997.

Fairchild, Henry Pratt. *The Melting Pot Mistake*. New York: Arno Press, 1977.

Fermaglich, Kristen. *American Dreams and Nazi Nightmares: Early Holocaust Consciousness and Liberal America, 1957–1965*. Waltham MA: Brandeis University Press, 2007.

Fredrickson, George. *The Black Image in the White Mind*. New York: Harper Torchbook, 1972.

———. *Race: A Short History*. Princeton NJ: Princeton University Press, 2003.

Fromm, Erich. *Escape from Freedom*. New York: Rinehart, 1941.

Gerstle, Gary. *American Crucible: Race and Nation in the Twentieth Century*. Princeton NJ: Princeton University Press, 2002.

Glazer, Nathan, and Daniel Patrick Moynihan. *Beyond the Melting Pot: The Negroes, Jews, Italian and Irish of New York City*. Cambridge MA: MIT Press, 1963.

Goffman, Erving. *Asylums*. Garden City NY: Doubleday Anchor, 1961.

———. *The Presentation of the Self in Everyday Life*. Garden City NY: Doubleday Anchor, 1959.

Goldberg, Chad Alan. "Robert Park's Marginal Man: The Career of a Concept in American Sociology." *Laboratorium* 4.2 (2012): 199–217.

Goldstein, Eric L. *The Price of Whiteness: Jews, Race and American Identity*. Princeton NJ: Princeton University Press, 2006.

Gordon, Milton M. *Assimilation in American Life: The Role of Race, Religion and National Origins*. New York: Oxford University Press, 1964.

Guterl, Matthew. *The Color of Race in America, 1900-1940*. Cambridge MA: Harvard University Press, 2001.

Handlin, Oscar. *The Uprooted*. New York: Little, Brown, 1951.

Heinze, Andrew R. *Jews and the American Soul: Human Nature in the Twentieth Century*. Princeton NJ: Princeton University Press, 2004.

Herberg, Will. 1951, *Protestant-Catholic-Jew*. Garden City NY: Doubleday, 1951.

Higham, John. *Strangers in the Land: Patterns of American Nativism*. New Brunswick NJ: Rutgers University Press, 1955.

Hollinger, David. "The 'Tough Minded' Justice Holmes, Jewish Intellectuals, and the Making of an American Icon." In *Science, Jews and Secular Culture: Studies in Mid-Twentieth Century American Intellectual History*, 42-59. Princeton NJ: Princeton University Press, 1998.

Howe, Irving. *World of Our Fathers*. New York: Touchstone, 1976.

Jacobson, Matthew Frye. *Whiteness of a Different Color*. Cambridge MA: Harvard University Press, 1998.

Jews in America. Edited by the editors of *Fortune*. New York: Random House, 1936.

Kallen, Horace. *Culture and Democracy in the United States*. 1924. Introduction by Stephen Whitfield. New Brunswick NJ: Transaction Books, 1998.

King, Richard H. *Race, Culture and the Intellectuals, 1940-1970*. Washington DC: Woodrow Wilson Center Press and Johns Hopkins University Press, 2004.

Lewin, Kurt. "Self-Hatred among Jews." 1941. In *Resolving Social Conflict: Selected Papers on Research Dynamics*, 186-200. New York: Harper and Bros., 1948.

Lifton, Robert Jay. "Protean Man." In *History and Human Survival*, 311-31. New York: Vintage, 1967.

Lindemann, Albert. *The Race Accused: Three Anti-Semitic Affairs. Dreyfus, Beilis, Frank, 1894-1915*. Cambridge: Cambridge University Press, 1991.

Lipset, Seymour Martin. "The American Jewish Community in a Comparative Context." In *Revolution and Counterrevolution: Change and Persistence in Social Structures*, 141-53. Garden City NY: Anchor Books, 1970.

Macdonald, Dwight. "The Responsibility of Peoples." In *Memoirs of a Revolutionist*, 33-72. New York: Meridian, 1958.

Marx, Gary. *Protest and Prejudice*. New York: Harper and Row, 1967.

Matthews, Fred H. *Quest for an American Sociology: Robert E. Park and the Chicago School*. Montreal: McGill-Queen's University Press, 1977.

Mitzman, Arthur. *Sociology of Estrangement: Three Sociologists of Imperial Germany*. New York: Knopf, 1973.

Morris-Reich, Amos. "Circumventions and confrontations: Georg Simmel, Franz Boas, and Arthur Ruppin and their responses to antisemitism." *Patterns of Prejudice* 44.2 (2010): 195-215.

Myers, D. G. *Annotated Bibliography of Holocaust Writing in American Jewish Magazines, 1945-1952*, http://www-english.tamu.edu/pers/fac/myers/annotated_bib.htm (accessed July 5, 2010; no longer active).

Myrdal, Gunnar. *An American Dilemma*. 2 vols. New York: McGraw, 1964.

Nelson, Benjamin. *The Idea of Usury: From Tribal Brotherhood to Universal Otherhood* 2d revised edition. Chicago: University of Chicago Press, 1969.

Parsons, Talcott. "The Sociology of Modern Antisemitism." In *Jews in a Gentile World*, edited by I. Graeber and S. H. Britt, 101-22. New York: Macmillan, 1942.

Pierpont, Claudia Roth. "The Treasure of America." *New Yorker*, March 18, 2004.

Rieff, Philip. *The Triumph of the Therapeutic: The Uses of Faith after Freud*. New York: Harper and Row, 1966.

Ross, Dorothy. *The Origins of American Social Science*. Baltimore: Johns Hopkins University Press, 1991.

Rosten, Leo. *The Joys of Yiddish*. New York: Washington Square Books, 1970.

Scott, Daryl. *Contempt and Pity: Social Policy and the Imagine of the Damaged Black Psyche, 1880-1996*. Chapel Hill: University of North Carolina Press, 1997.

Silk, Mark. "Notes on the Judeo-Christian Tradition in America." *American Quarterly* 36.1 (1984): 65–85.

Slezkine, Yuri. *The Jewish Century*. Princeton NJ: Princeton University Press, 2004.

Stocking, George W., Jr. *Race, Culture and Evolution: Essays in the History of Anthropology*. New York: Free Press, 1968.

Sumner, William Graham. *Folkways*. New York: Mentor Books, 1960.

Veblen, Thorstein. "The Intellectual Pre-eminence of the Jews in Modern Europe." *Political Science Quarterly* 34 (March 1919): 33–42.

Whitfield, Stephen J. "A Critique of Leonard Dinnerstein's *The Origins of Black Anti-Semitism in America*." *American Jewish Archives* 39 (November 1987): 193–98.

———. "Franz Boas: The Anthropologist as Public Intellectual." *Society* 47.5 (2010): 430–38.

Williams, Vernon H. *The Social Sciences and Theories of Race*. Urbana: University of Illinois, 2006.

Wilson, Edmund. "Holmes-Laski Correspondence" (1953)." In *The Bit between My Teeth: A Literary Chronicle of 1950–1965*, 78–100. New York: Farrar, Straus and Giroux, 1966.

Wirth, Louis. *The Ghetto*. Chicago: University of Chicago Press, 1982.

Woodward, C. Vann. *The Strange Career of Jim Crow*. 2d revised edition. New York: Oxford University Press, 1967.

8

Civilization(s), Ethnoracism, Antisemitism, Sociology

ROLAND ROBERTSON

In this chapter I undertake an interrogation of the principal uses of the concept of civilization. While this volume as a whole is primarily concerned with antisemitism and sociology, I attempt to frame this issue by consideration of a more encompassing theme, a theme in which I contend that the phenomenon of antisemitism and, more generally, ethnoracism can be fruitfully located. Nonetheless it has to be strongly emphasized that I am not in any way relativizing antisemitism, most certainly not the European Holocaust of the 1940s, as has increasingly become a political and intellectual habit.[1] In other words, I have no wish to consider antisemitism as "just" one form of discrimination—more strongly, racism. Rather I wish to locate this phenomenon in the broadest and most useful context possible. It should also be noted that the word *antisemitism* was apparently not coined until the late nineteenth century.[2]

It is difficult to draw a definite line between relativization, on the one hand, and contextualization, on the other. In any case one can, with sufficient analytic penetration, combine the two.[3] It has to be emphasized that the past few decades have seen a number of tragically cruel incidents of what has come to be called ethnic cleansing, such as those in the Balkans, various parts of Africa, and yet other places.[4] Indeed Ahmed has posed the question as to whether ethnic cleansing is what he calls a metaphor for our time, while the Israeli historian Ilan Pappe has spoken of the ethnic cleansing of Palestine.[5]

Patricia Hill Collins has cogently illustrated the problems involved in treating race and ethnicity separately in a global perspective, particularly since different national sociologies have had different definitions of race and ethnicity and have varied in their attention to or neglect of both of these phenomena.[6] The suggestion that ethnic cleansing is indeed a metaphor for the contemporary human condition casts some light on this particular problem. This is a perspective that will pervade the present discussion. In addition "ethnicity" and "race" are considered alongside "religion," "culture," "tradition," and "nation."[7]

Three Concepts of Civilization

For many years—particularly during the decades of the 1970s, 1980s, and 1990s—the theme of civilization had been more or less dominated in various academic and intellectual circles by discussion of the work of Norbert Elias, in spite of other important contributions to what some have called civilizational analysis. The Eliasian trend was, however, interrupted by the publication of Samuel Huntington's article on the clash of civilizations.[8] The latter phrase was apparently borrowed explicitly from the historian of the Middle East Bernard Lewis,[9] even though this general idea has had a very long history, going back at least as far as the Christian Crusades. The interruption came to a head—indeed a crash—with the destruction of the Twin Towers in New York and the attacks on the Pentagon in Washington DC and in Pennsylvania on September 11, 2001. These resurrected the theme of civilization dramatically, although in a very different way to that which had been undertaken by Elias and his followers or indeed the (rival) practitioners of what has been called civilizational analysis or the forerunners of the latter, such as Toynbee and his epigones, most notably Carroll Quigley.[10] For the most part the deployment of this theme in the writings of journalists and academics, not to speak of the pronouncements of politicians, became strikingly polemical in the aftermath of 9/11. In fact it quickly led to the so-called war on terror, involving the use of *civilization* in a highly normative sense.[11]

However, the novelty of this use of *civilization* should not be exaggerated, as the global trauma produced by 9/11 stood in a long line of deployments of this term to denote the Other. This has been particularly true of "European civilization" regarding Islam as the Other for many centuries, as well as viewing Islamic countries as potential or actual colonial possessions. There is also the case of the internal "Other," as for example Jews and Freemasons. In fact the ancient Greeks used the word *pharmakos*, meaning "magician" or "poisoner," to refer to the internal Other.[12] Nonetheless it has been "the Turk" who has been the most continuous and lingering Other for Europe. A parallel use of civilization as a way of representing the national or regional self against the Other is to be found in the history of Russia, where there has been continuing disagreement as to whether Russia is a civilization in and of itself in relation to either or both of the internal and external Others. The main cleavage in this respect has been between those who have thought of Russia as part of an expansive Eurasia, possibly forming a bridge into the West, and those who have thought of Russia as part of Western civilization.

Yet another use of this term is in reference to "a universal modern civilization," a phrase used by the sociologist Shmuel Noah Eisenstadt.[13] This, however, is one that I do not regard as being useful or sociologically helpful, although I will return to other crucial and much more constructive aspects of Eisenstadt's work toward the end of this chapter. While having significant reservations about Elias's oeuvre and not being concerned here with direct inspection and critique of Elias, I should stress that I certainly consider the contribution of Elias to the subject at hand of the greatest importance. It should also be kept carefully in mind that Elias suffered greatly from the death of both of his parents during World War II, it being believed that his mother died in Auschwitz in 1941.[14] There can definitely be no doubt that a concern with antisemitism and racism generally, whether explicit or implicit, has had a great impact on his sociology.[15] However, at the same time that interest in Elias's work increased rapidly during the 1970s, 1980s, and early 1990s there arose considerable opposition to the general use of the word *civilization* among those who took it to mean "the civilized world" in contrast to a "non-civilized world." In fact at one time the British Sociological Association actually forbade the use of *civilization* or *civilized*, but made a specific exception in contexts where they were employed in a definitely Eliasian mode.[16]

There is a broad parallel between the experiences of Elias and the French anthropologist Louis Dumont. The latter, when incarcerated as a Jew during World War II, apparently asked himself why it was that there was such a phenomenon as racism and that, insofar as he knew, it was confined more or less to Western societies. His response to this self-imposed query is far too complex to articulate here. However, very briefly stated, his answer was that the individualism of Western societies made for what he called an ideological rejection of hierarchy and an embrace of individualism.[17] The most important point here is that Dumont's ideas concerning the positive functional—the eufunctional—significance of hierarchy, particularly in its Indian context, has had a great influence on anthropology and, to a much smaller extent, sociology, where there has been a dominant but fallacious tendency to conflate hierarchy with class stratification.[18]

Civilization, Enlightenment, and Race

The beginnings of modern discussion of civilization in earnest probably began around 1500, with the assumption that it was the mission of Europe to civilize the world, even though, as Mignolo contends, a number of other civilizations—such as the Chinese, the Islamic, the Indian, the Incan, and the Aztec—had long been "in place."[19] From that time the very concept of civilization expanded all over the planet and, in the words of Mignolo, the European notion of civilization became "a yardstick by which to measure other societies."[20] In this respect civilization is double-edged: first, as the justification of European expansion; second, as the foundation of a field of study that located Europe as the yardstick for the consideration of all other civilizations or "pre-civilizations." As Eze states, "the numerous writings on race" by some enlightened philosophers played "a strong role in articulating Europe's sense not only of its cultural but also its *racial* superiority."[21] Furthermore it was frequently said of World War I (1914–18), the Great War, that it was a war *for* civilization. Much more recently the Israeli government has claimed that it is defending and fighting on behalf of Western civilization, a contention that has to be firmly recognized as in large part an aspect of contemporary Realpolitik.

The conjunction of the ideas of civilization, enlightenment, and race undoubtedly was crucial in the formation of the very ideas of sociology and anthropology during the nineteenth century, partly as a conservative reaction to the theme of enlightenment. This observation may be applied particularly to the positive philosophy and sociology of Auguste Comte and many of those who were influenced by him. Indeed the conservative aspect of the origins of sociology have often been overlooked in favor of the enormous influence of Karl Marx, whose own work played a very significant part in the controversy about the so-called Jewish question, a problem that was fairly central to the writings of the great foundational figures of modern sociology, notably Max Weber and, more indirectly, Durkheim.[22]

Associated with this consideration is the way a distinction has often been made between culture and civilization, which is best illustrated by their different uses in France and Germany. In France *civilization* tends to have a positive meaning, conceived as a process, more often than not a French civilizing mission.[23] In Germany civilization has been regarded as secondary to culture. As Mignolo puts it, "'Civilization' can be carried and expanded all over the planet, but not 'culture.'"[24] The consequence of this distinction is that German intellectuals have found it difficult to think of civilization without thinking at the same time of the obliteration of "local"—specifically, Germanic—cultures. In any case, the view gained ground in the interwar years that (European) civilization was the "*civitas maxima* of mankind."[25] Elias himself had become very familiar with the difference between the French and German uses while he was a member of the Weber circle in Heidelberg in the 1920s (hosted by Max Weber's widow, Marianne) and also as a result of his friendships with Karl Mannheim and Alfred Weber, Max's brother.[26]

Even though the principal focus of this chapter is civilization, it must be said that much of the conventional sociological wisdom concerning ascription and achievement, as well as particularism and universalism, has been radically modified in the past sixty years or so. It is now generally acknowledged that so-called ascriptive attributes can be altered and in this sense achieved, via body modification and cosmetic surgery, clothing, and generally changing one's identity. Groebner shows convincingly that much of this ability to modify oneself is, in fact, a very old but insufficiently recognized feature in the history of humanity.[27] What has rapidly changed in the recent past is the frequency, extent, and generalized awareness of this practice. Indeed it would not be too much to say that what presently tends to be called body modification has been globalized. To give but one example of a practice that is older than is often thought: the phenomenon of "passing" as being in one "racial" category as opposed to another is not particularly recent. One thinks of hair straightening in order to make black people look whiter, Jewish women having rhinoplasty to make them look less conspicuously Jewish, East Asian people having surgery on their eyes to make them look more Western, while Western female presentation of self is currently being greatly affected by West and East Asians by conscious emulation. In fact the vast growth in body modification is too complex to be treated here, even though it has a considerable bearing on what follows.

One must, however, add that the idea of "fakeness" is becoming increasingly the norm. In fact it may not be too much to say that it is a kind of equivalent of miscegenation, in the sense that ethnoracial difference is rapidly being obliterated or at least destabilized. Over a period of about fifty years the idea that one can have the body that one desires—that the body is a matter of choice—has become a virtually global phenomenon, with Brazil and Argentina being among the most prominent for this in contemporary societies. For example, there is evidence that many Brazilians, not necessarily of Japanese descent, have migrated to Japan after undergoing cosmetic surgery to make them look more Japanese—this, in spite of their being unable to speak Japanese.

Despite these trends with respect to body modification, one should insist that there are certain relatively autonomous forms of ethnoracism, one of which is undoubtedly antisemitism. In other words, some forms of ethnoracism have been sustained within long-term traditions, traditions that make one very skeptical about claims as to particular structural features of particular periods that may produce antisemitism or, to take another example, discrimination against "people of color." Clearly much contemporary discrimination against or hostility toward Muslims— whether in terms of ethnicity, religion, region, or tradition—also has a kind of cultural autonomy.

This is closely related to the currently very controversial and increasingly politicized topic of immigration, including the expulsion of Others. Much of the discourse concerning immigration is ultranostalgic and, in a sense, "utopian." The desire for a world without immigrants—a world without strangers—is a literally unobtainable wish, but one that is undoubtedly at the root of the rise, particularly in Europe, of racist rightwing movements in the early twenty-first century.

Civilization as a Contested Concept

The concept and idea of civilization is replete with problems of meaning and interpretation. In order to bring a semblance of conceptual and semantic order to this complexity, it is necessary, in the first place, to distinguish between civilization as a sociocultural complex—more loosely, a bounded, but not necessarily territorially bounded, form of life, on the one hand, and civilization as a process, on the other. This distinction is by no means clear-cut. While Elias concentrated very explicitly on the processual meaning of the term, his work does have some overlap with the notion of civilization as a complex.[28] But a particularly striking difficulty with Elias's work in this regard is his failure to recognize that what had become by the end of the nineteenth century to be called "the standard" of civilization was a relatively autonomous, transnational norm.[29] In other words, over and beyond Elias's *analytic* conception of the civilizing process there had developed a consciously recognized, prescriptive denotation of civilization. Whether or not Elias knew of this is a subject for a separate intervention. He certainly overlooked crucial aspects of world affairs, even though a number of his students have attempted to rectify this.[30]

For Elias, the civilizing process consisted in the way historically external constraints on human behavior became internalized. This process makes the conduct of social affairs less a matter of external control and more a matter of individual conduct. Essentially this means that over the long haul there is, in Elias's perspective, a trend toward what we would in everyday terms call "civilized behavior," notwithstanding periodic deviations from this trend. Indeed much of the work published by Elias's epigones has been concerned with the theme of decivilization.

Elias's work was undoubtedly influenced by Freud, who had talked roughly and much more briefly in the same kind of terms. Freud's ideas in this regard, while running through much of his work as a whole, were expressed succinctly in his late book *Civilization and Its Discontents* (1930). In any case, there has been considerable debate as to the degree to which the civilizing process, as defined by Elias, has taken different forms in different sociocultural contexts.[31] Of particular relevance here is the principle of civility.[32] While Cuddihy cited the work of Elias, Elias did not apparently even acknowledge the work of Cuddihy. On the other hand, Elias did deal extensively with manners, which can certainly be regarded as an aspect of civility.[33] It should be noted that Cuddihy was by no means the only sociologist to deal with the vital issue of civility. To take a major example, the influential (Jewish) American sociologist Edward Shils made civility a central aspect of his oeuvre.[34]

In contrast to the processual conception of civilization, the focus on civilization as a sociocultural complex, which has tended to be territorially bound, is—at least in an explicit sense—much older and probably much more familiar, in spite of the great prominence of Elias over the past fifty years or so in some Western academic circles. Having said this, a strong caveat must be stated in that the general ideas about barbarians, savages, and so on had permeated much historical writing, not only in the West, for a number of centuries.[35]

At the center of much of this was the question concerning the psychological and physical attributes of human beings. Different societies and cultures have displayed different "solutions" to this, along with varying conceptualizations of the Other, the stranger, and the "marginal man."[36] Interest in the issue of the distinction between human and nonhuman has a very long history, not least in the period of Western "discovery" of the Americas and the attendant "curiosity" about "the natives," and the Muslim, and then Christian use of slavery, in which Britain played a very conspicuous part.[37] Closely associated with the issue of the distinction between human and nonhuman was, historically, the matter of the origins of the idea of civilization.[38] Systematic concern with the attributes of humanity peaked with the rise of eugenics in the work of Frances Galton in the 1880s. Indeed it was Galton who coined the term *eugenics*, which he defined as "the science of improving stock, which is by no means confined to judicious mating, but which . . . takes cognisance of all influences that tend . . . to give the more suitable races . . . a better chance of prevailing speedily over the less suitable than they otherwise would have had."[39] Contemporary writers argued that this "eugenic wish" to control the biological constitution of the population underpins biological politics.[40] The national socialism of the Nazi Third Reich rested largely upon the deployment of eugenics, although it was the new field of genetics, devised in 1905, that gave this the full "authority" of "science."[41]

In addition to the deployments of *civilization* as process and entity two other uses may be identified. First, there is the tendency to use the notion of being civilized as marking the distinction between human and other forms of life, as when reference is made to "the beginning of civilization."[42] Second, there is the concept of civilizationalism, which involves the instrumentalization of the concept of civilization—which is what Chen has called "the ultimate expression of ethnic nationalism."[43] Chen himself associates civilizationalism with a postcolonial thrust, while in the present context this term is used to indicate the use of civilization as part of a much broader tendency to indicate the superiority of one large sociocultural formation as compared with others, for example, the claim that one nation is the true carrier or instigator of civilization as a whole.

Much of Elias's writing on the civilizing process had been published in German at the beginning of the Nazi domination of Germany, which many people have sometimes found to be both extremely ironic and courageous.

Civilization as a Complex

It is necessary to explore the idea of civilization as a complex, as an "entity," before coming more directly to its processual connotations, repeating that, in announcing this procedure, it will be essential later to bring the problems of the relationship between the two semantic tendencies into sharper focus. The conception of civilization as a complex with particular attention to its cultural content and associated practices was, as has already been noted, brought into particularly sharp political focus by the publication of Huntington's polemical book, *The Clash of Civilizations* (1996). This book was a much extended version of an article previously published in the American journal *Foreign Affairs*.[44] The fact that it was published in a journal devoted to world politics and foreign policy, notably U.S. foreign policy, is indicative of the way the very word *civilization* now carries with it considerable ideological baggage.[45] As previously stated, however, the idea of the clash of civilizations is much older than Huntington's work. A well-known example of this is Julien Benda's *The Treason of the Intellectuals* (1927). Lepenies used the term *war of cultures* ("guerre des cultures") to refer specifically to the great differences between German and French cultures, drawing attention to the different forms of antisemitism in those countries.[46]

In the late nineteenth century, particularly during the 1870s, there was a great wave of collective violence—or pogroms—against Jews in Russia and eastern Europe. This triggered a massive Jewish immigration to western Europe and the United States. As Alexander says, "In the 1890s, partly in reaction to this new wave of Jewish immigration and partly in response to the very gains Jews had been making in these Western societies, anti-Semitic social movements for the first time entered publicly into Western civil life."[47] Part of this circumstance was, however, the Dreyfus affair in France in the mid-1890s.

The Dreyfus affair had a considerable influence on intellectual life in France generally and is of most relevance here in the work of Durkheim.[48] Dreyfus was a Jewish captain in the French army who was convicted of treason in 1894 and imprisoned in French Guiana. The evidence against him was more or less nonexistent and led to profound polarization in France. It was, it should be emphasized, the moment when the word *intellectual* was coined; subsequently intellectuals became, according to Ruth Harris, opinion makers "in a way they never have in Britain."[49] Durkheim, himself Jewish, was deeply affected by the Dreyfus affair; many traces of this can be found in his highly influential writings, particularly on religion.[50] For example, his emphatic insistence that ritual preceded belief was in many ways the key to his sociology of religion. His Jewishness was part of his attraction to the significance of religious ritual, although it was the prominence of Judaism generally in the Dreyfus affair that more than consolidated Durkheim's focus on religion. Moreover the role of intellectuals in public life had great significance for Durkheim at a particularly acute phase in European society of the time.

Civilization and Empire

Another context is important for a discussion of the concept of civilization and its ambiguous relationship to race, including the antisemitic construction of "the Jews": many living in the often so-called Third World have for quite some time considered civilization an aspect of the Western imperial gaze.[51] The word *civilization* has been so inflated in political terms that much of its analytic purchase has been lost. However, this should by no means be taken as a rejection of the term, particularly since the more analytical use of this concept has never completely succumbed to ideological pressure and has in recent years been the subject of growing analytic concern, Huntington et al. notwithstanding. However, the decline in the analytic use of *civilization* should not be overestimated. An excellent recent example of the polemical—indeed ideological and instrumental—use of this is Niall Ferguson's *Civilization: The West and the Rest*.

Almost since the beginning of the U.S. republic there has been an American view that the United States itself represented the highest form of civilization—an aspect of the notions of American exceptionalism and America having a Manifest Destiny. Moreover this idea has been especially prominent in the past forty years or so among American Republicans and was a central ingredient of the rise of so-called neoconservatism at the turn of the present century.[52] Nonetheless the idea of a particular society being regarded as a civilization has by no means been confined to the United States. To take but a few examples, one can find this kind of idea being presented in Japan, Germany, Iran, Russia, and, more often than not implicitly, England.

In the case of Russia, Tsygankov gives particular attention to civilizationists who have "always seen Russian values as different from the West" and have consistently attempted to spread Russian values abroad.[53] Tsygankov dates civilizationism in Russia back to Ivan the Terrible's idea of the gathering of Russian lands after the removal of the Mongol "yoke" and to the dictum that Moscow is the Third Rome. Early civilizationists proposed the identity of the "Russian Empire," recommending that Russia extend its eastern and southern borders so as to make Russia into a Eurasian entity. Many aspects of present Russian foreign policy lean heavily in this direction, seeing Russia as "a constantly expanding land-based empire in [a] struggle for power against sea-based Atlanticism."[54] Neumann puts the issue rather differently, pointing out in 1999 that there were Russian arguments concerning the "disease" of "Europeanism" or "Westernism" that were to be overcome by Eurasianism. The latter was in fact a form of Russian nationalism with an internal, indigenous population—the Other—which was, in Neumann's words, "immediately recognizable as [meaning] 'the Jews.'"[55] He quotes Nikolay Trubetskoy: "Europe does not equal civilization; this is merely a formula of chauvinistic cosmopolitanism.... Europe is the product of the history of a specific ethnic group ... and the so-called European 'cosmopolitanism' ... should 'openly be called *common Romano-Germanic chauvinism.*'"[56]

With the proclaimed end of the cold war in the late 1980s and early 1990s, Huntington, among many others, considered that the Western world, and the United States in particular, would find it necessary to find an alternative Other. Opposition and resistance to the seeming threat of the old Soviet Union—more accurately the Russian Empire and indeed "civilization"—had become the basis of a considerable degree of the solidarity that existed within and among Western nations. In addition Huntington proclaimed that Islam in particular could and probably would come to be a threat to the Western world (at least in the

Northern Hemisphere), regardless of its Otherness. Particularly since the early 1970s the oil boom in the Middle East, coupled with the resurgence of the more "extreme" types of Islam, had already emerged in opposition to both Soviet communism and the "democratic capitalism" of the West.

Even without the collapse of Soviet communism, Islam would almost certainly have become a formidable factor in the world. Indeed in its extreme jihadist or Islamist form, some Muslims have envisaged that Islam could and should become the apex of a globe-wide Islamic civilization, often labeled Caliphate Islam. One of the contributing factors to the demise of the Soviet Union was in fact its unsuccessful venture into Islamic Afghanistan in the late 1970s and 1980s as well as the increasing signs of resistance to Soviet domination in the southern Islamic republics of the USSR. Here it should be kept carefully in mind that, over the long term, Islam had represented much more of a challenge to the Western "way of life" than what now seems to have been the relatively brief period of Marxist-Leninist expansionism from the time of the Russian Revolution of 1917 until the declining years of the twentieth century.

Civilization and the Barbarians

While the notion of civilization, both as a verb and as a noun, had been around for many centuries, notably in what we now call the West, extensive use of the term did not really occur until the late nineteenth century. This occurred in close connection with the beginnings of academic anthropology in two overlapping branches, the comparative and the evolutionary. It should be added, however, that it had significant, but highly complex, continuities with ideas propagated during the European Enlightenment of the second half of the eighteenth century.

As the imperial ventures of the most powerful Western countries gained momentum and reached their peak with the so-called scramble for Africa and the crowning of Queen Victoria as the empress of India at the end of the century, so did the view in political circles grow that areas of imperial expansion were uncivilized in terms of the ways of life of the "natives." This process resulted in the crystallization of rather clear-cut ideas as to the criteria for judging the degree to which the people occupying a particular territory were or were not civilized. Quite frequently the term *barbarian* was used as a synonym for the latter, although there is evidence that the ancient Greeks thought of those who insisted on ethnic homogeneity as barbaric.[57]

The development of the idea that non-Westerners were barbarians impinged a great deal on the work of religious missionaries, many of whom saw their task as being to civilize the indigenous, "primitive" inhabitants of colonized or to be colonized areas.[58] Indeed resistance to civilizing projects frequently resulted in nationalism, an ideology that rested strongly on the ideal of self-determination, an ideal that had strongly influenced the rise of Zionism and other movements of self-determination in Europe more than half a century before.[59]

Overall this was a period during which the Western imperial powers—including, to some extent, the United States—attempted not so much to conquer new territory but to open up new markets for their products and gain access to valuable and "exotic" raw materials, such as silk and other fabrics, as well as spices, tea, and coffee. The challenge posed to these areas was resisted with various degrees of success during the late nineteenth and early twentieth century. The idea grew in some of these countries that if they could become "civilized" they would not be so much at the mercy of such nation-states as Britain, France, Germany, the United States, and others. This meant that among political and intellectual elites in the threatened areas it was not at all uncommon to declare that they should calculatedly engage in their own projects of civilization.

Notwithstanding a superficial similarity with Elias's conception of civilization as a process, the notion of civilization as a *project* is not fully consonant with his idea of civilization as a *process*. Elias tended to neglect the reflexive and purposeful, not to say strategic significance of what I have called projects of civilization. This latter phenomenon is to be seen vividly in the case of Japan, where the aspiration to become a civilized nation-state grew rapidly in the declining years of the nineteenth century. Indeed the very notion of a bounded territory becoming a nation-state was in itself taken to be a hallmark of civilization, although some influential theorists of nationalism have identified the nation with modernity.[60]

The Japanese conception of civilization included such ideas as that a truly civilized nation should have its own empire. This aspiration grew steadily in the first half of the twentieth century, and in the case of Japan its leaders saw it as their mission to protect the entirety of what they called Asian civilization from Western intrusion by creating its own racially conceived empire.[61] In this perspective Japan would be the most civilized of the more superior Asian civilizations, with Western societies and certainly Africa and Latin America at the bottom of a racially conceived civilizational hierarchy. One may even speculate that the Japanese elite of the Meiji period acquired the notion of Jewish inferiority from their conception of a "proper" civilization.[62] In any case the "official" racism of Japan came to a peak with the onset of the Pacific War (1941-45), which Dower has aptly described as a racial war, in which the Japanese and the Americans described each other in very pejorative simian terms.[63] These reciprocal pejoratives constituted the centerpiece of propaganda in the early 1940s.

Among the various places where national elites thought that the Jews might be settled was Manchuria, a Japanese-controlled territory of China. This was advocated by the emperor of Japan, whose desire it was to build sympathetic ties to the American Jewish community in order to weaken America in the Pacific context.[64] However, this proposal was strongly rejected by the U.S. government on the grounds that Japan was as fascist as Germany and Italy, and although it should be noted that there were "good Germans," there were no good Japanese.[65] Of particular relevance at this point is the case of Kurt Singer. Singer was the German Jewish author of the highly influential *Mirror, Sword and Jewel* (1973) who was refused a contract renewal at Tokyo Imperial University and subsequently a lectureship at a high school in Sendai in 1939 at the instigation of the Nazi Teachers' Association.[66] According to Storry, Singer was later to remark, "In Japan all foreigners are treated as unwanted as soon as they cease to be *persona grata* in their own country." He left Japan for Australia—where his status as a Jewish refugee appears not to have been recognized—and was there interned as an enemy alien. His only close relative, a younger sister, was incarcerated in Lietzmannstadt internment camp in 1941, where she probably met her death.[67] The issue of antisemitism in the Japanese context is clearly of considerable interest. For many the case of Ben-Dasen's (1972) *The Japanese and the Jews* has constituted the fulcrum of this ongoing debate, particularly when seen against the background of the relationship between China and Japan. One should fully recognize that in the period of the Pacific War the issue of Japanese nationalism came to a peak in the work of the Kyoto School.[68] At that time the high visibility and sense of superiority of Japan as a nation was particularly evident. This was, of course, the time of great confidence in Japan in its presumption that it was the leader of the East Asian Co-Prosperity sphere. Even though Japan itself was founded as a nation-state in the mid-nineteenth century upon (Chinese) Confucian principles, it was by then in the very confident position of believing itself to be superior to China—and this, even after the Rape of Nanjing.

Almost certainly, one of the most acute commentaries on the China-Japan relationship has been written by Sakai. Quoting the work of Tetsuro Watsuji, Sakai says, "The Chinese are more Jewish than the Jews while the Japanese are more Greek than the Greeks." Sakai then remarks that Watsuji's antisemitic statements were first published before Marxism became particularly strong among a small group of intellectuals. "The oddity of Watsuji's anti-Semitism consists, above all, in the fact that it was announced in a country where the absolute majority of its population [can] hardly tell a synagogue from a church." Sakai's conclusion appears to be completely in line with the Japanese "tradition" of not being able or willing to distinguish between race, ethnicity, religion, and tradition. Sakai considers Watsuji's position to be best labeled "anti-Semitism/sinophobia."[69]

Even in the case of a relatively "advanced" and rapidly expanding nation or empire such as Russia the concern to be recognized as civilized was closely associated with the ambition to become politically, economically, and militarily powerful. Indeed Lenin proclaimed soon after the successful Russian Revolution of 1917 that in order to be accepted in the community of nations the newly founded Soviet Union had to be recognized as being civilized. This was also true of Ataturk's ambition when he founded the Turkish Republic in 1923.

This enables us to see with particular clarity why it was that the "standard of civilization" came to be a feature of international law during the period in question.[70] Whereas there has been a lot of resistance to the term *civilization* in recent decades among the peoples of "less developed" societies, the aspiration to become civilized was conspicuous in those same regions at the beginning of the twentieth century. This is why, in spite of many attempts to do otherwise, the concept of civilization cannot, when all is said and done, be entirely divorced from the theme of imperialism. Nor can it be divorced from the themes of race and racism. This partly explains why it was that the explicit, if a little reluctant strategy

to become civilized was to be found much more in the Northern Hemisphere than in the South. (This view, of course, was propounded well before the alleged Huntington thesis concerning the clash of civilizations.)

In the late nineteenth century the notion of civilization was bound up
in certain parts of the world, most notably East Asia, with the principle
of extraterritoriality. The latter referred to the ways imperial nations attempted to enforce the laws of the intrusive nation within certain regions
of the invaded territories. Such was the case particularly on the eastern
seaboard of China and in the central parts of Japan.

European Late Nineteenth-Century Elaborations of Enlightenment-Period Elements of Racism

Returning directly to the issue of "the native," there was considerable debate among Western intellectuals as to whether the black or red peoples
of Africa and the Americas, respectively, should be regarded as human at
all. In fact the debate about the human/nonhuman dichotomy has been
historically at the heart of the more normative discussions of civilization. The French novelist and philosopher Arthur de Gobineau argued
in *An Essay on the Inequality of the Races* (1853–55) that civilization in the
normative sense basically revolved around the question of racial superiority and inferiority, claiming that this was the only way we could explain why European societies had constituted the site of the production
of a superior way of life. At the heart of Gobineau's ideas on race was the
belief that some races were destined to remain incapable of mixing sociably with others, while superior races had a proclivity to produce such
peoples.[71] It is noteworthy that Gobineau considered that this theorem
could explain the rise and fall of civilizations. Moreover Gobineau was,
according to Schenk, certainly responsible for the invention of the Aryan
myth, in terms of which "the Aryans, who he oddly enough identifies with
the Teutons, form a racial elite destined to rule over the other races."[72]

Gobineau had a great influence on Richard Wagner, who had already
expressed strongly anti-Jewish feelings. Schenk writes:

> If the Germans could only rid themselves of the Jews, thus ran Wag-
> ner's argument in 1880, they might yet hope for a "pure race." . . .
> It really seems as though the Germans, with all their bewildering
> variety of dynastic, religious and other traditions, needed the Jew-

ish bogy for their national unification in the last third of the nineteenth century—that is two generations before Hitler was to use the
same device to cement the edifice of the National Socialist regime
in Germany and even of his so-called New Order in Nazi-occupied
Europe.[73]

One much-overlooked aspect of the notion that the world could be
divided essentialistically into superiors and inferiors is that this was a
rather strong feature of Enlightenment thought, most strikingly in the
work of none other than Immanuel Kant (the hero of those who have
unquestioningly subscribed to the so-called emancipatory Enlightenment project). In this connection it should be observed that there was a
considerable amount of what we would now call, very pejoratively, racism among Enlightenment thinkers, including such late Enlightenment
figures as Hegel. This was not simply implicit; it was quite open and un-
embarrassed, exemplified by Kant's statement "This fellow was quite
black . . . a clear proof that what he said was stupid."[74] Kant's pupil Johann
Herder was one of the few exceptions among Enlightenment thinkers to
resist the general consensus that the world could and should be divided
in terms of different racial characteristics.[75] Kant published three essays
on race but discontinued writing about this topic when he came to publish
Toward Eternal Peace.[76] Fenves remarks that what might here be called a
"failure" may have resulted from Kant's position concerning the proposition that "the white race is destined, after all, to dominate the planet."[77]

Gobineau's claim that the incapacity for some races to mix sociably
with others was a sign of their racial inferiority facilitates our returning
directly to the theme of the rise and fall of civilizations. Another Enlightenment thinker, Edward Gibbon, was, in a sense, the paradigmatic
figure in this regard; in his highly influential book *The Decline and Fall of
the Roman Empire* Gibbon blamed the introduction of Christianity into
this empire for having been primarily responsible for its downfall. This
theme of the negative effects of religion was a rather common feature of
Enlightenment thinking, although this tendency has been greatly exaggerated, as Cassirer cogently argued.[78]

Almost certainly the most well-known example of the revival of interest in the rise and fall of civilizations was Oswald Spengler's *The Decline
of the West* (first published in two parts in Germany in 1918 and 1923). This

book was partly based upon a very pessimistic, and what we would now call highly conservative, view of the rise of European modernity, particularly with regard to changes wrought by the changing ways of life to be seen in such "new" cities as Berlin, Vienna, Prague, and Budapest—as well as Paris and, to some extent, London. Spengler's pessimism and negativism rested on the new forms of life detected in a "tragic" way by such sociologists as Georg Simmel, who had a significant but unintended influence on Spengler.[79] However, it is crucial to recognize that Simmel's influence on Spengler was certainly not based on Simmel's being antisemitic himself; indeed Simmel suffered in German academia for his (perceived) Jewishness. What Spengler derived from Simmel was the latter's characterization of European modernity, including the increasing impersonality of social life, the growing distance between individual lives and bureaucratized societies, and the accelerating disjunction between individual "cultivation" and culture generally. Spengler regarded these characteristics as strong indications of Western decline, whereas Simmel may have regretted them but certainly did not see them as anything but inevitable attributes of "modernizing" Western societies, particularly the increasingly metropolitan cities of western and central Europe. In this somewhat complicated sense, antisemitism contributed immensely to the development of sociology, for Simmel's work has had a great and still-growing place in the latter, in spite of his being regarded by many as not as important as some of his contemporaries, notably Weber and Durkheim. What for Spengler constituted a decline was for Simmel a possibly unfortunate necessity, with no unequivocal value judgments involved.

Even though it was Spengler who specifically raised the issue of the decline and fall of civilization, it was actually Weber who came to this subject by inquiring what had made the West seem superior to the East—the Occident to the Orient.[80] Specifically Weber raised this matter in his two articles that, in combination, came to be known as *The Protestant Ethic and the Spirit of Capitalism*. Much of Weber's interest in this issue had been sparked by Sombart's *Der moderne Kapitalismus* (Modern capitalism). In fact the essays of 1904 and 1905 constituted Weber's reply to the latter. Davis has discussed the relationship between Sombart and Weber admirably, directly confronting the issue as to whether Sombart was an antisemite.[81] In this manner the issue of antisemitism came to play a huge part in the making of (historical) sociology. As Davis maintains:

Weber and Sombart were pioneers in developing a historical theory of the role of "culture" in stimulating or shaping change in economic behavior and institutions. They had much to go on—the work of Karl Marx and Georg Simmel's *Philosophy of Money* among others—but they were the ones who set out the task for historians. Their case was modern capitalism, to whose "spirit" they gave a single definition. (Sombart's heroic German capitalism was still a hope for the future.) They both assumed that here was *one* historical path by which to arrive at patterns of behavior and institutions informed by "rational" calculation of profits.[82]

Of all the sociological outcomes of a debate involving charges or refutations of antisemitism it is almost certainly the debate that was fully initiated by the dispute between Sombart and Weber that has had the widest, not to say the deepest impact.[83]

It is of much more than passing interest to note that Simmel clung to the notion of "the stranger." This was in considerable contrast to Weber's use of the term *pariah* (in which he was followed by Hannah Arendt). This issue has been taken up very perceptively by Abraham in his book *Max Weber and the Jewish Question*, in particular with reference to Weber's book on ancient Judaism.[84] In addition we have already noted that such themes as strangeness and marginality were pivotal in the work of the Chicago School. In turn these themes have become central in different ways to current concerns with immigration, multiculturality, and polyethnicity. Moreover continuity in each of these respects has been sustained by American concern with the so-called melting pot.

As Alexander notes, the motif of the melting pot has an intriguing genealogy, stretching back to the late eighteenth century.[85] Israel Zangwill, who was a Jewish immigrant from the East End of London, popularized the idea with respect to the northeastern American context, and this term persisted for a long period[86]—at least, until Glazer and Moynihan wrote *Beyond the Melting Pot* (1963). It is through such interconnections that antisemitism and the study of Jewish ethnicity have become central themes in contemporary sociology—if only indirectly. The issues of immigration, marginality, and multiculturality were profoundly influenced by the phenomenon of antisemitism. Much of this kind of sociology was developed by immigrant Jews, this being part of a general development of intellectual life in the areas of New York, Boston, and New Haven.

Direct sociological concern with antisemitism and the circumstance of Jews in society has been insightfully raised by Jeffrey Alexander in his book *The Civil Sphere,* a long contribution that is almost exclusively concerned with the United States.[87] Alexander emphatically focuses on the multiculturality of American society, which clearly contrasts with Ulrich Beck's numerous triumphalist statements on the superiority of what he sees as European cosmopolitanism.[88] Alexander's argument with respect to the place of Jews in America hinges upon what he calls the continuing dialectic between difference and identification. He concludes his lengthy discussion entitled "Before and after the Holocaust" by asking the question "What could more clearly signal the positive evaluation of Jewish qualities than the growing Christian interest in marrying Jews?" He continues by posing another question: "What could more graphically demonstrate how multicultural incorporation points to increasing solidarity, the deepening sentiments of respect and affection between members of core groups and out-groups?"[89] Multiculturalism in American sociology has largely—but certainly not exclusively—revolved around Jewishness. One of the major starting points for this interest was undoubtedly Glazer's *American Judaism* (1957, revised in 1989; Glazer later significantly altered his position in *We Are All Multiculturalists Now* of 1997).

Another way concern with Jewishness entered the mainstream of sociology was via Herberg's (1955) *Protestant-Catholic-Jew.* In this book Herberg emphasized that these religious cultures constituted the common religion of America. Subsequently the latter theme was to be taken up as a central issue in American sociology of religion by Robert Bellah. Bellah revitalized the idea of civil religion as it had appeared in the works of such people as Rousseau, Durkheim, and Gellner.[90] The larger proportion of the thousands of chapters, articles, and books that have been written about civil religion have not specifically incorporated attention to Jewishness or Judaism, although there has been a specialism in the study of Israeli civil religion.[91] All in all, the inclusion or exclusion of Judaism from studies of civil religion is in itself a kind of indicator of attitudes toward Jews in particular countries.

The American case has almost certainly received the greatest interest, largely because American Jewry moved from a situation of antisemitic prejudice before World War II to one of a "restricted" inclusion within the American Dream. Jacob Neusner has put this matter from the Jewish point of view: "The history of the third generation is this: Jewish but not too Jewish. Not so Jewish that you stop being an American."[92] In using the term *third generation* Neusner referred to the situation of American Jews who were too young to fight in World War II, were too old for Vietnam, and were excused from Korea by virtue of student deferments. One should add that following World War II the state of Israel was founded, with a great deal of political support from the American administration, in spite of the American neglect of the Holocaust in the 1940s.[93] This, however, is not to say by any means that antisemitism was greatly reduced. For example, without being particularly invidious, it could certainly be said that in the 1960s anti-Jewish feeling was "endemic among Negroes . . . because the Negroes [kept] bumping into the Jews in front and ahead of them."[94] This was said in particular reference to New York City, but it surely applied to many other parts of the United States and had as much to do with placement in the system of social stratification as with racial prejudice per se.

The Problem of Western Modernity

Many of these developments in American social science had been preceded by crucial changes in the position of Jews in European society. In fact it was such developments that stimulated and made possible both the instigation of much of American sociology and, in any case, thoroughly changed its direction.

It was in such contexts that the problem of modernity arose sharply, accompanied by the so-called *Kulturkampf*—the culture wars between Catholic and Protestant—wars that were somewhat different from those described by Lepenies in reference to the relationship between France and Germany that brought the problem of racism, particularly antisemitism, into great prominence. This was to be seen most notably in Vienna, which in a number of respects was the most crucial site of antisemitism. Indeed the characteristics noted by Simmel about the large cities that had grown so fast in western Europe were particularly in evidence in Vienna, even though Simmel said little about that city.

Even though antisemitism had been strongly in evidence in Austria generally, exhibitions in Vienna in the 1920s and 1930s brought modern

European and American art to great prominence; many of the influential painters, writers, and composers were Jewish. Meanwhile in Munich works by modern artists, such as Kokoschka, were included in the Degenerate Art exhibition. In fact Hitler specifically mentioned Kokoschka, Moll, and Klee as being among those who had "brought the poison of artistic nihilism to Germany."[95] After the annexation of Austria in 1938 (the Anschluss), arrests of numerous artists were made on an unprecedented scale. Following this so-called personnel cleansing, numerous artistic organizations were subsumed in Germanic forms and various art collections were confiscated and a central depot established for the holding of confiscated Jewish property, some items of which were removed to Germany.

Spengler was also much affected by what he perceived as the increasing power and global impact of such "inferior" areas of the world as East Asia, most notably to be seen in the meteoric rise of Japan from an isolated, more or less feudal society in the mid-nineteenth century to a rapidly changing, "modernizing" one by the beginning of the second decade of the twentieth century. One should say here that the problem of the rise and fall of civilizations came into even sharper focus when the relationship between Spengler's work and that of the English historian Arnold Toynbee was compared. The crucial difference between the two writers was that whereas the German, Spengler, paid no attention to the relationships between different civilizations—indeed he considered this as a sign of civilizational degeneration[96]—Toynbee, in direct criticism of Spengler, insisted on regarding world history in terms of the *mixing* of different ideas and different peoples. It is worth emphasizing that it has been rather common for German historians and social theorists to neglect mixing—specifically the issue of intercivilizational relationships and encounters—in comparison with their British and American counterparts.

This is probably the most appropriate point at which to discuss briefly the Frankfurt School in the development of American sociology, not least because it has some bearing upon the very prominent American sociologist Talcott Parsons. Whereas it has been suggested that Parsons was antisemitic, nothing could be further from the truth. Before, however, dealing directly with this problem, a few comments on the differences between California and New York perceptions of how Jewishness has been portrayed—or, more accurately, overlooked—are in order. This deficiency has been greatly rectified by Ehrhard Bahr in his book *Weimar on the Pacific*, in which he locates German exile culture in Los Angeles in relation to what he calls the crisis of modernism, an issue that is also prominent in Peter Gay's *Modernism: The Lure of Heresy*. Both Bahr and Gay explicitly show that there were intimate links between migration, marginality, modernism/modernity, and sociology.[97]

It should be noted that the encounter between Parsons's "systems theory" and the critical theory of the Frankfurt School, of which Hork-heimer and Adorno were leading members, is, as Uta Gerhardt has re-marked, one of the most vital events in the history of Western sociology. Gerhardt demonstrates in a long article that Parsons was of great assistance in obtaining positions in American academia for members of the Frankfurt School. During the war and immediate postwar peri-od, antisemitism was a theme both for Parsonian and critical theory.[98] Parsons took a sociological standpoint. He analyzed antisemitism as an expression of aggressiveness that resulted from structural tension in anomie-type coercive societies and tensions in the pluralist life-worlds in integration-type, Western democratic societies. In contradis-tinction, Horkheimer and Adorno took a psychoanalytically grounded standpoint. The Frankfurt School scholars analyzed antisemitism as a trait in the personality structure typical of "late" capitalism. They di-agnosed atavistic tendencies of the Id, displaced upon alleged enemies that governed the attitudes of the authoritarian-type personality, the ominous follower of fascist regimes.[99] As discussed by Gerhardt, the controversy between Parsons's general theory and the critical theory of the Frankfurt School came to a head at a conference at Heidelberg Uni-versity in 1962 that involved Benjamin Nelson, as it were, on Parsons's side, although he was not, in any strict sense, an adherent of Parsons's general position; much of the bitter dispute of that period revolved around the great hostility to Weber's concern with rationality and ratio-nalization. A highlight of the controversy was the mutual antagonism between Herbert Marcuse and Nelson, particularly as this was manifest in the exchange of letters between the two in the columns of the *New York Times Book Review*.[100]

In fact the inattention to civilizational encounters and cross-fertilization among civilization complexes is something of a hallmark of the German approach to the study of civilization and civilizations. This may well be why

German historiography and social and cultural theory has often attempted to negate the topic of globalization. There is, in any case, something of a tension between the civilizational perspective and the globalization standpoint—although this is certainly not necessarily so.[101] Increasingly the study of the processes of globalization in long-historical perspective involves emphasis upon the centrality of civilization analysis.[102]

The Future of the Concept of Civilization

Clearly the so-called war on terror has brought the notion of civilization as a *condition* into ever-sharper focus.[103] This development has in fact involved the fusion, or conflation, of civilization as process and civilization as complex. Now we are witnesses to, indeed participants in a fateful apocalyptic explosion of ideas concerning the future of humankind.[104] This development is not, however, at all incompatible with the globalization perspective.[105] Indeed the present phase in the overall globalization process may well be described as the human-conditional—or, better, the millennial—phase.[106]

An indication of the manner in which both the ideas of civilization and of empire are undergoing fundamental and rapid change is provided by McDonagh's exploration of what he calls "Iberian worlds." In spite of his inadequate conception of globalization, McDonagh "wanders" over the whole of planet Earth in order to find the way in which Iberian "civilization"—a word McDonagh himself (carefully) eschews—has penetrated virtually every aspect of modern life, including the multifarious fates of ethnoracial and religious "minorities." Indeed *Iberian Worlds* constitutes a paradigm for comprehending the complexity of the contemporary world as a whole, a paradigm that will undoubtedly prevail over both civilizational and imperialistic forms of analysis. McDonagh certainly exposes, if only unintentionally, how overly simplistic the notion of the clash of civilizations is.[107]

Moreover the flourishing of interest in indigeneity, particularly since the 1980s, has now come into great prominence—so much so that it may, in the long term, outweigh or surpass concern with racial, ethnic, and religious discrimination. This is not to say that we should neglect the latter issues—far from it. At the present time concern with ethnoracism—particularly antisemitism—needs even more attention than it has been getting of late. This is particularly true with respect to the status of Israel in the contemporary world. I refer here to the numerous ways many have seen fit to "enrich" criticisms of—indeed protests against—Israel's current foreign and domestic policy with anti-Jewish sentiment. There is considerable evidence that antisemitism—not to speak of "anti-blackness"—is on the increase in a number of Western societies. We presently face a situation in which racism is being intermeshed with discourses on culture, tradition, ethnicity, religion, and yet other human attributes. In fact this is where the vast issue of Islam comes into play.

The whole issue of civilization is becoming increasingly politicized— much more than it has ever been—and may therefore have to be rethought and reconceptualized, even abandoned by serious scholars of the contemporary world. A prominent dimension of this issue is exemplified by the extent of modern migration, which is presently the object of enormous political controversy and ideological complexity.[108] In the case of the latter, old distinctions between the Left and the Right are in a state of flux, when people who claim they are of the Left adopt rather conservative or even extreme right-wing ideologies. This phenomenon is intimately connected to the creation of numerous diasporas with attendant problems of belongingness and national membership.[109] The discourse on diaspora is leading, in many parts of the world, to additional controversies about what is frequently called multiculturalism, although the issues at stake would be better addressed as multiculturality or polyethnicity. The attempts to calibrate national identities in the face of "multiculturalism" is yet another seeming paradox of our time.

Finally, it should be stressed that much of the hostility to or exclusion of others involves the failure to recognize the enormous and increasing differences within "the Other." To take but one major example, the ethnic variation within Jewish communities, historically anywhere and certainly within modern Israel, is considerable. The "average" reader of commentaries on Israel could almost be forgiven for believing that Israel is an ethnically homogeneous nation-state, whereas the facts are that the original declaration of the establishment of the state of Israel in 1948 explicitly stated that there would be "complete equality of social and political rights to all its inhabitants irrespective of religion, race, or sex," including the Arab inhabitants of the state of Israel.[110]

In an important sense one can say that antisemitism has always been a globalized phenomenon. In other words, the phenomenon has been diffused as much as it has been autochthonous. More specifically it may well be that some civilizations other than Europe have emulated what they take to be a feature of a "normal" civilization. Or, at the very least, emulating antisemitism has often been added to already-existing antisemitism.

Notes

I am very grateful to Marcel Stoetzler for his encouragement, numerous insights, wisdom, and, not least, patience. I also wish to thank Victor Lidz for his very helpful comments on Talcott Parsons and for his long-standing friendship, much of which has been centered on the work of Parsons himself.

1. Goldhagen, *Worse than War*. An early example was Evans's book on (West) German historians, *In Hitler's Shadow*. Yet other examples are provided by the works of Nolte (e.g., *Fascism and Communism*).
2. Kornberg, *Theodor Herzl*.
3. Robertson, *Globalization*, 25–31.
4. Katz, *Post-Holocaust Dialogues*, 287–317.
5. Ahmed, "'Ethnic Cleansing'"; Pappe, *The Ethnic Cleansing of Palestine*.
6. Collins, "An Entirely Different World?," 208–22.
7. Yoshino, *Cultural Nationalism in Contemporary Japan*, 1–67; Smith, *The Ethnic Origins of Nations*; Smith, *Nationalism and Modernism*; Smith, "Zionism and Diaspora Nationalism."
8. Huntington, "The Clash of Civilizations?"
9. Benthall, "Distress of Nations."
10. Toynbee, *A Study of History*; Toynbee, *Civilization on Trial*; Quigley, *The Evolution of Civilizations*; Nelson, *The Idea of Usury*; Nelson, *On the Roads to Modernity*; Kavolis, "Civilizational Paradigms in Current Sociology"; Kavolis, "History of Consciousness and Civilization Analysis"; Walter et al., *Civilizations East and West*; Robertson, *Globalization*, 97–137. See also McNeill, *Polyethnicity and National Unity in World History*.
11. See, e.g., Barkawi, *Globalization and War*; Goldhagen, *Worse than War*; Fisk, *The Great War for Civilisation*; Aslan, *How to Win a Cosmic War*.
12. Neumann, *Uses of the Other*.
13. Eisenstadt, introduction to *Patterns of Modernity*, 1–11. Taken by his parents to what was then Palestine in the 1930s, Eisenstadt became one of the world's leading sociologists, greatly influenced by Max Weber and a close colleague of Talcott Parsons. He was a student of Martin Buber in Jerusalem, and, although he wrote on a vast array of topics, his major focus during the last thirty years of his career was civilization(s). Unlike most major sociologists of the twentieth century, Eisenstadt did not emigrate to the United States, even though he frequently visited and spent much of his life there. Whereas American sociology—

at least in the twentieth century—would have been entirely different and much more parochial were it not for Jewish immigration, Eisenstadt's contribution to sociology in the large was made from what became an Israeli base. His work on civilization is of the greatest importance, and it would be no exaggeration to say that, in conjunction with his more controversial work on multiple modernizations, it constitutes one of the major subjects of contemporary social science.

14. Mennell, *Norbert Elias*, 18.

15. Elias, "On the Sociology of German Antisemitism"; Mennell, *Norbert Elias*.

16. This prescription was contained in the pamphlet *Anti-Racist Language: Guidance for Good Practice* issued to members of the BSA in 1992. Eric Dunning quotes the relevant passage in his *Sport and Leisure in the Civilizing Process*: "Civilized/civilization: This term derives from a colonialist perception of the world. It is often associated with social Darwinist thought and is full of implicit value judgements and ignorance of Third World history. However, in some cases, such as the work of Norbert Elias, civilisation takes on a different meaning without racist overtones" (262).

17. See, e.g., Dumont, *Essays on Individualism*.

18. See Eisenstadt, *Power, Trust, and Meaning*, 291.

19. Mignolo, "Globalization, Civilization and Languages," 2–3.

20. Mignolo, "Globalization, Civilization and Languages," 33.

21. Eze, *Race and the Enlightenment*, 5.

22. Abraham, *Max Weber and the Jewish Question*.

23. Verges, "'There Are No Blacks in France.'"

24. Mignolo, "Globalization, Civilization and Languages," 34. See also Robertson, *Globalization*; Robertson, "Civilization."

25. Laski, *Nationalism and the Future of Civilization*, 21.

26. Mennell, *Norbert Elias*, 9–14.

27. Groebner, *Who Are You?*

28. Elias, *The Civilizing Process*, vols. 1 and 2.

29. Gong, *The Standard of "Civilization" in International Society*; Gong, "Standards of Civilization Today"; Robertson, *Globalization*, 114–28.

30. See, e.g., Mennell, *Norbert Elias*, 115–286; Robertson, *Globalization*, 115–28.

31. Mennell, *Norbert Elias*, 227–50.

32. Cuddihy, *The Ordeal of Civility*; Cuddihy, *No Offense*; Robertson, *Globalization*, 115–28.

33. Elias, *The Civilizing Process*, vol. 1.

34. Shils, *The Virtue of Civility*.

35. Isaac, *The Invention of Racism in Classical Antiquity*.

36. Park, "Human Migration and Marginal Man." It should be noted that Park, an American sociologist of the Chicago School, had studied in Germany and had become very familiar with the work of Georg Simmel, an ethnic Jew, who has become particularly well known for his use of the term *stranger* in much of his work.

37. Drescher, *Abolition*; Chanda, *Bound Together*, 145–243.

38. Vivanti, "The Origins of the Idea of Civilization."

39. Galton, *Inquiries into Human Faculty and Its Development*, 25.

40. Rose, *The Politics of Life Itself*, 56.

41. Stepan, "*The Hour of Eugenics*," 11.

42. Chanda, *Bound Together*, 1-33.

43. Chen, "Civilizationalism."

44. Huntington, "The Clash of Civilizations?"

45. Crockatt, "Anti-Americanism and the Clash of Civilizations"; Harris, *Civilization and Its Enemies*; Toynbee, *Civilization on Trial*.

46. Lepenies, *The Seduction of Culture in German History*, 100.

47. Alexander, *The Civil Sphere*, 488-89.

48. Harris, *The Man on Devil's Island*; Matthew Reisz, "A Tale of Two Frances," *Times Higher Education*, July 22, 2010, 48-49.

49. Harris, as quoted in Reisz, "A Tale of Two Frances".

50. Durkheim, *The Elementary Forms of Religious Life*.

51. Mignolo, "Globalization, Civilization and Languages"; Worsley, "Models of the Modern World-System."

52. See Beard and Beard, *The Rise of American Civilization*; Beard and Beard, *The Making of American Civilization*; Beard and Beard, *The American Spirit*; Boorstin and Goetzmann, *American Civilization*.

53. Tsygankov, *Russia's Foreign Policy*, 7.

54. Tsygankov, *Russia's Foreign Policy*: 8.

55. Neumann, *Uses of the Other*, 149.

56. Trubetskoy (1920) as quoted by Neumann, *Uses of the Other*, 173.

57. McNeill, *Polyethnicity and National Unity in World History*; Nussbaum, "Recoiling from Reason."

58. Chanda, *Bound Together*, 105-44; Pfaff, *The Wrath of Nations*, 132-60.

59. Moynihan, *Pandaemonium*, 63-106; Manela, *The Wilsonian Moment*. It should also be said that a rough distinction has to be made between colonial expansion in the Northern Hemisphere and areas south of the Equator, with the Southern Hemisphere, particularly Africa, allegedly more in need of civilization than other parts of the world. In this regard we should mention such regions as India, China, and other parts of East and, to some degree, Southeast Asia. Much of what we now call Latin America was an exception to this rule, in that by the end of the nineteenth century a considerable number of South and Central American countries, including Mexico, by virtue of a longstanding and dominating Spanish or Portuguese presence, had been largely "civilized," in spite of subsequent talk of much older Central American civilizations (Morse, "The Multiverse of Latin American Identity"; Hale, "Political Ideas and Ideologies in Latin America").

60. See, e.g., Greenfeld, *Nationalism*.

61. Heisig and Maraldo, *Rude Awakenings*.

62. See Goodman and Miyazawa, *Jews in the Japanese Mind*.

63. Dower, *War without Mercy*; Dower, *Ways of Forgetting*, 29.

64. Grose, *Israel in the Mind of America*, 111.

65. Dower, *War without Mercy*.

66. Storry, introduction to Singer, *Mirror, Sword and Jewel*, 11.

67. Storry, introduction to Singer, *Mirror, Sword and Jewel*, 11.

68. Heisig and Maraldo, *Rude Awakenings*.

69. Sakai, *Translation and Subjectivity*, 139, 141.

70. Gong, *The Standard of "Civilization" in International Society*; Gong, "Standards of Civilization Today"; Donnelly, "Human Rights"; Mozaffari, "The Transformationalist Perspective and the Rise of a Global Standard of Civilization"; Schwarzenberger, "The Standard of Civilization in International Law."

71. Harris, *Civilization and Its Enemies*, 76–77.

72. Schenk, *The Mind of the European Romantics*, 221.

73. Schenk, *The Mind of the European Romantics*, 222.

74. Eze, *Race and the Enlightenment*, 38–64; the quotation is from Kant's 1764 essay "Observations on the Feeling of the Beautiful and the Sublime."

75. Eze, *Race and the Enlightenment*, 65–78.

76. Fenves, *Late Kant*, 102; Eze, "The Color of Reason."

77. Fenves, *Late Kant*, 103.

78. Cassirer, *An Essay on Man*. See also Robertson, "The Development and Implications of the Classical Sociological Perspective on Religion and Revolution."

79. Hughes, *Oswald Spengler*.

80. Robertson, "Max Weber and German Sociology of Religion."

81. Davis, "Religion and Capitalism Once Again?"

82. Davis, "Religion and Capitalism Once Again?," 75.

83. Eisenstadt, *Power, Trust, and Meaning*.

84. Weber, *Ancient Judaism*.

85. Alexander, *The Civil Sphere*, 432.

86. Zangwill, *The Melting Pot*.

87. If only very recently there have been signs of "the Jewish question" becoming more or less central to contemporary sociology. This has derived mainly from the work of Alexander, who has revived this theme in particular reference to the *Problemstellungen* of American civil society. (The limitation of Alexander's work to the United States is a major lacuna.) Alexander's very highly praised work on this topic barely touches the theme of civilization or, for that matter, civility. Rather Alexander seeks to show that the European Holocaust should be treated more as a cultural trauma, or a trauma drama, than as a subject with a large variety of analytic consequences.

88. Robertson and Krossa, *European Cosmopolitanism in Question*.

89. Alexander, "On the Social Construction of Moral Universals," 552.

90. Bellah, "Civil Religion in America"; Bellah and Hammond, *Varieties of Civil Religion*; Robertson *Meaning and Change*, 148–85; Robertson, "Globalization, Theocratization, and Politicized Civil Religion."

91. See Ben-Yehuda, *Theocratic Democracy*.

92. Neusner, *Israel in America*, 185.

93. Grose, *Israel in the Mind of America*.

94. Glazer and Moynihan, *Beyond the Melting Pot*, 71.

95. Pippal, *A Short History*, 226.

96. McNeill, *Arnold J. Toynbee*, 101.

97. See also Gabler, *An Empire of Their Own*; Portuges, "Accenting L.A."

98. Gerhardt, "Worlds Come Apart," 14.

99. It should be added that in spite of Parsons having been helpful to Adorno in getting him placed in the United States, this gesture went unacknowledged when the Frankfurt School returned to Germany after World War II. While Horkheimer acknowledged such collegial help, "Adorno apparently did not show appreciation of the support given by Parsons, Allport, Lazarsfeld, Merton, and other Americans" (Gerhardt, "Worlds Come Apart," 14). The point here is that Parsons was very willing to assist a Jewish German academic who was imperiled by the Nazis for his thoughts, writings, and speech, regardless of his substantive disagreements with Adorno. Moreover many of Parsons's students and collaborators were Jewish—including, Robert Merton, Renee Fox, Jesse Pitts, Andrew Effart, Gerald Platt, Mark Gould (a Marxist Parsonian), Charles Lidz, Edward Shils, Harold Bershady, Arthur Jacobson (currently professor of law at Yeshiva University's School of Law in New York), and particularly his most dedicated and thoroughly informed graduate student, Victor Lidz. Benjamin Nelson, the important New York Jewish intellectual and sociologist, was also close to Parsons. There were numerous others, but the list is too long to specify here. For additional items by Gerhardt of relevance to this topic, see Gerhardt, *Talcott Parsons on National Socialism*; Gerhardt, *Agenda for Sociology*.

100. Among the many bitter exchanges following the Heidelberg conference was Adorno's charge "that Parsons's structural functionalism lacked sensitivity for the human needs of the individual" (Gerhardt, "Worlds Come Apart," 29).

101. Robertson, *Globalization*, 129–37; Barkawi, *Globalization and War*.

102. Sanderson, *Civilizations and World Systems*; Brotton, *The Renaissance Bazaar*; Goody, *The East in the West*; Gunn, *First Globalization*; Hobson, *The Eastern Origins of Western Civilization*; Jardine and Brotton, *Global Interests*; Mozaffari, "The Transformationalist Perspective and the Rise of a Global Standard of Civilization"; Mozaffari, *Globalization and Civilizations*.

103. Webel, *Terror, Terrorism, and the Human Condition*.

104. Aslan, *How to Win a Cosmic War*; Pearson, *A Brief History of the End of the World*, 86–290.

105. Robertson, *Globalization*; Osterhammel and Petersson, *Globalization*.

106. Robertson, "Globalization, Theocratization, and Politicized Civil Religion."

107. See also Nussbaum, *The Clash Within*.

108. Cohen, *Migration and Its Enemies*.

109. Cohen, *Global Diasporas*; Robertson, *Globalization*.
110. http://www.knesset.gov.il/docs/eng/megilat_eng.htm. (Accessed November 21, 2013)

References

Abraham, Gary A. *Max Weber and the Jewish Question: A Study of the Social Outlook of His Sociology*. Urbana: University of Illinois Press, 1992.

Ahmed, Akbar S. "'Ethnic Cleansing': A Metaphor for Our Time?" *Ethnic and Racial Studies* 18.1 (1995): 1–25.

Alexander, Jeffrey C. *The Civil Sphere*. New York: Oxford University Press, 2006.

———. "On the Social Construction of Moral Universals: The 'Holocaust' from War Crime to Trauma Drama." In *Cultural Trauma and Collective Identity*, edited by J. C. Alexander, R. Eyerman, B. Giesen, N. J. Smelser, and P. Sztompka, 196–263. Berkeley: University of California Press, 2004.

Arendt, Hannah. *The Human Condition*. Garden City NJ: Anchor Books, 1959.

Armitage, David. *The Declaration of Independence: A Global History*. Cambridge MA: Harvard University Press, 2007.

Aslan, Reza. *How to Win a Cosmic War*. New York: Arrow Books, 2010.

Bahr, Ehrhard. *Weimar on the Pacific: German Exile Culture in Los Angeles and the Crisis of Modernism*. Berkeley: University of California Press, 2007.

Barkan, Elazar, and Marie-Denise Shelton. *Borders, Exiles, Diasporas*. Stanford CA: Stanford University Press, 1998.

Barkawi, Tarak. *Globalization and War*. Lanham MD: Rowman & Littlefield, 2006.

Bar-Yosef, Eitan, and Nadia Valman, eds. *"The Jew" in Late-Victorian and Edwardian Culture: Between the East End and East Africa*. Basingstoke UK: Palgrave Macmillan, 2010.

Bauman, Zygmunt. *Modernity and the Holocaust*. Ithaca NY: Cornell University Press, 1989.

Beard, Charles A., and Mary A. Beard. *The American Spirit: The Study of the Idea of Civilization in the United States, 1880–1917*. Chicago: University of Chicago Press, 1942.

Beard, Charles A., and Mary A. Beard. *The Making of American Civilization*. New York: Macmillan, 1940.

Beard, Charles A., and Mary A. Beard. *The Rise of American Civilization*. New York: Macmillan, 1930.

Bellah, Robert N. "Civil Religion in America." *Daedalus* 96 (Winter 1967): 1–27.

Bellah, Robert N., and Phillip E. Hammond, eds. *Varieties of Civil Religion*. San Francisco: Harper & Row, 1980.

Beller, Steven. *Antisemitism: A Very Short Introduction*. Oxford: Oxford University Press, 2007.

———. *Vienna and the Jews, 1867–1938: A Cultural History*. Cambridge: Cambridge University Press, 1989.

Benda, Julien. *The Treason of the Intellectuals*. 1927. New York: Norton, 1969.

Ben-Dasen, Isaiah. *The Japanese and the Jews*. New York: John Weatherhill, 1972.

Ben-Raphael, Eliezer. "The Transformation of Diasporas: The Linguistic Dimension." In *Identity, Culture and Globalization*, edited by E. Ben-Raphael with Y. Sternberg, 336–70. Leiden: Brill, 2001.

Benthall, Jonathan. "Distress of Nations." *Times Literary Supplement*, August 13, 2010, 3.

Ben-Yehuda, Nachman. *Theocratic Democracy: The Social Construction of Religious and Secular Extremism*. Oxford: Oxford University Press, 2010.

Bethell, Leslie, ed. *Ideas and Ideologies in Twentieth Century Latin America*. Cambridge: Cambridge University Press, 1996.

Birnbaum, Pierre. "Becoming State Jews: From Visibility to Discretion." In *Identity, Culture and Globalization*, edited by E. Ben-Raphael with Y. Sternberg, 375–84. Leiden: Brill, 2001.

Bodemann, Y. Michal. "Ethnicity Cosmopolitanized? The New German Jewry." In *Identity, Culture and Globalization*, edited by E. Ben-Rafael with Y. Sternberg, 353–72. Leiden: Brill, 2001.

Boorstin, Daniel, and William H. Goetzmann. *American Civilization*. London: Thames and Hudson, 1972.

Brotton, Jerry. *The Renaissance Bazaar: From the Silk Road to Michelangelo*. Oxford: Oxford University Press, 2002.

Burckhardt, Jaacob. *The Civilization of the Renaissance in Italy*. New York: Harper & Row, 1975.

Cassirer, Ernst. *An Essay on Man*. New Haven CT: Yale University Press, 1944.

Chanda, Nayan. *Bound Together: How Traders, Preachers, Adventurers, and Warriors Shaped Globalization*. New Haven CT: Yale University Press, 2007.

Chen, Kuan-Hsing. "Civilizationalism." *Theory Culture and Society: Problematizing Global Knowledge: Special Issue* 23.2–3 (2006): 427–28.

Cohen, Robin. *Global Diasporas: An Introduction*. London: Routledge, 1997.

———. *Migration and Its Enemies: Global Capital, Migrant Labour and the Nation-State*. Aldershot UK: Ashgate, 2006.

Cohen, Steven M. *American Modernity and Jewish Identity*. New York: Tavistock, 1983.

Collins, Patricia Hill. "An Entirely Different World? Challenges for the Sociology of Race and Ethnicity." In *The Sage Handbook of Sociology*, edited by C. Calhoun, C. Rojek, and B. Turner, 208–22. London: Sage, 2005.

Cowen, Tyler. *Creative Destruction: How Globalization Is Changing the World's Cultures*. Princeton NJ: Princeton University Press, 2002.

Craig, Gordon A. *The Germans*. New York: Meridian, 1991.

Crockatt, Richard. "Anti-Americanism and the Clash of Civilizations." In *The Rise of Anti-Americanism*, edited by B. O'Connor and M. Griffiths, 121–39. New York: Routledge, 2006.

Cuddihy, John M. *No Offense: Civil Religion and Protestant Taste*. Englewood Cliffs NJ: Prentice-Hall, 1978.

──────. *The Ordeal of Civility: Freud, Marx, Levi-Strauss and the Jewish Struggle with Modernity*. New York: Basic Books, 1974.

Davidman, Lynn. *Tradition in a Rootless World: Women Turn to Orthodox Judaism*. Berkeley: University of California Press, 1993.

Davis, Natalie Z. "Religion and Capitalism Once Again? Jewish Merchant Culture in the Seventeenth Century." In *The Fate of "Culture": Geertz and Beyond*, edited by S. B. Ortner, 56–85. Berkeley: University of California Press, 1999.

Dawson, Christopher. *The Dynamics of World History*. New York: Sheed & Ward, 1956.

Dikötter, Frank, ed. *The Construction of Racial Identities in China and Japan*. London: Hurst, 1998.

Donnelly, Jack. "Human Rights: A New Standard of Civilization." *International Affairs* 74.1 (1998): 1.

Dower John W. *War without Mercy: Race and Power in the Pacific War*. New York: Pantheon Books, 1986.

──────. *Ways of Forgetting, Ways of Remembering: Japan in the Modern World*. New York: New Press, 2012.

Drescher, Seymour. *Abolition: A History of Slavery and Antislavery*. Cambridge: Cambridge University Press, 2009.

Dufoix, Stephane. *Diasporas*. Berkeley: University of California Press, 2008.

Dumont, Louis. *Essays on Individualism. Modern Ideology in Anthropological Perspective*. Chicago: University of Chicago Press, 1991.

Dunning, Eric. "Figurational Sociology and Sociology of Sport." In *Sport and Leisure in the Civilizing Process*, edited by E. Dunning and C. Rojek, 221–84. Basingstoke UK: Macmillan, 1992.

Durkheim, Emile. *The Elementary Forms of Religious Life*. 1912. Oxford: Oxford University Press, 2001.

Eisenstadt, Shmuel Noah. Introduction to in *Patterns of Modernity,* vol. 2: *Beyond the West*, edited by S. N. Eisenstadt, 1s–11. New York: New York University Press, 1987.

──────. *Japanese Civilization*. Chicago: University of Chicago Press, 1996.

──────, ed. *Martin Buber on Intersubjectivity and Cultural Creativity*. Chicago: University of Chicago Press, 1992.

──────, ed. *The Origins and Diversity of Axial Age Civilizations*. Albany: State University of New York Press, 1986.

──────. *Power, Trust, and Meaning*. Chicago: University of Chicago Press, 1995.

──────. *A Sociological Approach to Comparative Civilizations: The Development and Directions of a Research Program*. Jerusalem: Harry S. Truman Research Institute for the Advancement of Peace, 1986.

Elias, Norbert. *The Civilizing Process*. Vol. 1: *The History of Manners*. New York: Pantheon Books, 1978.

──────. *The Civilizing Process*. Vol. 2: *State Formation and Civilization*. Oxford: Blackwell, 1982.

———. *The Germans: Power Struggles and the Development of Habitus in Nineteenth and Twentieth Centuries.* Cambridge UK: Polity Press, 1996.

———. "On the Sociology of German Antisemitism." 1929. *Journal of Classical Sociology* 1.2 (2001): 219–25.

Evans, Richard. *In Hitler's Shadow: West German Historians and the Attempt to Escape from the Nazi Past.* New York: Pantheon Books, 1989.

Eze, Emmanuel C. "The Color of Reason: The Idea of 'Race' in Kant's Anthropology." In *Anthropology and the German Enlightenment*, edited by K. Faull, 150–75. Lewisburg PA: Bucknell University Press, 1995.

———, ed. *Race and the Enlightenment.* Oxford: Blackwell, 1997.

Feingold, Henry L. *Zion in America: The Jewish Experience from Colonial Times to the Present.* New York: Hippocrene Books, 1981.

Fenves, Peter. *Late Kant: Towards Another Law of the Earth.* London: Routledge, 2003.

Ferguson, Niall. *Civilization: The West and the Rest.* London: Allen Lane, 2011.

Fischman, Dennis K. *Political Discourse in Exile: Karl Marx and the Jewish Question.* Amherst: University of Massachusetts Press, 1991.

Fisk, Robert. *The Great War for Civilisation: The Conquest of the Middle East.* New York: Knopf, 2005.

Freud, Sigmund. *Civilization and Its Discontents.* New York: Norton, 1930.

Gabler, Neal. *An Empire of Their Own: How the Jews Invented Hollywood.* New York: Doubleday, 1988.

Galton, Francis. *Inquiries into Human Faculty and Its Development.* London: Macmillan, 1883.

Gay, Peter. *Modernism: The Lure of Heresy from Baudelaire to Beckett and Beyond.* London: Heinemann, 2007.

Gellner, Ernest. *Nations and Nationalism.* Ithaca NY: Cornell University Press, 1983.

———. *Thought and Change.* Chicago: University of Chicago Press, 1965.

Gerhardt, Uta. "National Socialism and the politics of *The Structure of Social Action*." In *Agenda for Sociology: Classic Sources and Current Uses of Talcott Parsons's Work*, edited by B. Barber and U. Gerhardt, 87–164. Baden-Baden: Nomos, 1999.

———. *Talcott Parsons on National Socialism.* New York: Aldine de Gruyter, 1993.

———. "Worlds Come Apart: Systems Theory versus Critical Theory. Drama in the History of Sociology in the Twentieth Century." *American Sociologist* 33 (2002): 5–39.

Gibbon, Edward. *The Decline and Fall of the Roman Empire.* Edited by D. A. Saunders. New York: Viking Press, 1952.

Gilbert, Martin. *In Ishmael's House: A History of Jews in Muslim Lands.* New Haven CT: Yale University Press, 2010.

Gilroy, Paul. "Fanon Amery: Theory, Torture and the Prospect of Humanism." *Theory Culture and Society* 27.7–8 (2010): 16–32.

Glazer, Nathan. *American Judaism*. Chicago: University of Chicago Press, 1957.

———. *We Are All Multiculturalists Now*. Cambridge MA: Harvard University Press, 1997.

Glazer, Nathan, and D. P. Moynihan. *Beyond the Melting Pot: The Negroes, Puertoricans, Jews, Italians, and Irish of New York City*. Cambridge MA: MIT Press, 1963.

Glazer, Nathan, and D. P. Moynihan, eds. *Ethnicity: Theory and Experience*. Cambridge MA: Harvard University Press, 1975.

Gobineau, Arthur de. *Selected Political Writings*. London: Jonathan Cape, 1970.

Goldberg, David J. *The Divided Self: Israel and the Jewish Psyche Today*. London: I. B. Tauris, 2011.

Goldhagen, Daniel. J. *Worse than War: Genocide, Elimination and the Ongoing Assault on Humanity*. New York: Public Affairs, 2009.

Gong, Gerrit W. *The Standard of "Civilization" in International Society*. Oxford: Clarendon Press, 1984.

———. "Standards of Civilization Today." In *Globalization and Civilizations*, edited by M. Mozaffari, 77–96. London: Routledge, 2002.

Goodman, David G., and Masanori Miyazawa. *Jews in the Japanese Mind: The History and Uses of a Cultural Stereotype*. New York: Free Press, 1995.

Goody, Jack. *The East in the West*. Cambridge: Cambridge University Press, 1996.

Graeber, Isacque, and Steuart Henderson Britt, eds. *Jews in a Gentile World: The Problem of Antisemitism*. New York: Macmillan, 1942.

Greenfeld, Liah. *Nationalism: Five Roads to Modernity*. Cambridge MA: Harvard University Press, 1992.

Groebner, Valentin. *Who Are You? Identification, Deception, and Surveillance in Early Modern Europe*. New York: Zone Books, 2007.

Grose, Peter. *Israel in the Mind of America*. New York: Knopf, 1983.

Gunn, Geoffrey C. *First Globalization: The Eurasian Exchange, 1500–1800*. Lanham MD: Rowman & Littlefield, 2003.

Hale, Charles A. "Political Ideas and Ideologies in Latin America, 1870–1930." In *Ideas and Ideologies in Twentieth Century Latin America*, edited by L. Bethell, 133–206. Cambridge: Cambridge University Press, 1996.

Harris, Lee. *Civilization and Its Enemies: The Next Stage of History*. New York: Free Press, 2004.

Harris, Ruth. *The Man on Devil's Island: Alfred Dreyfus and the Affair That Divided France*. London: Allen Lane, 2010.

Heisig, James W., and John C. Maraldo. *Rude Awakenings: Zen, the Kyoto School and the Question of Nationalism*. Honolulu: University of Hawai'i Press, 1994.

Herberg, Will. *Protestant-Catholic-Jew: An Essay in American Religious Sociology*. Garden City NY: Doubleday, 1955.

Hobson, John M. *The Eastern Origins of Western Civilization*. Cambridge: Cambridge University Press, 2004.

Hopkins, Antony G., ed. *Globalization in World History*. London: Pimlico, 2002.

Hughes, Henry S. *Oswald Spengler: A Critical Estimate.* New York: Scribner, 1952.

Huntington, Samuel P. "The Clash of Civilizations?" *Foreign Affairs* 72.3 (1993): 22–49.

———. *The Clash of Civilizations and the Remaking of World Order.* New York: Simon & Schuster, 1996.

Ifversen, Jan. "The Crisis of European Civilization: An Inter-war Diagnosis." In *Globalization and Civilizations*, edited by M. Mozaffari, 150–77. London: Routledge, 2002.

Isaac, Benjamin. *The Invention of Racism in Classical Antiquity.* Princeton NJ: Princeton University Press, 2004.

Janik, Allan, and Stephen Toulmin. *Wittgenstein's Vienna.* New York: Simon & Schuster, 1973.

Jardine, Lisa, and Jerry Brotton. *Global Interests: Renaissance Art between East and West.* London: Reaktion Books, 2000.

Jaspers, Karl. *The Origin and Goal of History.* New Haven CT: Yale University Press, 1953.

Juergensmeyer, Mark, ed. *Global Religions: An Introduction.* New York: Oxford University Press, 2003.

Julius, Anthony. *Trials of the Diaspora: A History of Antisemitism in England.* Oxford: Oxford University Press, 2010.

Katz, Steven T. *Post-Holocaust Dialogues: Critical Studies in Modern Jewish Thought.* New York: New York University Press, 1985.

Kavolis, Vytautas. "Civilizational Paradigms in Current Sociology: Dumont vs Eisenstadt." *Current Perspectives in Social Theory* 7 (1986): 125–40.

———. "History of Consciousness and Civilization Analysis." *Comparative Civilizations Review* 17 (Fall 1987): 1–19.

Konvitz. Milton R. *Judaism and the American Idea.* New York: Schocken Books, 1978.

Kornberg, Jacques. *Theodor Herzl: From Assimilation to Zionism.* Bloomington: Indiana University Press, 1993.

Laqueur, Walter. *A History of Zionism.* New York: Schocken Books, 1972.

Laski, Harold J. *Nationalism and the Future of Civilization.* London: Watts, 1932.

Lefkowitz, Mary R., and Guy M. Rogers, eds. *Black Athena Revisited.* Chapel Hill: University of North Carolina Press, 1996.

Lepenies, Wolf. *The Seduction of Culture in German History.* Princeton NJ: Princeton University Press, 2006.

Lipset, Seymour Martin, ed. *American Pluralism and the Jewish Community.* New Brunswick NJ: Transaction, 1990.

Lukacs, John. *Budapest 1900: A Historical Portrait of a City and Its Culture.* New York: Grove Weidenfeld, 1988.

Manela, Erez. *The Wilsonian Moment: Self-Determination and the International Origins of Anticolonial Nationalism.* Oxford: Oxford University Press, 2007.

Marrus, Michael R. *The Holocaust in History.* New York: Meridian, 1987.

Marx, Anthony W. *Making Race and Nation: A Comparison of the United States, South Africa, and Brazil*. Cambridge: Cambridge University Press, 1998.

McDonagh, Gary W. *Iberian Worlds*. New York: Routledge, 2009.

McNeill, William H. *Arnold J. Toynbee: A Life*. Oxford: Oxford University Press, 1989.

———. *Polyethnicity and National Unity in World History*. Toronto: University of Toronto Press, 1986.

Mennell, Stephen. *Norbert Elias: An Introduction*. Oxford: Blackwell, 1992.

Mignolo, Walter D. "Globalization, Civilization and Languages." In *The Cultures of Globalization*, edited by F. Jameson and M. Miyoshi, 32–53. Durham NC: Duke University Press, 1998.

Morawska, Ewa. "Ethnicity as a Primordial-Situational-Constructed Experience: Different Times, Different Places, Different Constellations." In *Ethnicity and Beyond, Theories and Dilemmas of Jewish Group Demarcation*, edited by Eli Lederhendler, 3–25. *Studies in Contemporary Jewry 25*. New York: Oxford University Press, 2011.

———. *Insecure Prosperity: Jews in Small-Town Industrial America, 1880–1940*. Princeton NJ: Princeton University Press, 1996.

———. "The Making and Remaking of a Sociologist." In *Sociologists in a Global Age: Biographical Perspectives*, edited by Mathieu Deflem, 115–29. Farnham UK: Ashgate, 2007.

———. *A Sociology of Immigration: (Re)making Multifaceted America*. Basingstoke UK: Palgrave Macmillan, 2011.

Morin, Edgar. "European Civilization: Properties and Challenges." in *Globalization and Civilizations*, edited by M. Mozaffari, 125–50. London: Routledge, 2002.

Morse, Richard M. "The Multiverse of Latin American Identity, c. 1920–c. 1970." In *Ideas and Ideologies in Twentieth Century Latin America*, edited by L. Bethell, 3–129. Cambridge: Cambridge University Press, 1996.

Moynihan, Daniel P. *Pandaemonium: Ethnicity in International Politics*. Oxford: Oxford University Press, 1993.

Mozaffari, Mehdi, ed. *Globalization and Civilizations*. London: Routledge, 2002.

———. "The Transformationalist Perspective and the Rise of a Global Standard of Civilization." *International Relations of the Asia Pacific* 1 (2001): 247–64.

Neiman, Susan. *Evil in Modern Thought: An Alternative History of Philosophy*. Princeton NJ: Princeton University Press, 2002.

Nelson, Benjamin. "Civilization of Complexes and Intercivilizational Encounters." *Sociological Analysis* 34.2 (1973): 79–105.

———. *The Idea of Usury: From Tribal Brotherhood to Universal Otherhood*. Princeton NJ: Princeton University Press, 1949.

———. *On the Roads to Modernity: Conscience, Science and Civilizations*. Edited by T. H. Huff. Totowa NJ: Rowman & Littlefield, 1981.

Neumann, Iver B. *Uses of the Other: "The East" in European Identity Formation*. Minneapolis: University of Minnesota Press, 1999.

Neusner, Jacob. *Israel in America: A Too-Comfortable Exile?* Boston: Beacon Press, 1985.

Nielson, Jens K. "The Political Orientation of Talcott Parsons: The Second World War and Its Aftermath." In *Talcott Parsons: Theorist of Modernity*, edited by R. Robertson and B. S. Turner, 217-233. London: Sage, 1991.

Niezen, Ronald. *The Origins of Indigenism: Human Rights and the Politics of Identity*. Berkeley: University of California Press, 2003.

Nolte, Ernst. *Fascism and Communism*. Lincoln: University of Nebraska Press, 2004.

Nussbaum, Martha C. *The Clash Within: Democracy, Religious Violence and India's Future*. Cambridge MA: Belknap Press, 2007.

———. "Recoiling from Reason." *New York Review of Books* 36:19 (1989, December 7).

Osterhammel, Jürgen, and Niels P. Petersson. *Globalization: A Short History*. Princeton NJ: Princeton University Press, 2003.

Pappe, Ilan. *The Ethnic Cleansing of Palestine*. Oxford: Oneworld, 2006.

Park, Robert E. "Human Migration and Marginal Man." *American Journal of Sociology* 33.6 (1928): 881-93.

Pearson, Simon. *A Brief History of the End of the World*. London: Robinson, 2006.

Pfaff, William. *The Wrath of Nations: Civilization and the Furies of Nationalism*. New York: Simon & Schuster, 1993.

Pippal, Martina. *A Short History of Art in Vienna*. Munich: Verlag C. H. Beck, 2001.

Portuges, Catherine. "Accenting L.A.: Central Europeans in Diasporan Hollywood in the 1940s." In *Borders, Exiles, Diasporas*, edited by Elazar Barkan and Marie-Denise Shelton, 46-57. Stanford CA: Stanford University Press, 1998.

Quigley, Carroll. *The Evolution of Civilizations: An Introduction to Historical Analysis*. Indianapolis: Liberty Fund, 1979.

Robertson, Roland. "Christian Zionism and Jewish Zionism: Points of Contact." In *The Politics of Religion and Social Change*, edited by A. Shupe and J. K. Hadden, 239-57. New York: Paragon House, 1988.

———. "Civilization." *Theory Culture and Society* 23.2-3 (2006): 421-27.

———. "The Development and Implications of the Classical Sociological Perspective on Religion and Revolution." In *Religion, Rebellion, Revolution*, edited by B. Lincoln, 236-265. London: Macmillan, 1985.

———. "Globalization, Culture and." In *The Blackwell Encyclopedia of Sociology*, vol. 4, edited by G. Ritzer. Oxford: Blackwell, 2007. Online access: http://www.sociologyencyclopedia.com/public/tocnode?id=g9781405124331_yr2012_chunk_g9781405124331113_ss1-54.

———. *Globalization: Social Theory and Global Culture*. London: Sage, 1992.

———. "Globalization, Theocratization, and Politicized Civil Religion." In *The Oxford Handbook of the Sociology of Religion*, edited by P. Clarke, 451-76. Oxford: Oxford University Press, 2009.

———. "Identidad Nacional y Globalizacion: Falacias Contemporaneas." *Revista Mexicana de Sociologia* 1 (January–March 1998): 3-19.

———. "Max Weber and German Sociology of Religion." In *Nineteenth Century*

Religious Thought in the West, vol. 3, edited by N. Smart et al., 263–304. Cambridge: Cambridge University Press, 1985b.

———. *Meaning and Change: Explorations in the Cultural Sociology of Modern Society*. Oxford: Basil Blackwell, 1978.

———. "Race." In *Encyclopedia of Globalization*, vol. 3, edited by Roland Robertson and Jan A. Scholte, 1007–11. New York: MTM/Routledge, 2007.

———. "S. N. Eisenstadt: A Sociological Giant." *Journal of Classical Sociology* 11.3 (2011): 303–13.

Robertson, Roland, and A. S. Krossa, eds. *European Cosmopolitanism in Question*. London: Palgrave Macmillan, 2011.

Rose, Nikolas. *The Politics of Life Itself: Biomedicine, Power, and Subjectivity in the Twenty-first Century*. Princeton NJ: Princeton University Press, 2007.

Rothberg, Michael. *Multidirectional Memory: Remembering the Holocaust in the Age of Decolonization*. Stanford CA: Stanford University Press, 2010.

Sacks, Jonathon "Judaism and Politics in the Modern World." In *The Desecularization of the World: Resurgent Religion and World Politics*, edited by P. L. Berger, 51–63. Washington DC: Ethics and Public Policy Center, 1999.

Sakai, Naoki. *Translation and Subjectivity: On "Japan" and Cultural Nationalism*. Minneapolis: University of Minnesota Press, 1997.

Sand, Shlomo. *The Invention of the Jewish People*. London: Verso, 2009.

Sanderson, Stephen K., ed. *Civilizations and World Systems: Studying World Historical Change*. Walnut Creek CA: Altamira Press, 1995.

Schenk, Hans G. *The Mind of the European Romantics: An Essay in Cultural History*. Oxford: Oxford University Press, 1979.

Schneer, Jonathon. *The Balfour Declaration: The Origins of the Arab-Israeli Conflict*. London: Bloomsbury, 2010.

Schorske, Carl E. *Fin-de-Siecle Vienna: Politics and Culture*. New York: Vintage Books, 1981.

Schwarzenberger, Georg. "The Standard of Civilization in International Law." In *Current Legal Problems*, edited by G. W. Keeton and G. Schwarzenberger, 212–34. London: Stevens and Sons, 1955.

Shils, Edward. *The Virtue of Civility: Selected Essays on Liberalism, Tradition, and Civil Society*. Indianapolis: Liberty Fund, 1997.

Singer, Kurt. *Mirror, Sword and Jewel: The Geometry of Japanese Life*. Tokyo: Kodansha International, 1973.

Sklare, Marshall. *Conservative Judaism: An American Religious Movement*. New York: Schocken, 1972.

Smith, Anthony D. *The Ethnic Origins of Nations*. Oxford: Blackwell, 1986.

———. *Nationalism and Modernism: A Critical Survey of Recent Theories of Nations and Nationalism*. London: Routledge, 1998.

———. "Zionism and Diaspora Nationalism." *Israel Affairs* 2.2 (1995): 1–19.

Sombart, Werner. *The Jews and Modern Capitalism*. New Brunswick NJ: Transaction, 1982.

Spengler, Oswald. *The Decline of the West.* New York: Knopf, 1932.

Stepan, Nancy L. *"The Hour of Eugenics": Race, Gender, and Nation in Latin America.* Ithaca NY: Cornell University Press, 1991.

Sternberg, Yitzhak. "Modernity, Civilization and Globalization." In *Identity, Culture and Globalization,* edited by E. Ben-Rafael with Y. Sternberg, 75–92. Leiden: Brill, 2001.

Stoetzler, Marcel. "For a Dialectical Concept of Culture." Paper given at the conference The Contentious Question of Culture(s) in Contemporary Society at University of Delhi, Department of Germanic and Romance Studies, March 1, 2007.

———. *The State, the Nation and the Jews: Liberalism and the Antisemitism Dispute in Bismarck's Germany.* Lincoln: University of Nebraska Press, 2008.

Storry, Richard. Introduction to Kurt Singer, *Mirror, Sword and Jewel: The Geometry of Japanese Life,* 9–21. Tokyo: Kodansha International, 1973.

Swain, Carol M., ed. *Debating Immigration.* Cambridge: Cambridge University Press, 2007.

Toynbee, Arnold. *Civilization on Trial.* Oxford: Oxford University Press, 1948.

———. *A Study of History.* Oxford: Oxford University Press, 1934–61.

Tsygankov, Andrei. *Russia's Foreign Policy: Change and Continuity in National Identity.* Lanham MA: Rowman & Littlefield, 2006.

Verges, Francois. "'There Are No Blacks in France': Fanonian Discourse, 'the Dark Night of Capitalist Slavery' and the French Civilizing Mission Reconsidered." *Theory Culture and Society* 27.7–8 (2010): 91–111.

Vivanti, Corrado. "The Origins of the Idea of Civilization: The Geographical Findings and Writings of Henri de la Popeliniere." *Comparative Civilizations Review,* no. 6 (Spring 1981): 15–39.

Walter, Eugene V., V. Kavolis, E. Leites, and M. C. Nelson, eds. *Civilizations East and West: A Memorial Volume for Benjamin Nelson.* Atlantic Highlands NJ: Humanities Press, 1985.

Wasserstein, Bernard. *On the Eve: The Jews of Europe before the Second World War.* London: Profile Books, 2012.

Webel, Charles P. *Terror, Terrorism, and the Human Condition.* New York: Palgrave Macmillan, 2004.

Weber, Max. *Ancient Judaism.* 1921. Glencoe IL: Free Press, 1952.

———. *The Protestant Ethic and the Spirit of Capitalism.* 1904–5. London: Allen & Unwin, 1930.

Weinberg, Robert. *Pogroms and Riots: German Press Responses to Anti-Jewish Violence in Germany and Russia (1881–1882).* Berlin: Peter Lang, 2010.

Worsley, Peter. "Models of the Modern World-System." *Theory, Culture and Society* 7 (1990): 83–95.

Yoshino, K. *Cultural Nationalism in Contemporary Japan: A Sociological Enquiry.* London: Routledge, 1992.

Zangwill, Israel. *The Melting Pot.* New York: Macmillan, 1909.

Part 3

*The Reformulation of Sociology
in the Face of Fascist Antisemitism*

9

Talcott Parsons's "The Sociology of Modern Anti-Semitism"

Anti-antisemitism, Ambivalent Liberalism, and the Sociological Imagination

JONATHAN JUDAKEN

> There are elements of anti-Semitism deeper than sociology or economics or even historical superstition. The Jew sticks like a bone in the throat of any other nationalism.
>
> GEORGE STEINER, *Language and Silence*

Zygmunt Bauman famously claimed in *Modernity and the Holocaust*, "Sociology is concerned with modern society, but has never come to terms with one of the most distinctive and horrific aspects of modernity—the Holocaust."[1] The Holocaust, he insists, is not just a remnant of barbarism; it was at the heart of modernity and the sociological processes that define it. Accepting this demands a rethinking of sociological theory, which his work undertakes. Bauman's *Modernity and the Holocaust* has, of course, been an important touchstone for many scholars in Jewish cultural and literary studies, the sociology of genocide, and the history and theory of antisemitism since it rethinks the Holocaust from a postmodern sociological perspective. But the hyperbole of Bauman's claim is evident from the entire program of conference participants who gathered in Manchester in November 2008 to address the topic Antisemitism and the Emergence of Sociological Theory.

I want to set Bauman's claim against one of the preeminent American sociologists of modernity, Talcott Parsons. While the numerous articles, radio broadcasts, speeches, addresses, and position papers dealing with Germany, national socialism, fascism, and the Jews written by Parsons between 1938 and 1945 never tackled the Holocaust per se, they do constitute a robust series of reflections on the constellation of forces that produced the Shoah by the leading pioneer of American sociology in the middle of the twentieth century.

Parsons's "The Sociology of Modern Anti-Semitism" (1942) and his other short sociological analyses on Hitlerism and the fascist movement, so helpfully gathered together by Uta Gerhardt in her collection, *Talcott Parsons on National Socialism*, are not generally depicted as central theoretical works in his development. But World War II clearly marked a crucial moment of change in Parsons's evolution, and his analyses of antisemitism were some of his only theoretical writings closely connected to empirical and historical events. The rise of the Nazis and the events of World War II were the context of the shift from Parsons's voluntarist theory of social action developed in his first major work, *The Structure of Social Action* (1937), to his systems theory, a structuralist-functionalist model of sociological theory that dominated the discipline of sociology from the postwar period to the mid-1960s, which he elaborated primarily in *The Social System* (1951), *Toward a General Theory of Action* (1951), and *Economy and Society* (1956).

This same period saw both a rise in sociological studies focused on antisemitism and an important influence of models drawn from the social sciences into the writing of history and consequently into analyses of the history of antisemitism. An investigation of Parsons's work is therefore important to consider in evaluating the categories that underlie the social history of antisemitism as well as the insights of sociological approaches to theorizing the underlying causes of antisemitism.

The focus of this chapter is an elucidation and critical analysis of Parsons's "The Sociology of Anti-Semitism." First, I locate this text within the unfolding discipline of sociology itself. Antisemitism and the sociological discipline have traveled the same paths. Contra Bauman, then, one could trace the evolution of the field from the perspective of the different accounts of antisemitism that sociologists have offered over time. My second point is that the rise of Nazism, World War II, and the Holocaust marked the moment of transition toward what I call "critical theories of antisemitism," and Parsons's text was on the cusp of this transformation and an important contributor to it. I make the case that it was only in this period that wholesale theoretical accounts were offered that provided a systematic explanation of antisemitism that ultimately did not place the blame for antisemitism on Jews and Judaism. This moment marked the shift from an emphasis on the object of hate as the cause of antisemitism toward an examination of the hating subject. The stress was now on explaining why antisemites hated, not how Jews could change to avoid antisemitism. Parsons found his own work caught in this shift.

I explain how in my third point, which encompasses most of the chapter. I show that Parsons was significantly influenced by Max Weber's sociological analyses of Judaism. Like Weber, Parsons's theory of antisemitism is riddled with the problems of an ambivalent liberalism, albeit with a distinctively American twist. His commitment to a set of liberal values that ultimately cannot affirm the historically embedded particularities of Jewish culture, religion, and rites leads him, at least in this text, to reiterate a series of typological constructions of Jews and Judaism despite his clear desire to contest and critique antisemitism and fascism.

This chapter seeks to explore why this tension exists in Parsons's work. I maintain against Gerhardt (Parsons's intellectual biographer and the leading scholar on this topic) that these stereotypes are not simply the result of the editorial tampering of the text by Isacque Graeber, the editor of the volume where Parsons's essay originally appeared. For Gerhardt, Graeber "unilaterally changed his writing and distorted his thought so as [to] make Parsons seem like an antisemite."[2] I want to show instead that Parsons's approach to the sociology of antisemitism highlights the problems with the imbrications of what I term "anti-antisemitism" and Enlightenment (i.e., liberal) responses to "the Jewish question." This tradition of Enlightenment liberalism was constituted, as David Ellenson has argued, by a "secularization of Christian universalism" evinced in Paul's epistles: the call to transcend the particularity of Jew or Gentile, slave or freeman, since all are "one in Christ Jesus" (Galatians 3:28).[3] In Parsons's universalist liberalism, the particularities of Christianity were also superseded but not without once more tripping over Jews along the way. My concluding remarks briefly discuss what this liberal tradition of anti-antisemitism teaches us about the sociological imagination and antisemitism.

Sociology and Antisemitism

Several of the classical figures of sociology contributed major works assessing the place of Jews in society, the role of Judaism in modernity, and the impact of this on Jewish existence. One might even draw a red thread through many of the canonic figures of the discipline by how they accounted for antisemitism as a social phenomenon and in turn theoretically constructed their systems of social thought. This is certainly the case most emphatically for Karl Marx, Émile Durkheim and the Durkheimians in France (Robert Hertz, Lucien Lévy-Bruhl, and later Marcel Mauss), Werner Sombart, Georg Simmel, and Max Weber.[4] As William Helmreich indicates in his brief overview, "The Sociological Study of Antisemitism in the United States," "There is no question that American sociologists have been aware of antisemitism as a social phenomenon throughout the history of the field."[5]

In *Geography of Hope* the historical sociologist Pierre Birnbaum has discussed how widespread the correlation was between the development of the value-neutral, objective rationality and scientificity of the social sciences as they emerged in the late nineteenth and twentieth centuries and the relegation of Jewish subjects to the margins, perhaps especially for aspiring Jews in the academy.[6] But nonetheless many of the major canonical sociologists have reflected on antisemitism, and consequently about Jews, Jewishness, and 'the Jewish question' as a jumping-off point to their sociological theories. The genealogical list could take one from the origins of social theory up to the present, beginning with Marx's *Zur Judenfrage*, to Durkheim's "L'individualisme et les intellectuels," through Weber's *Ancient Judaism* and *The Sociology of Religion*, into Sombart's *The Jews and Modern Capitalism*, and through to Simmel's famous excursus on the stranger.

In his own sociological project, then, Parsons was merely picking up on a sociological tradition that had long wrestled with antisemitism. As Marcel Stoetzler has shown, classical sociological theory and modern antisemitism have shared the same discursive space. Stoetzler points out that "sociologists developed a discourse that aimed to defend liberal society and modernization" while at the same time attacking the "utilitarianism" that they blamed for the dismal aspects of the emerging new form of society. During and after World War II, Parsons picked up this mantle. As a result, "post–Second World War sociology, especially due to the influence of Talcott Parsons who successfully amalgamated its main traditions . . . into liberal, progressivist modernization theory, could not but appear to be firmly of [*sic*] the side of western democracy and anti-fascism."[7]

Nazism as a Turning Point

Prior to the period of Parsons's writing, four key paradigms existed for explaining antisemitism: rabbinic, Christological, liberal, and Zionist.[8] What they each shared in common, however, was the notion that to overcome antisemitism, it would be necessary to change Jewish values, beliefs, or actions. Even the Chazal (the Jewish sages) adhered to this perspective. Why is there antisemitism in the world, according to the rabbis? "Halachah: Esau soneh l'Ya'acov": because Esau hates Jacob; non-Jews hate Jews. This rabbinic formula postulates antisemitism as eternal, until the messiah comes and the tears of Esau are dried.[9] Given the portrait of Jacob-Israel in the Bible, a measure of culpability is ascribed to Jews in this affair. After all, Jacob-Israel stole the birthright of Esau, as well as his father's blessing on his death bed. This is the cause of Esau's tears.

If this was the traditional Jewish perspective, in the Christian world before the modern period the range of attitudes to Judeophobia veered from ambivalence to hostility, with everyone from Augustine to Chrysostom agreeing that Jews existed in a state of subordination as a sign of their spiritual blindness.[10] Hostility toward Jews as a problem that Western civilization needed to address about itself really emerged only in the Enlightenment and was phrased as the so-called Jewish question. The solution to this question for liberals of the eighteenth and nineteenth centuries was to advocate tolerance for Jewish religious difference and equal rights. Civil equality was meant as a pathway toward Jewish assimilation, however. On the more radical extreme of liberalism, socialists were convinced that the Jewish problem would disappear with the victory of the social revolution. When they were not complicit in reworking anti-Jewish venom as a basis for their critique of capitalism (as was the case with Pierre-Joseph Proudhon, Charles Fourier, and Marx), they regarded antisemitism, in August Bebel's words, as "the socialism of fools," a "stratagem to distract the toiling masses from fighting their real enemies—the exploiters, capitalism, and the reactionaries."[11] Even the last response to antisemitism in the nineteenth century—political Zionism of the Herzlian stripe—concurred that Jews having a homeland of their own would enable them to become a nation like all other nations. The Zionist solution to the 'Jewish question' was that the transformation of the Jews affected by having a nation like all other nation-states would end antisemitism. Jews as they existed were still the problem.[12]

It was only with the rise of the Nazis in the 1930s that a new critical and social scientific emphasis emerged on the topic of antisemitism.[13] The work undertaken to explain the sociopsychological etiology of antisemitism that was led by the Institute for Social Research and sponsored by the American Jewish Committee would prove crucially important to this development. This work was significantly abetted by the psychologists Marie Jahoda, Bruno Bettelheim, Rudolph Loewenstein, Daniel Levinson, and Ernest Simmel and the historians Eva Reichmann, Aurel Kolnai, Paul Massing, and Joshua Trachtenberg.[14] The contribution of Talcott Parsons to the sociology of modern antisemitism was consequently undertaken just as the social and humanistic sciences began to offer a new series of studies on the topic of antisemitism, obviously under the impact of the rise of Nazism, and reflecting on its underlying causes.

Jews in a Gentile World

One such effort was the voluminous collection *Jews in a Gentile World: The Problem of Anti-Semitism*, edited by Isacque Graeber and Steuart Henderson Britt. Parsons's essay "The Sociology of Modern Anti-Semitism" was included in the book. The volume was a groundbreaking, early interdisciplinary effort to bring together eighteen sociologists, anthropologists, psychologists, political scientists, economists, and historians to "examine the problems of anti-Semitism in a dispassionate, objective manner."[15] After an introduction by the esteemed Harvard professor of government Carl Friedrich, among its chapters the book contained an open debate on whether Jews have a racial identity (with essays by Carleton Stevens Coon and Melville Jacobs taking opposing views), two chapters on "the history and sociology of antisemitism" (with essays by J. O. Hertzler and Parsons), a section on "the psychology of antisemitism" (with chapters by J. F. Brown and Ellis Freeman), and a section on "the mirage of the economic Jew" by Jacob Lestchinsky and Miriam Beard, daughter of the famed historian Charles Beard.

Putting all of this together was Isacque Graeber. Graeber was born in

Congress Poland. He emigrated to the United States with his family and later finished his studies at the University of Paris. Upon his return to America, Graeber was active in the League of American Writers, which was sponsored by the Communist Party USA.[16] He began work on *Jews in a Gentile World* as early as 1935, pulling together leading academics in a number of the social sciences to reflect on antisemitism as a social problem. He approached Parsons to participate in 1939, and Parsons wrote a manuscript that was over fifty pages long in early 1940. He sent it to Eric Voegelin for his comments and then sent off the final draft to Graeber. Upon request at the end of the year, he would follow up with a short précis of the argument. With no further communication between the two, Parsons received the galley proofs of his article, which had been shortened by Graeber.

Parsons was apparently horrified by the editorial intervention. Writing to Ben Halpern, who had served as an editorial assistant on *The Theory of Social Action*, Parsons declaimed, "Graeber, under the guise of shortening my manuscript, rewrote the article, and put in a great many statements to which I would not subscribe. . . . As it happens, that article represents the worst experience with editorial interference with an author's work I have ever encountered."[17] For his part, Graeber claimed that the editorial changes were a necessity imposed by the publisher's limits on the size of the book and in order to avoid the repetition of points made by the various authors. "I beg you not to castigate me for having cut your chapter," he beseeched Parsons. "In fact, I had instruction to rewrite yours as well as several others. Please believe that I did this—yours especially—with pains in my vitals."[18] Parsons responded by writing out eleven inserts that were supposed to be entered into the text, of which Graeber included only two in the final version. And Graeber kept most of the changes he had made to the chapter. Parsons was apparently displeased enough by the final product that he would not have the article reprinted in any of the five collections of his essays edited after 1949. This is the only case of all of his published pieces from the war years to suffer this fate. Moreover the article is today listed in the Harvard University Archives under unpublished manuscripts, as if it had never appeared.

Uta Gerhardt on Isacque Graeber

What accounts for Parsons's repression of "The Sociology of Modern Anti-Semitism"? This was, after all, his only substantial theoretical contribution to what has undeniably been a major social phenomenon. Moreover the essay was on the cutting edge of sociological work when it was published. On the basis of the account above Gerhardt suggests that Parsons was dismayed by the editorial changes made by Graeber, who ostensibly changed Parsons's own approach, insights, and conclusions.[19] In *Talcott Parsons on National Socialism*, edited by Gerhardt and which contains a collection of Parsons's published and unpublished articles from this period, she includes a version true to Parsons's original intent with the following footnote: "Chapter 4 of this volume omits these additions by Graeber and restores as much of the original of Parsons' text as could be reconstructed. The nine inserts unused in the printed article are put in. Where the manuscript from the Harvard University Archives deviates from the published version, the former is taken to be authentic."[20] Moreover she maintains that the article bothered Parsons enough to warrant his writing a posthumously published postscript in 1978. In *Talcott Parsons: An Intellectual Biography*, Gerhardt states that the key difference between Graeber and Parsons was methodological: "What was the conflict about? The issue was whether condemnation of antisemitism as amoral should stand at the end of the article, as Graeber found and wrote into the manuscript, replacing Parsons's insisting on the primacy of scientific analysis rather than an attempt to press any particular policy."[21]

But none of Gerhardt's claims stand up to scrutiny. Most of the changes that were made by Graeber were cosmetic. There are some alterations of phrasing and sentence order, but not one single fundamental theorem of Parsons's analysis differs in the version published by Graeber and that published by Gerhardt. The postscript that Parsons wrote in 1978 served to contextualize the original article and primarily to update it, not to recant it. The original article was written at the apex of Nazi power, Parsons explained in 1978, "after the fall of France and before the impact of Pearl Harbor and the American entry into the Second World War." It is important to note, as Parsons does, that "the Holocaust was not part of the historical record as early as that."[22] The focus of his postscript was a discussion of how the Jewish situation had changed in the intervening half-century, not a refutation of his earlier published piece. There is nothing in his 1978 article indicating a fundamental disavowal of his earlier work as it had appeared.

As to Gerhardt's claim about moral condemnation versus scientific analysis, Parsons unequivocally decried antisemitism in moral and political terms within the article. He insists in the concluding section *included in Gerhard's restored version*, "The attitude expressed in what follows is to be taken only as a personal view, no scientific authority being claimed for it. The author considers antisemitism of the type discussed here a pernicious and undesirable phenomenon which should be reduced to a minimum. He has strong moral sentiments regarding the importance and desirability of the universalistic patterns of equality of opportunity, so important in modern economic life."[23] Rather than the anecdotal and circumstantial evidence that Gerhardt provides, I maintain that what is troubling about Parsons's text stems directly from the theoretical axis that guides his orientation: his universalistic liberalism in the face of what he construes as Jewish particularity, intractable separateness, and difference. This was a position he shared, moreover, with Weber, whose work was the primary influence on Parsons.[24] To get at this we have to enter the text.

"The Sociology of Modern Anti-Semitism"

"The Sociology of Modern Anti-Semitism" is broken up into six sections, opening with an "introductory statement" and hinged together by a sociological account of the development of Judaism (called "The Character of the Jewish People"), moving into an analysis of "the position of the Jews in the modern world" that in turn is weighted against the "chief characteristics of Western society." The clash between these antinomies—between Jewishness and modernity—plays out in "the phenomenon of anti-Semitism." The article concludes with a section on "prognosis and policy," a concern that runs through all of Parsons's work in this period.

Parsons's operative thesis in "The Sociology of Modern Anti-Semitism" is that "the most important source of virulent anti-Semitism is probably the projection on the Jew, as a symbol, of free-floating aggression, springing from insecurities and social disorganization."[25] Antisemitism thus results from social disaggregation. The breakdown of a social system with clearly defined values, goals, and expectations results from the processes unleashed by the shift from the *Gemeinschaft* to the *Gesellschaft*, to use Ferdinand Tönnies's classic terms. The sociological processes of modernization—including urbanization, industrialization, the developing complexity and instability of the economy, increasing heterogeneity and mobility of the population, shifts in consumption patterns, the "'debunking' of traditional values and ideas," the expansion of popular education and mass means of communication—all result in the "large-scale incidence of anomie in Western society."[26]

Borrowing the notion of anomie from Durkheim's *Suicide*, Parsons defines it as "the state where large numbers of individuals are to a serious degree lacking in the kind of integration with stable institutional patterns which is essential to their own personal stability and to the smooth functioning of the social system."[27] Anomie is a state of rootlessness, disconnection, and social alienation. It results from the breakdown of norms or cultural expectations, which conflict with the social realities attendant upon the transformations brought about as a result of all that was solid melting into air, all that was holy being profaned, as Marx and Engels famously put it in *The Communist Manifesto*, discussing the experience of modernity. Parsons claimed that the result of anomie is social and psychological insecurity, frustration, and resentment, which is often expressed as aggression. The more heightened the anxiety, the more "free floating" the aggression. In these circumstances people act out this frustration and insecurity on a symbolic object. Parsons goes on to explain why it is that Jews constitute a particularly appropriate symbol "on which to project aggressive attitudes generated by a large-scale state of *anomie* in modern society."[28] The reasons for this, according to Parsons, are deeply rooted in the character both of the Jewish people and of the wider society in which they live.

Parsons and Weber

In order to explicate this "Jewish character," Parsons relates a historical narrative, largely based on Weber's writings on Jews and Judaism in *Ancient Judaism* and *The Sociology of Religion*. Indeed Parsons includes a footnote to the section "The Character of the Jewish People" that makes explicit that "the most important single source for the following sketch is Max Weber's study 'Das Antike Judentum,' in *Gesammelte Aufsätze zur Religionssoziologie*, Vol. III."[29] And in his correspondence with Voegelin about the article, he indicates that he had reread Weber's *Ancient Judaism* three or four times.[30]

Both Weber's narrative and Parsons's echo of it are, of course, complex accounts. But David Ellenson provides a useful summation of the key points of Weber's analysis, which were picked up wholesale by Parsons:

The authors of the Bible, by positing belief in a single God who was simultaneously both the purposeful creator of the world and a transcendent agent apart from nature, were able to secularize the cosmos. The prophets, in particular, with their message of moral rationalism, directed worship toward this one sovereign God who was above and beyond the universe. Their teachings not only disenchanted the world by ridding it of other gods; they also led people to focus on the meaning and import of human activity. God was not arbitrary, and the divine could be pleased and the people thereby rewarded through observance of the deity's commandments. In this way, the prophets and the Jewish people of ancient days laid the foundation for the construction of a social ethic of activity within the world that could inform all dimensions of human life. This foundation allowed Judaism to develop ritual and social guidelines for a highly systematic mode of daily conduct based upon a devotion to rationally consistent procedures and rules in the areas of commandment and law.[31]

The heart of this historical narrative was Weber's contention that Jews were what he famously called "a pariah people": "The Jews were a pariah people, which means . . . that they were a guest people who were ritually separated, formally or de facto, from their social surroundings. All the essential traits of Jewry's attitude toward the environment can be deduced from this pariah existence, especially its voluntary ghetto, long antedating compulsory internment, and the dualistic nature of its in-group and out-group morality."[32] In the *Sociology of Religion* Weber would develop this conception of Jewry into an ideal-typical construct: "Pariah people denotes a distinctive hereditary social group lacking autonomous political organization and characterized by prohibitions against commensality and intermarriage. . . . Two additional traits of a pariah people are political and social disprivilege and a far-reaching distinctiveness in economic functioning."[33]

Weber's "pariah people" thesis, as well as his history of Judaism, has been roundly critiqued. "Weber's analysis," writes Ephraim Schmueli, "disregards most relevant elements in Jewish history and accentuates a one-sided arrangement of the selected elements."[34] Freddy Raphael has also derided Weber for oversimplifying Judaism's attitudes toward non-

Jews.[35] Jay Holstein has taken Weber to task for relying on the skewed biblical scholarship of his era, steeped as it was in a set of cultural presuppositions about Jews.[36] In a more wholesale fashion, Gary Abraham's *Max Weber and the Jewish Question* has gutted Weber's writings on Jews and Judaism, showing how intrinsic they were to his whole sociological perspective.[37] Once more Ellenson usefully summarizes the key point for our purposes:

> Weber himself was a liberal who desired the Jew to participate fully in the civic and cultural life of Germany. He desired full Jewish integration into the life of Germany's majority culture. The continued Jewish insistence upon particularity—Jewry's "self-segregation" as a "pariah people"—disturbed Weber, who felt that the most appropriate Jewish response to the modern setting ought to have been full assimilation into German society. His writings on Judaism and his characterizations of the Jews reflect his impatience with and disapproval of this stance on the part of modern Jewry.[38]

It is interesting to note that in his later introduction to the English translation of *The Sociology of Religion*, Parsons would slight Weber for his contention that "ritual segregation" was an essential feature of Jewry's pariah people status, for in "The Sociology of Modern Anti-Semitism" he was wholly congruent with Weber on this point as on others.[39] After "the loss of their territory and national independence and consequent dispersion," the Jews would intensify "their tendency to exclusiveness," Parsons writes, by placing greater emphasis on "the Law and on those ritual elements which served to mark off the Jew from the non-Jew."[40]

Parsons's Typological Constructions of Jews

Indeed without referring to the Jews as a "pariah people" as such, like Weber, Parsons wove into the strands of his writing a series of stereotypical images. Since they are "a people without a country," they pose the threat of the nation within a nation. The result was that Jews developed "certain characteristics." Since Jews lived in humble circumstances, they puffed up their self-image with the arrogant pride of Jewish chosenness. This Parsons takes as a "natural" source of friction with Gentiles. The Jews' diasporic identity was unified as a "People of the Book," Parsons maintains, preoccupied with the Law, resulting in a "certain kind of rationalism or rather intellectualism" (this is the image of the Smart Jew). The strong predilection of Jews was for separatism and exclusiveness, Parsons insists. Moreover he states that while Jews maintained ethical obligations toward other members of the Jewish community, "it was only natural . . . that the Jews did not feel such responsibilities towards Gentiles," which he explains as "a transfer of the primitive in-group attitude, where outsiders are outside the law governing the group." Here Parsons reiterates the ancient image of the Jew as misanthrope or primitive or simply so clan-bound that he applies different standards to those inside and outside the group.[41]

The evidence that Parsons offers for this last point is that Jews would not take interest from Jews, but they could take interest from heathens or idolaters. This figure of the Jew as usurer—the Shylock Jew or Jewish banker—who exploits those outside his own tribe by charging interest on money loaned, has damned Jews perhaps more than any other image in modernity. It is interesting to note that Graeber and Britt insert an editorial footnote to Parsons's text indicating that "Maimonides, the great codifier of Jewish law and ritual, clearly differentiates between 'Non-Jew' and 'heathen,'" thus distancing themselves from Parsons's take on this.[42]

Parsons was clearly trying to debunk the myth of the Jewish businessman. It was explicable for him by the fact that Jews were forced to live in urban environments and concentrate on trade. He attacked the pernicious trope that Jews control "our whole economic life." But in doing so he assents to the notion that Jewish control of certain industries is "highly conspicuous . . . [in] the motion-picture industry, department stores, and the clothing industry. The Jews [also] play a relatively prominent role in the press, in the theater business, as well as in some of the professions—notably law and medicine." While he did not articulate it as such, he was laboring—albeit stumbling over certain stereotypes in the process—to suggest that Jewish *visibility* in these sectors of the modern economy, rather than *control* of the economy by Jews, as antisemites argued, made the Jewish situation precarious. As such, he was fully in accord with the liberal and Enlightenment tradition of thinkers from Wilhelm Dohm forward that shaped both his own and Weber's approach to Jewish emancipation. In accord with this liberal, Enlightenment position, Parsons's key policy program was that "any policy which tends to make

Jews as Jews more conspicuous and particularly those Jews who are at the same time vulnerable symbols in other respects would tend to be an invitation to antisemitic reaction."[43]

Parsons's position on antisemitism, it turns out, was in stark contrast to Graeber's understanding of antisemitism. Graeber placed full responsibility for antisemitism on the dominant culture. He maintained that antisemitism was deeply wound into the Christian tradition. The Church, he wrote, had dehumanized the Jew as "a 'monster,' a theological abstraction of superhuman cunning and malice," and Christians were raised with the "hostile myth of the cruel, greedy, treacherous, Christ-killing, Christ-rejecting Jew."[44] Still, both Judaism and Christianity were the twin pillars of Western civilization for Graeber. So he and Parsons both shared the view that what Nazism ultimately sought was to tear apart Western culture. And for Parsons, the modern West sat on the precipice of liberalism.

Parsons, Nazism, and Liberal Modernity

It is clear in the full gamut of Parsons's writings from 1938 to 1945 that he opposed Nazism and all forms of antisemitism on the grounds that they were a threat to the form of liberal democracy he was not only personally committed to defend but saw as the culmination of modernity itself. In "The Sociology of Modern Anti-Semitism" he largely identifies the "chief characteristics of Western society" with "liberal democracy" and "certain broad social values such as a modicum of equality of opportunity" and "a separation of church and state so that religion is a 'personal affair.'"[45]

Indeed his first effort to sound the alarm about the dangers of Nazism was a short article he published in the *Radcliffe News* just after the Kristallnacht pogrom of November 1938. In it he augured that Hitlerism was something radically new that was "rapidly coming to be the most formidable threat to many of the institutional fundamentals of western civilization as a whole which has been seen for many centuries." As such, antisemitism was the canary in the coal mine: "Seen in this perspective the treatment of the Jews, tragic as it is for the victims, is only a small part of the significance of the movement, perhaps even more of symptomatic importance than itself the major danger. For various reasons they, the most widespread and at the same time persistently 'unassimilated' cultural minority in Western society, are particularly vulnerable as a symbol and a scapegoat." In an unpublished article, "Academic Freedom," written in 1939, Parsons warned of the "tendency in the Nazi party to a basic anti-intellectualism which in principle questions the values of science." He argued that since professionalism depends upon liberality in the pursuit of knowledge, in certain circumstances an academic needs "to defend the liberal values which are essential to his own academic ethic, and to back up the forces in his society which maintain them."[46]

This commitment to a liberal vision of modernity guided Parsons's own involvement in a number of efforts from 1939 to 1945, including his active role on the Harvard Defense Committee and his biweekly radio broadcasts to combat American isolationism; in his efforts to urge intervention in the war effort and in his views about the war after Pearl Harbor; and finally in his thoughts about how to create conditions in postwar Germany that would foster a liberal democratic system to emerge from the ashes of the Nazi defeat. In accord with his liberalism, after the war Parsons would consistently oppose right-wing politics: he was a vehement critic of McCarthyism, strongly supported the civil rights movement,[47] opposed the Vietnam war, and robustly condemned the Nixon administration. In short, as Jens Nielsen has convincingly concluded about Parsons, "It is safe to classify him as a Left liberalist."[48]

It is clear from his unbridled opposition against fascism and Hitlerism in terms of a set of democratic values that the axis of Parsons's perspective was his liberalism. But it must be emphasized that his views on liberalism were not those of a Pollyanna. Parsons was not naïve about the tensions and antinomies of liberal modernity and the Enlightenment tradition that he embraced. He makes this evident in his article "Some Sociological Aspects of the Fascist Movements," originally given as his presidential address to the Eastern Sociological Society in 1942 and then published in *Social Forces*.

This article was an abstraction and elaboration of the same argument that he had made in "The Sociology of Modern Anti-Semitism." Supplementing his Durkheimian theory of antisemitism as a response to anomie with a Weberian spin, he argued that the solvent of modernity was a critical rationality that began with a series of Enlightenment promises calling for a "new and magnificent social order, for freedom against tyranny, for enlightenment against ignorance and superstition, for equality and justice against privilege, for free enterprise against monopoly and the irrational restrictions of custom."[49] Akin to the Frankfurt School, he argued that over time this Enlightenment program had degenerated.[50] As utilitarian measures are applied to more and more processes, he asserted, this has led to an overemphasis on a market-driven focus and the division of labor and the concomitant reduction of social relations to forms of a social contract. The result has been an "underestimating [of] the role of what Pareto has called the 'non-logical' aspects of human behavior in society, of the sentiments and traditions of family and informal social relationships, of the refinements of social stratification, of the peculiarities of regional, ethnic or national culture—perhaps above all of religion." In response to these contradictions experienced socially and individually as anomie, certain key targets have emerged. Both capitalism and communism have been depicted as twin enemies, and "the Jew serves as a convenient symbolic link between them."[51]

Most insightfully Parsons argues that the processes of modernity have come to stand in fascist discourse as the problem, and each is identified with the Jews: intellectualism; urbanism; economic, technological, and administrative rationalization; cultural emancipation in literature and the arts; and the perception of moral emancipation. Jews and Judaism stand in fascist discourse as proxies for their societal processes. Parsons put this succinctly and powerfully in "Democracy and Social Structure in Pre-Nazi Germany," another article from the same period: "The coincidence in Nazi ideology of the Jews, capitalism, bolshevism, anti-religious secularism, internationalism, moral laxity, and emancipation of women as a single class of things to be energetically combated is strongly indicative" of the Nazi's view of Jews. This approach is what Baum and Lechner call Parsons's "status insecurity and aggression theorem."[52] Parsons went on to argue that specific groups experienced the social dislocations of modernity more intensely, specifically the lower middle class because they are closest to achieving the promises of modernity. But the processes of rational-legal forms of rule combined with social stratification mean that only some actually achieve the goals of the social whole. Youth also suffer disproportionately from the "insecurities of competitive occupational adjustment," as do women.[53] Parsons had learned from his close colleague Edward Y. Hartshorne that these were some of the same groups that were followers of the Nazi Party.[54]

In closing the article, he perceptively suggested that nationalism is the ultimate incubator of the contradictions of modernity, for on the one hand the processes of state formation function as a major engine of what Weber called simply "rationalization." But nationalism is also a repository of all the traditional sentiments that are melting into air in the cauldron of modernization. Parsons avers that transformational processes are always going to challenge certain vested interests. Fascism harnessed these discontents and was able at the same time to bring into the movement not only a traditional elite but also the new business elite, since fascists were willing to fight organized labor. Here and elsewhere in Parsons's wartime analysis, we thus see a robust sociological analysis of the structures that undergirded the Nazi movement and the role that antisemitism played in it. Parsons appreciated that these were internal not only to the development of Germany but also to the contradictions of modernity itself and that liberals needed to manage these counterforces.[55]

Parsons on Racism

By 1945 Parsons had worked this material to the point of synthesizing his understanding of the dynamics of racism into a set of clear-cut propositions, best articulated in his article "Racial and Religious Differences as Factors in Group Tensions." Industrial modernity creates conditions of anomie, he stated, which lead to insecurity and aggression. To displace this aggression social groups either harness it or project it onto a pathologized out-group. As Parsons itemized it:

> There are (1) actually existent cultural and other differences between groups, creating barriers to communication and understanding. There are (2) elements of realistic conflict of value and interest. There are (3) internal tensions and insecurity in group life and structure, which create a need for the scapegoat reaction. There is (4) the relative adequacy or inadequacy of the other mechanisms of control or neutralization of the aggressive impulses generated by insecurity. There is (5) the symbolic appropriateness of an out-group as a scapegoat relative to particular tensions in the in-group. Finally, there are (6) the patterns of rationalization which justify scapegoating and make it subjectively acceptable to people.

These processes are as true for the black/white dyad as for the relationship between Jews and non-Jews, Parsons avows. But the situation of Jews was somewhat unique, he concluded:

Their appropriateness as a scapegoat is to an important degree a function of their association with those areas of modern society most rapidly rationalized and "emancipated" from traditional values. Their actual concentration in metropolitan centers, in intellectual pursuits, in the literary and artistic world, and in some areas of business lend this association plausibility. If Jews could be evenly distributed through the total social structure, antisemitism would probably be greatly reduced.[56]

Parsons's Allosemitism

As this quotation makes evident, Parsons's intervention depends upon what Zygmunt Bauman calls "allosemitism": "the practice of setting the Jews apart as people radically different from all the others, needing separate concepts to describe and comprehend them and special treatment in all or most social intercourse."[57] Parsons's allosemitism helps to reveal the limits of his liberal "anti-antisemitism."

As we have seen, like Weber's sociological analyses of Judaism, Parsons's theory of antisemitism is riddled with the problems of an ambivalent liberal universalism that ultimately cannot affirm the historical particularities of Jewish culture, religion, and practices. Consequently his solution to 'the Jewish question' was to caution against "any policy which tends to make Jews as Jews more conspicuous."

Sartre insightfully argued in *Réflexions sur la question juive* (*Antisemite and Jew*), written just after the liberation of France and so only a few years after Parsons's own reflections, that while the antisemite and the liberal unquestionably have a different political framework and agenda for Jews and Judaism, they converge insofar as "the former wishes to destroy him as a man and leave nothing in him but the Jew, the pariah, the untouchable; the latter wishes to destroy him as a Jew and leave nothing in him but the man, the abstract and universal subject of the rights of man and the rights of the citizen."[58] I conjecture, and one can do no more based on the evidence, that perhaps Parsons—like Adorno, Horkheimer, Arendt, and the other prescient critical theorists of antisemitism—came to recognize this convergence in the aftermath of the Holocaust and that this accounts for why he buried "The Sociology of Modern Anti-Semitism."

Still, Parsons's text, and the myriad other works of sociology on the problem of antisemitism, give the lie to the boldness of Bauman's claim about sociology never wrestling at least with antisemitism as a motor of the Holocaust that reveals the inherent contradictions of modernity.[59] It is more sage to think that Bauman built on a legacy that Parsons helped to establish. But Bauman's postmodern sociology of antisemitism does have the merit, where Parsons's approach did not, of orienting his understanding around an appreciation of Jewish alterity quite distinct from the liberal, Enlightenment, modernist tradition that undergirded Parsons's sociological imagination.

Notes

1. Bauman, *Modernity and the Holocaust*, cover. As he puts in his introduction, "Sociology after the Holocaust," "The Holocaust has more to say about the state of sociology than sociology in its present shape is able to add to our knowledge of the Holocaust" (3), a position he proposes to correct.
2. Porter, "Toward a Sociology of National Socialism," 507. In his review Porter summarizes the kernel of Gerhardt's argument.
3. Ellenson, "Max Weber on Judaism and the Jews," 94. Count Clermont-Tonnerre in a National Assembly debate about Jewish emancipation most famously articulated its catchwords: "The Jews should be denied everything as a nation, but granted everything as individuals. They must be citizens. . . . There cannot be one nation within another nation. . . . It is intolerable that the Jews should become a separate political formation or class" (Mendes-Flohr and Reinharz, *The Jew in the Modern World*, 115). In the words of Judah Leib Gordon, the modern Jew was thus enjoined to "be a Jew at home and a man in the street." Hannah Arendt takes this claim to be the leitmotif of the inherent paradoxes of Jewish assimilation. See Arendt's discussion in *The Origins of Totalitarianism*, 65. She discusses Leib's "excellent formula" as ironic, since for Jews "this actually amounted to a feeling of being different from other men in the street because they were Jews, and different from other Jews at home because they were not like 'ordinary Jews.'"
4. The role of Jews and Judaism in these other sociologists' work is more well known, so for Durkheim, see Strenski, *Durkheim and the Jews of France*; Birnbaum, *Geography of Hope*, chapter 2.
5. Helmreich, "The Sociological Study of Antisemitism in the United States," 134.
6. Birnbaum, *Geography of Hope*, 4.
7. Stoetzler, "Antisemitism, Capitalism and the Formation of Sociological Theory," 161, 164.

8. For a different taxonomy of theories of antisemitism at the time of Parsons's writing, see Adorno, "Research Project on Anti-Semitism," 125–26.

9. While not particularly sensitive to the Jewish religious interpretation of this scenario, see Lindemann's *Esau's Tears*, 3–6.

10. As Léon Poliakov put it in the first work of his summa on the history of anti-semitism, "From the first centuries, the various motifs of the original antagonism between Jews and Christians became interwoven, now in rivalries for proselytes, now in the effort to conciliate officialdom for its own advantage, or in the exigencies of theological thought; they are the nucleus of a strictly Christian anti-Semitism" (*The History of Anti-Semitism*, 21). See also Haynes, *Reluctant Witnesses*, which gives an overview of the historiography.

11. Quoted in Laqueur, *The Changing Face of Antisemitism*, 24.

12. See Boyarin, "The Colonial Drag," chapter 7; Stanislawski, *Zionism and the Fin de Siècle*.

13. See Langmuir's genealogy in *Toward a Definition of Antisemitism*, 315–26. This was also the case with racism more generally, as Frederickson points out in his "Appendix," 151–70.

14. See Smith, "The Social Construction of Enemies," 207.

15. Graeber and Britt, *Jews in a Gentile World*, v.

16. Folsom, *Days of Anger, Days of Hope*, 290.

17. Letter from Parsons to Ben Halpern, June 26, 1942, Parsons papers, 15.2, box 17, cited in Gerhardt, introduction, 21.

18. Letter from Graeber to Parsons, August 16, 1941, Parsons papers, 42.41, box 2, cited in Gerhardt, introduction, 21.

19. Relative to Parsons's oeuvre as a whole, there is only a small body of work on his writing from 1938–45. These include Baum and Lechner, "National Socialism"; Alexander, *The Modern Reconstruction of Classical Thought*; Buxton, *Talcott Parsons and the Capitalist Nation State*; Nielsen, "The Political Orientation of Talcott Parsons." But it is Uta Gerhardt that has most systematically interrogated the convergence of both Parsons's political and theoretical demarche and the only one to comment much on "The Sociology of Modern Anti-Semitism." In addition to Gerhardt's introduction, see Gerhardt, *Talcott Parsons: An Intellectual Biography*, chapter 2. She very usefully breaks down Parsons's intellectual biography in this period into five phases: "namely a pro-intervention stance prior to Pearl Harbor, an interest in issues of propaganda and power in the year 1942, a year of crisis in the Far Eastern and European theaters of operation, and a time when postwar democratization of the Axis countries, especially Germany, was pivotal prior to ve-Day. Last but not least, under the title of 'Beyond Victory,' I wish to highlight Parsons's contribution to re-education policy planning for Germany, as consultant to the Foreign Economic Administration Enemy Branch between March and October 1945" (61).

20. Gerhardt, introduction, 68, n. 105.

21. Gerhardt, *Talcott Parsons: An Intellectual Biography*, 84.

22. Parsons, "Postscript to 'The Sociology of Modern Anti-Semitism.'"

23. Parsons, *Talcott Parsons on National Socialism*, 149.

24. Parsons's "The Sociology of Modern Anti-Semitism" fits wholly into the *monumental* intellectual biography by Gerhardt. I mean this in two senses. First is the extraordinary reconstruction of Parsons's biographical and theoretical edifice undertaken by Gerhardt. She has painstakingly gone through the whole archive of his work—published and unpublished—and done so with mastery and attention to detail. Her task is to show that Parsons wrestled with a problem inherent in modern (liberal) democratic social systems: on the one hand, their capacity for integration, but on the other hand, their propensity toward anomie, which under the right circumstances can lead toward totalitarianism. But this commitment to preservation and veneration, what Nietzsche named an "antiquarian" spirit, sits alongside another sense in which Gerhardt's work is monumental: as a narrative of someone or "something exemplary and worthy of emulation—at the expense of the *causes*" (Nietzsche, *On the Advantage and Disadvantage of History for Life*, 59). What I hope to do is to suggest a critical turn necessary to a full appreciation of Parsons's contributions, one that I venture is perhaps at the heart of what he himself came to see as the limits of his analysis and perhaps suggests why he did not publish it again, although this claim cannot be wholly substantiated. For the senses of *antiquarian*, *monumental*, and *critical history* as I am using them, see Nietzsche, *On the Advantage and Disadvantage of History for Life.*

25. Parsons, "The Sociology of Modern Anti-Semitism," 121.

26. The itemization of the sociological processes of modernization listed here actually comes from "Some Sociological Aspects of the Fascist Movement," where Parsons develops some of the points he makes in "The Sociology of Modern Anti-Semitism" at greater length, focused less on antisemitism and more on fascism per se. See Parsons, *Talcott Parsons on National Socialism*, 203–18.

27. Parsons, *Talcott Parsons on National Socialism*, 204. Parsons elucidated the concept of anomie in *The Structure of Social Action*, 376–90.

28. Parsons, *Talcott Parsons on National Socialism*, 114.

29. Parsons, "The Sociology of Modern Anti-Semitism," 102.

30. Gerhardt, *Talcott Parsons: An Intellectual Biography*, 85.

31. Ellenson, "Max Weber on Judaism and the Jews," 80–95. This whole section on Weber and the Jews is thoroughly indebted to Ellenson.

32. Weber, *Ancient Judaism*, 3.

33. Weber, *The Sociology of Religion*, 109.

34. Schmeuli, "The 'Pariah People' and Its 'Charismatic' Leadership," 181.

35. Raphael, "Max Weber et le judaisme antique," 330.

36. Holstein, "Max Weber and Biblical Scholarship."

37. Abraham, *Max Weber and the Jewish Question.*

38. Ellenson, "Max Weber on Judaism and the Jews," 94.

39. Weber, *The Sociology of Religion*, lxii–lxvi.

40. Parsons, "*The Sociology of Modern Anti-Semitism*," 105–6.

41. Parsons, "*The Sociology of Modern Anti-Semitism*," 106.

42. Parsons, "*The Sociology of Modern Anti-Semitism*," 107.

43. Parsons, "*The Sociology of Modern Anti-Semitism*," 112, 121.

44. Cited in Bendersky, "Dissension in the Face of the Holocaust," 93. This important article by Bendersky wonderfully reconstructs the argument about antisemitism in the United States on the basis of the debate generated by the pamphlet on antisemitism *Nazi Poison*, produced the Council for Democracy under the leadership of Carl Friedrich at Harvard, which included Parsons and Graeber as contributors.

45. Parsons, *Talcott Parsons on National Socialism*, 108.

46. Parsons, *Talcott Parsons on National Socialism*, 81, 82, 95.

47. See, for example, Parsons and Clark, *The Negro American*.

48. Nielsen, "The Political Orientation of Talcott Parsons," 229. Nielsen's article is part of a growing body of revisionist scholarship on Parsons attempting to correct the impression of his work created in the 1960s and 1970s under the inspiration of the New Left that Parsons was a conservative, reactionary, cold warrior who legitimated bourgeois Western values. In addition to Gerhardt, this literature includes Loubser et al., *Explorations in General Theory in Social Science*; Alexander, *Theoretical Logic in Sociology*; Habermas, *The Theory of Communicative Action*; and the work of Brian Turner. My own effort is a post-revisionist account that seeks to understand Parsons's stance on antisemitism and, by extension, Nazi fascism and totalitarianism in terms of their own immanent limits, taking as a stepping-off point Parsons's liberalism.

49. Parsons, *Talcott Parsons on National Socialism*, 211.

50. On the Frankfurt School's views on antisemitism explored in a similar vein to this chapter, see Jonathan Judaken, "Between Philosemitism and Antisemitism."

51. Parsons, *Talcott Parsons on National Socialism*, 212.

52. Parsons, *Talcott Parsons on National Socialism*, 237–38. See Baum and Lechner, "National Socialism," 284.

53. Parsons, *Talcott Parsons on National Socialism*, 214.

54. See Hartshorne, *The German Universities and National Socialism*. On Hartshorne's influence on Parsons, see Gerhardt, *Talcott Parsons: An Intellectual Biography*.

55. For a fuller summation of Parsons's analysis of the historical and sociological elements that gave rise to national socialism, see Baum and Lechner, "National Socialism."

56. Parsons, *Talcott Parsons on National Socialism*, 284.

57. Bauman, "Allosemitism," 143.

58. Sartre, *Antisemite and Jew*, 57. For an overview on Sartre, see Judaken, *Jean-Paul Sartre and the Jewish Question*.

59. It is important to remember that chapters 2 and 3 of Bauman's *Modernity and the Holocaust* are focused squarely on theorizing the role of antisemitism as a by-product of the modernization process.

References

Abraham, Gary A. *Max Weber and the Jewish Question: A Study of the Social Outlook of His Sociology.* Urbana: University of Illinois Press, 1992.

Adorno, Theodor. "Research Project on Anti-Semitism." *Studies in Philosophy and Social Science* 9 (1941): 124–43.

Alexander, Jeffery C. *The Modern Reconstruction of Classical Thought: Talcott Parsons.* Berkeley: University of California Press, 1983.

———. *Theoretical Logic in Sociology. The Modern Reconstruction of Classical Thought: Talcott Parsons.* Vol. 4. Berkeley: University of California Press, 1983.

Arendt, Hannah. *The Origins of Totalitarianism.* 1951. New York: Harcourt Brace Jovanovich, 1973.

Baum, Rainer, and Frank J. Lechner. "National Socialism: Toward an Action-Theoretical Interpretation." *Sociological Inquiry* 51 (1981): 281–305.

Bauman, Zygmunt. "Allosemitism: Premodern, Modern, Postmodern." In *Modernity, Culture and "the Jew,"* edited by Bryan Cheyette and Laura Marcus, 143–56. Cambridge UK: Polity Press, 1998.

———. *Modernity and the Holocaust.* New York: Cornell University Press, 1989.

Bendersky, Joseph W. "Dissension in the Face of the Holocaust: 1941 American Debate over Antisemitism." *Holocaust and Genocide Studies* 24.1 (2010): 85–116.

Birnbaum, Pierre. *Geography of Hope: Exile, the Enlightenment, Disassimilation.* Translated by Charlotte Mandell. Stanford: Stanford University Press, 2008.

Boyarin, Daniel. "The Colonial Drag: Zionism, Gender, and Mimicry." In *Unheroic Conduct: The Rise of Heterosexuality and the Invention of the Jewish Man,* 271–312. Berkeley: University of California Press, 1997.

Buxton, William. *Talcott Parsons and the Capitalist Nation State.* Toronto: Toronto University Press, 1985.

Ellenson, David. "Max Weber on Judaism and the Jews." In *After Emancipation: Jewish Religious Responses to Modernity,* 80–95. Cincinnati OH: Hebrew Union College Press.

Folsom, Franklin. *Days of Anger, Days of Hope: A Memoir of the League of American Writers, 1937–1942.* Niwot: University Press of Colorado, 1994.

Frederickson, George. "Appendix: The Concept of Racism in Historical Discourse." In *Racism: A Short History,* 151–70. Princeton NJ: Princeton University Press, 2002.

Gerhardt, Uta. Introduction to *Talcott Parsons on National Socialism.* New York: Aldine de Gruyter, 1993.

———. *Talcott Parsons: An Intellectual Biography.* Cambridge: Cambridge University Press, 2002.

Graeber, Isacque, and Steuart Henderson Britt. *Jews in a Gentile World: The Problem of Anti-Semitism.* New York: Macmillan, 1942.

Habermas, Jürgen. *The Theory of Communicative Action. Lifeworld and System: A Critique of Functionalist Reason.* Vol. 2. Translated by Thomas McCarthy. Boston: Beacon Press, 1987.

Hartshorne, Edward Y., Jr. *The German Universities and National Socialism.* London: Allen and Unwin, 1937.

Haynes, Stephen. *Reluctant Witnesses: Jews in the Christian Imagination.* Louisville KY: Westminster John Knox Press, 1995.

Helmreich, William B. "The Sociological Study of Antisemitism in the United States." In *Approaches to Antisemitism: Context and Curriculum,* edited by Michael Brown, 134–41. New York: American Jewish Committee and The International Center for University Teaching of Jewish Civilization, 1994.

Holstein, Jay. "Max Weber and Biblical Scholarship." *Hebrew Union College Annual,* no. 46 (1975): 159–79.

Judaken, Jonathan. "Between Philosemitism and Antisemitism: The Frankfurt School's Anti-antisemitism." In *Antisemitism and Philosemitism in the Twentieth and Twenty-First Centuries: Representing Jews, Jewishness and Modern Culture,* edited by Phyllis Lassner and Lara Trubowitz, 23–46. Newark: University of Delaware Press, 2008.

———. *Jean-Paul Sartre and the Jewish Question: Anti-antisemitism and the Politics of the French Intellectual.* Lincoln: University of Nebraska Press, 2006.

Langmuir, Gavin. *Toward a Definition of Antisemitism.* Berkeley: University of California Press, 1990.

Laqueur, Walter. *The Changing Face of Antisemitism: From Ancient Times to the Present Day.* Oxford: Oxford University Press, 2006.

Lindemann, Albert. *Esau's Tears: Modern Anti-Semitism and the Rise of the Jews.* Cambridge: Cambridge University Press, 1997.

Loubser, J., et al. *Explorations in General Theory in Social Science.* 2 vols. New York: Free Press, 1976.

Mendes-Flohr, Paul, and Jehuda Reinharz, eds. *The Jew in the Modern World: A Documentary History.* 2d edition. Oxford: Oxford University Press, 1995.

Nielsen, Jens Kaalhauge. "The Political Orientation of Talcott Parsons: The Second World War and Its Aftermath." In *Talcott Parsons: Theorist of Modernity,* edited by Roland Robertson and Bryan S. Turner, 217–33. London: Sage, 1991.

Nietzsche, Friedrich. *On the Advantage and Disadvantage of History for Life.* Translated by Peter Preuss. Indianapolis: Hackett, 1980.

Parsons, Talcott. "Postscript to 'The Sociology of Modern Anti-Semitism.'" *Contemporary Jewry* 5 (1980): 31–38.

———. "The Sociology of Modern Anti-Semitism." In *Jews in a Gentile World,* edited by Isacque Graeber and Steuart Henderson Britt, 101–22. New York: Macmillan, 1942.

———. *Talcott Parsons on National Socialism.* New York: Aldine de Gruyter, 1993.

———. *The Structure of Social Action: A Study in Social Theory with Special Reference to a Group of Recent European Writers* Vol. 1. 1937. New York: Free Press, 1968.

Parsons, Talcott, and Kenneth B. Clark. *The Negro American.* Boston: Beacon Press, 1996.

Poliakov, Léon. *The History of Anti-Semitism. From the Time of Christ to the Court Jews.* Vol. 1. 1955. Translated by Richard Howard. London: Elek Books, 1965.

Porter, Jack Nusan. "Toward a Sociology of National Socialism." *Sociological Forum* 9.3 (1994): 505–11.

Raphaël, Freddy. "Max Weber et le judaïsme antique." *European Journal of Sociology / Archives Européenes de Sociologie* 11.2 (1970): 297–336.

Sartre, Jean-Paul. *Antisemite and Jew.* New York: Schocken Books, 1948.

Schmeuli, Ephraim. "The 'Pariah People' and Its 'Charismatic' Leadership: A Reevaluation of Max Weber's 'Ancient Judaism.'" *American Academy of Jewish Research Proceedings,* no. 36 (1968): 167–247.

Smith, David Norman. "The Social Construction of Enemies: Jews and the Representation of Evil." *Sociological Theory* 14.3 (1996): 203–40.

Stanislawski, Michael. *Zionism and the Fin de Siècle: Cosmopolitanism and Nationalism from Nordau to Jabotinsky.* Berkeley: University of California Press, 2001.

Steiner, George. *Language and Silence: Essays on Language, Literature and the Inhuman.* New York: Atheneum, 1967.

Stoetzler, Marcel. "Antisemitism, Capitalism and the Formation of Sociological Theory." *Patterns of Prejudice* 44.2 (2010): 161–94.

Strenski, Ivan. *Durkheim and the Jews of France.* Chicago: University of Chicago Press, 1997.

Weber, Max. *Ancient Judaism.* Translated and edited by Hans Gerth and Don Martindale. Glencoe IL: Free Press, 1952.

———. *The Sociology of Religion.* Translated by Ephraim Fischoff. Boston: Beacon Press, 1963.

10

The Irrationality of the Rational

The Frankfurt School and Its Theory of Society in the 1940s

EVA-MARIA ZIEGE

Recent years have seen a major reassessment of the forced migration of the 1930s and 1940s to the United States with regard to the history of the sciences and humanities. Mitchell G. Ash aptly phrased this reappraisal a scientific innovation through forced migration. This was not a new concept. The social scientist Paul Lazarsfeld, himself an émigré from Austria in the 1930s and a major figure in the innovation of the social sciences, stated as an autobiographical and, as it were, autosociological observation that innovation can often be traced back to individuals who belong to two worlds while belonging to neither unambiguously: "The best historical examples are Wilhelm von Humboldt who, as a hanger-on at Weimar, belonged to the lower Prussian aristocracy and created the University of Berlin in 1807. Another is Guillaume Budé, who was a hanger-on among the French humanists but who had access to the Court of Francis I and spent his life developing the Collège de France in opposition to the anti-humanistic Sorbonne (1515 to 1550)."[1] According to Lazarsfeld, individuals like these became "institution men," special cases of a well-known sociological phenomenon: the marginal person (not to be confused with Parkes's "marginal man"), who is part of two different cultures. In some cases precisely this marginality transforms itself into the propelling force to build up new institutions. These institutions offer their founders protection and at the same time a path to maintain their own identity.

This description may be used much more broadly in understanding scientific innovation. One can hardly envision the French sociologist

Pierre Bourdieu without his background in rural French Béarn and his experiences in Algeria that molded his perceptions of French high culture, perceiving it from the "outside" as he had perceived Algeria. We know how productive the Catholic Diaspora was in Protestant theology and vice versa. In the sciences innovation was repeatedly achieved by scientists who had to change from one discipline to another, a case in point being the physicists who left Nazi Germany and became biologists in their country of exile.[2]

The concept is useful also for understanding the Institute of Social Research (ISR) and its innovations in research on antisemitism. For the ISR, three aspects are of specific interest with regard to this approach. First, in the Weimar Republic the majority of associates of the ISR came from assimilated German Jewish families; an orthodox family background was the exception. Second, in the Weimar Republic all of them belonged to the Left, encompassing communists and in rare cases even anarchocommunists as well as Social Democrats. Third, irrespective of these differences, the inner circle shared as a paradigm Marx's critique of political economy. Perhaps what linked them was a discreet orthodoxy.

All of them were more or less influenced by Freud, who introduced the notion of the unconscious into the analysis of the individual and society. A distinct school of Freudian Marxism emerged. Precisely the intense success of differing schools of Freudianism in the United States was a major prerequisite of the success of the Institute of Social Research in this country. Its Marxism, though, was rendered nearly invisible.

For the Frankfurt School in the 1930s and 1940s, an esoteric form of communication has to be distinguished from an exoteric one. This distinction between what one can formulate explicitly and what one can articulate only very selectively, hoping that those "in the know" will recognize and understand all the same, had been important to Enlightenment thinkers and featured prominently in the thought of Leo Strauss (1899–1973), who emigrated to the United States in 1932 and argued that contemporary thinkers too needed to maintain this distinction in an age of persecution and dictatorship. At the core of critical theory, philosophical assumptions were presupposed that were nevertheless negligible in everyday research; they remained esoteric. It is possible to conceive of this distinction between esoteric and exoteric, as well as of the process of transcending Marxist orthodoxy, not as a corruption or decline of, let

alone a contradiction to, Marxism or critical theory but as the normal-
ity of any evolving school. The Marxist core paradigm in fact remained
paradigmatic for social thought with the key members of the Institute.
Nevertheless other associates did not necessarily share these tenets to
the same extent.

As Horkheimer defined it in the 1930s, the Institute's purpose was the
development of a theory of society based on the Marxist assumption that
the antagonism between labor and capital was the key driving force in
the dynamics of society. In 1937 Horkheimer published a famous article
entitled "Traditionelle und Kritische Theorie," juxtaposing traditional
and critical theory. It established the term *critical theory* for the Institute's
specific form of Marxist social theory. It aspired to a radical change of society but no longer accepted the Marxist prognosis that it was the working class who would bring about this change. This momentous theoretical shift was a response to the rise of Stalinism in the Soviet Union and
national socialism in Germany and the fact that there had been no successful revolution in Germany after 1918.

Antisemitism among American Labor

With *Dialectic of Enlightenment* by Horkheimer and Adorno (1947) and
The Authoritarian Personality (1950)—one of five volumes published in the
series Studies in Prejudice in 1949 and 1950—the Institute of Social Research became world famous.[3] Between these two classics of twentieth-
century social thought, however, a third major study was written: *Antisemitism among American Labor* (the *Labor Study*, 1945). This was the last
comprehensive study by the Institute of Social Research, and it remains
unpublished to the present day.[4]

In *Antisemitism among American Labor* hundreds of loosely structured
"screened interviews" conducted by American blue-collar workers with
coworkers under the combined guidance of social researchers from Europe and the United States looked at antisemitism in the United States in
the year 1944—attitudes toward Jews in the context of World War II, national socialism and the atrocities committed by Nazi Germany in Europe,
and the genocide of the European Jews that by then was a well-known
fact overseas. Based on qualitative analyses of these interviews, the hypothesis of the *Labor Study* was that the persecution and annihilation of
the Jews of Europe did not *decrease* but on the contrary significantly *in-*

creased antisemitic attitudes. This was the background of the concept of
the "guilty victim" later developed in *The Authoritarian Personality* and
that of "ticket-thinking" in *Dialectic of Enlightenment*. The *Labor Study*
forms, as it were, the "missing link" between *Dialectic of Enlightenment*
and *The Authoritarian Personality*.

These works by the Institute have to be seen in a broader context. In
the 1940s research on antisemitism was professionalized, primarily in
the United States, the major country of exile of European Jews. During
this decade, and mainly resulting from international conferences, pioneering work on antisemitism was published. Koppel Pinson edited the
volume *Essays on Antisemitism* (with a contribution by Hannah Arendt in
its second edition), and Graeber and Britt edited *Jews in a Gentile World*
(with a contribution by Talcott Parsons). The psychoanalyst Ernst Simmel
edited a volume entitled *Anti-Semitism*, including contributions by most
of the later authors of *The Authoritarian Personality*: Adorno, Else Frenkel-
Brunswik, and R. Nevitt Sanford, with a preface by Gordon Allport and
several mottos by the American president Franklin Delano Roosevelt.

Eugene Hartley (originally named Horowitz), who, like many of those
publishing in the field, was an exiled intellectual from Europe, published
Problems in Prejudice in 1946. The American Joshua Trachtenberg published *The Devil and the Jews* in 1943, and the American Carey McWilliams published *A Mask for Privilege: Anti-Semitism in America* in 1948.

Apart from Trachtenberg and, for example, Paul Massing's volume
Rehearsal for Destruction in the series Studies in Prejudice in 1949, historical studies were relatively rare compared to studies in psychoanalysis and social psychology, in social research and social theory. By its very
nature research on antisemitism was interdisciplinary. Major works were
published in philosophy and political theory, often by those who later became major figures of philosophical or political thought in the twentieth
century: Arendt, Adorno, Sartre, and Jacques Maritain.

This sudden proliferation of work on antisemitism cannot be explained
solely by the events in Europe and the genocide of the Jews. After Roosevelt was inaugurated president in 1933, antisemitism increased in the
United States. After the United States became part of the Allied Powers
in World War II, ethnic group antagonism as such was seriously exacerbated.[5] Interned Japanese Americans on the West Coast were attacked,
and African Americans became targets of violent assaults. In the infa-

mous case of "Sleepy Lagoon," Mexican Americans were falsely accused and convicted of murder. The Los Angeles Zoot Suit Riots were further proof of the hatred of white citizens against Mexicans.

Jews were targeted too. Jewish cemeteries were desecrated, synagogues damaged and defaced with swastikas, and antisemitic pamphlets distributed. Teenagers committed vicious assaults against Jewish children. Antisemitic incidents in the U.S. Army as well as Congress became known. The extreme violence of the Christian Front Hoodlums in October 1943 in Boston caused a police scandal. Roosevelt had been a target of antisemitism since 1933, so much so that his famous New Deal was nicknamed "Jew Deal" by those who inferred that Jews were unjustly privileged in his administration. This was the background for open antisemitism in the presidential campaign conducted by John Dewey, Roosevelt's rival candidate in 1944. The *Labor Study* commented, "The population is thoroughly saturated with antisemitism. One acquires it 'in the air.' Antisemitism, together with anti-antisemitism, is deeply ingrained in the whole American tradition."[6] In April 1943 one of the Institute's associates wrote in a letter to Horkheimer:

> I do not know how closely you follow the New York papers. Also whether the Jewish Project is of interest to you only because one can earn a couple of thousands of dollars with it. If your interest exceeds this you will want to know that during the last months here in New York State, in New York & other places millions of antisemitic leaflet[s] (à la Hitler) were distributed in all the factories involved in the war effort to workers, women, youths. The authorities do nothing; the FBI does not act, nobody was arrested, the Dies Committee remains silent. You can see from the press cuttings I enclose in this letter how far antisemitic propaganda has gone. Seeing this I am convinced that this is not the time for a theoretical study of antisemitism. It is the time for immediate political action by the Jews. We know enough about the motives of fascist antisemitic agitation. One must act and one can act. If the Jews are not to do that, no scholarly project is going to help (however great its merits may be).[7]

American antisemitism was part of the American experience of the exiles. The Institute of Social Research closely monitored an increasing number of surveys and polls conducted since the late 1930s. In addition empirical research like *Middletown* (1929), *An American Dilemma* (1944), and *The People's Choice* (1944) became more and more sophisticated. Having been prepared by its own qualitative and quantitative studies in Europe, the Institute searched for new methods to perceive and analyze American society.

Especially *An American Dilemma*, a study of race relations and African Americans in society, became an influential model for the work of the Institute. In 1938–42 the young Swedish economist Gunnar Myrdal had been commissioned and lavishly funded by the Carnegie Foundation to direct a comprehensive study on how African Americans were being discriminated against and the implications of their position in society for American democracy as such. Thus the "idea of a textbook à la Myrdal" emerged as a guiding idea of Horkheimer's for the Institute, aspiring to a comprehensive study on the situation of the Jews in the modern world.[8] The working hypothesis for the early 1940s became that, while antisemitism could be understood only through society, society at that particular time in history could henceforth be understood only through antisemitism.

Since the early 1940s the Institute had continually but unsuccessfully tried to acquire funding for various projects on antisemitism by the major U.S. funding bodies, the Rockefeller Foundation and the Carnegie Foundation. After years of failed efforts, however, two Jewish defense organizations, the American Jewish Committee and the Jewish Labor Committee, agreed to finance the Institute's work on popular antisemitism.

The leadership of the Jewish Labor Committee, an umbrella organization of the Jewish labor unions founded to coordinate public responses of the political Left toward Nazi Germany in 1934, recruited from the Bund, a secular Jewish socialist party originating in Lithuania, Poland, and Russia. It maintained the idea of a distinct Jewishness against the ideal of the American "melting pot." Specifically and programmatically it adhered to maintaining the use of the Yiddish language. Its most famous political leaders were Baruch Charney Vladeck and later David Dubinsky. The Jewish Labor Committee represented migrants from the Eastern European laboring classes and brought from Eastern Europe a moderate version of socialism that is best compared to Austromarxism in Europe. The American Jewish Committee, founded in 1906, was the organization of the German Jews. Its members were part of the influential economic elite, governed by the paradigm of assimilation (or acculturation) and "Americanism" in accordance with the famous dictum by Woodrow Wilson: "America does not consist of groups."[9]

Politically as well as sociologically, the American Jewish Committee and the Jewish Labor Committee represented two counterparts, two opposite poles, as it were, among the secular Jews of America. Equally opposed were their immediate strategies as to how to deal with the defense against antisemitism at home and abroad. The Jewish Labor Committee from the very beginning pursued a politics of boycott of the National Socialists, organizing mass rallies and, for example, a high-profile counter-Olympics as a form of protest against the 1936 Berlin Olympics, the World Labor Athletic Carnival. Later they actively supported armed resistance in Europe, active rescue operations, and media work.

The American Jewish Committee, by contrast, favored a policy of appeasement toward Germany well into the later 1930s and a strategy of silent diplomacy. While according to them, Jews in the United States should prove themselves by becoming Americans first and foremost, playing down antisemitism and resisting Jewish "particularism," the Jewish Labor Committee opted for the opposite. The two organizations epitomized antagonistic positions, sharing, however, two main tenets: Jewish existence in Diaspora and the willingness to cooperate with the German Jews who had fled Germany.

The Institute of Social Research had to manage a difficult tightrope act between these two organizations, trying to maintain its academic autonomy against the heteronomy of these contradictory political influences. This contributed to a concerted effort of the academic and the political fields, of exiled Europeans and of American Jews, and this was a new phenomenon. It was also due to an emerging cognitive demand addressing some of the most urgent political and existential questions of the time. In this process the Institute in its mainly marginal position within the academic field became a connecting cog. The social scientist Nathan Glazer commented on this significant development already in 1946: "The 'intellectual current' is not the only force moving scientists to concern themselves with prejudice. The large Jewish domestic defence and community relations groups . . . are now sponsoring scientific research on prejudice."[10]

The Jewish Labor Committee and the American Jewish Committee as organizations were quite different with regard to their social structure and political aims, yet they shared this conviction with the Horkheimer circle: "Our aim is not merely to describe prejudice but to explain it in order to help its eradication. . . . Eradication means re-education."[11]

The Irrationality of Society's Rationality

In his book *Reflections on America*, Claus Offe showed that the descriptions of America by Tocqueville, Max Weber, and Adorno always contained European self-descriptions. This holds true also for *Antisemitism among American Labor*. Here was a task Horkheimer had declared in his 1939 article "The Jews and Europe" to be virtually impossible: "That the exiles show a mirror to a world that innately produces fascism precisely in those places where asylum is still granted to them, that is something nobody can ask of them."[12] Accordingly the Institute presented its own work on antisemitism with modesty, suggesting it should be considered a preparatory exploration of the subject, a first approach as to how antisemitism might be researched in the future. In these approaches Horkheimer and Adorno were influenced by the followers of Franz Boas in American cultural anthropology, particularly Ruth Benedict's famous concept of "cultural pattern."[13] In the *Labor Study* the concept of "cultural pattern antisemitism," adopting Benedict's concept, was used to distinguish between the forms of antisemitism they encountered in the United States and the antisemitism of Europe in the 1940s, which they termed "exterminative antisemitism."

The irrationality of society's rationality, according to Horkheimer, should be considered key for a theory of current antisemitism both in Europe and the United States:

Fascism is the caricature of social revolution. . . . The monopolistic elimination of competition takes within the fascist states radically destructive forms only against the Jews, on the outside against colonial or national groups. Apart from that this trend is only a side effect of the new subordination of the masses into the machine of production. The unchecked brutality of the individual entrepreneur will be checked in the age of working contracts and social welfare and be replaced by more rational relations within society. To understand the rationality of this, to understand the irrationality of this rationality, is our most important task. On the solution of this task depends also a theory of current antisemitism to a very large extent.[14]

This theory of current antisemitism was founded on a theory of so-called state capitalism. It included a theory of the role of the Jews in late capitalism. Horkheimer wrote the passage quoted above in November 1944, while the writing of *Antisemitism among American Labor* was in its early stages. The *Labor Study* was the first large-scale empirical study of antisemitism in the United States. It was written in the dire apprehension of an imminent outbreak of fascism in North America after the war and the instabilities arising from the postwar situation. Their European experience led the authors to believe that totalitarian antisemitism did not grow out of any constitutional peculiarities of any people or race. It was regarded not as a genuine product of a particular country but as a particular system of domination that had a political function as class-manipulated antisemitism for undermining democracy in unstable political situations such as the aftermath of a war. In the United States antisemitism as part of a "totalitarian" strategy might thus parallel the European model because during the war antisemitism in America had become, as Massing phrased it, a "staple commodity" and might be used after the war for political purposes.[15] According to Leo Löwenthal, it was the antisemitic agitator who sold this commodity to the people.[16]

Thus the ISR reached a conclusion contrary to that of Talcott Parsons in his 1942 essay "Sociology of Modern anti-Semitism." According to Parsons, antisemitism in North America would never reach an intensity comparable to the destructive force it had attained in Germany: "Two factors are particularly responsible for the spread of anti-Semitism in Germany. One is the extreme form of nationalism of the German people, and the other is the Nazi movement. . . . It seems exceedingly unlikely that nationalism can be brought to such a pitch of intensity in the United States."[17] Nevertheless it was Parsons, not the Institute of Social Research, who on this question and at this point in time held a minority position. The assessment of the European exiles was by no means European alarmism: it was shared by many social scientists and philosophers as well as large parts of the labor unions and public intellectuals like the writer Sinclair Lewis and, later, Thomas Mann.

Labor Antisemitism and Class Society

Antisemitism among American Labor was a qualitative, not a quantitative study. Unlike *The Authoritarian Personality* and the other works in the series Studies in Prejudice, it was based on neither psychoanalysis nor social psychology. Six major chapters were written by Massing, A. R. L. Gurland, Löwenthal, and Friedrich Pollock, and edited by Adorno: "Incidence of Antisemitism among Workers," "The American Worker Looks at the Jew," "War, Fascism, Propaganda," "Image of Prejudice," "Opinions and Reactions of Union Officers," and methodological consequences to be drawn from the study. The study was supervised in its empirical parts by Herta Herzog and Paul Lazarsfeld. Unlike other works in the Studies in Prejudice series that had an often extensive number of academic advisors, this study was accompanied by a single advisor from outside the Institute: Horace M. Kallen, the famed advocate of the concept of cultural pluralism in the United States.

In the course of the study approximately 4,500 questionnaires were distributed, and in the final instance approximately five hundred blue- and white-collar workers declared themselves willing to conduct "screened" undercover interviews according to the guidelines of these questionnaires and to write them up with the support of field workers. Eventually 270 interviewers wrote up 613 interviews that had been conducted in the industrial centers of the American West, Midwest, and East, in New York City, Philadelphia, Camden, Newark, and other parts of New Jersey, Pittsburgh, Los Angeles, Detroit, San Francisco, Massachusetts, Maryland, and Wisconsin. Not included were the South and the Farm Belt. This large-scale operation became possible only with the active help of the huge organizational capacities of the labor unions.

The *Labor Study* was based on the Marxist idea of society as an inherently antagonistic totality, according to Horkheimer's dictum "He who does not speak of capitalism should not speak of fascism, either."[18]

In the 1970s the German sociologist Niklas Luhmann declared the concept of class society obsolete, assessing it as part of a semantics of transition. Luhmann explained its overwhelming influence and reception with its very transitoriness. The idea of class society in his assessment meant not having to give up completely on the notion of society as a vertically organized hierarchy while at the same time giving it up insofar as crucial aspects of modern society could be absorbed by it. Though obsolete, one characteristic of the concept of class proved to be still useful to sociology: its particular suitability as a theoretical framework for raising empirical data. Even though the paradigm of the factory, according to Luhmann, had become obsolete, the factory gave access to empirical data.[19]

Indeed the theoretical assumption of class, based on the politically generalized distinction between labor and capital, guided the theoretical framework of the *Labor Study*. In January 1944 Adorno wrote to his parents, "On Thursday, I will give my very first talk to a group of Jewish workers, with discussion to follow. It is going to be an interesting experience." Briefly afterward he reported, "My speech to the workers really went very well. I had to apologise that I did not speak Yiddish, the language of the meeting."[20]

In the course of the actual fieldwork, communication sometimes proved to be much more difficult than that. In July Löwenthal wrote to Horkheimer, "[Massing] is so meek and depressed at the present because of the enormous difficulties which he encounters in forming study groups and getting interviews that he stays very clear from any new contacts which do not lead directly into the next factory."[21] Even though class theory was a core aspect of the theory of the Frankfurt School, its Marxist paradigm remained esoteric in *Antisemitism among American Labor*. It was made virtually invisible even though it was written by a group of authors who (with Löwenthal, Massing, and Pollock)—like no other group of authors in the Institute of Social Research in the United States—embodied the "old" Marxist Institute as it had existed in Frankfurt in the 1920s. While the critique of capitalism was weakened in the *Labor Study*, the critique of totalitarianism became very pronounced. (As if Horkheimer and Adorno themselves were quite aware of this, in *Dialectic of Enlightenment* they went on ostentatiously to use the vocabulary of orthodox Marxism. This, however, was to be softened for the 1947 publication of their book.)

Precisely this made possible productive innovations of the *Labor Study*. This study established entirely new perspectives in the analysis of antisemitism. Differences in antisemitic attitudes between different national, cultural, and ethnic groups in the United States and, most notably, differences in attitudes of white non-Jews as compared to those of African Americans toward Jews, and attitudes of Mexicans, Irish, Japanese, and other immigrant groups were looked at as the stereotypes of individuals belonging to groups who themselves were stereotyped. The study showed in great empirical detail through the analysis of interviews conducted by workers with fellow workers that inequality, distinctions, and stereotypes evolved not necessarily along the lines of class antagonism. Although this may seem to contradict its underlying theoretical frame of class theory, the study did not negate the reality of class as such. Rather it differentiated within the concept of class with regard to age cohorts, gender, educational level, and migratory background.

Thus class remained crucial in the *Labor Study*. It gained special importance because the existence of a "proletariat" in the United States was not self-evident. In Europe the working class was a fixed entity; in the United States it was fluid. Perhaps it was precisely this openness that made it possible to broaden the concept of class. The *Labor Study* conceptualized manifold "fine distinctions": between men and women, blue- and white-collar workers, religious and nonreligious affiliations, and multiethnic and multicultural differences by virtue of country of origin, first, second, or third generation, education, sex, age cohort, and so on.

In the analyses of the interviews, however, there clearly emerged a specific type that seemed most susceptible to antisemitism: white male workers with neither vocational training nor education, the core membership of the Congress of Industrial Organizations (CIO). There also emerged just as clearly one group in the interviews as most resistant to antisemitism: the African American interviewees.

According to Horkheimer and Adorno in *Dialectic of Enlightenment*, enlightenment, historically speaking, was specific to a certain class: the bourgeoisie. Therefore, Adorno assumed, prejudice could not be analyzed without the category of class. Workers formed the other of the bourgeois class, as it were. They could produce ideological elements that were products of the bourgeois consciousness only in an indirect manner. The production of the elements of antisemitism, as well as the specific changes they underwent when reflected in the minds of a non-bourgeois group, was one of the implicit guiding questions of *Dialectic of Enlightenment*.

From the interviews conducted for the *Labor Study* Adorno drew the conclusion that for the "true labourer," "the Jew" mainly represented the bourgeois. Gurland and Massing showed in their analyses of the interview material that workers saw "the Jew" as the representative of the economic sphere, as the executor of capitalism. The Jew to them was he "who presented the bill," as Adorno later phrased it in *The Authoritarian Personality*.[22] In the *Labor Study* Gurland analyzed this in detail with regard to perceptions of "Jewish power," "Jewish bosses," "Jewish traders," "Jewish workers," and "the Jew as middleman" in line with *Dialectic of Enlightenment*.

What was the impact of war and genocide on the antisemitism encountered in factories and shipyards? There were two questions in the *Labor Study* directly addressing this aspect: "How do you feel about what the Nazis did to the Jews in Germany?" and "Do people think the Jews are doing their share in the war effort? What do you think?" The following selected quotations illustrate the material the researchers were to interpret:

Interviewee: a son of immigrants from Sweden, married, no children, High School Graduate, union member, welder in San Francisco Shipyard: "He thinks the Nazis were 'fairly reasonable' in their treatment of Jews, 'the thing had to be done.' Maybe the Nazis 'went too far.'"

Interviewee from American South, three children, union member, machinist in Los Angeles, Seventh Day Adventist: "'The Bible says they should be persecuted.'"

Interviewee from Poland, Catholic, no vocational training, works with Ford in Detroit, union member: "Steve knew 'plenty' of Jews in his hometown and elsewhere. 'They are all the same. . . . Type of work not important but getting ahead is. The Aryan, so to speak, has a pride beneath which he won't stoop. With Jews—nestegg, profit, etc.'" Interviewer asks whether Hitler "did the right thing, then. . . . No, says Steve, 'He didn't do enough. He should have exterminated all of them."

"'Capital started this war,' says a plumber in a shipyard on the East Coast. . . . 'They owned too much. . . . If it hadn't been for this war, the country would have cracked up. . . .' He distinguishes between 'two kinds of Jews—capital Jews and working Jews.' But his 'class consciousness' leaves him right there and he continues in the best antisemitic fashion: 'The Jews own most everything and they won't share'–and '[Hitler] got rid of the capital Jews.'"

Control interview with housewife: "Woman, 58, 5 children, 8th grade, born in New Jersey, father German, mother Irish, Catholic (no regular churchgoer), married to metal engraver who is an old union member (041).... 'They [Jews] deserved what they got [in Germany]. No one can trust them. Father Coughlin has their number. Roosevelt and the American and British Jew bankers got us into this war.'"

Looking at these quotes, Massing wrote in the *Labor Study*, "Immeasurable damage was done by the extermination of millions of Jews through the Nazis. The weakness of the Jewish group was thrown into bold relief when they were slaughtered as so much cattle. It is noteworthy that only once in our interviews reference was made to the Jews' death battle in the Warsaw ghetto."[23]

Evaluating the interviews, two groups were distinguished in the report. Individuals in Group A say "they do not like mass murder but the Jews brought it on themselves":

"Linesman, telephone company, San Francisco, 37, Italian descent, Californian-born, member, IBEW-AFL: 'Don't approve of Nazism in any form but wonder if [the] Jews did not bring it on themselves by controlling the business and professions.'"

"Woman worker, machine plant, Los Angeles, (no further information available): 'Of course, the Nazis have been far too harsh in their methods of destroying a Jewish monopoly in Germany but I do not entirely blame Germans for hating Jews.'"[24]

Those in Group B "reject mass killing but favor discriminatory measures against Jews":

"Shipfitter leadman, shipyard, Los Angeles, 24, 2-3 years college, Anglo-Saxon from Arizona, member, Boilermakers, American Federation of Labor: 'Extermination of the Jews is not the solution, but economic and social control; had Hitler stopped there, would have caused no outcries from non-Jews in the rest of the world.'"

"'Don't believe that Germans would do such a thing . . . ,' says a German-born machinist in a tool- and die-making plant in New Jersey. 'Won't believe the newspaper accounts. Cannot believe that a white man could be as cruel and intolerant as Hitler,' says a Tennessean machinist-helper in a rubber-plant in Detroit."

"Woman, former worker, 32, married, ex-Catholic, born in Los Angeles, of Irish-German descent: 'Ten years from now we shall know it is all a gross exaggeration and merely propaganda.'"

"'Germany was right in driving out the Jews,' says a machinist in an aircraft plant in the New York area. . . . He adds: 'I don't approve of killing them, but I don't believe the reports are true. If you would have taken these reports day by day and added them up, every Jew in Germany would have been killed.'"[25]

What was the political relevance of these results in the assessment of the European scholars? According to Massing, it was not antisemitic agitators like Charles Coughlin who exacerbated antisemitic attitudes in the United States but the events in Europe, or rather the reports on these events in media and war propaganda: "The coldblooded and unpunished annihilation of a part of world Jewry has exposed the rest to a new type of violence and contempt never experienced in modern times."[26]

This interpretation gave added complexity to the idea in *Dialectic of Enlightenment* that antisemitism was an instrument of manipulation of the working class.[27] It was crucial to Adorno's hypothesis of the "guilty victim" in *The Authoritarian Personality*:

The mere fact that Jews were hunted down, slaughtered, burned alive and suffocated in gas chambers, and that all this was done on a scale never before witnessed nor held possible, has separated the Jews from the human race. . . . One cannot emphasize this point too strongly. The American worker, as he appears in this survey, shows little if any understanding of the purpose of totalitarian antisemitism. He tries to make sense of what he hears about it in terms of his own experience. The result of his thinking processes often is that "you don't just torture or kill a man, unless there is a reason." The less comprehensible the Nazi actions are, the more the explanation of their motives is looked for and found with the Jews.[28]

Press reports publicizing stories of Jewish persecution in Europe, according to the workers who volunteered as interviewers for the *Labor Study*, had been to the detriment of fighting prejudice, because "atrocity stories" were usually disbelieved. Were there significant differences between minorities with regard to their attitudes toward the genocide in Europe? Comparing interviewees of Scandinavian, British, Irish, Mexican, Hungarian, Polish, German, and Italian origin, only one group clearly emerged with very high degrees of support for the National Socialists: the Irish. Those who condemned the Nazi persecution of the Jews most consistently were Mexicans, even more than Scandinavians.

The most surprising reaction for the researchers was that of the black interviewees. What did black Americans think about the Jews? Among all interviewees 7.2 percent were black; this represented a proportion only a little lower than that in the general U.S. population. The result was unequivocal: "Negroes among our interviewees . . . reacted more favorably to working with Jews than other national or ethnic groups." Compared to white people, only half as many black people declined to work with Jews. Also significant was the difference between whites and blacks in their answer to question 7: "Do people think the Jews are doing their share in the war effort?" Whereas only 53.1 percent of whites condemned the Nazi genocide, 65.9 percent of blacks did so; 17.9 percent of whites supported Nazi race policies, but only 9.7 percent of blacks. Almost two-thirds of the black interviewees were unconditionally against the Nazi genocide. Negative reactions were observed, however, when Jews as a persecuted group were strongly emphasized: "As a persecuted minority, Negroes are as sensitive to social discrimination as are Jews. . . . When working with Jews and hearing them talk emphatically about the persecution of Jews, Negroes easily resent the publicity given to persecution of Jews abroad while no attention is being paid to the persecution of Negroes at home."[29] On the whole, however, blacks expressed themselves with less animosity and did not hold a "mythical concept of 'the Jew.'"[30] A connection between the prejudices that whites held against blacks *and* Jews seldom appeared plausible to black interviewees. To them, there did not seem to be a connection. Because of the shared history of persecution, however, black workers often suggested that Jews should show more solidarity with African Americans and fight for equal rights for all. The *Labor Study* concluded, "Negroes in America are subject to discriminatory treatment at all times and on any occasion. . . . Negroes do not need substitute targets."[31]

According to the ISR researchers, antisemitism did not fulfill the specific function that it did, psychologically speaking, for a significant percentage of whites. In part this was linked to religious orientations among African Americans derived from the Old Testament. The picture of the patriarchal Jew, the representative of the people chosen by God, was well known to them. Influential was the idea that the blacks should be the next chosen people of God.[32] The next Messiah would not be Jewish, but black. That was the basis for their identification with the first chosen people of God.

Summary

As a marginal institution in exile, the ISR was perhaps able to develop and bring to a close precisely those projects that American research groups could not achieve. After Massing contacted an American union activist with regard to the antisemitism projects, he wrote to Horkheimer and Pollock in 1944, "When I told him about our project and our approach he got very excited and said: 'I have been telling that to my American friends for years and it takes you, a German, to do it!'"[33]

Despite this, the problems of the ISR researchers in their fieldwork were highly complex. The following reflection by Ruth Benedict may serve as a point of departure: "Americans can poll Americans and understand the findings, but they can do this because of a prior step which is so obvious that no one mentions it: they know and take for granted the conduct of life in the United States. The results of polling tell more about what we already know. In trying to understand another country, systematic qualitative study of the habits and assumptions of its people is essential before a poll can serve to good advantage."[34] With Benedict's idea in mind, one can return to the hypothesis of Lazarsfeld on innovation by persons on the margin, cited earlier. In his *Reflections on America* Offe developed this theme with regard to Tocqueville, Weber, and Ador-

no, showing that their descriptions of America always included European self-descriptions. This can also be said for the studies conducted in
exile by the ISR. In these studies the Marxist paradigm of critical theory
remained esoteric. The *Labor Study* was not only the blue-collar but also
the multicultural complement to *The Authoritarian Personality*. After the
Labor Study the Institute's hypothesis of the relevance of antisemitism
for the understanding of society irrevocably changed. The *Labor Study*
forms the missing link between *Dialectic of Enlightenment* and *The Authoritarian Personality*. Without this missing link, the differences between
these two works cannot be understood. According to the ISR, after World
War II antisemitism could no longer be regarded as the key to a theory of
society because its social function had changed. In the following quote,
the Marxism that used to be esoteric becomes exoteric for once:

> Our hypothesis of what causes anti-semitism is the following: It is
> due to the total structure of our society or, to put it more sweeping-
> ly, to every basically coercive society. This totality manifests itself
> in numerous aspects, all of which are comprised in it and appear as
> particular "causes" only to the kind of thinking which, naively fol-
> lowing the pattern of natural sciences, forgets that all social facts
> bear the imprint of the system in which they appear and which can
> never be explained satisfactorily by atomistic enumeration of vari-
> ous causes.[35]

Notes

1. Lazarsfeld, "An Episode in the History of Social Research," 302.
2. Fleming, "Émigré Physicists and the Biological Revolution."
3. Horkheimer and Adorno, *Dialektik der Aufklärung/ Dialectic of Enlightenment*;
   Adorno et al., *The Authoritarian Personality*.
4. A full table of contents is transcribed in Ziege, *Antisemitismus und Gesellschaftstheorie*, 323–37. On *Antisemitism among American Labor*, see Ziege,
   Antisemitismus und Gesellschaftstheorie, 7–18, 180–228; Ziege, *Patterns within
   Prejudice*; Jay, *The Dialectical Imagination*, 224–66; Bonß, *Die Einübung des
   Tatsachenblicks*, 208–11; Wiggershaus, *Die Frankfurter Schule*, 409–12; Worrell, *Dialectic of Solidarity*; Walter-Busch, *Geschichte der Frankfurter Schule*,
   126.
5. Dinnerstein, *Antisemitism in America*; Diner, *The Jews of the United States*.
6. Institute of Social Research, *Antisemitism among American Labor*, 1157.

7. Henryk Grossman, letter to Horkheimer, April 30, 1943, in Horkheimer, *Gesammelte Schriften*, 443. Unless otherwise noted, all translations are mine.

8. Horkheimer, letter to Adorno, January 21, 1945, in Adorno and Horkheimer, *Briefwechsel*, 3:32.

9. Arad, *America, Its Jews and the Rise of Nazism*, 77.

10. Glazer, "The Social Scientists Dissect Prejudice," 79.

11. Horkheimer and Flowerman, "Foreword to Studies in Prejudice," vii.

12. Horkheimer, "Die Juden und Europa," 115.

13. Benedict, *Patterns of Culture*.

14. Horkheimer, letter to Adorno, November 13, 1944, in Adorno and Horkheimer, *Briefwechsel*, 2:351.

15. Massing in Institute of Social Research, *Antisemitism among American Labor*, 699.

16. Löwenthal and Guterman, *Prophets of Deceit*.

17. Parsons, "Sociology of Modern Anti-Semitism," 119.

18. Horkheimer, "Die Juden und Europa," 115.

19. Luhmann, *Die Gesellschaft der Gesellschaft*, 1057.

20. Adorno, letter to his parents, January 1944, in Adorno, *Briefe an die Eltern*, 238, 242.

21. Horkheimer-Pollock-Archive of the City of Frankfurt, Germany, VI 17, LL 1/4-7/44.

22. Adorno et al., *The Authoritarian Personality*, 638.

23. Institute of Social Research, *Antisemitism among American Labor*, 1259, 86, 75, 76, 77, 633, 832, 645.

24. Institute of Social Research, *Antisemitism among American Labor*, 712.

25. Institute of Social Research, *Antisemitism among American Labor*, 715, 716, · 782, 805, 783.

26. Institute of Social Research, *Antisemitism among American Labor*, 780.

27. See Horkheimer and Adorno, *Dialektik der Aufklärung*, 200.

28. See Adorno et al., *The Authoritarian Personality*, 631, 780.

29. Institute of Social Research, *Antisemitism among American Labor*, 519, 1259, 521, 539. "'I didn't feel very sorry about them because I thought about what happens to Negroes in the South every day and the lynching and horrible things that have happened there—and nobody is interested'" (540).

30. Institute of Social Research, *Antisemitism among American Labor*, 530, 1135. "A young drugstore attendant, URWDSEA [United Retail, Wholesale, and Department Store Employees of America], in Harlem indignantly states: 'I lived in Harlem all my life, and Harlem is run by Irish cops and Jewish pawnbrokers. Don't ask me how I like them because then I become very insulting. One Jew cost my father his job because he complained to his boss that Dad could not pay his rent. So he was fired'" (523).

31. Institute of Social Research, *Antisemitism among American Labor*, 542.

32. "'This preacher believes that the second coming of Christ will occur as a physical rebirth and that the Messiah will be born to a Negro. . . . This belief is

widespread among the Negroes out at the Rouge [Ford Rouge Plant] and . . . it has affected their attitude toward the Jews. Those who believe in this doctrine are friendly to the Jews for the most part and show a marked tendency to identify themselves with Jews'" (Institute of Social Research, *Antisemitism among American Labor*, 544).

33. Massing, "Memorandum to Horkheimer and Pollock."
34. Benedict, *The Chrysanthemum and the Sword*, 18.
35. Adorno, "Remarks on 'The Authoritarian Personality,'" 81.

References

Adorno, Theodor W. *Briefe an die Eltern*. Frankfurt am Main: Suhrkamp, 2003.

——. "Remarks on 'The Authoritarian Personality' by Adorno, Frenkel-Brunswik, Levinson, Sanford (1948)." Horkheimer-Pollock-Archive of the City of Frankfurt, Germany, VI 1 D. 71–100, 81.

Adorno, Th. W., Else Frenkel-Brunswik, Daniel J. Levinson, and R. Nevitt Sanford, in collaboration with Betty Aron, Maria Hertz Levinson, and William Morrow. *The Authoritarian Personality*. Social Studies Series III. New York: Harper & Brothers, 1950.

Adorno, Th. W., and Max Horkheimer. *Briefwechsel*. Vol. 2: *1938-1944*. Frankfurt am Main: Suhrkamp, 2004.

Adorno, Th. W., and Max Horkheimer. *Briefwechsel*. Vol. 3: *1945-1949*. Frankfurt am Main: Suhrkamp, 2005.

Arad, Gulie Ne'eman. *America, Its Jews and the Rise of Nazism*. Bloomington: Indiana University Press, 2000.

Benedict, Ruth. *The Chrysanthemum and the Sword: Patterns of Japanese Culture*. Rutland VT: Tuttle, 1946.

——. *Patterns of Culture*. Boston: Mentor Books, 1934.

Bonß, Wolfgang. *Die Einübung des Tatsachenblicks: Zur Struktur und Veränderung empirischer Sozialforschung*. Frankfurt am Main: Suhrkamp, 1982.

Diner, Hasia R. *The Jews of the United States 1654 to 2000*. Berkeley: University of California Press, 2004.

Dinnerstein, Leonard. *Antisemitism in America*. New York: Oxford University Press, 1994.

Fleming, Donald. "Émigré Physicists and the Biological Revolution." In *The Intellectual Migration: Europe and America, 1930-1960*, edited by Donald Fleming and Bernard Bailyn, 152–89. Cambridge MA: Belknap Press of Harvard University Press, 1969.

Glazer, Nathan. "The Social Scientists Dissect Prejudice: An Appraisal of Recent Studies." *Commentary* 1 (May 1946): 79–85.

Graeber, Isacque, and Steuart Henderson Britt, eds. *Jews in a Gentile World: The Problem of Anti-Semitism*. New York: Macmillan, 1942.

Hartley, Eugene L. *Problems in Prejudice*. 1946. New York: Octagon Books, 1969.

Horkheimer, Max. "Die Juden und Europa." *Zeitschrift für Sozialforschung/Studies in Philosophy and Social Science* 8.1–2 (1939): 115–37.

———. *Gesammelte Schriften*. Vol. 17: *Briefwechsel 1941–1948*. Frankfurt am Main: Fischer, 1996.

Horkheimer, Max, and Theodor W. Adorno. *Dialectic of Enlightenment*. Stanford CA: Stanford University Press, 2002.

Horkheimer, Max, and Theodor W. Adorno. *Dialektik der Aufklärung*. Amsterdam: Querido, 1947.

Horkheimer, Max, and Samuel Flowerman. "Foreword to Studies in Prejudice." In Th. W. Adorno, Else Frenkel-Brunswik, Daniel J. Levinson, and R. Nevitt Sanford, in collaboration with Betty Aron, Maria Hertz Levinson, and William Morrow, *The Authoritarian Personality*, v–viii. Social Studies Series III. New York: Harper & Brothers, 1950.

Institute of Social Research. *Antisemitism among American Labor: Report on a Research Project Conducted by the Institute of Social Research (Columbia University) in 1944–1945*. May 1945. 4 mimeographed vols. Horkheimer-Pollock-Archive of the City of Frankfurt, Germany, MHA IX 146, 1–23.

Jay, Martin. *The Dialectical Imagination: A History of the Frankfurt School and the Institute of Social Research, 1923–1950*. 1973. Berkeley: University of California Press, 1993.

Lazarsfeld, Paul F. "An Episode in the History of Social Research: A Memoir." In *The Intellectual Migration: Europe and America, 1930–1960*, edited by Donald Fleming and Bernard Bailyn, 270–337. Cambridge MA: Belknap Press of Harvard University Press, 1969.

Lazarsfeld, Paul F., Bernard Berelson, and Hazel Gaudet. *The People's Choice: How the Voter Makes Up His Mind in a Presidential Campaign*. New York: Dnell, Sloan, and Pearce, 1944.

Löwenthal, Leo, and Norbert Guterman. *Prophets of Deceit: A Study of the Techniques of the American Agitator*. New York: Harper & Brothers, 1949.

Luhmann, Niklas. *Die Gesellschaft der Gesellschaft*. Frankfurt am Main: Suhrkamp, 1999.

Massing, Paul. "Memorandum to Horkheimer and Pollock." June 23, 1944. Horkheimer-Pollock-Archive of the City of Frankfurt, Germany, VI 17, 47.

———. *Rehearsal for Destruction: A Study of Political Anti-Semitism in Imperial Germany*. New York: Harper & Brothers, 1949.

McWilliams, Carey. *A Mask for Privilege: Anti-Semitism in America*. Boston: Little, Brown, 1948.

Myrdal, Gunnar, with Richard Sterner and Arnold Rose. *An American Dilemma: The Negro Problem and Modern Democracy*. New York: Harper & Row, 1944.

Offe, Claus. *Reflections on America: Tocqueville, Weber and Adorno in the United States*. Cambridge: Cambridge University Press, 2005.

Parsons, Talcott. "Sociology of Modern Anti-Semitism." In *Jews in a Gentile World: The Problem of Anti-Semitism*, edited by Isaacque Graeber and Steuart Henderson Britt, 101–22. New York: Macmillan, 1942.

Pinson, Koppel S., ed. *Essays on Antisemitism.* Jewish Social Studies Publications 2. 2d enlarged edition. New York: Conference on Jewish Relations, 1946.

Simmel, Ernst, ed. *Anti-Semitism: A Social Disease.* New York: International Universities Press, 1946.

Trachtenberg, Joshua. *The Devil and the Jews: The Medieval Conception of the Jew and Its Relation to Modern Antisemitism.* New Haven CT: Yale University Press, 1943.

Walter-Busch, Emil. *Geschichte der Frankfurter Schule: Kritische Theorie und Politik.* Munich: Wilhelm Fink, 2010.

Wiggershaus, Rolf. *Die Frankfurter Schule: Geschichte—Theoretische Entwicklung—Politische Bedeutung.* 1988. Munich: dtv, 2008.

Worrell, Mark P. *Dialectic of Solidarity: Labor, Antisemitism, and the Frankfurt School.* Chicago: Haymarket Books, 2009.

Ziege, Eva-Maria. *Antisemitismus und Gesellschaftstheorie: Die Frankfurter Schule im amerikanischen Exil.* Frankfurt am Main: Suhrkamp, 2009.

———. "Patterns within Prejudice: Antisemitism in the United States in the 1940s." *Patterns of Prejudice* 46.2 (2012): 93–127.

11

Gino Germani, Argentine Sociology, and the Study of Antisemitism

DANIEL LVOVICH

Translation by Lars Stubbe and Maria Valeria Galvan

Gino Germani is unanimously considered to be the founding father of modern Argentine sociology, even though the origins of the discipline in that country can be traced back to the beginning of the twentieth century. The objective of this chapter is to reflect upon the ways Germani approached the study of antisemitism in Argentina, describing the results and the theoretical and methodological assumptions and putting them into the overall context of his work. The first two sections outline Germani's background and general development; the third section describes his theoretical and empirical work on antisemitism, which was largely inspired by some of the work on the subject by the Frankfurt School in the United States (especially the series *Studies in Prejudice*); and the fourth section points to some issues that have been relevant to the reception of Germani's work.

Germani's Background and General Development

Germani was born in Rome in 1911 as the only child of a working-class couple. His father was a tailor sympathizing with socialism, while his mother was a fervent Catholic from a peasant family. Germani studied accountancy at a technical school and was meant to study economics at the University of Rome. In 1930 he was caught distributing antifascist propaganda and was incarcerated for more than a year on the island of Ponza. After his father died in 1931, he and his mother decided to emigrate to Argentina, where some close relatives were already living, but they were not to arrive in Buenos Aires until 1934.[1] After spending some time at the School of Economics at the University of Buenos Aires, he changed schools in 1938 and graduated with a degree in philosophy. Soon after that Germani started collaborating with the Instituto de Sociología of the University of Buenos Aires (UBA), while at the same time earning his living as an employee at the Office of Agriculture. Since his arrival in Argentina, Germani had established a close working relationship with exiled Italian antifascist groups.[2]

After the coup of 1943 and the subsequent election of General Juan Perón as president, the government took over control of the national universities, and many members of the faculty either resigned or were removed from their posts. In 1947 Germani himself was expelled from the UBA. Until the fall of the Peronist government, he taught social psychology and sociology at the Colegio Libre de Estudios Superiores, which had become a refuge for many liberal and socialist intellectuals who opposed Perón. He also worked as an editor and translator of the main sociological works of that time.

After the coup of 1955 that ousted Perón, Germani became director of both the newly created School of Sociology and the Institute for Sociological Research at UBA. Through these posts he became a key figure in the process of cultural and academic modernization that took place in Argentina between 1955 and 1966.[3] His daughter Ana sums up his work during this period in these words:

> Germani's theoretical and empirical contributions were particularly productive between 1955 and 1966. His texts were of paramount importance for opening up a set of intellectual spaces that until then had remained unexplored. His works on the social structure and the system of stratification initiated the tradition of social research in Argentina. . . . He took care of the whole labor of promotion, direction and supervision of the research. The social, economic, political, cultural and psychological dimensions of modernization: social mobility, changes in the social structure and in the system of stratification, the impact of a massive immigration, processes of urbanization and marginalization, political participation, the integration of the masses, possible explanations of the "Argentine paradox," the emergence and the failure of the nationalist-populist movements, constituted some of the issues that he developed in the new institutional field.[4]

Beginning in the early 1960s Germani regularly traveled to the United States to teach at Harvard University, and in 1966, shortly before the coup of Onganía, which toppled President Arturo Illia, he accepted a chair at that institution. He eventually moved to Rome in 1976 but kept his chair at Harvard. Shortly afterward he was offered a chair at the University of Naples; he died in Rome in 1979.[5]

Sociology and Social Research inside and outside the University

There is a long-standing tradition of sociological research in Argentina and Latin America. In 1877 the Institute for Social Sciences was founded in Caracas, Venezuela, and in 1892 one of the first sociology courses worldwide was established at the University of Bogotá.

Sociology courses became established in Buenos Aires in 1898, and in 1907 at the University of Córdoba. By the 1920s sociology as a discipline had become established in nearly all Latin American countries; in Argentina it was taught at the universities of Buenos Aires, Córdoba, Tucumán, La Plata, and the Littoral. However, sociology as an academic discipline was akin to social philosophy rather than to scientific research. Empirical social research in Argentina had not originated in the universities but was carried out by state authorities as part of a plan of the political elites to administer the social question and the public policies of social reform.[6]

Beginning in the 1940s the tradition of academic sociology in Argentina became strongly institutionalized. In 1940 the first Instituto de Sociología was created at the Faculty of Philosophy at the University of Buenos Aires. Two years later its first bulletin was published. In 1943 the National University of Tucumán underwent a similar process of institutionalization through the creation of the Institute of Economical and Sociological Research, headed by the Italian exile Renato Treves.[7] As head of the Institute of Sociology of the UBA, Ricardo Levene started an important network with different institutes of sociology based in the United States, Mexico, and Brazil. As Alejandro Blanco has shown, this institution was concerned with developing empirical social research following the supposedly paradigmatic American experience. In fact Germani's first research projects were developed within this institutional context. In spite of sociology's relatively secure institutionalization as an academic discipline, it lacked a defined theoretical orientation and had as yet neither obtained a clear object nor boundaries that would separate it from history or philosophy.[8]

Following the military coup of 1943 and the subsequent presidential elections, which returned General Perón to power, the majority of the most renowned intellectuals, most of whom were liberals or left-wingers, were expelled from the national universities, and sociology was taught by supporters of Catholic nationalism. Even if their theoretical and empirical contributions were relatively modest, they developed intense organizational activities and liaised with the most important international organizations of their discipline.[9] In spite of this background, Argentine sociology did not become fully institutionalized until 1957, when the Department of Sociology was founded at the UBA and the first degree course in sociology was created. From this moment onward the links between teaching sociology and doing social research were intensified. In this process Germani played a fundamental role.

During the period when Germani was banned from the national universities, his contribution to the social sciences in Argentina stemmed from other areas, such as editorial work and the Colegio Libre de Estudios Superiores. Starting in 1944 he developed an intense activity as director of the series Ciencia y Sociedad, published by Abril, and the Biblioteca de Psicología y Sociología, published by Paidós, over a period of twenty-five years. During this time he also worked as a translator and wrote preliminary studies and introductions to many foreign works. Among these were *U.S. Foreign Policy: Shield of the Republic* by Walter Lippmann, *Liberty in the Modern State* and *The Danger of Being a Gentleman and Other Essays* by Harold Laski, *Escape from Freedom* by Erich Fromm, *Studies in Primitive Psychology: The Oedipus Complex* by Bronislaw Malinowski,[10] *Sigmund Freud: An Introduction* by Walter Hollischer, *The Feminine Character* by Viola Klein, and *Mind, Self and Society from the Standpoint of a Social Behaviorist* by George Mead. He also was responsible for the publications in Spanish of *The Neurotic Personality of Our Time* by Karen Horney, *Anti-Semitism and Emotional Disorder: A Psychoanalytic Interpretation* by Nathan Ackerman and Marie Jahoda, *Character and Social Structure: The Psychology of Social Institutions* by Hans Gerth and C. Wright Mills, *The Lonely Crowd* by David Riesman, and *The Democratic and the Authoritarian State* by Franz Neumann. This list of publications reveals that Germani maintained a dialogue with diverse intellectual traditions, such as culturalism, symbolic interactionism, the Frankfurt School, psychoanalysis, anthropology, political theory, as well as the work of Talcott Parsons and structural functionalism, all of which must be seen as sources of inspiration of the Italian Argentine sociologist.[11]

As Blanco states, the work of Germani as an editor reveals a strong concern for the imbalance between the progress of technical knowledge and the prevalence of irrationality in social and moral life. This question, which echoes Karl Mannheim's concerns described in *Diagnosis of Our Time* (1943), turn up in Germani's works of the 1940s and the 1950s. Additional areas of concern for Germani were modernization processes, the relation between social change and personality, totalitarianism and authoritarianism, and democratic planning. Germani's editorial work, adds Blanco, must be considered as a strategy designed to introduce the question of the relationship between mass society and totalitarianism and the future of democracy into sociological thinking in Argentina. The aim of this was to widen the theoretical and conceptual horizons of sociology in order to put it into the broader context of the social sciences.[12] On the other hand, for those intellectuals banned from the universities under Peronism, the publishing industry was a means of expression for their intellectual concerns, as well as a space of sociability, "an alternative intellectual community opposed to official culture, through which new internal solidarity networks were built to be extended later to other intellectual fields, such as the Colegio Libre de Estudios Superiores."[13] In this institution Germani taught sociology. He first taught in Buenos Aires and, when the course was prohibited by the government in 1952, in Rosario. In these courses Germani outlined some of the topics that would be central to his later work: the transition from traditional society to mass society and the maladjustments derived from it, the contrast between individuation processes and self-determination, and the rise of "propaganda, the forms of entertainment and mass consumption . . . that show a growing standardization of the individuals, a tendency opposed to what might be expected from the process of external liberation of the individual."[14]

The problems of mass society are obviously linked to the question of authoritarianism. This was very important for Germani for theoretical reasons, as well as because of his own personal experience under the fascist regime in Italy and under the Peronist regime, puzzled as he was, like so many Argentine intellectuals, by the workers' massive electoral support for Perón during the presidential elections of 1946. Thus in his

1947 prologue for *El miedo a la libertad* (*Escape from Freedom*) he brought up the question of adjustment to structural changes, pointing out that "one of the most important characteristics of the contemporary scene has been the irrationality of such adjustments."[15]

Authoritarianism, Totalitarianism, Antisemitism

As his daughter Ana recalls, the question of antisemitism in Argentina was a constant preoccupation for Germani. In his personal archives there is "an impressive collection of materials related to different aspects of this phenomenon, in particular newspaper cuttings on antisemitic attacks and ideological pamphlets of the Frente Nacional Socialista Argentino and other extremist groups."[16] Such concern was consistent with Germani's antifascism, and it was probably encouraged by the imposition of the racial laws of 1938 in Italy, which, among other things, led a considerable number of Jewish Italian emigrants to look for exile in Argentina. Among these were the renowned intellectuals Renato Treves and Rodolfo Mondolfo.

The Argentine liberal and socialist intellectuals of the 1930s and 1940s, a period in which anti-Jewish prejudice spread widely within Catholic and nationalist ranks, had regularly voiced their concern over and organized public interventions against antisemitism.[17] However, Germani was to be the first intellectual to address the problem of antisemitism as a research subject of the social sciences.

As stated earlier, in 1954 Germani translated and edited for Paidós the Spanish version of *Anti-Semitism and Emotional Disorder: A Psychoanalytic Interpretation* by Nathan Ackerman and Marie Jahoda, with a preface by Max Horkheimer and Samuel Flowerman (in Spanish, *Psicoanálisis del antisemitismo*). This was one of the volumes of the series Studies in Prejudice, directed by Horkheimer and Flowerman and sponsored by the American Jewish Committee. It was also the most strictly psychoanalytical of the five volumes of Studies in Prejudice.[18] Germani had been interested in the Frankfurt School since the 1940s, as demonstrated by the recurring references in many of his works to *The Authoritarian Personality* by Theodor Adorno, Else Frenkel-Brunswik, Daniel Levinson, and R. Nevitt Sanford. Blanco observed that Germani's affinity with the research work of the Institute of Social Research resided as much in its methodological as in its conceptual aspects. On the one hand this involved developing an approach to the social sciences based on an intensive exchange with psychoanalysis, while on the other hand taking up the questions resulting from the emergence of mass society, the breakdown of the democratic system, and totalitarianism.[19] Once Germani directed the Instituto de Sociología, his search for analytical instruments bringing together both social and psychological aspects adequate to the study of prejudice therefore led him to publish the edited volume *Psicología social del prejuicio* (1960; The social psychology of prejudice) by Eliseo Verón. The volume included "La personalidad autoritaria" (The authoritarian personality) by Else Frenkel-Brunswik, Daniel Levinson and R. Nevitt Sanford; "Las causas del antisemitismo: Una investigación de siete hipótesis" (The causation of antisemitism: An investigation of seven hypotheses) by N. C. Morse and F. Allport, and "Problemas psicosociológicos de un grupo minoritario" (Psycho-sociological problems of a minority group) by Kurt Lewin.[20] The aim of this volume was to contribute to the systematization of "the existing materials on racial prejudice and ethnocentrism, from both a methodological and a theoretical perspective," in the search for a theory of prejudice that would allow understanding of "how variables relating to the different levels of analysis are interrelated and integrated into the dynamic of prejudicial behaviour."[21]

Germani's most important initiative in the study of antisemitism was developed in the context of an extraordinary drive of empirical social research developed by the Instituto de Sociología of the UBA. Since 1957 he had headed the research project "Etnocentrismo y actitudes autoritarias" (Ethnocentrism and authoritarian attitudes) that crystallized in 1961 in a broad research project on antisemitism in Argentina. The results of this research were published in 1963.

Germani's research project suggested the existence of two levels of antisemitism: an antisemitism embraced by the "general public," which consisted of "certain adverse verbally expressed stereotypes," and a political antisemitism expressed through movements "similar to the European totalitarian right-wing movements," known in Argentina as *nacionalistas*. Despite their minor influence on national elections (less than 5 percent of the vote in Buenos Aires), these groups were formed by upper- and middle-class individuals and had "particularly tight relations" with the Catholic Church and the armed forces. They were able to expand the influence they might have been able to exert on account of these connections due to two characteristics of the Argentine working classes ascertained by Germani: the adherence to a form of popular nationalism as a "vague feeling capable of eliciting contradictory political expressions" and "certain psychosocial elements liable to promote authoritarian political attitudes."[22]

The first of these characteristics was linked to the analysis of Peronism, considered by Germani to be a form of totalitarianism, albeit with significant differences from its European versions. Their respective social bases constituted a key difference: while the social base of the Peronist party was made up of lower social classes, with the industrial workers forming its most dynamic core, totalitarianism in Europe found its followers, said Germani, among the middle classes. Further contrasts derived from this difference: "Although the political and social background of the leader and a large part of the ruling elite could be considered as being right-wing totalitarian similar to the European form, the official Peronist ideology was egalitarian, stressing not only a 'social justice' reasoning but also calling for 'free elections,' participation of the masses in government, nomination of union leaders by shop-floor activists, etc."[23]

Since the coup in 1930, only governments based on fraud or on the exclusion of the Union Cívica Radical from the elections succeeded one another. As the Peronist party assured the country, it would formally organize free elections for the first time in fifteen years, and Perón was able to rely on the traditional confidence the lower classes had in universal suffrage as a solution to national problems. This led the working classes to perceive Peronism not as a dictatorship but as the first form of democracy that gave them some kind of participation:

> The "objective" reality was different, but what is of interest here is the subjective experience, the "psychological" reality as experienced by men and women belonging to this class. Therefore, although many of the psychological elements that characterized European totalitarianism are present in Peronism, it must not be forgotten that there was also the subjective experience of self-determination and democratic participation that was probably absent in the European movements.... Peronist ideology became inoculated with elements traditionally belonging to socialist movements (and also to a specific stage of European totalitarianism) not only with regard to

the labour unions, but also with regard to the limitation of property rights, the nationalization of industries and economic planning.[24]

In a famous work published in 1956 entitled *The Integration of the Masses into Political Life and Totalitarianism*, Germani stressed that the massive internal migration caused by the process of rapid industrialization begun in the 1930s brought the rural masses, lacking trade unionist or political experience, into Buenos Aires, where they became a loose mass susceptible to manipulation, through a form of *ersatz*[25] participation.

In his analysis, Germani stated that, despite its alliance with strongly antisemitic nationalist sectors, "Peronism does not appear to have been antisemitic." This could be due to strategic considerations arising from the outcome of World War II, "but we should also ask whether the absence of racism in the Peronist ideology was a result of the specific egalitarian ideology of its peculiar human base."[26] At the time this assertion, as well as the differentiation between Peronism and fascism, strongly contrasted with widely held views within the Argentine liberal progressive circles of that period.

The second issue, the authoritarian psychosocial characteristics, referred to Germani's modernization theory. The transition from traditional to industrial or developed societies generates, among other changes, personality changes, as it means a move from forms dominated by the internalization of prescriptive rules to other types with a predominantly "elective structure with universal, specific and emotionally neutral roles." The coexistence of divided social structures affected differently by the process of change can lead to a series of situations that depend, among other things, on the kind of reaction that occurs in the "underdeveloped" groups and on the forms of adjustment they generate.[27] Based on the ideas and empirical work of Seymour Martin Lipset and Juan Linz, Germani argued that the lower classes of a country, or certain subgroups, "are both more prone to supporting authoritarian movements (from left or right) the later their political integration and the more traumatic the transition experience from pre-industrial to industrial society and the process of 'fundamental democratization.'"[28]

On the other hand, the same process explains the social foundation of what Germani called "political antisemitism" in 1957. When recently developed countries enter the stage of *fundamental democratization*, ideological traditionalism, which mainly expresses the position of groups that belong to the elite linked to the traditional structure of preindustrial society, is one of the transition phenomena that may emerge. Although these groups do not reject changes in the economic structure but rather accept or even promote them, they reject the extension of these changes to other areas, such as the family, political institutions, or social stratification. In Germani's view, the traditional or ideological character of a specific mode of thinking lies less in its content than in how it is rooted within a group. Thus its character will follow from its relationship with *elective* or *prescriptive* frameworks of action. So "if the traditional content is the result of an ideological commitment, it must be called 'ideological traditionalism,' a phenomenon completely different from traditional life as the only possible reality where dissent neither exists nor is perceived."[29]

The antisemitic attitude is one of the examples of ideological traditionalism found by Germani, for which an inverse correlation in relation to the economic, social, and educational field could be shown to exist in various countries. However, this perspective is insufficient to give an account of the phenomenon, since "the psychological research of Adorno and reflections of other observers, such as Sartre, have tended to prove the existence of an 'authoritarian syndrome,' which also finds expression in antisemitism and constitutes a manifestation of neurotic tendencies." He goes on to hypothesize the existence of two types of antisemitism: "The first one [is] of a 'traditional' character and devoid of special psychological significance (this kind of antisemitism would diminish with increased education and greater participation in the 'modern' culture through social advancement), whereas the second [is] of an ideological type characterized by the psychological elements described by Fromm, Adorno and others."[30]

In certain situations *traditional* antisemitism may be *ideologically* exploited. Germani warns of the potential ideological use of traditionalism as an instrument by the elites given its "highly variegated possibilities for *manipulating* the popular masses recently incorporated into industrial society. These new workers are bearers of traditional attitudes and, above all, continue to act within the normative framework in line with this kind of society."[31]

The 1957 project aimed at establishing a typology applicable to the Argentine population, taking into account the linkages and possible distinctions between what he called "authoritarianism (and ethnocentrism) as a 'cultural trait' and as an 'ideology.'"[32] In order to accomplish this, he based the project on *Dynamics of Prejudice* by Bettelheim and Janowitz, particularly with regard to the need for covering the cognitive, affective, and conative attitudes observed, and to pay attention to the degree of organization of such an attitude within the individual, thereby distinguishing between "a) organization as a result of individual, conscious thinking; b) as an unconscious result of some underlying personality structure, c) as a reflection of existing patterns in the cultural milieu."[33]

A modified version of the F Scale, developed by Adorno and his research group in *The Authoritarian Personality*, adapted to the Argentine case, and a brief questionnaire were applied in order to analyze the distribution of authoritarian and ethnocentric attitudes.

Given the differences between the contributions of Bettelheim and Janowitz on the one hand and those of Adorno and his group on the other, merging their approaches brought forth something sui generis. While the former believed that intolerance prevailed among those who resisted society and rejected its values, the researchers in California established a relationship between prejudice and the individual's conformity to society.[34]

The project envisaged the realization of a survey including between 1,000 and 1,500 cases. A first implementation of a test version of the F Scale, using the shortened version applied by Mackinnon and Centers to investigate the spread of authoritarian tendencies in different social urban classes in a community in Los Angeles, was part of it.[35] The questionnaire also contained a question about selection of immigrants of different ethnic backgrounds and nationalities (eleven were included) and data on sex, age, nationality, occupation, and education and a self-assessment on the interviewee's own social class affiliation. The questionnaire was handed out to three groups of students belonging to either the Faculty of Arts, the Faculty of Law, or an industrial school. The sample covered a total of 124 individuals.

The results of the test established a very strong correlation between authoritarianism and the tendency to exclude migrant groups. Among these, the Jews and Russians belonged to the groups excluded most strongly.[36] Students from the industrial school (working-class members of around sixteen years of age) showed a higher degree of authoritarianism and ethnocentrism than the university students surveyed, which was consistent with Germani's theoretical perspective.

Given this confirmation, the methodological conclusion indicated that the F Scale (short version) was highly predictive of ethnocentric tendencies and, following some necessary adaptations, might prove to be a starting point for studying the authoritarian tendencies of Argentina's urban population.[37]

The main research was conducted in 1961 and sponsored by the American Jewish Committee. Following the capture of Adolf Eichmann in Buenos Aires and his subsequent trial in Jerusalem, a broad wave of antisemitic actions carried out by extreme right-wing organizations was unleashed in Argentina. However, the survey was conducted before this wave reached its highest intensity, which led Germani to state that the results reflected the "normal level" of antisemitism.[38]

The survey was conducted on a random sample of 2,078 adults, mostly male, in the area of Buenos Aires. It included questions on antisemitism and other forms of ethnocentrism. Other questions were included to gather data on occupations, social class, and mobility. Based on a list of national, ethnic, and occupational groups, the interviewees were asked to single out both the most harmful and most beneficial groups in order to establish the degree of ethnocentric attitudes and were asked their opinions on the policies (to attract, keep out, exclude, or proceed according to individual cases) most suitable for treating citizens belonging to one of ten different given nations. The survey included several tests of authoritarianism: the abridged version of the F Scale, which measures some features of the authoritarian character; a measure of political authoritarianism (determining the preference for pluralism or a one-party regime); and a projective test to observe attitudes toward authority.

The result showed 22.1 percent of antisemitic answers, which located Buenos Aires below New York and Chicago, according to studies carried out in the 1950s in those cities. The survey showed that the most widespread hostility in the population of Buenos Aires was directed against economic, political, and religious groups: landowners were deemed harmful by 44.8 percent of the sample, the military by 38.4 percent, politicians by 30.2 percent, and priests by 23.5 percent. However, the Jews generated the greatest proportion of rejection from among ethnic or national groups.[39]

Once again Germani proved through his research that the propensity to antisemitism was greater in social groups with a lower economic and educational status. Thus the group "of the unskilled workers, which lack or have undergone formal schooling for at most one or two years, and which live relatively isolated from modern urban life is also the group showing the largest proportion of antisemitism; in groups having occupations or roles of greater prestige or importance that ratio tends to be lower."[40]

Germani's hypothesis, consistent with his overall theoretical perspective, was that the results reflected two types of antisemitism: the *traditional*, consisting of the passive acceptance of widespread stereotypes about Jews, and the *ideological*, which acquires a much more precise and elaborate form. While the former does not necessarily correspond to a specific type of personality, the second is the result of the "authoritarian syndrome." While interviewees belonging to lower social strata gave answers that could be categorized as "traditionalist," those belonging to the middle and upper classes expressed forms of hostility toward Jews that characterized them as "ideological" antisemites. At the same time, there is an issue of class in the relation between authoritarianism and antisemitism. While no difference could be found with respect to authoritarianism between antisemites and non-antisemites of lower social strata, a marked difference is found in members of the middle and upper classes. There is a high degree of authoritarianism in the lower social classes (63.8 percent, according to the F Scale) as a result of the persistence of traditional attitudes. In the middle and upper classes, authoritarianism is lower (52.5 and 36.2 percent, respectively), but within the group of antisemites it is much higher than in the average of those social groups (71.3 and 71.4 percent, respectively).

After Germani

As in many other areas of sociological studies, the research on antisemitism led by Germani was pioneering. However, although his work became a standard reference, new studies that were to question his research assumptions and his theoretical findings soon developed. Thus the research developed in 1967 by the Center for Social Studies of the Delegation of Argentine Jewish Associations, headed by Joaquín Fischerman, strongly questioned the categories of traditional and ideological antisemitism on the assumption that it was unjustified to attribute rationality to the second, while at the same time considering every form of antisemitism a form of ethnocentrism. The average percentage of antisemitism in the sample (one thousand cases in Buenos Aires) was higher in this research than in Germani's. For Fischerman this was explained by an increase in the activity of extreme right-wing groups in the period between the two works—but contrary to the findings of 1961, the investigation of 1967 concluded that "the likelihood of finding antisemitic subjects increases the higher one rises in the socio-economic level, regardless of the degree of ethnocentrism."[41]

Although I do not intend to assess the relative merits of either investigation, it may be asked whether the critique of the design of the F Scale as an instrument the findings of which were strongly colored by the political bias of their creators could not also be extended to the work of Germani.[42]

In other areas of social research, and in particular with regard to the link between the working classes and Peronism, the positions of Germani opened one of the most fruitful sociological and historiographical debates in Argentina. In this sense and as a more general questioning of modernization theory, different studies challenged the view of the working class as irrational and heteronomous, the notion of a lack of political and trade union experience and the classification of internal migrants as belonging to traditional societies, and the notion of manipulation of the masses by Perón—which was contradicted by the evident continuity of much of the pre-Peronist trade union leadership after 1946.[43]

While other contributions of Germani, such as on the centrality of the previous experience of workers and the consideration of the elements of subjectivity, found their continuity in works that were also inspired by other traditions, such as the British tradition of cultural studies,[44] the conclusions of this debate highlight the difficulty in sustaining the existence of an authoritarianism inherent in a structurally determined working class and require a reconsideration of some of the empirical elements that supported the work of the Italian Argentine sociologist.

In the field of studies on antisemitism, this necessarily requires a revision of some of the conclusions of Germani's contribution, which can be done only in the light of the criticism of modernization theory to which his theoretical conceptions were strongly linked. However, some of the contributions of Germani—particularly those that emphasize the links between ideology and tradition and between authoritarianism and antisemitism— inspire new research on prejudice and hostility against Jews up to this very day. Indeed even the most superficial overview of the sociological and historical literature on antisemitism in Argentina bears evidence of the perspectives opened up by Germani.

Notes

1. A. Germani, *Gino Germani*, 37–41.
2. Fanesi, *El exilio antifascista en la Argentina*, 61; Treves, *Sociologia e socialismo*, 96–101.
3. Terán, *Nuestros años sesenta*, 33.
4. A. Germani, *Gino Germani*, 192.
5. Of his numerous works, these are the most significant: *Estructura social de la Argentina* (Social structure of Argentina, 1955); *Política y sociedad en una época de transición* (Politics and society in a period of transition, 1967); and *Authoritarianism, Fascism and National Populism* (1978).
6. Blanco, *Razón y Modernidad*, 58.
7. Blanco, *Razón y Modernidad*, 52.
8. Blanco, *Razón y Modernidad*, 62.
9. Blanco, *Razón y Modernidad*, 65, 71.
10. This is a compilation in Spanish of three originally separate monographs: *Myth in Primitive Psychology, The Father in Primitive Psychology*, and *The Matriarchal Family and the Oedipus Complex*.
11. Blanco, *Razón y Modernidad*, 83–86.
12. Blanco, *Razón y Modernidad*, 115.
13. Blanco, *Razón y Modernidad*, 103, 104.
14. "Notes for a Course," quoted in A. Germani, *Gino Germani*, 111.
15. Erich Fromm, *El miedo a la libertad*, versión y presentación de la edición castellana por Gino Germani (Buenos Aires: Paidos, 1947), 17.
16. A. Germani, *Gino Germani*, 327.
17. Lvovich, *Nacionalismo y antisemitismo en Argentina*.
18. Jay, *La imaginación dialéctica*, 362–83. In 1965 Paidós published the translation of *Antisemitism* by James Parkes in its series Biblioteca del Hombre Contemporáneo. Though Germani was not the editor of this collection, it is likely that his advice influenced the decision to publish this text (communication with Alejandro Blanco, September 20, 2008).
19. Blanco, *Razón y Modernidad*, 138.
20. The following articles completed it: Milton Rokeach, "La rigidez mental generalizada como factor del etnocentrismo" (Generalized mental rigidity as a factor in ethnocentrism); J. Greenblum and L. Pearlin, "Movilidad vertical y prejuicio: Un análisis sociopsicológico" (Vertical mobility and prejudice: A sociopsychological analysis).
21. Verón, *Psicología social del prejuicio*, 215, 225.

22. Germani, "Etnocentrismo y actitudes autoritarias," 3.
23. Germani, "Etnocentrismo y actitudes autoritarias," 5.
24. Germani, "Etnocentrismo y actitudes autoritarias," 6.
25. [German in the original.—Translator.]
26. Germani, "Etnocentrismo y actitudes autoritarias," 6.
27. Germani, *Política y sociedad en una época de transición*, 79, 101.
28. Germani, *Política y sociedad en una época de transición*, 142. In 1960 Germani published Seymour Lipset's "El autoritarismo de la clase obrera y la democracia" (Democracy and working-class authoritarianism) and "Ideologías autoritarias de izquierda, derecha y centro" (Authoritarian ideologies, left, right and center) in the *Cuadernos del Boletín de Sociología* 24.
29. Germani, *Política y sociedad en una época de transición*, 115.
30. Germani, *Política y sociedad en una época de transición*, 115.
31. Germani, *Política y sociedad en una época de transición*, 115.
32. Germani, "Etnocentrismo y actitudes autoritarias," 9. ["Cultural trait" and "ideology" in English in the original.—Translator.]
33. [English in the original.—Translator.]
34. Jay, *La imaginación dialéctica*, 386.
35. Mackinnon and Centers, "Authoritarianism and Urban Stratification." The scale consisted of the following statements:

    1. Human nature does not change. There will always be struggles and conflicts.
    2. The most important thing a child must learn is to obey its parents.
    3. For most countries it would be better to have a strong ruler than so many laws and speeches.
    4. Most of those who failed to succeed in life do not really have the willpower.
    5. Women should not meddle in politics.
    6. No one should forgive an insult to one's honor.
    7. One can generally put trust in people.

36. As the Jewish population of Argentina is popularly referred to as "Russian" given that they are predominantly of Eastern European origin, it can be concluded that the strong tendency toward the exclusion of these two groups indicates the presence of antisemitic tendencies.
37. Germani, "Etnocentrismo y actitudes autoritarias," 19.
38. Germani, "Antisemitismo ideológico y antisemitismo tradicional," 180.
39. Germani, "Antisemitismo ideológico y antisemitismo tradicional," 183.
40. Germani, "Antisemitismo ideológico y antisemitismo tradicional," 186.
41. Fischerman, "Etnocentrismo y antisemitismo," 197.
42. Jay, *La imaginación dialéctica*, 396–401.
43. Murmis and Portantiero, *Estudio sobre los orígenes del peronismo*; Halperin Donghi, "Algunas observaciones sobre Germani"; Torre, *La vieja guardia sindical y Perón*; Torre, "Interpretando (una vez más) los orígenes del peronismo."

44. James, *Resistencia e integración*. [The term used here is "culturalismo Inglés," a Latin American term that refers to the tradition that includes E. P. Thompson, Raymond Williams, and others.—Editor.]

References

Blanco, Alejandro. *Razón y Modernidad: Gino Germani y la Sociología en la Argentina*. Buenos Aires: Siglo XXI, 2006.

Fanesi, Pietro Rinaldo. *El exilio antifascista en la Argentina*. Buenos Aires: Centro Editor de América Latina, 1994.

Fischerman, Joaquín. "Etnocentrismo y antisemitismo." 1967. In *La cuestión judía en la Argentina*, edited by Juan José Sebrelli, 191–204. Buenos Aires: Tiempo Contemporáneo, 1973.

Germani, Ana Alejandra. *Gino Germani: Del antifascismo a la sociología*. Buenos Aires: Taurus, 2004.

Germani, Gino. "Antisemitismo ideológico y antisemitismo tradicional." 1963. In *La cuestión judía en la Argentina*, edited by Juan José Sebrelli, 177–90. Buenos Aires: Tiempo Contemporáneo, 1973.

———. *Authoritarianism, Fascism and National Populism*. New Brunswick NJ: Transaction Books, 1978.

———. *Estructura social de la Argentina: Analisis Estadístico* (Social structure of Argentina). Buenos Aires: Raigal, 1955.

———. "Etnocentrismo y actitudes autoritarias." Proyecto 6. Texto del proyecto e informe de algunos ensayos con la escala F. Trabajos e investigaciones del Instituto de Sociología. Facultad de Filosofía y letras, University of Buenos Aires, Publicacion interna 1, 1957.

———. *Política y sociedad en una época de transición: De la sociedad tradicional a la sociedad de masas* (Politics and society in a period of transition). Buenos Aires: Paidós, 1967.

Halperin Donghi, Tulio. "Algunas observaciones sobre Germani, el surgimiento del peronismo y los migrantes internos." *Desarrollo Económico* 14.56 (1975): 765–81.

James, Daniel. *Resistencia e integración*. Buenos Aires: Sudamericana, 1990.

Jay, Martin. *La imaginación dialéctica: Una historia de la Escuela de Frankfurt*. Buenos Aires: Taurus, 1991.

Lipset, Seymour. "El autoritarismo de la clase obrera y la democracia" (Democracy and working-class authoritarianism). Translated by Gino Germani. *Cuadernos del Boletín de Sociología* 24 (1960): 345–70.

Lipset, Seymour. "Ideologías autoritarias de izquierda, derecha y centro" (Authoritarian ideologies, left, right and center). Translated by Gino Germani. *Cuadernos del Boletín de Sociología* 24 (1960): 410–40.

Lvovich, Daniel. *Nacionalismo y antisemitismo en Argentina*. Buenos Aires: Ediciones B, 2003.

Mackinnon, William, and Richard Centers. "Authoritarianism and Urban Stratification." *American Journal of Sociology* 61 (1956): 610-20.

Murmis, Miguel, and Juan Carlos Portantiero. *Estudio sobre los orígenes del peronismo*. Buenos Aires: Siglo XXI, 1973.

Parkes, James. *Antisemitism*. London: Vallentine Mitchell, 1963.

Terán, Oscar. *Nuestros años sesenta: La formación de la nueva izquierda intelectual en la Argentina, 1956-1966*. Buenos Aires: Puntosur, 1991.

Torre, Juan Carlos. "Interpretando (una vez más) los orígenes del peronismo." *Desarrollo Económico* 28.112 (1989): 525-48.

———. *La vieja guardia sindical y Perón*. Buenos Aires: Sudamericana, 1990.

Treves, Renato. *Sociologia e socialismo: Ricordi e incontri*. Milan: Franco Angeli, 1990.

Verón, Eliseo, ed. *Psicología social del prejuicio*. Buenos Aires: Cuadernos del Instituto de Sociología, no. 23, 1960.

12

Antisemitism and the Power of Abstraction

From Political Economy to Critical Theory

WERNER BONEFELD

The Nazi ideologue Arthur Rosenberg formulated the essence of modern antisemitism succinctly when he portrayed it as an attack on communism, Bolshevism, and "Jewish capitalism," by which he and his fellow antisemites, then and now, understand a capitalism not of productive labor and industry but of parasites: money and finance, speculators and bankers.[1]

There is of course a difference between the antisemitism that culminated in Auschwitz and the antisemitism of the post-1945 world. However, whether antisemitism persists because of or despite Auschwitz is ultimately an idle question. The terms *despite* and *because* give credence to the notion that Auschwitz, this factory of death, destroyed antisemitism too. In a differing but connected perspective antisemitism is viewed as a phenomenon of the past that merely casts its shadow on the present but has itself no longer any real existence in it. In this perspective overt expressions of antisemitism are deemed ugly merely as pathological aberrations within an otherwise civilized world. Those viewing antisemitism in this way often either belittle and dismiss its critique as an expression of "European guilt," or they reject it as an expression of bad faith—a camouflage for insulating Israel from criticism.[2]

The chapter argues that modern antisemitism is the "rumour about the Jews" as incarnation of hated forms of capitalism, which implies that antisemitism expresses resistance to capitalism. This chapter expounds this deadly notion. The following section examines some contemporary expressions of antisemitism, while the third and fourth sections explore Adorno's and Horkheimer's as well as Postone's conception of Nazi antisemitism.[3]

Radicalism and the Elements of Antisemitism: After Auschwitz

The projection of the Jew as the external enemy within, as communist, financier, speculator, and banker, remains potent to this day. For example, the former prime minister of Malaysia, Mahathir Mohamad, assessed the root causes of Malaysia's financial collapse in 1997 by stating, "I say openly, these people are racists. They are not happy to see us prosper. They say we grow too fast, they plan to make us poor. We are not making enemies with other people but others are making enemies with us."[4] What is meant by "we," and who are "they"? "The Jews," he says, are not happy to see Muslims progress; "they have promoted socialism, communism, human rights and democracy so that persecuting them would appear to be wrong, so they may enjoy equal rights with others. With these they have now gained control of the most powerful and they . . . have become a world power." They "rule the world by proxy." Mahathir Mohamad's stance, including his idea that the crisis of 1997 was a Jewish "plot,"[5] does indeed appear, as the *Financial Times* (October 23, 2003) rightly suggested, to have taken its cue from *The International Jew*, a book commissioned by Henry Ford in the 1920s. In its structure, the conception of "speculators" as the external enemy within bent on destroying relations of the national harmony of interest belongs to modern antisemitism. It summons the idea of finance and speculators as merchants of greed and, counterposed to this, espouses the idea of an otherwise "healthy," "industrious," and peaceful national community that arises from the "soil," furnishes the homeland with indestructible force and permanence, and is united by characteristics of race and the bond of blood.

Then there is Pat Buchanan's defense of supposed American values and virtues that he sees to be in crisis because of the nefarious effects of "critical theory," for which he holds "those trouble making Communist Jews" responsible.[6] Intelligence based on reason and critical judgment appears here as a powerfully destructive force that is ascribed to the cunning "Jew." Antisemitism projects the Other as rootless. Instead of having roots in nature, this Other is deemed to be lacking in nature. The "Jew" has no concrete roots and is thus "unnatural": his roots are in books. Instead, then, of being rooted in the supposed values of the nation, its soil and tradition, the Jew is possessed of a rootless intelligence and cunning that is destructive of tradition and organic social matter. The Jew seems to come from nowhere; he is a cosmopolitan, rootless, forever wandering in a borderless world. "Antisemitism is the rumour about the Jews."[7] They are seen to stand behind phenomena. Ascribed to this rootless Other is an immensely powerful, intangible, international conspiracy.[8] It cannot be defined concretely; it is an abstract, invisible power, which hides in such contradictory phenomena as communism and (hated forms of) capitalism, or in any case, universal, abstract values.

Then there is the anti-imperialist Left. As one of its more critical and distinctive thinkers, Perry Anderson argued, "Entrenched in business, government and media, American Zionism has since the sixties acquired a firm grip on the levers of public opinion and official policy towards Israel, that has weakened only on the rarest of occasions."[9] The Jews, then, have not only conquered Palestine; they have also taken control of America, or as James Petras sees it, the current effort of "U.S. empire building" is shaped by "Zionist empire builders."[10] For Anderson, Israel is a Jewish state, its nationalist triumphs are Jewish triumphs, and its economy is a Jewish economy, making Israel a "rentier state" that is kept by the United States as its imperialist bridgehead in the Middle East.

Originally, as Immanuel Wallerstein has argued, orthodox Marxism was hostile to the concept of national liberation and "quite suspicious of all talk about the rights of peoples, which they associated with middle-class nationalist movements." It was only at the Baku Congress in 1920 that the emphasis on class struggle "was quietly shelved in favour of the tactical priority of anti-imperialism, a theme around which the 3rd International hoped to build a political alliance between largely European Communist parties and at least those of the national liberation movements . . . that were more radical." After Baku anti-imperialist struggles were "given the label of 'revolutionary' activity."[11] The seminal text that informed this displacement of class struggle for general human emancipation onto anti-imperialist struggle for national liberation is Stalin's *Marxism and the National Question*, written in 1913. Defining a nation as a "historically evolved, stable community of language, territory, economic life, and psychological make-up manifested in a community of culture," he declared that "it is sufficient for a single one of these characteristics to be absent and the nation ceases to be a nation."[12] The Great Purges, as Leon Trotsky commented as early as 1937, espoused antisemitic demagogy to such an extent against the Marxists of internationalist persuasion that it almost amounted to a science. In the Soviet understanding of class struggle as anti-imperialist national liberation, the Jew appeared in many disguises—liberal, freemason, social democrat, Trotskyist, fascist, or Zionist—but regardless of its projected image, he embodied everything that was defined as capitalist, imperialist, Western, and above all non-Russian.[13]

What makes a state Jewish? For Marx the state was the political form of bourgeois society; crudely put, the purpose of capital is to make profit, and the state is the political expression of this purpose. He thus saw the state as the executive committee of the bourgeoisie. Max Weber argued that the state cannot be defined by its functions, let alone imagined national characteristics, but solely by its means: the legitimate use of physical violence. He conceived of the modern state as a machine. The great theorist of the autonomy of the state, Thomas Hobbes, conceived of it as the result of a social contract that allowed the warring social interests to flourish on the basis of mutual protection. His state appeared akin to a mortal God. Adam Smith defined the state as a market-enabling power; it polices the law-abiding conduct between the private interests to secure the relations of perfect liberty, where each pursues her own ends in a context in which everybody is obliged to all, but nobody is absolutely dependent upon anybody in particular. For the economy to be free, the state needs to be strong, as market police. None of these approaches defines the state in terms of the supposed or imagined national characteristics of a homogenized people. Such forging of national identity is a political task. Indeed the flip side of anti-imperialism is the demand for national liberation, national autonomy, and national self-determination—a mere abstraction of a classless, imagined community that is rendered effective by political power, not posited by nature. The identification of a people in terms of assumed national characteristics tends to rebound politically. It rejects universal values in favor of "difference," be it national, local, tribal, or merely parochial. If difference "has become the hallmark of theoretical anti-reason, 'the Other' has become the hallmark of practical anti-reason."[14] The Other provides the excuse for a damaged life and as such a scapegoat and becomes the object of resentment. Perry Anderson is therefore absolutely right when he argues that the potential of violence against the Other is intrinsic to nationalism; one would wish that Anderson's anti-imperialist stance be conscious of this insight.[15]

The mounting scale and sheer extent of contemporary antisemitism especially in the Middle East has blurred any distinction between the critique of the state of Israel and the concrete human beings that sustain Israel in their social relations. The anti-imperialist Left tends to dismiss Islamist antisemitism as a mere epiphenomenon of justified anger at Israel and U.S. imperialism and seeks to work in alliance with the "respectable Islamic clergy" in order to "radicalise the anti-capitalist movement by giving it an anti-imperialist edge."[16] Symptomatic here is the call for solidarity with the Muslim Brotherhood by *International Socialism*: "We say we have to work with the Muslim Brotherhood over specific issues [Palestine or Iraq]."[17] Against this Slavoj Žižek has argued that there should be no attempt to "'understand' Arab anti-Semitism . . . as a 'natural' reaction to the sad plight of the Palestinians." It has to be resisted "unconditionally." To "understand" Islamic antisemitism as a "justified" expression of anger against imperialism is to claim, by implication, that antisemitism articulates resistance to capitalism. Similarly there should be no attempt to "understand" the measures of the state of Israel "as a 'natural' reaction against the background of the Holocaust."[18] Such understanding accepts the utilization of the barbarism of the Holocaust as a legitimation for military and state action. Every state seeks to justify its policies by exploiting the past for its own legitimacy.[19] Such utilization of the past does not redeem the dead. Following Benjamin, redemption entails the recovery of the past in contemporary struggle for human dignity, which is both singular and universal, indivisible and priceless.[20] It is associated with refuseniks, heretics, dissenters, and dissidents, not the good offices of the state.

Islamic fundamentalism can be seen as a reaction against the "heavy artillery" of global capital to create a world after its own image. Against this it espouses the quest for authenticity, seeking to preserve through the purification of imagined ancestral conditions and traditions existing social structures, repeating with deadly and deafening force the "paradigmatic Fascist gesture" that seeks a "capitalism without capitalism."[21] The fight against "westoxication," as Khomeini had called the ideas of liberalism, democracy, socialism, and communism, involves the depiction of Israel as an imperialist bridgehead of "Jewish" capitalist counterinsurgency, fueling the hatred of Israel as a "Jewish" state. The attribute "Jewish" in this phrase does not refer to concrete human beings, be it Ariel Sharon or Karl Marx, Albert Einstein or Emma Goldman, Rosa Luxemburg or Leon Trotsky, Michael Neumann or Esther Rosenberg. It disregards social distinctions, be they of class, gender, or ethnicity, and instead assumes everybody to be of the same invariant nationalized type, whether they are anarchists, communists, refuseniks, capitalists or workers, conservatives, religious fanatics, warmongers, peace lovers, beggars, or just plain and boring average Joes.[22] Instead of recognizing contradictions, distinctions, antagonisms, struggles, and conflicts, it projects onto a nationalized people those abstract, reason-defying, imagined "qualities" on which antisemitism rests, substituting the critique of existing social relations for totalitarian conceptions of the national friend and the national foe. Within this relationship reason is suspended and thought is led to the further, equally irrational belief that the enemy of my enemy is my friend. Socialism, though, is the alternative to barbarism, its determinate negation; it is not its derivative. That also means, however, that the only way to fight resurgent antisemitism is not to preach liberal tolerance, which, say, accepts that nobody, neither woman nor man, should be stoned to death, but represses this principle in relation to the adopted Other: liberalism's civilized humanity is in fact inhuman toward people it secretly regards as uncivilized. It befriends the "respectable clerics" and political warlords in wonderment, gazing without thought.[23]

In Marx's *On the Jewish Question* and the writings of the Frankfurt School, the category "Jew" is a social metaphor that focuses anticapitalist resentment from the standpoint of capitalism. In contrast, however, to Perry Anderson's affirmative categorization, Marx and the Frankfurt School approached the "Jewish question" through the lens of the critique of the fetishism of bourgeois relations of production.[24] Expanding on Marx's critical question, "Why does this content [human social relations] assume that form [the form of capital]?," it asks, Why does the bourgeois critique of capitalism assume the form of antisemitism?[25] In contrast, the affirmative use of the category "Jew" rationalizes antisemitism as a manifestation of hated forms of capitalism, and through this rationalization is complicit in the "rumour about the Jews." Such complicity partakes in the paradigmatic fascist gesture of an anticapitalism that seeks a capitalism without capitalism.

Ulrike Meinhof articulated succinctly this rationalization of antisemitism as hatred of capitalism when she said, "Auschwitz meant that six million Jews were killed, and thrown on the waste-heap of Europe, for what they were: money Jews. Finance capital and the banks, the hard core of the system of imperialism and capitalism, had turned the hatred of men against money and exploitation, and against the Jews. . . . Anti-Semitism is really a hatred of capitalism."[26] In her view, then, "antisemitism is in its essence anti-capitalist."[27] Given the omnipresence of this idea in left antisemitism, what do antisemites attack when they claim to attack capitalism? The following sections explore this with reference to Nazi antisemitism.[28]

On the Time of Abstraction

Antisemitism does not "need" Jews. The "Jew" has powers attributed to it that cannot be defined concretely. It is an abstraction that excludes nobody. Anyone can be considered a Jew. The concept "Jew" knows no individuality, cannot be a man or a woman, and cannot be seen as a worker or beggar; the word *Jew* relates to a nonperson, an abstraction. "The Jew is one whom other men consider a Jew."[29] For antisemitism to rage, the existence of "Jews" is neither incidental nor required. "Antisemitism tends to occur only as part of an interchangeable program," the basis of which is the "universal reduction of all specific energy to the one, same abstract form of labor, from the battlefield to the studio."[30] Antisemitism belongs to a social world in which sense and significance are sacrificed in favor of compliance with the norms and rules of a political and economic reality that poses sameness, ritualized repetition, and subjectified economic things as forms of human existence. Time is money, said Benjamin Franklin. And we might add that therefore money is time. "The economy of time: to this all economy ultimately reduces itself."[31] If, therefore, everything is reduced to time, an abstract time, divisible into equal, homogeneous, and constant units that move on relentlessly from unit to unit, and that though dissociated from concrete human activities, measures these whatever their content, then "*man is nothing; he is, at the most, time's carcase.*"[32] Time is of the essence. Everything else is a waste of time. Indifferent to social content and human purposes, such time is interested only in two things: "How much?" and "How long did it take?"[33] The mere existence of difference, a difference that signals happiness beyond life as a mere personification of labor-time, fosters the blind resentment and anger that antisemitism focuses and exploits but does not itself produce. "The thought of happiness without power is unbearable because it would then be true happiness."[34]

Antisemitism differentiates between "society" and "national community." Society is identified as "Jewish," whereas community is modeled as a counterworld to society. Community is seen as constituted by nature, and nature is seen to be at risk because of "evil" abstract social forces. The attributes given by the antisemite to Jews include mobility, intangibility, rootlessness and conspiracy against the—mythical and mythologized—values of the imagined community of an honest and hardworking people. The presumed "well-being" of this community is seen to be at the mercy of evil powers: intellectual thought, abstract rules and laws, and the disintegrating forces of communism and finance capital. Both communism and finance capital are seen as uprooting powers and as manifestations of reason. Reason stands rejected because of its infectious desire to go to the root of things, and the root of things can only be Man in her social relations. Reason is the weapon of critique. It challenges conditions where Man is degraded to a mere economic resource. For antisemitism independence of thought and the ability to think freely without fear is abhorrent. It detests the idea that "Man is the highest being for Man [*Mensch*]."[35] Instead it seeks deliverance through the furious affirmation of its own madness. The antisemites' portrayal of the Jew as evil personified is in fact their own self-portrait. "Madness is the substitute for the dream that humanity could organize its world humanely, a dream that a man-made world is stubbornly rejecting."[36]

Antisemitism manifests a perverted urge for equality. It seeks an equality that derives from membership in a national community, a community of *Volksgenossen*. This equality is defined by the mythical "property" of land and soil based on the bond of blood. The fetish of blood and soil is itself rooted in the capital fetish, where the concrete in the form of use-value obtains only in and through the abstract in the form of exchange-value. Antisemitism construes blood, soil, and also machinery as concrete counterprinciples of the abstract. The abstract is personified in the category "Jew."[37] For the apologists of market liberalism, the reference to the invisible hand operates like an explanatory refuge. It explains everything with reference to the Invisible. "Starvation is God's way of punishing those who have too little faith in capitalism."[38] For the antisemites, however, the power of the invisible can be explained: the Jew is its personification and biologized existence. It transforms discontent with social conditions into a conformist rebellion against the projected personification of capitalism.

The nationalist conception of equality defines society as the Other, a parasite whose objective is deemed to oppress, undermine, and pervert the "natural community" through the "disintegrating" force of the abstract and intangible values of—bourgeois—civilization. The category "Jew" is seen to personify abstract thought and abstract equality, including its incarnation, money. The Volksgenosse, then, is seen as somebody who resists "Jewish" abstract values and instead upholds some sort of natural equality. Their "equality" as Jews obtains as a construct, to which belong all those who deviate from the conception of the Volksgenosse, that is, mythical concrete matter. The myth of the Jew is confronted with the myth of the original possession of soil, elevating nationalism's "regressive egality" to a liberating action.[39] The Volksgenosse sees himself as a son of nature and thus as a natural being. He sees his natural destiny in the liberation of the national community from allegedly rootless, abstract values, demanding their naturalization so that everything is returned to "nature." In short, the Volksgenosse portrays himself as rooted in blood and ancestral tradition to defend his own faith in the immorality of madness through the collective approval of anger. This anger is directed toward civilization's supposed victory over nature, a victory that is seen as condemning the Volksgenosse to sweat, toil, and physical effort, whereas the Other is seen to live a life as banker and speculator. This the Volksgenosse aspires for himself. The Volksgenosse speculates in death and banks the extracted gold teeth.

The efficient organization and the cold, dispassionate execution of the deed is mirrored by its disregard for individuality: corpses all look the same when counting the results, and nothing distinguishes a number from a number except the difference in quantity—the measure of success. The mere existence of distinction is a provocation. Judgment is suspended. Everybody is numbered and assessed for use. "The morbid aspect of anti-Semitism is not projective behaviour as such, but the absence from it of reflection."[40] Auschwitz, then, stands for the "stubbornness" of the principle of not only "abstraction" but also "abstractification." The abstraction "Jew" is also *made* abstract: all that can be used (concretely) is used, like teeth, hair, skin; labor-power; finally, the abstract remainder is destroyed: the invisible hand of the market, identified as the power of the "Jew," is transformed into smoke.

Antisemitism: Finance and Industry

Nazi antisemitism is different from the antisemitism of the old Christian world. This does not mean that it did not exploit Christian antisemitism. Christian antisemitism constructed "the Jew" as an abstract social power: "the Jew" stands accused as the assassin of Jesus; those apparently descending from the assassins of Jesus are thus persecuted as the descendants of murderers. In modern antisemitism the Jew was chosen because of the "religious horror the latter has always inspired."[41] In the Christian world the "Jew" was also a social-economic construct. The one who was forced to fulfill the vital and hated economic function of trafficking in money was called a Jew. The economic curse that this social role entailed reinforced the religious curse.

Modern antisemitism uses and exploits these historical constructions and transforms them: the Jew stands accused and is persecuted for following unproductive activities. His image is that of an intellectual and banker. "Bankers and intellectuals, money and mind, the exponents of circulation, form the impossible ideal of those who have been maimed by domination, an image used by domination to perpetuate itself."[42] In this context the mythologized possession of the soil and of ancestral tradition based on the bond of blood is counterposed to the possession of universal, abstract phenomena. The terms "*abstract, rationalist, intellectual . . .* take a pejorative sense; it could not be otherwise, since the anti-Semite lays claim to a concrete and irrational possession of the values of the nation."[43] The abstract values themselves are biologized, and the abstract is identified as "Jew." Thus both the concrete and the abstract are biologized, one through the possession of land (the concrete as rooted in nature, blood, and tradition) and the other through the possession of "poison" (the abstract as the rootless power of intelligence and money). The myth of national unity is counterposed to the myth of the Jew. Jewry is seen to stand behind the urban world of crime, prostitution, and vulgar, materialist culture. Tradition is counterposed to reasoning, intelligence, and self-reflection, and the nationalist conception of community, economy, and labor is counterposed to the abstract forces of international finance and communism.[44] The Volksgenossen are thus equal in blindness. "Anti-

Semitic behaviour is generated in situations where blinded men robbed of their subjectivity are set loose as subjects."⁴⁵ While reason subsists in and through the critique of social relations, the Volksgenosse has faith only in the efficiently unleashed terror that robs the alleged personifications of capitalism of everything they have—cloth, shoes, teeth, hair, skin, life—and even the dead will not be safe from torture. The collection of gold teeth from those murdered, the collection of hair from those to be killed, and the overseeing of the slave labor of those allowed to walk on their knees for no more than another day requires only effective organization. "How much?" "How long did it take?" Time is of the essence.

Nazism's denunciation of capitalism as "Jewish capitalism" thus allowed the relentless development of capitalist enterprise while seemingly rejecting capitalism as a system of finance, money-grabbing speculation, accumulation of parasitic wealth, as a rootless, mobile, intangible annihilator of space through time, undermining concrete enterprise on the altar of money, and so on. The critique of capitalism as "Jewish capitalism" argues that capitalism is in fact nothing more than an unproductive money-making system—a rentier economy that lives off and, in doing so, undermines the presumed national community of creative, industrious individuals, subordinating them to the rootless and therefore ruthless forces of global money, or as Mahathir Mohamad had it, 'They are not happy to see us prosper."

For the antisemites, then, the world appears to be divided between hated forms of capitalism, especially finance and money capital, and concrete nature. The concrete is conceived as immediate, direct, matter for use, and rooted in industry and productive activity. Money, on the other hand, is not only conceived as the root of all evil; it is also judged as rootless and existing not only independently from industrial capital but also over and against the industrial endeavor of the nation: all enterprise is seen to be perverted in the name of money's continued destructive quest for self-expansion. In this way money and financial capital are identified with capitalism, while industry is perceived as constituting the concrete and creative enterprise of a national community. Between capitalism as monetary accumulation and national community as industrial enterprise, it is money that calls the shots. In this view, industry and enterprise are "made" capitalist by money: money penetrates all expressions of industry and thus perverts and disintegrates community in the name of finance capital's abstract values. The force and power of Money is seen to under-mine the individual as entrepreneur; the creative is perceived in terms of a paternalist direction of use-value production; the rooted in terms of *Volk*; the community in terms of a natural community. For the antisemites, "the Jew" is money personified. Instead of community's natural order of hierarchy and position, money's allegedly artificial and rootless force is judged to make the world go round by uprooting the natural order of the Volksgenossen. In this way, then, it is possible for the Volksgenossen not only to embrace capitalism but also to declare that the forced labor creates freedom: *Arbeit macht frei*. "They declared that work was not de-grading, so as to control the others more rationally. They claimed to be creative workers, but in reality they were still the grasping overlords of former times."[46] By separating what fundamentally belongs together, that is, production and money, the differentiation between money on the one hand and industry and enterprise on the other amounts to a fe-tish critique of capital that, by attacking the projected personification of capital, seeks its unfettered expansion by means of terror.

The approval of the Volksgenosse as the personification of the concrete, of blood, soil, tradition, and industry, goes hand in hand with the elimi-nation of the cajoling and perverting forces of the abstract—the "cunning Jew" stands condemned as the destructive incarnation of capitalism. In this way the ideology of blood and soil on the one hand and machinery and unfettered industrial expansion on the other are projected as images of a healthy nation that stands ready to purge itself from the perceived perversion of industry by the abstract, universal, rootless, mobile, intan-gible, international "vampire" of "Jewish capitalism." Extermination is itself an industrial effort of concrete nature and thus industrialized. Ex-termination manifests "the stubbornness of the life to which one has to conform, and to resign oneself."[47] As Volksgenossen they have all com-mitted the same deed and have thus become truly equal to each other; their efficiently discharged occupation only confirmed what they already knew: that they had lost their individuality as subjects.

Everything is thus changed into pure nature. The abstract was not only personified and biologized; it was also "abstractified." Auschwitz was a factory "to destroy the personification of the abstract. Its organization was that of a fiendish industrial process, the aim of which was to 'liber-ate' the concrete from the abstract. The first step was to dehumanize, that is, to strip away the 'mask' of humanity, of qualitative specificity, and reveal the Jews for what 'they really are'—shadows, ciphers, numbered abstraction." Then followed the process to "eradicate that abstractness, to transform it into smoke, trying in the process to wrest away the last remnants of the concrete material 'use-values': clothes, gold, hair, soap."[48]

Summary: Critical Theory and the Constituted World

Adam Smith was certain in his own mind that capitalism creates the wealth of nations and noted that "the proprietor of stock is properly a citizen of the world, and is not necessarily attached to any particular country. He would be apt to abandon the country in which he was exposed to a vexatious inquisition, in order to be assessed to a burdensome tax, and would remove his stock to some other country where he could either carry on his business, or enjoy his fortune more at his ease."[49] David Ricardo concurred, adding that "if a capital is not allowed to get the greatest net revenue that the use of machinery will afford here, it will be carried abroad," leading to "serious discouragement to the demand for labour."[50] He thus also formulated the necessity of capitalist social relations to produce "redundant population." According to Hegel, the accumulation of wealth renders those who depend on the sale of their labor power for their social reproduction insecure in deteriorating conditions. He concluded that despite the accumulation of wealth, bourgeois society will find it most difficult to keep the dependent masses pacified, and he saw the form of the state as the means of reconciling the social antagonism, containing the dependent masses.[51]

Marx developed these insights and showed that the concept of equal rights is in principle a bourgeois concept. "The power which each individual exercises over the activity of others or over social wealth exists in him as the owner of exchange value, of money. The individual carries his social power, as well as his bond with society, in his pocket."[52] Against the bourgeois concept of formal equality, he argued that communism rests on the equality of individual human needs. Adorno and Horkheimer argued that antisemitism articulates a senseless, barbaric rejection of capitalism that makes anticapitalism useful for capitalism. "The rulers are only safe as long as the people they rule turn their longed-for goals into hated forms of evil." Antisemitism channels discontent with conditions into blind resentment against the projected external enemy within. This rejection of capitalism, then, "is also totalitarian in that it seeks to make the rebellion of suppressed nature against domination directly useful to domination. This machinery needs the Jews." That is, "no matter what the Jews as such may be like, their image, as that of the defeated people, has the features to which totalitarian domination must be completely hostile: happiness without power, wages without work, a home without frontiers, religion without myth. These characteristics are hated by the rulers because the ruled secretly long to possess them."[53] Antisemitism urges the mob on to dehumanize, maim, and kill the projected Other; participation in the slaughter suppresses in the exploited themselves the very possibility and idea of happiness and distinction.

The anti-imperialist critique of Israel as the bridgehead of U.S. imperialism in the Middle East and of modern Zionism as the ideology and the far-reaching organizational system and political practice of U.S. capitalism displaces anticapitalist motives on a *false* conflict and encourages friendship with *false* friends. Originally the critique of ideology sought to reveal the necessary perversion of human social practice in its appearance—as relations between things and as a mere human agent of the "logic of things," be they capital, value, price, money, or nation. Enlightenment was its critical intent. Rendered helpless in the face of abject misery, blinded by desire for action, and shaken by events, it now appears as a mere Weltanschauung that, having no principle to call upon, is subject to political calculation and opportunism. Alex Callinicos's robust defense of Al Qaeda against its description as fascist expresses this well. He rejects this description as "an extraordinary assertion" and then goes on the say that the "Muslim concept of the *ummah*—the community of the faithful—is precisely a transnational one, something that the Al Qaeda network has strictly observed (whatever respects in which its interpretations of Muslim doctrine may differ from those of others), incorporating as it does activists from many different national backgrounds."[54] Since for Callinicos, Al Qaeda is transnational by virtue of its strict observance of the ummah, he declares that it cannot be described as fascist.[55] On this definition even national socialism would score well. It too was a transnational movement; its main death squad, the ss, was in fact an international brigade, and its followers adhered strictly to the doctrine of the faithful. The anti-imperialist idea that the enemy of my enemy is my friend is irrational. It accepts barbaric rejections of capitalism as anticapitalist and finds worthwhile the quest for a "capitalism without capitalism."

This chapter has argued that displaced modes of anticapitalism do not question the character of capitalist social relations; they merely interpret them differently and seek to reconfigure negative human conditions in another way. Antisemitism is the official ideology of a barbaric rejection of capitalism that makes anticapitalism useful for capitalism. It offers an articulation for resentment and anger, and an enemy. Antisemitism is all-embracing—because it comprehends nothing.

Notes

This is a revised version of a paper given at the conference Antisemitism and the Emergence of Sociological Theory, held at the University of Manchester in November 2008. I am grateful to all participants for their comments, and especially to David Seymour, who acted as discussant, and Marcel Stoetzler for his many insightful comments. The usual disclaimers apply.

1. Rosenberg, *Der staatsfeindliche Zionismus.*
2. See, for example, Keaney, review of *Human Dignity.*
3. Horkheimer and Adorno, "Elements of Antisemitism"; Postone, "Anti-Semitism and National Socialism."
4. Quoted in "Malaysia Acts on Market Fall," *Financial Times*, September 4, 1997.
5. Quoted in "Mahathir's Dark Side," *Daily Telegraph* (London), October 24, 2003.
6. Buchanan, *Death of the West.* Buchanan is a former senior advisor to American presidents Nixon, Ford, and Reagan. He is a distinguished conservative thinker.
7. Adorno, *Minima Moralia*, 141.
8. On this, see Postone, "Anti-Semitism and National Socialism."
9. Anderson, "Scurrying towards Bethlehem," 15.
10. Petras, "Empire Building and Rule," 201.
11. Wallerstein, *After Liberalism*, 156, 211.
12. Stalin, *Marxism and the National and Colonial Question*, 8.
13. Leon Trotsky, quoted in Poliakov, *Vom Antizionismus zum Antisemitismus*, 47.
14. Rose, *Judaism and Modernity*, 5.
15. Anderson, "Scurrying towards Bethlehem."
16. Callinicos, "The Grand Strategy of the American Empire."
17. "Egypt," 31. See also Boron, *Empire and Imperialism*, who praises the "patriotic resistance" in Iraq and Afghanistan (9–10) against what he terms a "villainous," "fascistic," and "genocidal" United States (see, e.g., 123). Callinicos, *An Anti-Capitalist Manifesto*, 107, argues that anticapitalism has to "meet the requirements of (at least) justice, efficiency, democracy, and sustainability," and in order to radicalize the anticapitalist movement demands that

moral support is given to anti-imperial "resistance" groups that are openly hostile to the anticapitalist ends he advocates. See Callinicos and Nineham, "At an Impasse?" See also Harman, "Hizbollah and the War Israel Lost." Devoid of content, radicalism becomes an end in itself. The critique of ideology has itself become an ideology.

18. Žižek, *Welcome to the Desert of the Real*, 129.

19. On this, see Tischler, "Time of Reification and Time of Insubordination."

20. Benjamin, *Illuminations*.

21. Žižek, *Welcome to the Desert of the Real*, 131.

22. I owe this phrase to Marcel Stoetzler.

23. The support given by sections of the Left to Islamist resistance groups is a case in point. Under the guise of anti-imperialism, solidarity is extended to the Muslim Brotherhood, who are openly hostile to socialism and feminism, to the point of murder. Who, then, extends solidarity to the socialists and feminists in, say, Iran, Iraq, Palestine? Another case of mistaken identity can be found in Žižek's critique of antisemitism, which is ambivalent. He says that in the face of antisemitism one should not "preach liberal tolerance" but try to "express the underlying anti-capitalist motive in a direct, non-displaced way" (*Welcome to the Desert of the Real*, 130). He assumes that antisemitism expresses an anticapitalist motive that needs to be brought out and expressed clearly. He also assumes that the hidden anticapitalist motive is in fact a progressive one, worth fighting for. What, though, really is the anticapitalism of, say, the Muslim Brotherhood? Then there is Judith Butler. When asked by *Online Magazin für Frauen* to clarify her statement that Hamas and the Hezbollah are progressive social movements (http://radicalarchives .org/2010/03/28/jbutler-on-hamas-hezbollah-israel-lobby/) she remarks that "groups like Hamas and Hezbollah should be described as left movements. . . . They are 'left' in the sense that they oppose colonialism and imperialism" (http://www.aviva-berlin.de/aviva/Found.php?id=1427323, accessed July 20, 2010). Since she does not condone the use of violence, she rejects their tactics, but she accepts them nevertheless as members of the global Left because they reject imperialism. Her definition of the Left is indifferent to social ends and contents and includes most unsavory bedfellows, historically as well as contemporary.

24. Marx, "Zur Judenfrage."

25. Marx, *Das Kapital*, 95.

26. Ulrike Meinhof, quoted in Watson, "Race and the Socialists," 23. Meinhof was the cofounder of the German Red Army Faction.

27. Ulrike Meinhof, quoted in "Mörder wie die Väter," *Der Spiegel*, May 10, 2010.

28. In what follows I have freely borrowed from Horkheimer and Adorno, "Elements of Antisemitism" and Postone, "Anti-Semitism and National Socialism." See also Werner Bonefeld, "Notes on Antisemitism" and "Nationalism and Anti-Semitism in Anti-Globalisation Perspective."

29. Sartre, *Anti-Semite and Jew*, 69.

30. Horkheimer and Adorno, "Elements of Antisemitism," 207.

31. Marx, *Grundrisse*, 173.

32. Marx, *The Poverty of Philosophy*, 127, emphasis in the original.

33. On different forms of time, from the time of happiness to the time of mourning, and their connection to concrete human events, see Ecclesiastes 3:4. See also Alliez, *Capital Times*. On abstract labor as a temporal category, a category of a time made abstract, see Bonefeld, "Abstract Labour."

34. Adorno and Horkheimer, "Elements of Antisemitism," 172.

35. Marx, "Contribution to the Critique of Hegel's Philosophy of Law," 182.

36. Adorno, "What Does Coming to Terms with the Past Mean?," 124.

37. On this, see Postone, "Anti-Semitism and National Socialism."

38. John D. Rockefeller Sr., quoted in Marable, *Race Reform and Rebellion*, 149.

39. Adorno, *Minima Moralia*, 56.

40. Horkheimer and Adorno, "Elements of Antisemitism," 189.

41. Sartre, *Anti-Semite and Jew*, 68.

42. Horkheimer and Adorno, "Elements of Antisemitism," 172.

43. Sartre, *Anti-Semite and Jew*, 109.

44. This point is most clearly brought out by Postone, "Anti-Semitism and National Socialism."

45. Horkheimer and Adorno, "Elements of Antisemitism," 171.

46. Horkheimer and Adorno, "Elements of Antisemitism," 173.

47. Horkheimer and Adorno, "Elements of Antisemitism," 171.

48. Postone, "Anti-Semitism and National Socialism," 313–14.

49. Smith, *The Wealth of Nations*, 848–49.

50. Ricardo, *On the Principles of Political Economy and Taxation*, 39.

51. Hegel, *Philosophy of Right*, 122–29.

52. Marx, *Grundrisse*, 156–57. On money as a social form that expresses exploitation in the form of equivalence, see Bonefeld, "Money, Equality and Exploitation."

53. Horkheimer and Adorno, "Elements of Antisemitism," 199, 185.

54. Callinicos, "The Anti-Capitalist Movement after Genoa and New York," 140.

55. Whether the fascist label is appropriate or not is beside the point. The ticket mentality that attaches labels to things is, however, a concern. It labels things without telling us what they are, and by leaving the thing undisturbed, thought is reduced to mere conviction. It is a well-known fact that in the world of convictions, the social world does not need to be changed. All that needs to be done is to interpret it more favorably. Reality becomes a matter of conviction.

References

Adorno, Theodor. *Minima Moralia: Reflexionen aus dem beschädigten Leben.* Frankfurt: Suhrkamp, 1951.

———. "What Does Coming to Terms with the Past Mean?" In *Bitburg in Moral and Political Perspective*, edited by G. Harman, 114–29. Bloomington: Indiana University Press, 1986.

Alliez, Eric. *Capital Times*. London: University of Minnesota Press, 1996.

Anderson, Benedict. *Imagined Communities*. London: Verso, 1991.

Anderson, Perry. "Scurrying towards Bethlehem." *New Left Review*, 2d series, no. 10 (2001): 5–30.

Benjamin, Walter. *Illuminations*. New York: Harcourt, Brace & World, 1968.

Bonefeld, Werner. "Abstract Labour: Against Its Nature and On Its Time."*Capital and Class* 34.2 (2010): 257–76.

———. "Money, Equality and Exploitation." In *Global Capital, National State and the Politics of Money*, edited by W. Bonefeld and J. Holloway, 178–209. London: Palgrave, 1996.

———. "Nationalism and Anti-Semitism in Anti-Globalisation Perspective." In *Human Dignity: Social Autonomy and the Critique of Capitalism*, edited by W. Bonefeld and K. Psychopedis, 147–71. Aldershot UK: Ashgate, 2005.

———. "Notes on Anti-Semitism." *Common Sense*, no. 21 (1997): 60–76.

Boron, Atillio. *Empire and Imperialism*. London: Zed Books, 2005.

Buchanan, Pat. *The Death of the West*. New York: Dunne, 2002.

Callinicos, Alex. *An Anti-Capitalist Manifesto*. Cambridge UK: Polity, 2003.

———. "The Anti-Capitalist Movement after Genoa and New York." In *Implicating Empire*, edited by S. Aronowitz and H. Gautney, 133–50. New York: Basic Books, 2003.

———. "The Grand Strategy of the American Empire." International Socialism Journal 97 (2002), pubs.socialistreviewindex.org.uk/isj97/callinicos (accessed July 29, 2010).

Callinicos, Alex, and Chris Nineham. "At an Impasse? Anti-Capitalism and the Social Forums Today." *International Socialism* 115 (2007), http://www.isj.org.uk/index.php4?id=337&issue=115 (accessed May 31, 2013).

"Egypt: The Pressure Builds Up." *International Socialism*, no. 106 (2005), http://www.isj.org.uk/index.php4?id=90&issue=106 (accessed July 29, 2010).

Harman, Chris. "Hizbollah and the War Israel Lost." *International Socialism* 112 (2006), http://www.isj.org.uk/index.php4?id=243&issue=112 (accessed May 31, 2013).

Hegel, Georg Wilhelm Friedrich. *Philosophy of Right*. Oxford: Clarendon Press, 1967.

Horkheimer, Max, and Theodor Adorno. "Elements of Antisemitism." In *Dialectic of Enlightenment*, 168–208. London: Verso, 1989.

Keaney, Michael. Review of *Human Dignity*. *Review of Radical Political Economics* 39.4 (2007): 606–9.

Marable, Manning. *Race Reform and Rebellion*. 2d ed. Jackson: University Press of Mississippi, 1991.

Marx, Karl. *Capital*. Vol. 3. London: Lawrence & Wishart, 1966.

———. "Contribution to the Critique of Hegel's Philosophy of Law: Introduction." In *Marx/Engels Collected Works*, 3: 157–87. London: Lawrence & Wishart, 1975.

———. *Grundrisse*. London: Penguin, 1973.

———. *Das Kapital*. Vol. 1. In *Marx-Engels Werke*, vol. 23. Berlin: Dietz, 1962.

———. *The Poverty of Philosophy*. In *Marx/Engels Collected Works*, vol. 6. London: Lawrence & Wishart, 1976.

———. "Zur Judenfrage." In *Marx-Engels Werke*, 1: 347–77. Berlin: Dietz, 1964.

Petras, James. "Empire Building and Rule: U.S. and Latin America." In *The Politics of Imperialism and Counterstrategies*, edited by P. Chandra, A. Ghosh, and R. Kumar, 197–248. Delhi: Aakar Books, 2004.

Poliakov, Leon. *Vom Antizionismus zum Anti-Semitismus*. Freiburg: Ça ira, 1992.

Postone, Moishe. "Anti-Semitism and National Socialism." In *Germans and Jews since the Holocaust: The Changing Situation in West Germany*, edited by A. Rabinbach and J. Zipes, 302–14. New York: Holmes & Meier, 1986.

Ricardo, David. *On the Principles of Political Economy and Taxation*. Cambridge: Cambridge University Press, 1995.

Rose, Gillian. *Judaism and Modernity*. Oxford: Blackwell, 1993.

Rosenberg, Alfred. *Der staastsfeindliche Zionismus*. Munich: F. Eher Nachfahren, 1938.

Sartre, Jean-Paul. *Anti-Semite and Jew*. Translated by G. J. Becker. New York: Schocken Books, 1976.

Smith, Adam. *The Wealth of Nations*. Vol. 2. Indianapolis: Liberty Fund, 1981.

Stalin, Josef. *Marxism and the National and Colonial Question*. New York: International Publishers, n.d.

Tischler, Sergio. "Time of Reification and Time of Insubordination." In *Human Dignity*, edited by W. Bonefeld and K. Psychopedis, 131–43. Aldershot UK: Ashgate, 2005.

Wallerstein, Immanuel. *After Liberalism*. New York: New Press, 1995.

Watson, George. "Race and the Socialists." *Encounter*, November 1976, 15–23.

Žižek, Slavoj. *Welcome to the Desert of the Real*. London: Verso, 2002.

Conclusion

The Dialectic of Social Science and Worldview

DETLEV CLAUSSEN

Translated by Marcel Stoetzler

> Scholarly consciousness must not reduce the riddle of antisemitic irrationality to a formula that is itself irrational: the riddle demands to be resolved at the level of society, and this is not possible in the sphere of national peculiarities.
>
> HORKHEIMER AND ADORNO, VORWORT TO PAUL W. MASSING, *Vorgeschichte des Politischen Antisemitismus*

Everything begins in France: sociology and, hard to believe, antisemitism too. Auschwitz, the epitome of the National Socialist mass murder of European Jews between 1942 and 1945, has obstructed our perspective on the history of antisemitism. Only reflection in the mode of social theory can open it up again. Such reflection was pioneered by the critical theorists, exiled in the United States, whose epochal key text, *Dialectic of Enlightenment* (1944), throws its light also on the present volume and its exploration of the genetic connection between sociology and antisemitism. In August 1940 Adorno wrote to Horkheimer, "Thanks also to the latest news from Germany, I am less and less able to free myself from having to think about the fate of the Jews. It often seems that everything that we used to see under the aspect of the proletariat has been concentrated today with frightful force upon the Jews."[1] Horkheimer replied in September 1940, "I am convinced that the Jewish Question is the question of contemporary society—in this we agree with Marx and with Hitler."[2]

These remarks ask for interpretation—not only interpretation in terms of intellectual history but also with respect to their own substantive content. Neither Marx nor Hitler was a sociologist, but while Marx was accused of antisemitism unjustly, Hitler was a declared antisemite of a particular kind, referring to his own antisemitism as the "antisemitism of reason," which he strove to distinguish from pre-bourgeois, Christian Jew-hatred as much as from the antisemitic one-issue movements of the nineteenth century, the "antisemitism of sentiment."[3] He was not interested in sociology, the study of society. He wanted to change society radically, and the National Socialists' most radical deed, the mass murder of European Jews, has in fact changed society irreversibly. Interpreting this crime as the realization of one man's fantasy would mean to rationalize it. One can attempt to comprehend the incomprehensible only by trying to understand the society that made it possible and that produced the perpetrators.

Throughout most of its history, sociology has not been able to develop other than rationalistic theories of antisemitism. This might have to do with the fact that from its beginnings, sociology was intertwined with bourgeois society, its object of study, and considered antisemitism a pre-bourgeois relic rather than a genuine and continuous element of modern society itself. There is concrete historical urgency in examining antisemitism as a constitutive and unexamined aspect of the history of sociology, especially as the social scientific mainstream considers the critical traditions of social theory and psychoanalysis to be somewhat outdated.

Sociologists and Marxists used to see themselves as inheritors of the Enlightenment; both share a rationalism that limits their perspectives on societal developments. In the case of sociology, an affirmative-positivistic habitus is the problem; in the case of Marxism, the trust in history. Auschwitz and the gulag archipelago have made it impossible any more to trust the quiet "voice of the intellect,"[4] as Freud still did in 1927, although not without skepticism. Both sociology and the various traditions of Marxism failed already in their nineteenth-century forms to understand the dialectic of Enlightenment, and this fact has resulted in an inherent antitheoreticism in sociology and, in the area of philosophy, has facilitated a resurrection of ethics (transpiring in the day-to-day business of the mass media more modestly as "the dispute on values"). To the extent that sociology had been inspired by the longing for emancipation, the latter has given way to the drive to order that had already been contained in Comte's programmatic formula "order and progress." The sociology of the present period is in danger of regressing to a science of order.

The Enlightenment of the seventeenth and eighteenth centuries had been ambivalent toward the Jews, and sociology, a child of the long nineteenth century, inherited this ambivalence. Jewish traditionalists, not unlike later Zionists, felt threatened by bourgeois society's tendency toward enlightenment and secularization. After the civilizatory catastrophe of Auschwitz, a body of literature emerged, mostly in the area of intellectual history, that looked back and focused on the anti-Jewish tendency in the Enlightenment without realizing that giving up on the Enlightenment meant giving up on the only intellectual antidote to antisemitism.[5] The rationalist, and politically deliberate, distortions of the intellectual history of the bourgeois era can be rectified only by adopting the dialectical perspective on the Enlightenment. The consolidation of bourgeois society during the long nineteenth century, the emergence of sociology as a scholarly discipline, and the formation of modern antisemitism are closely connected phenomena. Without examining the mass murder of European Jews one cannot contemplate the destruction and self-destruction of the bourgeois world during the "short century," the twentieth. Other than through this perspective the twentieth century cannot be understood. Sociology has long hesitated and has left this perspective to the historians.

In the long nineteenth century the Jews owed to sociology's rationalistic pedigree their disappearance from it. More often than not the Enlightenment had demanded from the Jews that they should change: the members of a religious sect should turn into equal citizens. The Jews as a pre-bourgeois nation were negated; emancipated as individuals, though, they were welcomed by the *citoyens* of the bourgeois commonwealth. The sociological perspective on facts confirmed to those happy to believe it that the emancipated Jews had amalgamated into bourgeois society. The antisemitic perspective, though, saw Jews everywhere—in their disguised form as secularized moderns and undisguised as an immigrant flood from the East. While the early sociologists prided themselves of their scientificity, the first modern antisemites spoke the language of realism. As the present volume shows, both competed at the end of the long century, especially in Germany and France, for the mantle of value-neutral objectivity. Still, throughout the "short century" the anti-antisemitic argumentation was weakened by its focus on denouncing antisemitism (and subsequently also racism) for lacking scientificity rather than taking the opportunity to reflect critically on its own rationalistic scientism. The so-called scientific socialism followed bourgeois rationalism on the path of credulity toward science. Antisemitism appeared to be a dated prejudice that would best be refuted through the accumulation of facts. The famous formula of antisemitism as the "socialism of fools" is expressive of this rationalist context that tried to get at the antisemites in terms of a practical-political sociology.

Insufficient, though, as the Marxist rationalism of the period of the Second International might seem today, one must acknowledge that it challenged antisemitism as a political phenomenon and recognized it as a problem of political practice. Early French sociology, by contrast, aimed to emancipate itself from the political philosophy of the early socialists that carried a significant antisemitic heritage. This can be seen in the figure of Auguste Comte (1798–1857), who in his younger days had been the private secretary of Saint-Simon. The Jews were no topic for Comte; his concern was the great disorder in the wake of the French Revolution. Sociology was meant to replace the practical Enlightenment philosophy that he had identified as a metaphysical troublemaker. What Adorno later called secondary antisemitism can already be discerned in Comte, without reference to Jews, though: Comte pronounces on phenomena that (primary) antisemitism identifies with Jews, such as rootlessness, exaggerated intellectuality, secretiveness, lack of loyalty against the established powers. These are the core themes of the Dreyfus affair, during which Émile Durkheim (1858–1917) clearly acted as a Dreyfusard. His essay "L'individualisme et les intellectuels" of 1898 unequivocally takes sides with the persecuted Jewish officer.[6] In his enormous oeuvre, though, whose importance for the constitution of sociology as an independent discipline can be compared only to that of Max Weber, Jews seem to disappear from society, except for those who are clearly identified. Durkheim turns all social relationships that he examines into spiritual facts to be treated without sentiment and prejudice as things. His partisanship for Dreyfus contradicts his theoretical *chosisme*, which prioritizes *conscience collective* over individualism. Durkheim's sociology thus lacks the intellectual means to understand antisemitism.

The repercussions of this deeply ingrained flaw of sociologism, the reduction of the societal to the spiritual, can still be felt in contemporary research on antisemitism. This can be partly explained with the function sociology chose for itself in the long nineteenth century, namely that of being the antidote to revolutionary theory. Comte positioned himself against the ideologists of the French Revolution, whereas in the cases of Durkheim and especially Weber the intellectual enemy was given the name Marx. Bourgeois society was threatened not by antisemitism but by social revolution, as whose prophet they saw Marx. Marx had seen himself not as a sociologist but as a theoretician of social revolution, first of all in a country that was relatively backward compared to England and France. When Marx wrote his pathbreaking essay "On the Jewish Question" in 1843, Germany did not exist—or, at best, she existed in the "airy realm of dreams," as Heinrich Heine put it.[7] Not in the context of the pre-1848 period but only toward the end of the century Marx's essay was much read when antisemitic movements increasingly competed with the labor movement. At the same time the Zionist movement emerged, whose ideologues thought Marx's text could be easily dismissed as antisemitic. It was then ignored that Marx's text constituted a critique of the left-Hegelian Bruno Bauer, who represented an actual antisemitism avant la lettre within the German democratic pre-1848 movement, trying to displace the responsibility for emancipation onto the Jews themselves rather than seeing it as a question of social change. Before 1848, in backward Germany, at the top of the agenda was still bourgeois revolution; civic discrimination against the Jews was a pre-bourgeois everyday reality. When dealing with the "Jewish question" that pre-bourgeois estate society was not able to solve without giving up its own claim to absolute dominance, Marx shifted the focus from the problem of consciousness to that of socially necessary change: a secular bourgeois society should replace the Christian state. The weakness of Marx's text lies in its abstract character, not in its allegedly being directed against actual Jews, as many subsequent misinterpretations claimed.

In his letter of 1940 Horkheimer reminds Adorno that Marx's essay on the Jewish question posits the question about the good society—a question that was as urgent in the middle of the short century as it had been in the 1840s. The fortune of bourgeois society can be read off the fortune of the Jews. Both are doomed. The sociology of the past one hundred years considered the Jewish question outdated, a matter of history. Not so the antisemites. The conjuring up of the Jewish danger had the function of designating a group who could be held personally liable for an anonymous bourgeois society's proneness to crisis. The French antisemites of the nineteenth century are as much a postrevolutionary phenomenon as is the sociology of Comte and Durkheim. Durkheim, who carefully studied Germany after 1871, is additionally concerned with the competition offered by the young German nation-state. The growth of the antisemitic movements in continental Europe in the last third of the nineteenth century is indeed connected to that of nationalism, which was as absent from classical sociology as were antisemitism, racism, and colonialism. One of the reasons for this negligence is that when nationalism and antisemitism were taken seriously at all, they were considered to be ideologies and not forms of social praxis. This misconception is based on a model rooted in deformed Enlightenment thinking, the engineer's model: you first make a plan, and then you put it into operation. Sociological theorizing has a tendency to rationalize antisemitic explanations of anti-Jewish violence as spiritual entities rather than recognizing them as legitimizations of verbal and physical violence against Jews. The intellectual phenomena that accompany antisemitic violence should be understood as a worldview that legitimizes rather than causes the violence, a depraved form of superstition that at the end of the long century presented itself in the scientific form that Zeitgeist then demanded. Like an empirical social researcher, the antisemite bases his discourse on an accumulation of facts which he then categorizes in keeping with his worldview.[8] Marcel Stoetzler, using a formulation by Reinhard Rürup, describes the character of this kind of antisemitism succinctly in his essay in this volume as the "travesty of a social theory."

Sociology was contested in Europe in the long nineteenth century and found a home in the United States in the short twentieth century. Postwar poverty, world economic crisis, and the National Socialist attempt at world domination drove many continental European intellectuals to the United States in the first half of the short century. To their greatest horror they experienced antisemitism as a social phenomenon in the day-to-day life of the new country. When it might have seemed plausible enough in Europe to interpret antisemitism as an epiphenomenon of the transition from feudal to bourgeois society, in America it could not but be understood as the intrinsic product of bourgeois society itself. In America, unlike in Europe, Jews could not be perceived as a group whose traditional domination—rather confusingly—also involved elements of privilege, but they were unmistakably an immigrant group, like others, although perhaps not quite like others. The American experience of the exiled scholars showed bourgeois society as a whole in a new light: it appeared as a genuinely antisemitic society. Antisemitism could no longer be dismissed as an archaic relic of bourgeois prehistory but had to be analyzed as a phenomenon of the bourgeois present. Initially, though, American sociology failed to take antisemitism any more seriously than classical European sociology had done. Only under the harmless-sounding heading "research on prejudice" did the examination of antisemitism enter academe in the middle of the short century. The series *Studies in Prejudice* that Horkheimer helped organize achieved the breakthrough, and next to the more dominant race question, the Jewish question became an object of serious social scientific research, culminating in 1951 in *The Authoritarian Personality*. In spite of its great success, Adorno always remained conscious of its insufficiency; he continued to reference *Dialectic of Enlightenment* because it

> best obviates a misunderstanding *The Authoritarian Personality* was exposed to from the outset and for which it was perhaps not entirely without responsibility on account of its emphasis: namely the criticism that the authors had attempted to ground antisemitism, and beyond that fascism as a whole, merely subjectively, subscribing to the error that this political-economic phenomenon is primarily psychological.[9]

By contrast, "Elements of Antisemitism" (in *Dialectic of Enlightenment*) "theoretically shifted racial prejudice into the context of objectively oriented critical theory of society." Within the discipline of sociology interest in a critical theory that is directed at the objective while relying on the mediation by an analytically oriented social psychology seems to be diminishing, while the latter does not currently seem to be a central concern of the discipline of psychology either. In the dispute of the faculties, antisemitism seems to become, in theory and empirically, an object distorted by disciplinary divisions. The continued existence of antisemitism after Auschwitz, even its universalization in a globalized world, urgently demands sociological-historical reflection, though, on the demise of bourgeois society. Its urgency becomes evident even after only cursory comparison of nineteenth-century France, Germany, and the United States to the present. The memory politics that emerged at the end of the short century have imprisoned historical studies again in the paradigm of nationalist historiography from which critical social theory's attempt at mediating objective theory with analytical social psychology had liberated it. Looking back again at the genesis of sociology and modern antisemitism can serve as a step toward the self-reflection and self-clarification among the dispersed scholarly disciplines that is necessary in order to face the object: antisemitic practice and the worldviews that accompany it.

Notes

1. Adorno to Horkheimer, August 5, 1940, in Adorno and Horkheimer, *Briefwechsel*, 2: 84.
2. Horkheimer to Adorno, September 24, 1940, in Adorno and Horkheimer, *Briefwechsel*, 2: 103.
3. See Hitler, "Brief an Adolf Gemlich."
4. Freud, *Die Zukunft einer Illusion*, 377.
5. See especially Léon Poliakov's rich oeuvre *Die Aufklärung und ihre judenfeindliche Tendenz*.
6. Durkheim, "Individualism and the Intellectuals."
7. This formulation is from Heine's 1844 poem *Deutschland, Ein Wintermärchen*.
8. I deliberately choose the word *worldview* (*Weltanschauung*) rather than *ideology*, as ideology is centered around a kernel of truth. Those intellectual phenomena that accompany antisemitic practice that can be grasped only in terms of social psychology I try to capture with the concept of "quotidian religion" (*Alltagsreligion*), which is based on Adorno's notion of "faithless faith" (*glaubenslosen Glauben*) in his "Beitrag zur Ideologienlehre."
9. Adorno, "Wissenschaftliche Erfahrungen in Amerika," 722; Adorno, "Scientific Experiences of a European Scholar in America," 230 (translation amended). My own monograph *Grenzen der Aufklärung* (Limits of Enlightenment) attempts to extend and continue the approach Adorno and Horkheimer developed in "Elements of Antisemitism."

References

Adorno, Theodor W. "Beitrag zur Ideologienlehre." In *Gesammelte Schriften*, edited by Rolf Tiedemann, vol 8: 457-77. Frankfurt am Main: Suhrkamp, 1995.

————. "Scientific Experiences of a European Scholar in America." In *Critical Models, Interventions and Catchwords*, translated by Henry W. Pickford, 215–42. New York: Columbia University Press, 2005.

————. "Wissenschaftliche Erfahrungen in Amerika." 1968. In *Gesammelte Schriften*, edited by Rolf Tiedemann, vol. 10.2, 702–38. Frankfurt am Main: Suhrkamp, 2003.

Adorno, Theodor W., and Max Horkheimer. *Briefwechsel*. Vol. 2: *1938-1944*. Frankfurt am Main: Suhrkamp, 2004.

Adorno, Theodor W., and Max Horkheimer. *Dialectic of Enlightenment. Philosophical Fragments*. 1944. Stanford CA: Stanford University Press, 2002.

Claussen, Detlev. *Grenzen der Aufklärung: Die gesellschaftliche Genese des modernen Antisemitismus. Erweiterte Neuausgabe*. 1987. Frankfurt am Main: Fischer, 2005.

Durkheim, Emile. "Individualism and the Intellectuals." 1898. In *On Morality and Society*, edited by Robert N. Bellah, 43–57. Chicago: University of Chicago Press, 1973.

Freud, Sigmund. *Die Zukunft einer Illusion*. 1927. In *Gesammelte Werke*, 14: 325–80. London: Imago, 1948.

Heine, Heinrich. *Deutschland, Ein Wintermärchen*. 1844. Edited by Joseph Kiermeier-Debre. Munich: Deutscher Taschenbuch Verlag, 1997.

Hitler, Adolf. "Brief an Adolf Gemlich." 1921. In Detlev Claussen, *Vom Judenhaß zum Antisemitismus*, 190–93. Darmstadt: Wissenschaftliche Buchgesellschaft, 1987.

Horkheimer, Max, and Theodor W. Adorno. Vorwort to Paul W. Massing, *Vorgeschichte des Politischen Antisemitismus*, v–viii. Frankfurter Beiträge zur Soziologie 8. Frankfurt am Main: Europäische Verlagsanstalt, 1959.

Marx, Karl. "Zur Judenfrage." In *Marx Engels Werke*, 1: 347–77. Berlin: Dietz, 1964.

Poliakov, Léon. *Geschichte des Antisemitismus*. Vol. 5: *Die Aufklärung und ihre judenfeindliche Tendenz*. Worms: Verlag Georg Heintz, 1983.

Contributors

Y. Michal Bodemann is a professor of sociology at the University of Toronto. He has published numerous books on German Jewry, immigration, and sociological theory, including *A Jewish Family in Germany: At Home in the Geography of Time* (Duke University Press, 2005).

Werner Bonefeld is a professor of politics at the University of York UK. Among his numerous publications are the three volumes of *Open Marxism* (Pluto Press, 1992, 1993, 1995), of which he was a coeditor.

Detlev Claussen is a professor of social theory and sociology of culture and science at the University of Hannover. He is the author of *Grenzen der Aufklärung, Die gesellschaftliche Genese des modernen Antisemitismus* (Fischer, 1987, 1994), and *Adorno: One Last Genius* (Harvard University Press, 2008).

Robert Fine is emeritus professor of sociology at the University of Warwick. His numerous books include most recently *Cosmopolitanism* (Routledge, 2007).

Chad Alan Goldberg is an associate professor of sociology at the University of Wisconsin. He is the author of *Citizens and Paupers: Relief, Rights, and Race, from the Freedmen's Bureau to Workfare* (University of Chicago Press, 2008).

Irmela Gorges is a professor of sociology at the Freie Universität, Berlin. She is the author of *Sozialforschung in Deutschland 1872–1914: Gesellschaftliche Einflüsse auf Themen-und Methodenwahl des Vereins für Socialpolitik* (Hain, 1980).

Jonathan Judaken holds the Spence L. Wilson Chair in Humanities at Rhodes College. He is the author of *Jean-Paul Sartre and the Jewish Question: Anti-antisemitism and the Politics of the French Intellectual* (University of Nebraska Press, 2006), the editor of *Race after Sartre* (State University of New York Press, 2008) and *Naming Race, Naming Racisms* (Routledge, 2009), and a coeditor of *Situating Existentialism: Key Texts in Contexts* (Columbia University Press, 2012).

Richard H. King is a professor of American intellectual history at the University of Nottingham. He is the author of *Race, Culture and the Intellectuals, 1940–70* (Johns Hopkins University Press, 2004) and coeditor of *Hannah Arendt and the Uses of History: Imperialism, Nation, Race, and Genocide* (Berghahn, 2007).

Daniel Lvovich is a professor of history at the Universidad Nacional de General Sarmiento, Buenos Aires. He is the author of *Nacionalismo y Antisemitismo en la Argentina* (Vergara, 2003).

Amos Morris-Reich is a senior lecturer in the Department for Jewish History and Thought and director of the Bucerius Institute for the Study of Contemporary German History and Society at the University of Haifa. He is the author of *The Quest for Jewish Assimilation in Modern Social Science* (Routledge, 2007).

Roland Robertson is the chair in sociology and global society at Aberdeen University. He is the author of numerous books, including *Globalization* (Sage, 1992).

Marcel Stoetzler is a lecturer in sociology at the University of Bangor. He is the author of *The State, the Nation, and the Jews: Liberalism and the Antisemitism Dispute in Bismarck's Germany* (University of Nebraska Press, 2008).

Eva-Maria Ziege is a professor of political sociology at the University of Bayreuth. She is the author of *Mythische Kohärenz: Diskursanalyse des völkischen Antisemitismus* (UVK, 2002) and *Antisemitismus und Gesellschaftstheorie: Die Frankfurter Schule im amerikanischen Exil* (Suhrkamp, 2009).

Index

CPSIA information can be obtained at www.ICGtesting.com
Printed in the USA
BVOW03*0135080514

352889BV00002B/2/P